The Complete Book of Pub Catering

Edited by
John Fuller

Hutchinson
London Melbourne Sydney Auckland Johannesburg

Hutchinson and Co. (Publishers) Ltd
An imprint of Century-Hutchinson Limited
Brookmount House, 62–65 Chandos Place, London WC2N 4NW

Hutchinson Publishing Group (Australia) Pty Ltd
16–22 Church Street, Hawthorn, Melbourne, Victoria 3122

Hutchinson Group (NZ) Ltd
32–34 View Road, PO Box 40–086, Glenfield, Auckland 10

Hutchinson Group (SA) (Pty) Ltd
PO Box 337, Bergvlei 2012, South Africa

First published 1986

© Virtue & Company Ltd 1986

Set in VIP Palatino by
D. P. Media Limited, Hitchin, Hertfordshire
Printed in Great Britain at The Bath Press, Avon

British Library Cataloguing in Publication Data
The Complete Book of Pub Catering

British Library Cataloguing in Publication Data
The McCormick Book of Pub Catering
  1. Hotels, taverns, etc. – Food service
  I. Fuller, John, *1916*–
  642'.5   TX950.7

ISBN 0 09 161571 2

Hutchinson Catering and Hotel Management Books
Series Editor: John Fuller

Other books by John Fuller

Modern Restaurant Service
Guéridon and Lamp Cookery
The Waiter (with A. J. Currie)
A Hotel and Catering Career (with D. Gee)
H. P. Pellaprat's L'Art Culinaire Moderne (ed.)
Meat Dishes in the International Cuisine (ed.)
Catering and Hotelkeeping (ed.)
Professional Kitchen Management
The Chef's Compendium of Professional Recipes (with E. Renold)
Catering Management in the Technological Age (ed.)
Productivity and Profit in Catering (ed. with James Steel)
The Caterer's Potato Manual
Hotelkeeping and Catering as a Career

Contents

List of contributors 5
Editor's preface 8
Acknowledgements 9

Part One Meeting Market Demand

1 **Pubs in the catering context** 13
  H. A. Monckton

2 **Concepts and systems** 19
  James Fuller

3 **Promoting pub food** 27
  Anthony M. Perry

4 **A promotional case study** 38
  Anthony M. Perry

5 **Factors in layout and planning** 49
  Robert Humphreys

6 **Equipment for catering** 69
  Anthony Milson and David Kirk

7 **Decor and design for dining** 80
  Bruce Braham

Part Two Policy and Operations

8 **Menus and their compilation** 97
  J. J. Morel

9 **Purchasing food for pubs** 116
  J. J. Morel

10 **Receiving, storing and issuing food** 133
   James Steel

11 **Selling functions** 149
   James Fuller

12 **Functions and outside catering** 152
   Michael R. Small

13	**Costing, pricing and control** *James Steel*	176

Part Three Meal Service

14	**Snackbars, counter and informal service** *Brian Cheesman*	197
15	**Formal dining service** *Brian Cheesman*	213
16	**Sales and service of wine with food** *J. G. Miles*	226

Part Four Recipes for Pubs

17	**Soups, sauces and dressings** *Michael Davidson and Daniel Stevenson*	241
18	**Egg, pasta and fish dishes** *Michael Davidson and Daniel Stevenson*	257
19	**Roasts, ethnic and featured dishes** *Michael Davidson and Daniel Stevenson*	270
20	**Vegetables and savoury pastries** *Michael Davidson and Daniel Stevenson*	293
21	**Buffet items, sandwiches and cheese** *Michael Davidson and Daniel Stevenson*	305
22	**Pastry, puddings and sweets** *Michael Davidson and Daniel Stevenson*	319

Index 333

Contributors

Professor John Fuller, Honorary Catering Adviser to the RAF, is now Editorial Director at Virtue and Editorial Consultant at Hutchinson. Formerly Professor of Hotel Management and Director of Strathclyde University's Scottish Hotel School, he also headed similar departments at Battersea Polytechnic (now Surrey University) and Oxford Polytechnic. He is the author of *Professional Kitchen Management* (Batsford), *Modern Restaurant Service* (Hutchinson) and a dozen other textbooks.

Bruce Braham is Senior Lecturer in the Department of Tourism, Catering and Hotel Administration at the Dorset Institute of Higher Education, Bournemouth. He is a regular contributor to the trade press and author of *Hotel Front Office* (Hutchinson). He is also engaged in consultancy work for international hotel companies as well as being Chairman of Poole's Tourism Committee, a Director of the Southern Tourist Board and an Executive Member of the Dorset Tourism Association.

Brian Cheesman, Principal Lecturer in Food and Beverage Studies at the Westminster Hotel School, is also Course Tutor for Licensed Trade Diploma Courses and a consultant for the Institute of Innkeeping Pub Business Programmes. All the college bars and cellars come under his direct control.

Graham Cromack worked for several years at Truman Ltd where he set up Ben's Larder, a fast food operation. He was Regional Director of Managed Houses at Courage Central Ltd.

Michael Davidson is Catering Adviser since 1966 with Chef and Brewer South, part of the Grand Metropolitan Group. Trained as a chef at Hastings Hotel and Catering School, his experience includes the Rembrandt Hotel in South Kensington.

Eric Ellmes is responsible for food purchasing for Imperial Inns and Taverns. Previously he was for fourteen years in the UK hotels division of Grand Metropolitan Hotels as Food and Beverage Purchasing Manager. His catering education was in Ealing Technical College.

James Fuller, BA, FHCIMA, is now Research and Development Manager for Imperial Inns and Taverns, following experience in other divisions of Imperial Leisure and Retailing. He was previously with Grand Metropolitan County

Contributors

Hotels, mainly in food and beverage management but finally as a hotel manager. He is a graduate of Strathclyde University's Scottish Hotel School.

Peter M. G. Hime, formerly Managing Director of J. Lyons Catering, is now developing his own group as Chairman of Pilla Pilla. Among previous appointments he was Director of Operations Centre Hotels (Cranston), Regional Director of Berni Inns Group and Hotels Controller of the Reo Stakis Organization, and he held various management posts of a progressive nature with Trusthouse Forte.

Robert Humphreys, BSc.(Econ.), FHCIMA, a graduate of Portsmouth Hotel School and the London School of Economics, has spent the twenty years since leaving college in both the hotel and licensed trades, including periods in West Africa and the Caribbean. His current responsibilities include supervising and advising a group of publicans and restaurateurs on effective catering.

David Kirk is a graduate in food technology. His interest in applying food technology to the design and operation of catering appliances started during his period as the Charles Forte Research Fellow in the Department of Hotel and Catering Administration at the University of Surrey. He is currently Principal Lecturer in Food Engineering in the Department of Hotel and Catering Studies and Home Economics at Sheffield City Polytechnic.

John Miles, MBII, is Retail Secretary of the Brewers' Society and Secretary of the British Institute of Innkeeping. He joined the National Trade Development Association as Assistant Secretary in May 1964, moving to the Brewers' Society in 1969. He edited the standard work *Innkeeping*.

Anthony Milson, who was Vice Principal of Queen's College, Glasgow, died suddenly in February 1984. His impact on catering education will not be forgotten through his involvement with Sheffield City Polytechnic and the Food, Accommodation and Related Subjects Board of CNNA as well as with the Glasgow college.

H. A. Monckton is the author of *A History of English Ale and Beer* and *A History of the English Public House*, and numerous other publications about the brewing industry. H. A. Monckton recently retired after a lifetime with Whitbread (last appointment Assistant Managing Director, Whitbread East Pennines). He is currently Chairman and Managing Director of Publishing and Literary Services.

Julian Morel, an HCITB registered Training Officer and Tutor in Food Studies with Metropolitan College, HCIMA correspondence course, is the author of several catering books. He trained with the Savoy Hotel Group, held appointments with Gordon Hotels, the LNER Hotel Services, the Pullman Car Company (later the Pullman Division of British Transport Hotels) and the Hotel and Catering Industry Training Board.

Anthony M. Perry, a journalist member of a hotel family, was for ten years editor of various catering publications, incluing *Catering Times*, *Catering*

Contributors

Management and *Hotel and Restaurant Management*. He spent eleven years as a practising hotelier with his family and won a special commendation in the British Tourist Authority's 'Come to Britain' competition for marketing his hotel services. He served for four years as elected commercial representative on the executive of the North West Regional Tourist Board.

Nigel Pullan is Chairman of The Ebury Wine Company which was started in 1973, when he and three others purchased The Ebury Wine Bar in Ebury Street, SW1. The Ebury Wine Bar is one of the best-known wine bars in London and has a particularly good reputation for its food, all of which is prepared daily on the premises. Prior to 1973 Nigel Pullan held a senior marketing position at Hedges and Butler, the wine and spirit subsidiary of Bass Charrington and he was also Deputy-Chairman of The Wine Development Board.

Mike Small is currently in charge of catering at a large college of the University of London. He began his career in the banqueting department of Grosvenor House Hotel, Park Lane, and then became a trainee manager with a small hotel group. He has written many articles for the trade press. He was editor of *Buffets and Receptions* (Virtue, 1978) and the second edition of his own book *Catering for Functions* (Hutchinson) was published in 1983.

James Steel is Director of Catering Studies in Strathclyde's Scottish Hotel School. He had early experience of pub catering in management posts with a large brewery company. He is author of *Control in Catering* (Hutchinson).

Daniel R. Stevenson is Senior Lecturer in Oxford Polytechnic's Department of Catering Management and formerly headed the catering department in Stornaway. He is closely associated with the development of the process approach to food production and is the author of the authoritative text *Professional Cookery: The Process Approach* (Hutchinson).

Editor's preface

Already in 1950, just after the founding of the then Hotel and Catering Institute, the licensed trade was an important sector of catering and was playing a leading part in developing staff training to meet new demands in preparing and serving food as well as liquor. At that time, thirty-five years ago, I first wrote (in the Institute's journal) about pub catering. Twenty years later, chairing the National Catering Inquiry, I was associated with a study into the British eating out in pubs, which again underlined the ever-increasing importance of the licensed trade in the growth of the food service industry.

In short, long involvement in the catering industry and in education for it has continually indicated to me the significance of pubs in British catering. In introducing the report on our National Catering Inquiry into pub catering in 1970, I wrote that 'most customers will rejoice that half of our publicans (according to the survey) plan to develop their catering . . . because our pubs reveal the special hospitality talents of the British. Dr Johnson, a great pub user, triumphed over the French "for not having in any perfection the tavern life".' Those plans have surely matured.

Since then we have seen how abroad the British pub has penetrated into many parts of Europe; at home, we are still witnessing imaginative diversification of food and beverage enterprise in our own pubs. The changes and the continuing trends are identified by our contributors in this book and there is no need, therefore, in this preface further to emphasize the opportunities and challenges for the publican caterer both to enhance profits and gain job satisfaction.

Indeed, the varied background of the contributors indicates the richness of the food service pattern in pubs. Represented are top, middle and specialist management from brewery and substantial companies and individual licensees and entrepreneurs. Even a contributor from a university hotel school has past catering experience with a brewery company.

I trust that this book, which concentrates the experience and knowledge of those in and associated with the licensed trade, will provide support to those now continuing to develop the important catering facet of pub activity. The years since 1950 have been stimulating ones for those so involved. The next twenty up to the century's end will be just as exciting. They will still demand a core of know-how such as that contributed here.

John Fuller
Oxford, 1985

Acknowledgements

In addition to the contributors whose names are attached to chapters, acknowledgement is due to the following whose material has been incorporated: M. J. Boella, J. B. Simpson, Doris Hatfield, Eric Jolly, M. H. McDougall, Peter Shill, M. H. Nicholson, David Gee, John Gregson, C. J. M. Horsman, Valerie Mieczowski and Desmond White.

The preliminary work of Martin Blunden of Virtue Publishers and his continuing assistance is gratefully acknowledged, as is the help of J. R. Valentine of Oxford Polytechnic in checking metric conversions and other details in several chapters.

Finally, the editor wishes to record with appreciation the collaboration at all stages of his wife and especially her substantial aid in assembling, typing and checking manuscripts.

Part One

Meeting Market Demand

1 Pubs in the catering context

H. A. Monckton

At the end of the Second World War there were about 82,000 fully licensed public houses and hotels in the UK. They represented 65 per cent of all classes of on- and off-licences. By 1980 the number of fully licensed public houses had fallen to about 74,500 to represent about 46 per cent of all classes of licence. This reduction reflected social change. There has been not only a deliberate swing towards fewer and better public houses, but also a significant number of pub closures in demolition areas. Fewer new public houses have been built on housing estates and other urban and suburban developments. In some cases, public houses have even been built into large municipal blocks of flats.

Ownership, tenancy and management

There has also been a change in the ownership of pubs. In 1945 about 90 per cent of all public houses were either owned by, or tied to, brewing companies. Again by the early 1980s that figure had dropped to about 68 per cent, although this percentage varies from one part of the UK to another.

Of the brewery-owned public houses about 28 per cent are run by managers appointed by the brewing company and 72 per cent by tenants selected by the owning company. Tenancy and management, as two complementary ways of running pubs, are both long established. In general there has been, and still is, a preponderance of tenanted houses, but in certain areas and for certain purposes management has historically been preferred. Sometimes the preference was that of the brewing companies because they considered that management gave them better control; sometimes it was that of the licensing magistrates, faced (as for example in Liverpool at the turn of the century) with an urgent need to improve standards of liquor retailing in their area.

There is a clear place for both management and tenancy in brewery-owned pubs. Management is logical where a large investment has to be made in a pub which, in order to earn a commercial return, would involve an unacceptably high rent for most tenants. This is particularly so in the case of new pubs costing something in the order of £200,000 to build at current prices. It is also logical where specialized management is required, for example in large-scale catering houses built to cope with the increasing popularity of eating out. At the other end of the scale, a pub which is running down because of urban redevelopment and the threat of compulsory purchase may often be placed under management by the brewing company simply because it would not be possible to attract a tenant to the house.

Meeting Market Demand

In between these two extremes the tenancy system offers a broad band of advantage to both the licensee and the brewery. The system has stood the test of time and has enabled many people to acquire businesses as going concerns with a comparatively small capital investment. The mix of the two systems provides a choice which is widely recognized as being in the public interest.

The pub tradition

The British pub has long been one of the most cherished threads in the fabric of our national way of life, and there can be little doubt that, since the Second World War, its position has been further strengthened. Owners have invested enormous sums of money to raise the standard of pubs to keep pace with the needs of social evolution.

Although in many instances the architecture may have changed, the basic precepts of fellowship and good cheer have remained to keep alive the traditional role of the pub. Many pubs have disappeared as a result of urban demolition programmes and new highway schemes, but considerable numbers have been built in areas where new local communities have sprung up. New pubs and older pubs alike have good facilities today and standards of comfort and decor reflect the requirements of a more demanding society. In the cellars and behind the bars there have been many technological advances in recent years.

Change in sales and service

Over the last thirty years no change in pubs has been more noteworthy than the growth of catering. Contrary to popular belief, the provision of food in pubs was not widespread before the Second World War. The pub is more sensitive to social change than many of our other national institutions. That it is able to be flexible is remarkable when one considers the jungle of licensing and other laws which control its activities.

An example of licensed trade sensitivity to the dictates of social evolution is the pubs' response to the widespread public demand for catering in bars following the end of food rationing. This is to be seen in the vast number of pubs which today offer good fare ranging from simple snacks to hot meals (see Figure 1).

The British licensee's reputation for ingenuity is demonstrated by the variety of food which is offered from pub to pub according to the facilities installed and the neighbourhood needs. Standards vary from poor to good, but levels of excellence and service are improving all the time. Competition between one pub and another for a market share of the catering turnover has become a positive feature of contemporary times. It is not to be inferred that sophisticated dishes are the main attributes of a pub catering operation, because bread and cheese, ham sandwiches etc. which are fresh and well presented still represent the most popular requirements of pub customers.

Pubs in the catering context

Figure 1 *Today, most pubs offer food ranging from simple snacks to hot meals* Courtesy Charrington & Co. Ltd Brewers. Photograph by LPA International Photo Services Ltd

Types of operation

Platter dishes, which include home-made pies and pastries, frequently testify to the interest and skill of the licensees in recognizing and responding to a growing demand. Fast food operations in wide variety are making their appearance in an ever-increasing number of pub bars. Licensed premises are being adapted and refurbished to provide steak bars and grill rooms to cater for a more affluent society in which eating out by the family once a week, or more often, is rapidly becoming an accepted way of life.

Purpose-built public houses with the planned aim of combining eating and drinking in comfortable and imaginatively designed surroundings have entailed a heavy investment on the part of the owners of public houses who have recognized the need for change. Pub entrepeneurs are likely to be encouraged by the success of such ventures and, spurred on by the need to be competitive, will invest their money in response to customer demand for many years ahead.

Trends, influences and competition

An interesting post-war development in retail catering operations was the creation of the non-licensed Wimpy Bars. This chain introduced on a big scale the concept of sophisticated fast food retail outlets backed by system catering. In the late 1950s Berni Inns created their famous steak bar chain in licensed outlets which was unique in terms of decor, menu, service and price. They gave the lead to similar catering operations to follow.

The Licensing Act 1961 was the first general revision of licensing law for forty years, and profoundly affected licensed catering. Effectively the Act created three new types of licence, the most significant of which, in the context of this account, was the restaurant licence. It became the trigger for a new range of catering opportunities. Individual entrepreneurs took advantage of the situation and thousands of such licences were granted by the justices. This caused public house owners to review their own operations.

Among the challenges that have faced pubs have been oyster bars, wine bars and a large number of ethnic food operations with liquor licences. Leading this particular field are Chinese restaurants (including the large numbers of non-licensed take-away Chinese food operations), followed by Indian and Pakistani restaurants. Also to be reckoned with are significant numbers of Italian, Spanish, Greek and Turkish restaurants. The popularity of ethnic restaurants is probably accounted for by the fact that Britain is becoming far more cosmopolitan and our introverted traditional views are less strongly held. In Britain today there is a readiness to be adventurous in sampling unfamiliar dishes and to acknowledge that they make interesting, if occasional, alternatives to our traditional fare.

As beef-dominated menus are becoming beyond the financial reach of many people, we can detect the beginning of a less expensive range of food specialities. Apart from fish bars there are to be seen restaurants which focus upon chicken, pizza, crêpes and omelettes.

Response to changed demand

Demand patterns of consumers are constantly changing and there are various behavioural and economic explanations for this. Variations to eating habits owe something to changing patterns of work. Progressively, in recent years, we have seen an extension of staggered start times, flexitime, and an increase in shift working. Business people travel more extensively and this, coupled with a more generous attitude by employers towards fringe benefits, has combined to bring about greater use of luncheon vouchers. Thus further demands have been made upon catering resources.

The fact that more women are at work means that they have less time to purchase food and prepare meals at home. This has led to an enormous increase in recent years in take-away shops and the use of frozen foods, but it has meant good news for the catering industry in general. These changes across the whole spectrum of catering combined with a more broadly based affluence have inevitably led to increased demands upon pub catering, a process likely to continue for the foreseeable future.

Changes in consumer demand in pubs have not gone unnoticed by the brewing companies, which predominate in the ownership of licensed houses. Often their investments in catering have been heavy, and under these circumstances it is not surprising that the houses concerned are frequently controlled by salaried house managers who enjoy additional financial incentives. The owners of licensed premises have encouraged catering operations to meet local consumer requirements. In so doing they recognize public appreciation for individuality, varied cooking and good personal service.

Brewery-owned houses Nearly three-quarters of brewery-owned houses are operated by tenants. They offer significant opportunities for individual licensees who may be likened to other people in business on their own. Between tenant and brewer is a rather special partnership in which the tenant enjoys many advantages not found with other business arrangements. This partnership is evolutionary and is continually subject to change. For example, traditional tenancy agreements are increasingly being replaced by lease and lend arrangements with the owning brewer. In such circumstances both parties are the gainers and the licensee may, according to the terms of the agreement, be the beneficiary of a capital gain upon the expiration of the lease. Arrangements between brewers and licensees are becoming many and varied, and of late we have seen examples of brewers concluding deals where licensees are taking up multiple licences. The spouses of licensees frequently bring their special skills to bear upon the total operation of a pub, and the partnership of a married couple adds a versatility which could not otherwise have been achieved.

Free houses In public house ownership, free houses represent some 24,000 of the 75,000 fully licensed premises. The free house owner has a number of advantages over the tenant licensee. He has total freedom in the way he styles his business, adapts his premises and negotiates terms of supply of goods. He is in a strong position to take the quickest advantage of neighbourhood needs.

He can choose a style of operation reflecting his own individuality across a broad span of opportunities. He may decide to convert a bar, for the lunchtime trade, which offers meals at various levels of sophistication with waitress service. He may choose to serve plated meals of steak or egg and chips across the counter, down to more simple fare such as a ploughman's lunch. He may opt for the only real fast food operation in pubs – hot and cold food served off the counter direct to the customer. Although a licensee may have freedom of choice in the matter of catering, there can be no freedom when it comes to standards; they have to be high if the venture is to be successful.

Prospects for pub catering

In order to attempt a prediction about the future, it is helpful to understand the level of esteem that the pub currently enjoys among members of the public. An attitude survey of those over the age of sixteen carried out by Market Opinion and Research International for the Brewers' Society in 1979 revealed that about half the men and a quarter of the women in the UK go to the pub at least once a week. The survey confirmed that the pub enjoys a remarkable degree of sustained goodwill and dedicated customer support. In comparison with other forms of leisure and entertainment the pub heads the list above licensed restaurants, dances, cinema and theatre. It is the focal point for people to gather, meet their friends and enjoy themselves in pleasant and convivial surroundings.

The attraction of the pub in the future will be influenced by what it will offer as a social centre within expanding leisure facilities. A pub must reflect of social needs, the most pressing of which is that of more and improved catering. Of the three major threads in pub catering – restaurant, grill room and snack bar – all stand to benefit from the future. Restaurants are only likely to succeed if they are of a high standard since the competition from licensed restaurants is fierce. There will come a time, perhaps not too far off, when saturation level is reached. Grill room operations of a high standard appear still to have scope, to judge from the support they now receive. Their menus may have to change if the cost of meat continues to rise as it has done in the recent past; non-steak foods are likely to supplement the menu, thereby changing the present characteristics a little.

The greatest scope for the future would seem to lie in snack catering, where the possibilities are many and the pub is well placed to take advantage of them. There is scope for the greater use of microwave ovens and toasted sandwich equipment which are easy to install.

Perhaps the most important lesson to be learned by the licensee is that of putting food on display so that customers can actually see that it is good. The future will also require that snacks are served on demand rather than by order. As in the past, so it is likely in the future that a good pub meal will represent better value for money than most of its competitors.

Further reading

Monckton, H. A., *A History of English Ale and Beer*, The Bodley Head, 1966.

2 Concepts and systems

James Fuller

The terms 'concept' and 'system' are commonplace in catering. Systems catering implies a total catering strategy aimed at maximizing sales and profits and minimizing costs, and spread across marketing, operational and supply aspects. Although all catering requires a system, no chain food operation can prosper without a totally planned system which should integrate all operational factors from marketing through production to service. Such a system aims to obtain volume sales of maximum throughput, whether take-away food or seat turnover ratios.

A totally planned system depends for success on researched attention to menus, decor, exteriors, interiors, staff and their appearance, billing, storage, layout, cooking and services as well as purchase specifications and suppliers able consistently to meet them. Additionally, successful catering must include standards and methods to measure and control them.

Systems may apply technology but this does not mean that licensees need a deep understanding of it, for such application may be achieved through suppliers. Food processors and equipment manufacturers bring the fruits of technology to catering through developments in commodities (convenience foods) and newer equipment (convection and microwave ovens, for example).

Components and advantages

Any system can only be described in general terms, since implementation must take into account the facilities each publican has at his disposal. The publican must also gauge the variety and quality of food acceptable to his customers. Following his research he can decide on a step by step programme to establish his system. Essential components are:

Quality must match customers' expectations.
Food must be served at the correct temperature.
Control procedure must be adequate to avoid wastage.
Capacity must cope equally well with peaks and troughs.
Minimal skills are required by pub staff (because food production and processing are carried out elsewhere).
Labour costs are reduced significantly.
Reduced space is normally required (because smaller preparation, kitchen and service areas are needed).

Achieving objectives

A catering system's objectives should include maximum operational efficiency, anticipate operators' needs, create routines, and ensure low overhead costs, high turnover and hence a satisfactory return on capital investment. To achieve such goals, managerial skill must be applied. In a systemized food operation, method study (in however simple, home-made a style) must be used to:

Identify each task and step in the production process.
Develop the most effective methods and especially seek to eliminate variables.
Group tasks to create appropriate jobs.
Monitor work and method performance, constantly assessing and reassessing effectiveness.

A system working properly should ensure that dishes are readily available when required and are of a quality comparable with accepted or traditional standards. Customers should be attracted to, and retained by, the appeal of the concept. This should be achieved with a service that is easy to operate and with minimum skills, labour, equipment and space usage to keep costs at an acceptable level.

Many characteristics of a system are to be observed in pub catering though they may have been slow in coming. Many 'systems' in pubs are based on concepts tested over decades: for example, the selection of an appropriate site and the carrying out of the operation in an attractive, albeit simple, setting. Other aspects include:

The selection of an appropriate food product, normally familiar (steak, fried fish or chicken are examples) but alternatively made familiar by good promotion (hamburgers or pizzas, for example).
A production method which is as foolproof as possible and service that is speedy, efficient and sophisticated, yielding dishes of consistent quality at an acceptable price.
The back-up of production and service by controls that yield information speedily, and market and merchandise the product effectively.

Examples of systemized catering chains based upon the foregoing concepts are Berni, Imperial Inns and Taverns, The Host Group, Chef and Brewer, Schooner Inns, Trophy Taverns, Cavalier Steakhouses and Beefeaters. The customer in such houses knows what to expect: a warm and interesting atmosphere, a limited menu offering popular, freshly cooked fare at a fair price, speedy and informal service. Customers have a positive understanding of the routine, the menu and the final bill.

Background to development

This indicates that the brewery companies who own 50,000 pubs include many which are aware that they must look beyond wholesale and retail profits on beer for revenue to maintain their large estates. As a consequence catering, both as a significant source of revenue in its own right and as an attraction to boost flagging liquor sales, is recognized as important by major brewers,

Concepts and systems

many of whom are already well down the catering road. Yet many judge that initial progress was slow.

In brewery-owned public houses, managers are governed by brewery policy. Relative slowness to realize the potential of food sales within their houses was presumably because brewers historically saw profits being made from liquor sales and were reluctant to complicate the operation by food sales.

Food production on site brought problems. Needs included dry storage space for groceries; refrigerated stores for meat, fish and dairy products; trained staff; and dish costing skill (partly due to varying yields of raw materials). A high staff level was required. Overproduction could lead to costly waste. Expensive equipment was needed to cope with menus and cooking. 'Finishing' had to be achieved in restricted trading periods (two hours at lunchtime and three hours in the evening).

Technology now bypasses many of these problems because manufacturers can produce acceptable portioned and prepared dishes of consistent quality and known cost, easily made ready with a minimum of skill.

However, many landlords long ago recognized the potential profitability of food and were allowed to sell it at profit to themselves provided that it did not affect their liquor sales adversely. Profit from catering was a licensee's perk and the brewery left any catering operation to his discretion. Profits were often hidden from the brewery by tenants to avoid the chance of an increased rent. This secrecy is no longer widespread owing to the increased ratio of managed to tenanted houses.

Challenge of competition

Today the vast majority of the country's 77,000 pubs serve food of some description. This volume of outlets should mean a lion's share of the consumer pound spent on eating out. This is not the case.

Competition for business is fierce, both from other pubs and from other sectors of the retail trade. Fast food outlets offering often superior food at greater perceived value, and ready prepared meals sold through supermarkets, are among the obvious competitors. These outlets are selling not just food but also hygiene and consistency, both highly rated by consumers. The development of pub catering at any level must recognize this.

As consumers look more to their leisure time for entertainment, pubs must provide more than just a good pint and a dartboard. Television and foreign travel make consumers more aware of what is available, and caterers often underestimate their sophistication. Why should anybody spend an evening in a dingy pub when at home with friends they can enjoy a take-away meal and watch a video? There will, of course, always be demand for traditional pubs serving good food and drink, and, indeed, many such 'locals' trade exceedingly well. But many sites still do not realize their full potential.

Steak house pitfalls

The Berni Inn Group is popularly credited with pioneering the identification and marketing of a need and concentrated on identifying food as the priority within its branches. The most successful market mix in steak house operations is 60 per cent food to 40 per cent liquor. Ironically, once this mix is obtained, barrelage is normally greater than was originally obtained when the premises were run simply to sell liquor.

Many imitators of a successful brand mistakenly sited a steak bar at the back of the premises. Access was through a tortuous passage; the steak bar was impenetrable because customers were propping up the drinks bar which dominated both concept and floor area. Their next mistake was to believe that there is no demand except for Fridays and Saturdays. They then closed the restaurant outside this time or operated a limited menu for the customer brave enough to ask whether the steak bar was open. The licensees, believing Saturday to be a good morning for weddings, might decide to have a wedding reception in the steak bar. Before long the premises were used for everything other than the original concept. This highlights some difficulties in first creating a concept that meets the apparent marketing profile and then establishing it by working to disciplined marketing principles. How can we avoid the pitfalls outlined?

Setting standards

In past, present and future concepts, standards dominate all else. In any business, if the standards set do not meet consumers' requirements or are allowed to drop below an acceptable level, then consumers will eventually withdraw custom. No consumer, no business.

Most beer cellars have detailed wall charts on cellar management; most licensees have attended cellar management courses. How many trade kitchens display recipe cards and presentation specifications for the dishes offered? How many breweries run catering courses? The introduction and maintenance of standards in already good catering operations will make them better.

The bulk of a pub's food business is normally conducted at lunchtime, even in a successful one. The development of evening trade is a natural follow-on. We should look for more aggressive retailing in extending hours of catering trading. Fostering business outside traditional trading hours has already started with bar/café concepts opening for breakfast and continuing to trade throughout the day. They are proving successful. Hence the emphasis on tightening standards and the further development of the business within successful outlets.

Total merchandising

The greatest challenge comes from developing sites within the managed house estates which are falling short of achieving a return on capital employed. This prompts the establishment of concepts for both liquor and catering, and the creation of brands. Themed pubs are not a new phenomenon and the breweries will continue to formulate one-off concept houses, capitalizing on the unique features of a particular house or its location. Examples of this include the Old Rangoon in Barnes, London, where the old billiard room has been converted into a colonial style restaurant overlooking landscaped gardens. Such theming resulted in a massive increase in trade; there was undoubtedly a stimulation of wet sales even though the theming was led by food. This result is similar to the benefit in liquor sales experienced by the early steak houses.

From one-off concepts will come replicable themes to be adopted in other sites within the estate. This embraces a whole house approach, i.e. one in which a site is developed in total and a comprehensive change is achieved. Less drastic conceptual theming is also occurring whereby a catering concept is adopted within an existing outlet to establish a competitive edge in catering, to make the pub more appealing than other pubs in the area.

The Pizza Hut concept in Whitbread pubs is just one example. Imperial Inns and Taverns have developed catering concepts to be adopted within successful Tavern sites, ranging from 'Pantry' traditional pub food to Chicago style hot dogs (see Figure 2). Where such concepts are introduced, the full package goes beyond purchase, cooking and presentation specifications to include full merchandizing. This will be achieved by strong external and internal signage and by integrated uniforms, menus, etc. compatible with the concept.

Identity factors

Development can be in two significant ways. First, the concept is taken over by the pub, but the identity of the pub is the stronger and the concept is themed to fit the pub. For example, a pub with a strong name, such as the Robin Hood, if developing a pie concept would adopt names linked with Robin Hood to describe its menu items, such as Friar Tuck's Pie and Maid Marian's Pasty. Conversely, a strong concept could be put into a pub of little identity and the new concept creates an identity.

The adoption of concepts on a local basis will provide the competitive edge already mentioned, but as repeats of the concept are introduced elsewhere then brand loyalty needs to be developed. This is exactly the same as has happened with the multiple catering outlets, such as Happy Eater, McDonalds and Little Chef. This is still some way off within the pub estate, but with 50,000 brewery-owned sites and with a natural limitation of concept variant this must eventually happen.

Whole house theming in terms of branding is well under way. Berni Inns were early forerunners within the Watney Truman estates, and Beefeaters are now firmly established. The new American diner concepts, such as the Exchange Restaurants operated by Allied Breweries' Vittle Inns and the Sullivan's operated by Imperial Inns and Taverns, are backed by high investment programmes to create a significant number of outlets with their own brand identity in a relatively short time.

For the family

Whether in whole house theming or concept catering, most innovations take into account the importance of the valuable family market. Pubs by their nature often occupy prime sites with high-volume passing traffic, including

Meeting Market Demand

INNS

	Harvester	Falstaff	Sullivans	Pier House Restaurants
Style and menu	The logo says "steak houses" but the object is to develop a well-defined, branded, chain of family restaurants. Skilful architectural titivation — weather boarding and artificial shutters — makes the outside of the pub look plush but rural.	A chain of popular priced steak bars with no pretentions to be anything other than restaurants in pleasant public houses. Peter Webber says the chain is aiming for the part of the market which Berni captured 30 years ago.	As a family pub — with soda fountain for children — the first unit now open in Ilford, Essex, is already reckoned to be a winner.	A small organisation of restaurants ranging across the spectrum of contemporary styles which do not invite definition. It will include the Old Rangoon, Barnes, and The Dome at Hampstead
Average spend	£6.50 excluding drinks	£4.40 excluding drinks	£6 excluding drinks	Wide range
Staffing	50-60 inc part-time	35-40	60	Wide range
Cost	£250,000+	Up to £100,000	£250,000+	£250,000+
Anticipated No. of units	50 in four years	30 in first year	20 in first year	50 in four years

TAVERNS

	Little Jack's Pie Shop	The Hot Potato	The Pantry	Slica Pizza
Style and menu	The menu features a selection of pies baked in individual dishes on the premises. The first opened in the Robin Hood, Newport, South Wales.	Potatoes baked in their jackets and served with a choice of hot or cold fillings. Serveries of a standard design are cut into the counter.	A selection of traditional pub food, but subject to strict control. It's pub grub, but managers will have no choice in what they serve, being required to follow the specifications.	Complete pizzas are cooked on the premises in open pizza ovens and sold by the slice. The slices are cut to order and presented in foil packages which allow them to be eaten in the fingers.

	Meat and Eat	Old Time Deli	Chicago Hot Dog	The Magic Pan
	A basic steak bar operation suitable for small upstairs pub restaurants offering four different cuts and weights of steaks with all selling at the same price.	A New York-style sandwich bar featuring salt beef sandwiches and Chicago-style hot dogs. Imperial has an American supplier to ensure authenticity.	Genuine frankfurters served in a seeded roll garnished with cucumber relish, onion, mustard, gherkins and tomato. They're served from carts by girls wearing T-shirts.	A call-order omelette and salad bar. Omelettes are cooked in front of the customers. The unit is of standard design.

Figure 2 *Imperial Inns and Taverns — twelve concepts in pub catering.* Caterer & Hotelkeeper *has compiled this table to show at a glance how the Courage-owned group is setting about changing its pubs by launching new food service systems*
Courtesy *Caterer & Hotelkeeper*, 2 February 1984

pedestrians; much of this traffic cannot be turned into business simply because of the licensing laws. Within a decade there must surely be relaxation of the licensing laws that will allow children into what are now no-go areas.

Generally, the average British person feels comfortable with a British pub. The general public can sometimes feel apprehensive walking into a restaurant or hotel, but does not see the pub environment (usually much less imposing) as hostile. All pub catering concepts and systems are likely to bear in mind this fundamental factor. If licensing restrictions are removed, the business flood gates will open.

The licensee's response

The independent licensee can begin to meet the catering challenge of major operators simply by adopting a similar approach.

Undertake a simple market exercise to establish what market segment would be served to best advantage. Generally, markets should not be mixed; attempts to attract two or more invariably attract none. Scrutinize competitors' activity closely. Evaluate how much catering business you want and how much area you can devote to it, including space at the back of the house. Catering should not conflict with liquor sales. Do not lose valuable liquor trading areas to less profitable food trading areas.

Having established the market and your available space, decide on a range of products that will meet your customers' needs. If the market has been clearly identified, then the product range need not be very wide to satisfy it. Successful steak bars sell steaks and not much more. Kentucky Fried Chicken sell chicken and not much more. In addition it is normally much easier to prepare a few products to a consistent standard than a large number.

Where possible the range of products should include one or more key dishes. Such 'signature' items need not be the most expensive, but should be a memorable experience for customers that will encourage repeat custom and gain repute. This can be achieved by the inherent quality of the food itself, for example fine traditional cheeses, or by spectacular presentations, such as the enormous baked jacket potatoes sold at the King's Head, Woodstock. In either case, the products must represent value for money.

The more you can guarantee consistency, the more successful you will be in building your reputation and business. Most licensees would never brew their own beer even if they were allowed to; and the same reasoning can and should be applied to food. If a manufacturer is producing the product that is required to the right standard and the right price, then it is better to buy it than produce it on site. The case for convenience food has already been stated. The need to deskill, to control payroll costs and maintain standards has long been identified by major operators. The same rules apply to licensees.

Whatever type of food is purchased, it must be bought to a specification agreed and understood by both buyer and supplier. Monitor these specifications rigorously. Likewise, fully determine and document the storage, handling and preparation of materials.

If available funds permit major theming of the pub and the site is ideal for a particular concept, this will have been considered fully at the preliminary marketing stage. In most cases 'theming' will take place during or after the establishment of the product range and signature dishes, often by linking dishes with local place names or activities and the name and feel of the pub.

Methods of food service, style of crockery etc. are equally important in contributing to the total package. Every aspect of food service must therefore be documented, from purchasing through to portioning, dish presentation and service methods. A licensee will then have operating standards of performance against which to train staff and to control and monitor his catering business.

Obviously staff need only be trained to a standard of performance sufficient to cover their job. In larger establishments there might be a distinction between food production, food service and cleaning staff; but in small establishments all three jobs may be rolled into one. In either case reference to operating standards should be as quick and as easily understood as possible. An inexpensive and effective method is photography, not only of all dishes but also of table setting, food displays, and correct fridge and dry stores layout. Standards at the back of the house are as important as in the front.

The time you devote as a licensee to food operation should be directly linked to its value to the business as a whole. If not systemized, catering can be time consuming, costly, unprofitable and, to the consumer, inconsistent. By developing a system for catering you will be better placed to meet the challenge of the major operators.

Further reading

Cooper, Derek, *British Eating Out in Pubs*, National Catering Inquiry, 1970.
Kotas, R. (ed.), *Market Orientation*, Surrey University Press, 1975.

3 Promoting pub food

Anthony M. Perry

Material from Peter Hime is included in this chapter.

Colourful advertising surrounds us – on television, in magazines and newspapers, on hoardings and in cinemas. Any business unaware of the effects of advertising on the consumer is doomed to failure.

The challenge facing every consumer trade – and catering is no exception – is how to create a credible and colourful image for an establishment. An image in this sense does not just mean an outside view of how the caterer would like his operation to be viewed; it is the reality of its total public face at a time when visual images projected by the media create ever greater expectations.

Marketing the image

Publicity and advertising are important factors in image building, but it is of little practical use to business if publicity creates public awareness and demand for a product that cannot reasonably be provided. Indeed, in the days of consumer protection legislation, ill-advised publicity can easily step across the bounds of illegality. The building and environment in which the catering service is offered is as important to the image conscious caterer as the means by which he promotes his products.

In the advertising world, before a product is marketed, those responsible look for and work upon what is termed the unique selling proposition or USP. In plain English, this is what makes the product a uniquely better buy than its competitors. It shapes the direction the advertising takes, the way the packaging is developed, and the method by which the product is offered to the consumer. In brief, it dictates the final public image of the product or service.

A small business – and the pub caterer will usually fall into this category – has to mount its own advertising campaigns. It does not usually have the assistance of advertising men, agencies and the other experts who are available to big business. One of the benefits of the franchised operation such as Wimpy and Kentucky Fried Chicken is that the total number of outlets can contribute sufficient publicity funds to create their own brand-building publicity campaign.

For success in this highly competitive field, there is still room for the small operator who can combine imagination with the use of some general principles. Unfortunately the catering industry has been notoriously backward in self-promotion over the years. The principles which make for successful catering promotion are not always clear, and it can be a valuable exercise for the small businessman to take serious notice of other people's advertising.

Meeting Market Demand

Advertising What such an exercise reveals is how the agencies who produce advertisements for familiar products view those factors which make the products most desirable. From this they build the visual and public picture for their sales pitch.

An example has been seen in the bread industry in recent years. Factory sliced breads started to meet consumer resistance, and to counteract this the bakers promoted the Victorian virtues of freshness, home-made shapes and old time taste. In areas where resistance to supermarket bread was at its highest, retail bakery shops with their own ovens (producing pies, not bread) were opened to provide credibility to the image of 'home-madeness'.

In beer marketing, the most successful recent example of this has been the regionality of taste: the advertisements promote 'your local beer' because the brewers had found consumer resistance to national brand name marketing.

After becoming thoroughly familiar with how to spot the USP, it is a short step to identifying it in one's own business. The food and drink may be good, but is that really the reason why customers come to your establishment rather than the one down the road? Perhaps it is the speed of service; perhaps they do not feel cramped or crowded; or perhaps they feel that the service is used by what they regard as a 'better type of customer'. Rarely is the USP of a catering establishment the product that is actually served, unless it is very unusual. Once identified, the USP is a factor on which one can build a successful advertising and publicity campaign.

In licensed premises and small hotels there are limits to the extent to which an image can be created that is singularly different from the run-of-the-mill competitors. But every manager worth his salt and concerned with the creation of his public image should first consider colour and symbolism and the way it can be worked throughout a catering establishment to give a sense of

Figure 3 *An example of a merchandized snack lunch offer in pubs that is proving its worth*
Courtesy Rank Hovis Limited

Promoting pub food

identity. A name or an inn sign is a good starter, but co-ordinated decor should also be considered.

Co-ordination As a guideline, colour decor and publicity material for the hotel industry is most successful when co-ordinated in reds, oranges and browns because these are the colours of welcome. Blues and greens are the colours of clinical cleanliness and, although they can play a part in catering decor (in cafeterias etc.), they should be avoided in the licensed sector.

Decor apart, co-ordination is important. All too often licensed caterers are persuaded into using a mass of printed material from suppliers (drip mats, posters, stickers etc.). These all project different images, and the establishment's own image can be destroyed.

The most important aspect of the caterer's business life is the one most often left to chance: how to get an increasing number of customers to enter the establishment. Once inside, the caterer should be trying to persuade each customer to spend his money, and at the same time provide that customer with satisfaction. If the mix of those three aspects of business life is right, regardless of how the product is produced, the caterer is well on the way to success.

Premises checklist

To establish whether every aspect of marketing your establishment, in the broadest sense, has been covered, run through the following:

Outside
(a) Are the exterior signs clean and freshly painted; are they clearly illuminated at night?
(b) If the local authority does not permit illumination, have you used luminous paint?
(c) Are the signs visible from all angles and approaches on the road?
(d) Are there clear signs to available parking space?
(e) Are the car parks in good order, clearly lit at night, and marked for maximum efficient accommodation?
(f) Are the grass edges overgrown? Long grass looks uncared for and may reflect the general attitude of the pub.
(g) Is the pavement outside the premises clean? It is unlikely that the council will maintain it in a spotless state.
(h) Is the paintwork of your premises clean and fresh or showing signs of dilapidation? It is not essential to redecorate the exterior every year but the ground floor window and door frames should have regular attention.
(i) Are the windows clean?
(j) Are there adequate signs to guide the customer to the various bars and facilities of your premises? Don't assume that it is obvious and that the customer will find them on his own.

Inside
(a) Is the lobby covered with posters of long past events or badly displayed material, tacked up with bits of sellotape and drawing pins at odd heights

and angles? If you want to publicize local events, do so with pride to show that you care and wish to lend support to them.
(b) Is the lighting right? The correct lighting at lunchtime will not do for the evening. Are the lampshades straight and the bulbs all functioning?
(c) Are the chairs safe, and the cushions clean and not frayed? Are the pictures and other furniture clean and therefore achieving the objective for which money was spent on them in the first place?
(d) Is there a telephone available to customers? It is negative to point out that it is vandalized: the main problem for telephones is siting. A telephone tucked away in an odd dark corner or corridor is ripe for attack.
(e) Look at the bar: is the counter and front scuffed and tatty? Is the footrail burnished? Are the beer taps and pump handles clean?
(f) Is the back of the bar just a jumble of bottles, glasses and other items, or is it a positive aid to selling? This is your main selling area and opportunity to merchandize your wares.
(g) Price lists should be readable to short-sighted people and should be displayed next to the bar where customers can get close to them and bar staff can refer to them.

Fitting the market

As inflation and advertising make increasing demands on the consumers' discretionary income, the old reliance upon regular customers may not prove sufficient to keep a business viable. What a caterer has to do is to build his service to fit a market, create an image around it, and project that image through advertising, point of sale material, and word of mouth. Five years, in these ever-changing times, is about the maximum time a service, decor style or idea can be expected to survive changing consumer taste. Permanent success is no longer guaranteed in the public house business.

If a service idea catches on in a pub, and is properly promoted, it will take about a year to build up to its true potential because of the cyclical and seasonal nature of the business. A good idea should remain at a high level of business for about three years, after which the management should be seeking a radical change. During those three years it is essential to write off all special equipment and underwrite all advertising costs. By the fifth year, if the idea is good enough, it will have been copied and competition which was not there at the start will have been created.

It can prove a productive exercise in preparing any sales or marketing programme to analyse the range of services provided within the establishment during the week. Measure these against the clientele, their age group, their social class, whether they are at work or leisure, where they come from, and their general occupations.

Opportunities for custom It will become obvious from such a survey that there are at least twenty-one clearly defined opportunities for custom during the week (see later); the clientele may vary in type and age, but a pattern will form. Those premises lucky enough to have a party or function room separated from the main public areas may have another fourteen periods in the week when they can find extra business. There is nothing to say that each of these business opportunities will be maximized, but it is a good start to constructing a sales campaign, and incidentally makes the most of available staff.

As drink takings are a fairly stable factor in averaging business patterns, management wanting a more complete business pattern assessment should take bar till readings at set and different times of the day over a week, irrespective of cashing-up times. This information can be linked to clientele information to build a fairly complete picture of existing sales patterns.

When are these opportunity times? There are seven lunchtime licensing sessions during each week. Added to this there is a potential for party business for seven lunchtimes. The evening falls into two clearly defined periods – early and late.

Often a pub with a good lunchtime trade, sited near places of work, also enjoys a sound early evening trade which peters out as customers go home. In a case like this the weekend is often slack. Such a pub could profitably put on a special event on Saturday and Sunday nights. The result would probably be a considerable increase in takings and, if the overheads have already been met by the regular weekly trade, the uplift in profits will be considerable.

In a rural location, party bookings on Monday to Thursday lunchtimes may be infrequent, whereas the demands of weddings and functions at the weekends are heavy. A campaign aimed at parties of pensioners, who do take days out in the country at this time of the week, could offer reduced prices. As this would generate extra rather than bread and butter business, every penny after basic staff, material and energy costs are met is profit. Cut prices in such a situation can be a critical sales attraction.

Assessing demand

All licensed premises are unique. Nevertheless several factors make public houses and small hotels similar in their pattern of trading. Management in this vast sector of business has an overwhelming tendency to give the customers what they think the demand should be. It is unusual to find a publican or small hotelier who has assessed the demands of his clients rationally rather than with the emotion of his own prejudices. Added to this, the licensing laws affecting the drinking area and alterations, times of opening and sometimes even the style of the liquid product have, down the years, been a severe depressant on trade. Management has thus been deflected from a much more positive attitude to sales. Changes in social behaviour and attitudes towards drinking continue, with the pub now reckoned to be the leisure time playground of the under twenty-fives.

If this is the case, as some recent research suggests, the place of the pub in society must be reassessed. A service and product analysis along the lines regularly conducted by other consumer industries is an appropriate base from which to make this reassessment. A realistic and successful promotion campaign cannot be shaped unless a fairly exact market definition has been reached.

Defining the pub market

Pubs fall into quite clear and defined categories:

The city and town centre pubs
Secondary and town pubs near housing estates and new building developments
Country pubs in main road locations
Country pubs in rural locations.

The city centre pub now attracts high rents. Almost always it is in the hands of a brewery or other well-financed operator. If these pubs are on a worthwhile site and not in an area of urban decay, the brewers inevitably choose to operate them directly or through subsidiary companies.

Pubs in secondary town sites or strategically sited near housing or other developments, as with all country pubs, can only really afford to avoid a long-term rethink of the former pub management methods of drink, snacks and a little food if they enjoy a high level of passing trade. Rents, rates, staff overheads and energy costs have turned what were relative gold mines into marginal profit-makers. The gold is created by the business attracted after these basic costs have been met.

Potential custom The key factor in determining whether the licensee should aim his promotional activities towards point of sale advertising, or whether a more widespread and subtle approach is necessary, is the number of potential customers passing his front door.

It is difficult to lay down precise guidelines on the count that justifies a retailing approach to attracting business. As most premises outside the brewers' control will be in secondary locations, a fair average could be at least 1000 people per hour passing by in peak periods. If the count is below that figure this establishment should consider whether to provide a more elaborate product than 'this is a pub; we sell good food; welcome'. Where pedestrian or car counts are high, presentation and external advertising is an essential factor in attracting the greatest number of clients.

Good marketing demands an awareness of the social class and category into which potential custom may fall. Whereas a town pub may have a potential middle class and business clientele during the day, at night it could well be that the under twenty-fives from a wider social spectrum are looking for pub services. Mix the two groups and neither will be satisfied.

Matching service and demand To match the service to customer demand is where the identified USP plays its most vital role. The two most easily identified reasons for lunchtime eating in a pub or licensed restaurant, whether during work or leisure, are either that the food is inexpensive, the service is quick and the surroundings and atmosphere are congenial, or that the food is up-market and is served with a minimum of fuss but with the element of single-table privacy that the general bar situation cannot provide.

The ideal mix for an average busy lunchtime pub may be a two-level service offering snacks and light meals in the bar area, with a clearly defined restaurant area elsewhere providing a more expensive menu.

Promoting pub food

There is much to commend a merchandizing approach to pub lunches. In years to come the change in lunchtime habits will become even more marked than it is today. At the moment too many licensed premises are old buildings unsuited to providing modern medium-price service and at the same time taking account of modern building legislation. In any case the most critical factor in building a good customer relationship is to maintain an even standard of food and service.

Types of fare Consequently there is considerable merit in offering a set of clearly identified, inexpensive snack platters. These can be prepared in the kitchen to a set pattern which should not be varied either in standard or content. Prices may have to increase but it can be potentially disastrous to avoid a price increase by skimping portions. Already there are examples of merchandized snack lunches in pubs that are proving their worth. They are offered under such names as Pub Grub and Ploughman's Lunch (see Figure 3). Fisherman's Lunch is a variation of the latter; the possibilities are endless for the imaginative.

One way of attracting custom is to offer ethnic dishes. They can be introduced into a menu by promotional means. Why not have a French week – or month – in which the snack counter offers French pâtés, French cheeses and French wines? Afterwards the most popular items could be incorporated into a Frenchman's Platter. This adds excitement to a menu, and breaks the menu monotony for regular lunchtime clientele.

Another idea for a holiday area, near to the sea, is to offer a plate of mussels in their shells. This has the virtue of being a dish that can be cooked *en masse* inexpensively, attracts a return higher than its relative raw material price would normally command, and can be served with a minimum of fuss.

Food signs If the customer is passing the door, the best and cheapest way to attract him is by a visual sign. If this sign is a fixture, beware of planning regulations. If it is possible to place a sign that is portable without causing an obstruction, then this is the best point of sale advertisement. It should be more attractive than just a square name sign or menu board; it might perhaps be chef shaped. It must not be so portable that thieves can steal it, vandals wreck it, or the wind blow it over.

After the external board the most powerful form of promotional material is at the place where the sale is made: where the customer sits when he is handed a menu. This might seem obvious but it is the most often forgotten fact. Here the opportunity exists for communicating to an already captured audience not only the products, dishes and services then on offer, but also future offerings.

Media and material Table mats are an obvious medium. Made attractive enough they will leave the premises with customers, a most useful way of spreading your message – and remember that there are two sides to a place mat.

With modern instant print litho so readily available, providing table mats with a printed menu, even if inflation does not always allow a printed price, is economic. If you are unsure of design, use your inn sign or symbol as a basis and ask the printer to work out an inexpensive design which can be changed or updated as the business develops. There is no need to order more than 1000 or 2000 mats at a time. If the house has other attractions at night, perhaps in the way of entertainment, or there are party facilities, a place mat that is used subtly to describe these services can be powerful.

When and where to advertise

For the more adventurous, media advertising can reap rich rewards or it can be an expensive flop! As advertising rates become ever higher, even in local newspapers, those businessmen attracted by the idea of advertising their wares should be aware of what advertising can do for single premises. This is vital when deciding how much to spend and when and where to spend it.

There are several ground rules that from experience apply to pub and small hotel advertising, whatever the medium. Advertising for a single attraction – a definite artiste appearing for a fixed night or period – may or may not work, but advertising in the media is the only safe way of attracting sufficient business to justify the expense of staging such an event. Advertising for overall services has to be more clearly defined than just stating the establishment's name, to give any possibility of achieving results.

If a single attraction is advertised, particularly where there is a door or table fee, the space purchased should not be more than 10 per cent of the total possible turnover generated by this source. It is also better to have a wide spread of similar spaces in a variety of newspapers; weekly local papers are the most suitable.

The second type of advertising is for a repeated service; this may be to 'Try our steak', to 'Have a fish dish with us', or for party services. The more general the service, the less likely it is that the results of the advertising will prove worthwhile.

Tourists and party groups

In any situation where a high proportion of outside visitors is evident, it is generally possible to identify that groups of people from the same locality, or with the same interests, make a regular habit of visiting another different locality in quite substantial numbers. This should indicate where advertising can be placed with some hope of a result.

Whether the catering establishment is on a main road or in a rural location, by the sea or on a housing estate, if there is a significant tourist movement in the district, there are business possibilities which can be exploited by judicious advertising.

The most productive tourist business to be found is party groups. Chance tourists are a risky business and weather and other diversions can create completely unpredictable trading patterns. But a tourist trade based upon group business is more reliable and the chance traveller is the jam on the bread and butter.

The advertising pitch to get party business must be aimed not so much at the party group itself but at the organizer. One step nearer to the caterer is the coach operator, with whom personal face to face contact is often the only way of successful selling. Coach operators have their own special restriction of choice by the laws under which they operate.

Publicity events and the media

Radio, television and cinema are expensive media which should only be used with one's eyes fully open. Cinema advertising should be avoided unless the establishment's clientele is under twenty-five. Television and radio can be worthwhile if there is a really special message to put across.

Production costs of these advertisements can be high if left to the programme companies to organize on your behalf. What is required is a tape of broadcasting quality or, in the case of television advertising, a transparency slide with what is known as a 'voiceover'. Video or film is so expensive that it can never be justified for the catering and licensed trades.

'Let's have some publicity' is a feeling that strikes many businesses from time to time. Although advertising can work, good free publicity, carefully constructed and worked out, can hit the jackpot. It may result in far more long-term business than any advertisement. If a feature article appears that is really pleasing, a reprint should always be carried and distributed widely to customers.

To achieve results there are a few golden rules. Never go for a gimmick. Never upset the press; if a mistake or misstatement is serious enough, write a courteous letter to the editor for publication, explaining your view. If you provide a worthwhile story and gain a reputation among local pressmen as a source of good reliable stories, you will be rewarded with all the publicity you desire.

The press have a job to do. If the catering establishment cultivates their goodwill it will find itself mentioned increasingly often, as a place where such-and-such a function was held, or so-and-so had their wedding reception, or where such-and-such celebrity stayed. Over a long period this publicity can do much to create a solid local reputation that is worth its weight in gold.

Publicity events in hotels and pubs must be as carefully thought out and programmed. There is no finer way of publicizing your business than to show it off to opinion moulders, party organizers and tour operators. It can take as much as five years for a regular flow of business to emerge from such a move but, accompanied by a well-run publicity campaign, this long-term promotion can also be valuable as public relations.

Do not have any preconceived ideas about where publicity or business may be found. Tourism is organized on a nationwide level throughout the UK. There are increasing demands from tourist boards for facility visits for tour organizers, VIPs and others. One successful facility trip can generate others; it can be seen beforehand that they may not generate any direct business. Either way they can be turned to good effect as a vehicle for press publicity.

Groups Visitors in a group always interest the local press and radio. Management should make sure that the press knows of the time, itinerary and personal details of such visitors in good time. Build into the itinerary a time slot for interviews with the visitors.

The hospitality you offer does not need to be lavish or to be a gastronomic experience. A facility visit may cost a few pounds in free food, wine and extra staff, but set this against the potential publicity value and the cost of advertising even in a local weekly and costs quickly fall into perspective.

Invite at least some local dignitaries to meet and greet the visitors. On the day the management should be too busy making everything run smoothly to socialize casually with the visitors. Make sure that each visitor has a literature pack about the establishment and its services on his seat, and include literature on the locality and a small memento of the visit. This may be a souvenir place mat, a small personalized chocolate box or a stamped beer glass; the range of items is immense.

The food For a press occasion like this offer regional food from your locality, preferably in a buffet rather than as a formal meal. Make sure that the guests do not sit in cliques. Although you offer a buffet service, make a seating plan so that the pressmen and local VIPs are able to meet the visitors. If the object of the exercise is to obtain publicity, the one way to fail to get the coverage you want is to have a set dinner with top table formality.

Invitations Invitations should go out to the press not more than seven days before the event, and each person from the media should be contacted if an RSVP has not been sent. Every invitation list will be different, but as a broad generalization include the news editor of the local radio station, the editor of the local weekly newspaper, and the editor of the local evening newspaper. If the visit is sufficiently important, invite regional television.

Invitations are best in the form of a letter explaining in as much detail as possible what is to take place; it is worth mentioning that a guest with each press representative would be welcome, as would photographers. The guest invitation is rarely taken up, but it creates a feeling of goodwill which is the essence of good press relations. Press people have deadlines to meet, and the informality of the buffet lunch allows them to come and go more easily.

One tip to bear in mind with all facility visits is that it is in your own interests to offer the service without charge and free of all strings. Tourist boards do have money to pay for some of their facility visits, and if they offer to pay use the money to provide something extra. A free party gives the host hotelier a much freer hand in menu selection and on the press side if the tab is not then picked up by an official organization.

A presentation At the end of the meal, during coffee, stage-manage a small presentation to the group leader, and to the local VIPs. Give a small memorable personal present, and also make a presentation of something which can make a good press picture. Successful publicity lunches stage-managed by the author include the presentation of a giant fish from the Fleetwood market to a leading British politician, the largest black pudding in Lancashire dressed in red and yellow ribbons for the leader of an official Russian delegation, a drink of sarsaparilla for a group of pensioners on a trip organized by a television company, and tripe and onions for a party of Dutch journalists.

The reactions, the pictures – all of it is good harmless copy for the press. But if you hit on a good press idea, never repeat it. And once you have organized an event it is important to make sure that the press can get the facts and the names of those involved accurately. Write a press release, give details of all involved with initials and titles of the main personalities. At the bottom of each piece of press literature give the name, title and telephone number of the person or persons in your organization most concerned with the detailed planning of the event. Given good luck, a well-planned event gets good publicity.

Vending machines

These cover anything from cigarettes to sweets and cakes. There is little doubt that machines serving a variety of hot and cold snacks and drinks will become available in many pubs before this decade is over. People are no longer adhering rigidly to particular meal times or eating habits, and a vending machine is more cost effective during slack times than the use of catering staff.

Further reading

Kotas, R. (ed.), *Market Orientation*, Surrey University Press, 1975.

4 A promotional case study
Anthony M. Perry

The ideas in this chapter for exploiting and marketing pub opportunities have been drawn from the author's own experience in a small country pub. Those successful and those that failed over a decade are the bases for suggested ways in which a licensee can exploit market opportunities, whether his pub is in town or country.

The market and merchandising

The key to success in pub catering is to identify the exact market segment for which the establishment is best suited. For many a licensee the pub is not only his business, but also his life. Therefore, whatever his background, his interests and his circle of friends often reflect the business he conducts. They often reflect the type of business the publican believes is best for his house on evidence no better than hunch.

Whereas this may have been the route to pub success in the past, the landlord who can treat the bar and dining rooms as his private domain, and the resort of his friends, is lucky indeed. If the landlord's social attitudes reflect the type of pub he runs, and he is successful, it is due more to coincidence than a plan. In this consumer age the successful pub, like any successful business, has to use all the wiles and skills of the modern retail merchandiser. In essence the modern pub is a retail establishment in which the product is the service, and it has to be moulded to fit the market in which it finds itself.

The fundamental fact behind the brand names on the doors and facias of Britain's pubs – Schooner Inns, Berni, Cavalier and Duttons Bistros – is that in every aspect of pub service, merchandising and brand identification has become important.

The marketing objective in licensed premises will vary according to whether the multiple owner or individual is more interested in the 'great God' barrelage or in the overall profitability of the enterprise.

An examination of a number of pubs in a national chain would quickly identify those operations which are making a realistic return on the total value of the site. This is particularly so when you consider that the principal justification for running a pub is to create an outlet for the brewer's product. Although a considerable number of brewers develop catering operations within their premises, some may still make the fundamental error of measuring success purely on barrelage.

A promotional case study

Brewery catering policies

There are four main catering operations used by the breweries and pub owners:

Snack bar: sandwiches, hot and cold snacks, coffee
Limited menu served at table (e.g. steak bars, pie parlours)
A la carte restaurant, either fresh or convenience foods
Party catering

Packaging aims to eliminate all the negative aspects of the selling operation in a given situation. For example, if you take a car as a product, its specification might include four wheels, five seats, 45 m.p.g. at 60 m.p.h., top speed of 110 m.p.h., 0–60 m.p.h. in 11 seconds, and all at a price between £4250 and £4750. However, you would not be impressed by a car which achieved all this but was wrapped up in a 1950 style body. Sales impact would be lost. The product would not sell.

Just as there is no value in creating a product which is not going to sell, there is no merit in selling a product which makes no profit. There is no such thing as a loss leader; it is merely a product which makes less profit than others. It is normal, therefore, for the food gross profit on a snack bar operation to be no higher than 50 per cent overall. This does not mean that no product will be sold with a 20 per cent only mark-up. Averaging creates a variety of products for the customer to choose from and enables a display at the snack bar counter to have maximum effect.

The principal aim of a pub snack bar is to create a greater volume of consistent trading revenue through the whole of the licensing hours. Snack bar equipment costs are such that there is little point in equipping the premises unless you believe you will exceed a revenue of £300 per week from the snack bar.

As businesses showing a real return on capital, many pubs are redundant but survive because of the restrictions on competition imposed by the licensing acts.

Competition

In the North of England, where it has become far easier to open a club with barely a pretence at a regulated membership, competition in the licensed trade has become more intense. Many brewery-owned houses have found their way on to the open market and are now operated as free houses, more for their value as property rather than for trading profits.

Before the creation of the big brewery combines, many pubs across the country were either inns or staging posts on important cross-country routes, taverns for entertainment, or attached to farms or other small enterprises, with beer brewed in the cellar. Consequently they provided a service to what was a fairly steady market. Many pubs retailed a home-made product – beer – with a high added value and high profit level, or they were in partnership with the brewery whereby their rent, generally low by any standards, was linked to sales. In the country the service was carried out by the women while the man of the house ran his farm and looked to the business side of the pub.

Motorways, entertainment complexes and even the problem of retailing and looking after real beer, as opposed to keg, have left wide swaths of Britain with large numbers of what are really redundant pubs – redundant in that their role in modern society has not been truly redefined.

A case history The case history of trading at the Bayley Arms in the Lancashire fellside village of Hurst Green highlights many of the problems facing a number of modern pubs and some of the solutions. At the time we acquired the Bayley Arms, one of two local pubs in the hands of our family for some thirty years previously, it had long been regarded as a loss maker impossible to fill. It was one of no less than fourteen licensed premises within a four-mile radius in an area with a population of only 600.

The problems What we can see in retrospect from our experience is that the problems of running a profitable country pub parallel those of creating a viable rural community. As the infrastructure of the rural community collapses, leaving many houses used only for weekends or converted into solitary hideouts for the rich, the rural pub's normal livelihood is threatened. Greater mobility among country people has destroyed the corps of regulars any country establishment must hope to rely upon; the same drift away from rural living among poorer families has destroyed the pool of potential staff. Permanent skilled resident staff find living in remote country areas unattractive.

That there is a demand at certain times of the week for the catering services of a country pub there can be no question. What is far more debatable is whether it is economic to provide investment, space and equipment to meet this demand, which by its nature is affected by unpredictable factors such as weather.

The Bayley Arms was facing this classic dilemma in 1969. The society which had been based for so many years on drinking, and which had its local pub as a centre, had disappeared. Could a new market be created? If skilled resident staff could not be found, how could this pub provide service beyond the physical capacity of the management? What type of service could be provided by unskilled staff? What wage structure could be imposed, irrespective of the Wages Council rates? These were some of the basic problems facing us at the Bayley Arms; what happened shows how we surmounted these various hurdles to success, or just accepted the situation and changed the product accordingly.

Staff As staff is the basis of any successful catering business, a few words on our success in this sector are appropriate. No trained catering worker was ever employed by us. We were never lucky enough to receive an application for a job from anyone with training. When we acquired the Bayley Arms it had a staff of three part-time cleaners and a barmaid, also part-time, who soon afterwards left the district. When we sold the pub ten years later the same three members of staff were still working for us, together with part-time employees fluctuating in number from five to twenty-five. By this time, our three cleaners were skilled enough to carry out any single service function capably, whether in the kitchen, restaurant or bar.

A promotional case study

We found that willing sixth formers or local students were the best and most reliable extra labour. They needed the money and were available at precisely the times when the country pub catering for leisure business wanted staff. To deal with these students, several ground rules were observed. We never asked them to do anything we were not prepared to do ourselves, and within reason we always tried to make their working periods with us fun. Pay for everyone was fixed at a certain sum per working session; on a weekday there might be little work to do, at weekends a great deal, but the pay was the same regardless. A bonus for each session was paid for each year worked. This ensured that our long-established workers received more than the youngsters, but nobody felt exploited. Tips by and large were discouraged.

Some catering employers using student labour complain about their unreliability and their tendency to want nights off at the most inconvenient times. All our student staff knew there was a job for them as long as we were never let down. If they wanted a night off that was in order provided that it suited us or they found someone else to take their place. In ten years the system worked so well that we were never short of good staff. The system of replacements provided a regularly replenished pool of youngsters from year to year as individuals left college to take up their careers.

The product Having created a happy working environment, the next challenge was to create a product to the satisfaction of customers, served by people unwilling to take a catering course and for whom the acquisition of any real catering skills was of no interest. Behind every move made in the operational side of the Bayley Arms in ten years was this one fact.

The potential we found when we took over was uncertain. The number of cars passing the door was spasmodic. Bedroom business, on which a high percentage of the turnover had always rested, was threatened by the Fire Precautions Act and the construction of a number of new motor hotels in the district. The cost of providing residential fire precautions in a 600-year-old building was beyond the possible return of sales. Change or closure was clearly inevitable. This unedifying choice is similar to that facing many publicans today, where soaring inflation and overheads create the ever-present danger of having to increase prices to the point where they discourage existing clientele.

Food In this climate we assessed the market for the Bayley Arms. There was clearly a demand for food; in catering for the residual bedroom business there was a small demand for restaurant meals. Under the new fire laws it was possible to accommodate up to six guests without a certificate. Ultimately we found that, if we offered minimum bedroom service in warm cosy rooms at a minimum price, we had appreciative regular residents and passing holiday-makers, and we made more profit and gave more satisfaction than we ever did offering complete hotel services from breakfast to dinner.

Saturday night and Sunday morning provided our big business opportunity. The question was how best to achieve a menu mix that was economic, viable and possible given the pool of willing but unskilled staff.

Equipment The equipment available and the space for preparation was limited: a 2 kW microwave oven, a deep fat fryer, a grill, a toaster, a two-pot bain-marie, three infrared lights for keeping food awaiting service warm, a hot cabinet for warming plates, and a quartet of bain-marie containers for soups and vegetables. Available seating in the restaurant gave, at most, thirty customer places. The type of tables we found ideal for our small service situation were small square polished wood ones with a central pedestal, having a surface area not more than 51 × 51 cm (20 × 20 in). They could be combined into a larger party or split up according to demand.

Service All food was personally prepared by the management in the kitchen, where service was supervised. Service in the restaurant was also supervised by management. With a limited number of tables it was vital to achieve at least a two-times turnaround on Saturday if sufficient turnover was to be generated.

Promotion and advertising brought in the people; but could the system stand the pace? Could unskilled staff in a conventional restaurant situation cope? They could not. At the critical peak point of turnround, chaos would start from a small mistake such as a wrongly set table. Service would be delayed and customers become angry.

Diners in the North Country do not wish to spend more than a spare hour on eating, even if they have booked their meal months in advance. They do not understand that good cooking takes time. Even using microwave ovens, the margin between service success and chaos on a busy night, given this situation, is at its narrowest. One suspects that many a half empty British restaurant is suffering from the same problem.

The menu Bar snacks were served in the small comfy bar. Pub food had become stereotyped from Birmingham to Carlisle, the standard offerings being scampi or chicken in the basket and a selection of uninspired dishes with chips, or pies and pasties. In many places the unexciting menu is completed by a ploughman's lunch or its marine equivalent, fisherman's lunch. This is a menu mix hardly likely to entice the average customer from his fireside on a cold winter's night to take a five- or ten-mile car ride to reach the pub. That is the measure of the real marketing challenge facing many country and even urban pubs today. It was the problem at the Bayley Arms.

One answer was to give the bar snacks menu its own special character: to take a selection of basic ingredients and make them more interesting. It had to be possible to serve them at any time within a few minutes. Our secret was to use rice, not chips, and to have a wide range of dishes that were boil-in-the-bag or could be created in our kitchen and retained under freeze or fridge conditions.

From coq au vin and scampi Newberg to chicken and mushroom casserole – all these dishes proved popular and profitable. Knives and forks were pre-wrapped in attractive serviettes and each dish was served on its own bed of rice in earthenware oven-to-table dishes. Portion cost and control could be exactly determined. As an alternative we offered a range of curries given the grandiose name of Bayley Bengalis, although they had no Bangladeshi connections – beef, chicken or prawn. For customers choosing curry there was a

A promotional case study

large platter of side dishes offered, with a range of items from chutney, chopped onions and garnished tomato to peanuts. Access to this platter, in itself as popular as the curry, was free except on Saturday nights; this was an incentive to visit us on other days. What all these dishes and the way they were served had in common was that, if for any reason management was not available, they could be served speedily and efficiently by our unskilled staff in just the same way as we would have served them. Our standards did not drop.

The restaurant problem remained. How could we solve the business conundrum of finding a way to serve a full house without creating chaos, or at least the mental torment of management facing uncertainty at the peak of 9 p.m. on a Saturday night? Cut the numbers and there was no real profit to be made at the popular price levels at which our menu was pitched. Increase the numbers by accepting the actual demand for dinners, and chaos resulted. Raise the price levels and the establishment was all too likely to lift itself to a new, more sophisticated market that its ambience and surroundings could never hope to satisfy. Disaster that way was certain.

Reet Good Do

Curiously it was the miners' strike of 1972 that provided the answer. Coal was unobtainable; electricity was subject to power cuts. Customers used to planning their night out, sometimes weeks ahead, could not be convinced that a hot meal would be provided. Overnight, the Bayley Arms, like all its local competitors, lost all its advance bookings. From a busy weekend business we were reduced in that bitter winter to a blank diary.

If Saturday was normally successful, could we fill Friday night with a special promotion? The strike provided an opportunity to experiment, something we could never have afforded to do in a time of uninterrupted trading. Armed only with a belief in brand name merchandising and the effect of advertising, we established an entirely new product to be known as the 'Reet Good Do'.

The first thing we did before we even considered what the product would be was to place a few judicious advertisements in the local newspaper just saying that if you came to the Bayley you would 'have a Reet Good Do', adding that despite the gloom then enveloping the country, our customers would be having a good time at a price they could afford. In retrospect this is an advertising line which could be redeveloped in the dismal 1980s.

To surmount the problem of energy we provided a cold buffet lit by candlelight and added a folk duo named the Bayley Buskers, with guitars, singalong and folk music (see Figure 4). It was an immediate success. Although in later years our marketing approach of a Reet Good Do became the copy line for coach operators in the South of England, for our local customers the evening soon became known as the Lancashire Night Out.

By 1974 it had become a stylized product, but when it started it was experimental. Once the strike was finished it became a weekday or Friday night product as we felt we required the more substantial turnover of the restaurant for Saturdays. Always ready to learn, we felt there were aspects of the evening out that could with some benefit solve our restaurant service problems. Could we, for example, charge double price, keep people amused all evening and thus deliberately slow down service to increase efficiency? Entertainment with food seemed to be an ideal mix, and so was born another

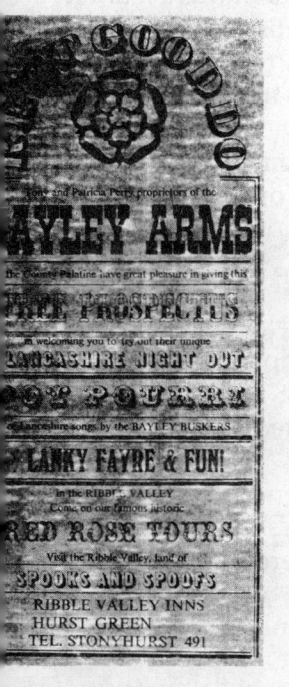

Figure 4 *The 'Reet Good Do' poster*

Meeting Market Demand

idea, Country Serenade. The price levels were £1 for a Reet Good Do and £2.50 for Country Serenade.

Costings   During the first three months every available space in both services was sold out. Costings were monitored and astoundingly it was discovered that although the Country Serenade was at a price 250 per cent higher than the Reet Good Do, turnover and profits on those nights out was significantly lower. In both services there was a high level of repeat business. The floor space was the same, but whereas customers at Country Serenade were given chairs and a degree of space and comfort, the Reet Good Do customers were made to accept a degree of deliberate discomfort. They sat on stools which would never have been acceptable to restaurant customers. Folding chairs were introduced because they were easiest to handle in a crowd.

How, if both services were a sell-out, could the profits and turnover be higher in the less expensive of the two events? The answer was drink sales. In the cheaper service, for every £1 taken for food £3 was spent on drink. On the other hand, although wine sales were relatively high for Country Serenade, other drink sales were so small as to be insignificant in their relation to the total turnover.

Country Serenade was served exactly as a restaurant meal, with entertainment being offered during and after the meal, but the Reet Good Do was the antithesis of a restaurant meal. Its development over the next few years does indicate the potential of an entirely new approach to pub catering. The Reet Good Do was precisely the sort of event which, by personality and persuasion, those involved in the management of the Bayley Arms would have avoided at all costs as their type of leisure enjoyment. To the public at large the Bayley Arms reflected the public face of the management, but it was a marketing façade created, as are most consumer products, to satisfy demand.

What did the product, one refined to a saleable service, really amount to? Party groups could buy a night out from their home back to their home. Direct mail advertising and, most important, recommendation were the main sales weapons. Mailing to social club secretaries over a wide 100 mile radius, backed up by free nights offered to potential organizers or to coach operators together with their twenty-five best party customers, each with a guest, produced enormous dividends.

Coach parties   Coaches are the only realistic form of party transport. Undoubtedly here lies the secret marketing weapon of any pub caterer seeking night-time party business. Licensees who make an effort to examine the effects of transportation on their business may find it a useful background. The breathalyser undoubtedly affects drink sales; if the law is further tightened, this situation will deteriorate. People in coaches need have no worries about that law. Coaching no longer means uncomfortable charabancs; there are now executive coaches with tables, toilets and small kitchens (no bars – drink on licensed coaches is against the law) that can make a party-time journey a continuation of the event until the arrival home.

Once a party secretary had been convinced that an evening out was a good idea, we found the success of the evening was dependent on our making the

A promotional case study

organizer look efficient to friends and members. The greatest single problem any social secretary faces in organizing a night out is price; the catering price can be fixed, but the coach price may vary. It is all too easy to estimate numbers wrongly and for the committee to face a potential loss-making event. That means cancellation and loss all round.

Costs One answer to this was based on the fact that it cost more or less the same amount to run a twenty-nine (smaller) seater coach as to run one for fifty people or more. Having identified major areas from which it was possible to draw substantial business, in our case from the cities of Manchester, Liverpool and Leeds/Bradford, it was no problem to find coach operators ready to give a fixed price for a coach for the evening. Any party organizer with more than twelve people in his group could be quoted an all-inclusive price from home back to home, with numbers up to fifty presenting no problem. With a group of under twelve a minicoach provides a ready answer.

If a party of twenty-five was aboard a coach for fifty, the advertising allocated for that specific night would be in the media covering the same geographical area, designed to find an extra twenty-five passengers for that evening; we rarely failed to do so. Once the coach cost was covered, the extra seats paid for the advertising. Smaller parties using a coach provided by us in this way found a considerable price advantage in using our service, because as energy prices rose the price of coach tickets for a small or half-filled coach, even for a relatively local run, could cost as much as the entrance to a cabaret club or even a dinner out.

There was also an operational advantage. Regular business from us put us in a better position with coach operators. We provided the drivers with a meal and television so that they co-operated with us in making the customers' night out a memorable one from the time they left home.

Booking A small deposit per person was demanded for the booking; payment in total was always required, except by special arrangement, by the morning of the party in question. This had a useful effect on cash flow. Coach operators were given a flat per person discount or a percentage, and they always received their money in advance. We expected the same, or we made acceptance of the booking subject to a considerable (and often hidden) price surcharge – hidden in the sense that our published prices were invariably higher than we were prepared, in fact, to accept to allow for discounts.

Any licensee organizing dinner dances or any special party event at seasonal occasions could do well to study this question of getting the parties to his door at the minimum of cost and with a minimum of fuss. It is crucial to success, particularly in remote districts.

On arrival a member of our family would personally board the coach and give a few words of welcome. This was always appreciated; but there was an operational reason too. By doing so it was possible to persuade people to leave their coats on the coach and avoided congestion in the cloakroom. Very occasionally some coach parties are the type of customers to be avoided. At the point of welcome, before they entered the establishment, experience would identify the situation and we would suddenly have made a mistake in the booking and become overbooked. It could mean considerable financial loss for the night but it made certain there was never a real chance of customer misbehaviour on the premises.

Simplifying service   All glasses were government-stamped plastic of a stacking type, stored in boxes under the bar. In a space for storing, say, fifty conventional glasses, we could keep 500 plastic ones, so that service of drink was uninterrupted by washing up, an important factor in party catering. Small columns of glasses could be collected with safety when people were clapping their hands, singing or otherwise enjoying themselves.

The meal was simple. Soup was served in earthenware beakers, twenty-four to a tray, poured from a jug and garnished with parsley. Beaker service halved the time it took for soup service. This was followed by individual Lancashire hot-pots, made under contract by a local baker and garnished with red cabbage. At the same time as the hot-pot was served, each table was given a bowl of black puddings.

The next course was a large bowl of chips portioned out to numbers on a single or party group, together with fish cakes at an average of one and a half cakes per person. This strange choice was popular and it slowed down the next course, a help-yourself buffet, because by this time many were full; at the same time it helped to discourage people from taking more than they wanted from the buffet.

It was here that we made a feature of Lancashire foods; each dish appearing on the buffet is a story in itself, but briefly there was a range of foods including stew'n'hard, steak and cowheel served on oat cakes, Morecambe Bay seafoods, Eccles cakes and, of course, apple pie (which, as the Lancastrians say, without cheese is like a kiss without a squeeze). Tripe and onions and many other Lancashire specialities were there for the tasting.

Entertainment   Towards the end of dinner, while tables were being cleared, light dialect folk songs telling the story of industrial Lancashire were sung by a single guitarist. Once everybody had finished dinner, the singers increased the tempo until the Bayley Arms became a cross between a German beer hall, a Spanish barbecue and a Victorian English tavern.

Anything went, but good humour and manners were what we asked in return. The author organized a nightly 'go-go' contest for the ladies, a 'knobbly knees' for the men and a ritual singing of 'You'll never walk alone,' the Liverpool FC song. A conga and a hokey-cokey allowed staff to move in and collect glasses.

If the night's customers wanted a singalong it was easy to tell by this time, and this was what our buskers would give them. If they were quieter, perhaps more elderly, and we had many a party of pensioners, always early in the week, then our boys would sing old Lancashire songs from a tradition that runs through from the cotton mills to Formby and from George to Lennon and McCartney.

That was the Reet Good Do. As a special event it would attract an individual customer who liked the atmosphere, say, four times a year. Could he, we wondered, be enticed to visit us at other times? Most important, a factory

A promotional case study

social secretary or the party organizer in a large office complex has far more potential customers to attract again, if they could be reached.

Marketing and presentation

To capitalize on this opportunity we had to market our services to already satisfied customers while they were actually in the pub. Each place setting was stylized with selling in mind. Cutlery was wrapped in serviettes of orange, our house colour. The mix might be thought strange, consisting as it did of a plastic knife and fork and silver-plated knife, fork and spoon; when we used all silver we found our cutlery losses were very high. If cutlery was laid out before the customers arrived in a party group, it created a problem if tables had to be changed to suit individual cliques; prewrapped changes could be made without mistakes. Each setting had a place mat with the menu; on it were printed details of the other products we offered as we developed them, and on the reverse was a song sheet. Each setting consisted of a small plate laid with a bread roll, a large plate and two saucers, one for the soup and one for the hot-pot. With two kitchen staff, two waitresses and a management supervisor we could serve the whole dinner for 130 people, have it cleared up and the entertainment in full swing within an hour and a half. We reckoned that twenty-six persons per staff member was a high rate of productivity.

Tours

Our other main product developed over the years was a day-time tour with a Lancashire lunch based on the Reet Good Do buffet, and the provision of a guide through some of Lancashire's most beautiful fell country, visiting historic monuments, churches and ghost haunts. To make this work we prepared a guide script, and paid some retired local people to act as guides. It assisted coach operators who brought us night-time business in finding a new view for a country day out, and further cemented relations with them. With these tours we soon found ourselves becoming a stop on the international tourist route. From the special welcome register in the church we used at the little village of Slaidburn, we found that we had welcomed forty different nationalities on these small tours during one year. What we got out of them was a great deal of pleasure in meeting a widely different collection of people, and the sale of lunch to each one of them. It was a good regular basis on which to pay summer overheads, whatever the weather.

Promotion

As I mentioned at the start, pubs benefit by good retail merchandising. As part of our everyday promotion we produced window stickers for coach operators' vehicles and windows, a souvenir poster for agents' windows and as a purchased souvenir from the pub itself, and souvenir glasses. The English Tourist Board included our tour and snatches of the Reet Good Do in a record on England's heritage which included the Tower of London and York Minster. We were filmed for television on several occasions, and our proudest moment was the award of a Special BTA Commendation in the 'Come to Britain Award' scheme.

Some publicity was a double-edged sword because a few writers were sufficiently impressed to describe an event that was in their mind but did not in reality happen. Every night was different because every group of customers was different, and reacted to us and to each other's company in a different way. But we suspect that what the Bayley Arms really was during those years was a down-to-earth social centre, charging prices people could afford, without class or pretension, but capitalizing on every opportunity that came along by using well-tested public relations and advertising methods.

Further reading

Kotas, R. (ed.), *Market Orientation*, Surrey University Press, 1975.

5 Factors in layout and planning

Robert Humphreys

Where there has been little or no past provision of food, some alteration to licensed premises and addition of equipment is likely to be necessary.

Planning alterations

Planning such change is a task which varies according to the size and type of the enterprise, the amount of new work needed and the structural or financial constraints.

Consent for extensive alteration work may have to be obtained from numerous authorities. This is a time consuming and complex task. For this reason and because overlooking minor requirements can lead to extra cost, both in lost trade and in extra payment to contractors or staff, licensees should seek professional help.

This may be available from the owning brewery in the case of a tied house, or it may be appropriate to find and pay a freelance architect or designer. In such circumstances a personal recommendation for the person or firm chosen is desirable, since on their competence and reliability will depend the standard and progress of the work. Although such outside help can be costly, licensees considering major work can offset any fees which they pay against the cost of their own time in conducting and supervising the project, and against the cost of any extension of the contract or substandard workmanship which might result. For those determined to do the work unaided, and for those carrying out less substantial changes, the following are guidelines.

Obtaining consent Any extension of the premises which exceeds one-tenth of the volume of the original building, up to 115 cubic metres maximum, will generally require planning consent, although the rules are not quite as simple as this and advice may be obtained from the planning office of the local authority. Also from this office may be obtained advice on the precise procedure required in this operation, but drawings will need to be submitted so that both the existing and proposed layouts are clear. In some cases, the parish council is also involved in the approval process. If consent is refused then an appeal may be lodged.

The local Fire Officer must be notified if structural changes to the premises are contemplated. His prime concern will be satisfactory means of escape, but he will usually take the opportunity offered to consider whether or not the premises as a whole comply, in his view, with the Fire Precautions Act 1971. The Fire Officer should be consulted at an early stage, so that time is not wasted, and a meeting at his office, with preliminary drawings, can usually be arranged and conducted relatively informally. Among other things, he will advise on adequate, appropriate, and suitably sited fire fighting appliances either before or after any changes are made.

Where licensed houses employ more than twenty staff, or ten or more above ground floor level, then a fire certificate for the premises must be sought, and more stringent requirements will be applied. If the grant of a fire certificate is awaited, then a copy of the application must be kept on the premises, for inspection at any time.

Building and other regulations Statutory regulations govern building standards and those relating, for example, to the provision of gas and electrical services and equipment. Any work carried out should conform in both workmanship and materials to such regulations. The work of any reputable building or other contractor and that of the utility authorities should comply with the relevant requirements, but this does not in itself affect the obligation on the property owner to ensure that this is so. An architect employed to superintend work would normally place this obligation on the builder in his contract.

When minor work is carried out, drainage arrangements in particular must be correct, and advice may be obtained from the Building Regulations department of the local authority. Building Regulations also specify flame spread standards for wall and ceiling surfaces, and advice may be sought.

Licensing justices The consent of the local licensing justices must be sought if an alteration will change the size of the licensed area, or the line or arrangement of a bar counter. Any change to the premises' entrance also requires their consent.

Such an application involves an appearance in court and is therefore often handled by a solicitor, although many licensees do represent themselves. 3.175 mm (⅛ in) or 1:100 scale drawings showing the proposals must be submitted to the justices twenty-one clear days before the transfer session at which the application is to be heard, and some (but not all) courts still require one set of drawings for their permanent record to be on linen. Additional copies will be inspected by the surveyor to the justices, the local Fire Officer, the Environmental Health Officer and the police. Any observations or objections which they may have can be raised in court. Most solicitors send the copies for the local authority and police direct.

The sort of issue likely to interest licensing justices, particularly if consent is sought to enlarge the trading area, is adequate provision of lavatory accommodation in accordance with modern minimum standards. Since what at first appears to be a small project (such as to squeeze six or eight extra covers into an eating area) may turn into a major and costly scheme, this question must be carefully considered, particularly when existing facilities are old and barely adequate. Enquiries about an application should be made of the clerk to the local licensing justices.

Factors in layout and planning

Environmental Health Department There is a statutory requirement to notify the local Environmental Health Officer (EHO) if a work area is to be changed, although he is unlikely to be displeased by an enlargement. A reduction in working area is normally regarded as acceptable if the remaining space appears adequate, and other standards are to be maintained or improved, and particularly if the layout is to be improved.

EHO consent is required for a significant change in the standard of wall or floor surface. No objection is likely if normal recommendations are followed, but a proposal to carpet a kitchen would be unlikely to find favour.

When a sizeable alteration is conceived, consult the local EHO before going too far. Inevitably he will visit the house, and making good deficiencies later will be disruptive and more costly than incorporating the requirements in the original scheme. However unwelcome may be extra work or expenditure, the EHO's advice is intended to improve vital standards of hygiene. An oversight might render the licensee liable to prosecution. In addition to the Food Hygiene (General) Regulations, the EHO is also responsible for ensuring compliance with the Public Health Act, the Health and Safety at Work Act, the Offices, Shops and Railway Premises Act and the Local Government (Miscellaneous) Provisions Act, all relevant to licensed premises.

Local legislation Some local Environmental Health Departments issue their own codes of practice, free on request. These are worth reading before the EHO is called in.

Local requirements may go beyond the general standard. In Greater London, for example, compliance with the London Building Act is policed by a number of District Surveyors operating independently from the local authority (the GLC), and their involvement is necessary over any structural alteration.

There are many categories of licensed premises which are governed by more rigorous controls. In these cases advice on proposed alterations should be sought from the relevant authority. Examples are: buildings listed as of special historical or architectural interest; any house with a current music and dancing licence; and any house carrying a fire certificate.

Owning brewery Many public houses are brewery owned and are let under tenancy or lease. The form of tied tenancy or lease usually granted requires the written consent of the brewery to any alteration, and any tenant licensee should ensure that this authority to proceed is secured before work is begun.

Kitchen planning

The best planning of a kitchen should efficiently use space in which it is as easy and safe to work as possible, which is satisfactorily connected to the rest of the business, and which conforms with or exceeds statutory requirements. The kitchen should be a pleasant, comfortable workplace in which staff and licensee enjoy working.

Kitchen planning rules have been devised to achieve these objectives, although since they are not always compatible a compromise is generally sought.

Schedule

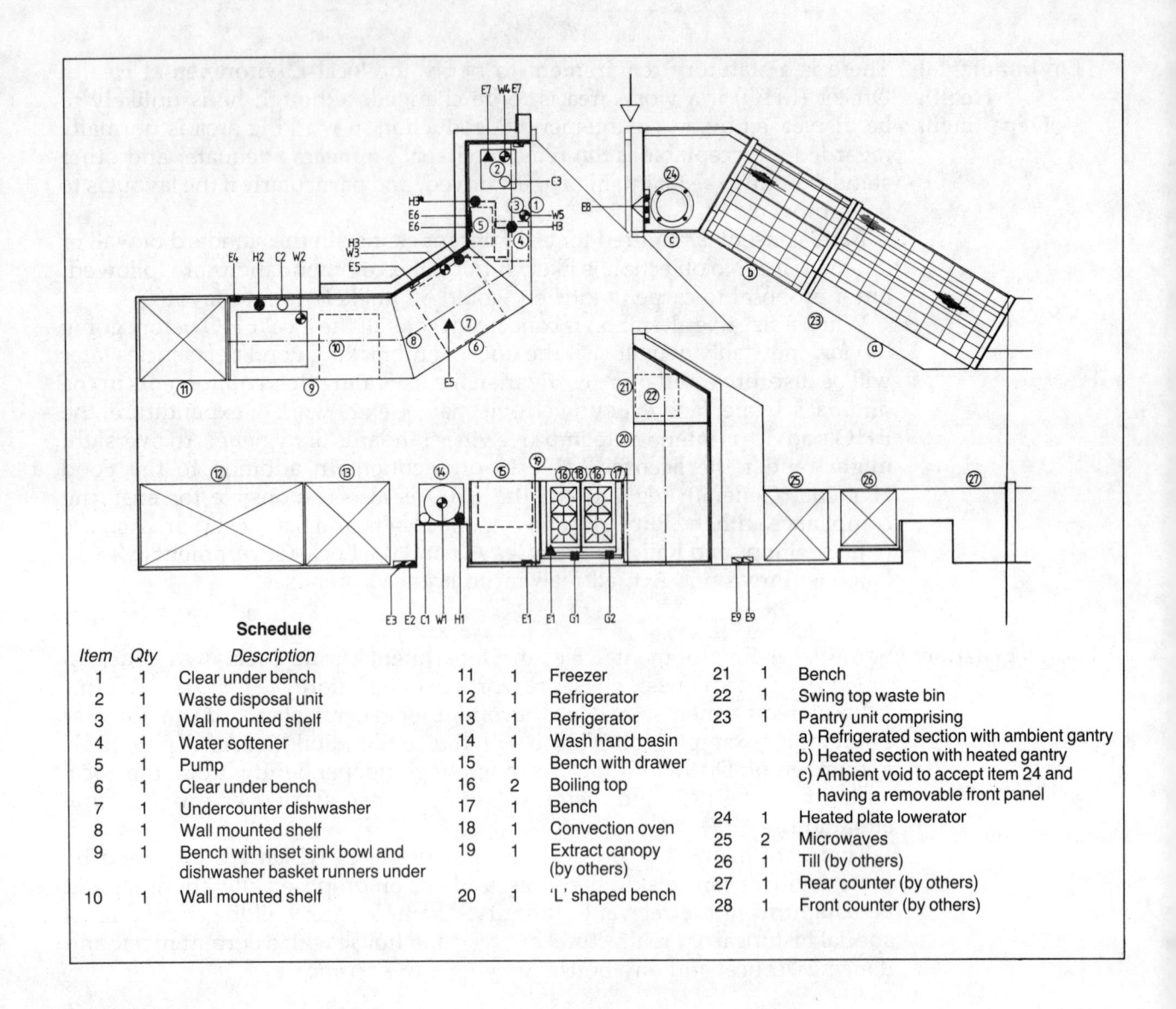

Item	Qty	Description
1	1	Clear under bench
2	1	Waste disposal unit
3	1	Wall mounted shelf
4	1	Water softener
5	1	Pump
6	1	Clear under bench
7	1	Undercounter dishwasher
8	1	Wall mounted shelf
9	1	Bench with inset sink bowl and dishwasher basket runners under
10	1	Wall mounted shelf
11	1	Freezer
12	1	Refrigerator
13	1	Refrigerator
14	1	Wash hand basin
15	1	Bench with drawer
16	2	Boiling top
17	1	Bench
18	1	Convection oven
19	1	Extract canopy (by others)
20	1	'L' shaped bench
21	1	Bench
22	1	Swing top waste bin
23	1	Pantry unit comprising a) Refrigerated section with ambient gantry b) Heated section with heated gantry c) Ambient void to accept item 24 and having a removable front panel
24	1	Heated plate lowerator
25	2	Microwaves
26	1	Till (by others)
27	1	Rear counter (by others)
28	1	Front counter (by others)

Figure 5 *An imaginative and efficient utilization of an otherwise awkward corner and small ancillary room off. This very compact scheme also highlights the significance of display. A sizeable unit has been given an excellent corner spot for the maximum effect*

The first aim should be to minimize movement in the course of working. Analyses of actual kitchen working have separated tasks regularly performed and measured the number of times each one occurs. This helps determine the order of priority of tasks in differing types of kitchen and the likely occurrence of different combinations of these tasks. Ideal layouts aim to reduce to a minimum the walking done during the day's work (see Figure 5).

Also important is minimizing accident risk. For example, collisions may occur in a kitchen. Thus in drawing the shortest lines between pieces of equipment, the intersections of lines and the type of task involved must be considered. A collision of two workers each moving from one completed task to another is relatively unimportant, whereas the collision of one carrying a knife with another carrying a container of hot liquid could be serious.

Economic use of space is vital. Space is economically used if gangways have equipment along both sides rather than on one side only. The saving of space in such cases may be set against the extra costs associated with the provision of gas, electricity and ventilation services.

Factors in layout and planning

Kitchen area is usually especially limited in public houses and can be as little as 3 m × 2.75 m (10 ft × 9 ft). Thus work flow is important and at this stage menu plans should be finalized.

Work flow and work triangle

Theoretical kitchen planning has a number of general concepts. One is that of work flow, i.e. describing the arrangement of a series of tasks into a predictable order of performance. Potatoes will be taken from store, removed from the sack, peeled, eyed, cooked and served in a sequence which cannot be rearranged. For most tasks, though not all, right-handed people work easier from right to left. Since work sequence may be predicted, and preferable directions of flow determined, the ideal order in which to line up equipment can be calculated for the most frequently recurring sequence of tasks.

A useful concept, sometimes known as the 'work triangle', is based on the frequency of use of the cooker, the sink and the refrigerator in domestic kitchens. The closer these three are, the easier will be working in the kitchen. For the domestic standard, the total of the three sides of the triangle should be not more than 7 metres, and the sink and cooker should not be more than 2 metres.

Energy, ventilation and heat

The most efficient use of energy is of considerable and growing importance. Heat, light and power should be used as sparingly as possible and, as far as is feasible, diffused energy should be recovered and re-employed. Discharging to the atmosphere all heat and steam extracted from a kitchen should be minimized and must be considered in the earliest design stage.

A clean, reasonably dry, working atmosphere is required by law and is desirable for the health and comfort of kitchen staff. Fat and steam in particular must be extracted without the formation of cold draughts which might cause just as much discomfort. Kitchen air should not normally be recirculated if a large amount of cooking is done, but no offence should be caused to others by allowing kitchen air to escape into neighbouring customer areas.

Natural ventilation, or three air changes per hour are satisfactory other than in traditional cooking or washing-up areas, where at least twenty air changes per hour are sought. When no traditional cooking or steam discharge occurs, less mechanical ventilation, if any, will be needed.

The recovery of heat traditionally discharged to the atmosphere along with odours, fats and dust may be achieved by a number of devices. Suitable for pubs is the 'heat wheel' which revolves slowly, partly in the discharge duct and partly in the supply duct, picking up heat from the discharge air and transferring it to the supplied air. Gas and electricity boards, and ventilation consultants, can advise on this and other equipment.

With the development of better insulated equipment, more microwave and infrared cooking, enclosed and pressure cooking, heat recovery systems on washing-up machines, and other plant which lose less energy in performance, space heating in kitchens will become essential. Radiators or warm air supply grilles should be so sited as to provide general warmth without hot or cold pockets, and to be as far as possible from extraction points. A temperature of 16 °C is considered satisfactory in working areas, and 18 °C is more suitable for changing rooms, offices etc.

Space and other factors The area required for a group of people working constantly together would obviously be greater than if members of the group came and went and were mainly absent, but too great a level of congestion even for very short periods increases the risk of accident. The most commonly used minimum figure is 11 cubic metres of space per person.

Traffic areas of the kitchen should not be obstructed. An obstruction has to be avoided every time it is passed, and that takes time and encourages accidents.

When food is cooked to order the distance between the finishing of cooking and the customer should be as small as possible. Any intermediate delay or obstruction should be avoided.

If it is feasible, tasks at which much time is spent, such as washing up or vegetable preparation, should be sited before the windows affording the best possible view.

Often storage space is limited, and goods received areas may be used for storage. Exploit every part of a kitchen for fitting in lockable cupboards, adequate shelving and worktop surfaces.

Lighting Lighting should be diffuse but ample in all working areas and, ideally, not of a markedly different colour from that in contiguous rooms with which there is traffic interchange. Areas such as under stove extraction hoods must not be forgotten. Lighting levels should be at least 200 lux generally and 400 lux in work areas (i.e. 10 and 20 W/m² fluorescent).

Fit, or direct, lighting over working and cooking areas.

Application of principles to pubs

Publications dealing with kitchen planning (see the further reading at the end of the chapter) may be of use to the specialist student or to those involved in planning larger commercial premises. But most work carried out to public house kitchens is to adapt or alter the style of existing facilities. Basic principles must be borne in mind, but more important is their incorporation into a practical and economical scheme to fit the premises available. Demands on an average public house kitchen are closer to those on a domestic rather than a large commercial kitchen.

Theory is all very well, but putting it into practice is another matter. It may be ideal to avoid obstruction in the work area but, faced with a column in the middle of our kitchen, do we then demolish the house and start again? Obviously not. The principles, once grasped, must be adapted to the individual circumstances and every case is different.

Common to every case, however, are constraints of one kind or another, and these must be assessed with the kitchen plan from the outset. Many minor constraints can be overcome by modifying the plan, but some cannot be circumvented.

Objectives First decide what is required, based on careful analysis of those aims which appear most desirable and also of the alternatives and their implications, so

Factors in layout and planning

that the best compromise can be devised. Theoretical objectives can be effectively turned into practical decisions if important issues are separated and considered one after another.

Market sector This decision should always be the first. Defining the type of clientele sought (the 'customer profile') begins the process of answering all the other questions.

Number of covers This is determined by simple physical considerations such as the size of the eating or food preparation areas, or the current staff.

Price levels This decision should follow from the first two, but some choice may still be apparent.

Food style Fundamental to the kitchen design, this question may be the hardest to answer. Although the earlier decisions will be determining factors, there will still be a broad area of choice. In addition to general principles of style and range of food to be offered, it is also necessary to determine whether the food will be hot, cold or both. It may be decided to offer one kind at one time of day or week, and another or others on different occasions.

Menu It should be possible to draft a selection of sample menus in keeping with the decisions, in principle, so far reached.

None of these questions can be isolated from the real constraints faced in the house. To find the answer, each issue should be separately considered in a sensible sequence, so that the right priorities are grasped. Each question should be examined in relation both to the other questions and to any relevant difficulties. Possible constraints include the following.

Size of kitchen This may be significant in relation to the number of staff to be accommodated or the size of the equipment to be fitted in. Although it may, if small, reduce the possible options, it will not necessarily prevent better exploitation of the enterprise. For example, if the kitchen will not take a traditional stove, salamander grill and deep fryer, then an alternative menu based on ready prepared fresh or frozen food, which can be microwave oven finished for hot service, or even passed straight to a bar display counter, is a more feasible alternative. This will generate the required increase in trade without demanding more space (see Figure 6).

The size of the bar area will also determine some of the options relating to customer capacity, and to styles of food, but this is related to kitchen size just as much as to servery space, extent of lavatory facilities or cellarage.

Layout The present layout of the premises and the ease of conversion are critical factors. Many town and city public houses have kitchens sited above the bar, usually in a direct line above it but often two or even three floors up, and invariably interconnected by a manually operated service lift. In such cases it is unlikely that freshly prepared hot food can be cooked to order in the kitchen and served successfully. Hot food sent down in the lift to the bar would be likely to be cool on arrival, bar staff would be interrupted to empty the lift, and communication difficulties would compound the problems. Any licensee who allowed his enthusiasm to blind him to the logistical difficulties deriving from such an arrangement would be foolish. Far better to consider alternative ways

Meeting Market Demand

of successfully serving hot food. It could, for example, be supplied in batches throughout service, although this sytem has its own problems. Better still the food could be displayed cold in the bar and then cooked or finished to order in the bar by microwave, sandwich toaster or grill.

Available skills Whether or not existing staff could cope with new equipment, a new and more difficult menu, or new customers from a different market sector may appear trivial in relation to the major plan as conceived. Surely any training or retraining trouble will be transient and capable of solution, given a little patience, persistence and perhaps one or two redundancies? Often this may be the case, but the matter should nevertheless be considered. In spite of other shortcomings, a long-serving member of staff's personality or reputation with customers may render it undesirable to dispense with his or her services. It may be that there is little alternative in the area, or that the cost of changing staff could not be justified by any possible gain.

Services The availability and layout of utilities and services are frequently important determinants of the cost of feasibility of a scheme. If mains gas is not available, then bulk LPG or electricity may be easy alternatives. The capabilities of the sewage disposal system, the adequacy of the water supply, or even the ease of installing new waste and other runs may all be significant. Ventilation can also be costly. If new ventilation hoods, ducting, and plant have to be installed from scratch, then the cost can be considerable, since it is often necessary to carry a kitchen discharge to roof level before terminating to the atmosphere. Even minor modifications to the kitchen layout can involve expenditure on ductwork and hoods and, even worse, can sometimes necessitate upgrading of the whole system.

Mixed use in kitchen A difficulty in city houses, and one which will become general, is that environmental health departments are discouraging the use of the licensed house kitchen for domestic purposes. In many cases a separation of the functions – the commercial and the domestic – is impossible within the existing building, and in other instances the distinction is of no practical relevance, but proposed alterations to extend the business may raise this question. It should be anticipated. In particular, keeping food destined for customers beside that for domestic consumption, and even more so that for domestic pets, in one refrigerator is strongly discouraged and should be avoided. At least then a separate domestic refrigerator should be incorporated in an improvement scheme.

How living-in staff are fed and how they may store food which is their own property is relevant. As staff living conditions improve, providing private storage, cooking and washing-up facilities for them inevitably arises.

Total costs The final major constraining influence is likely to be the overall cost of work. This is related to all other questions. The kitchen equipment chosen as most suitable to satisfy all other aspects of the scheme on examination may prove to

Factors in layout and planning

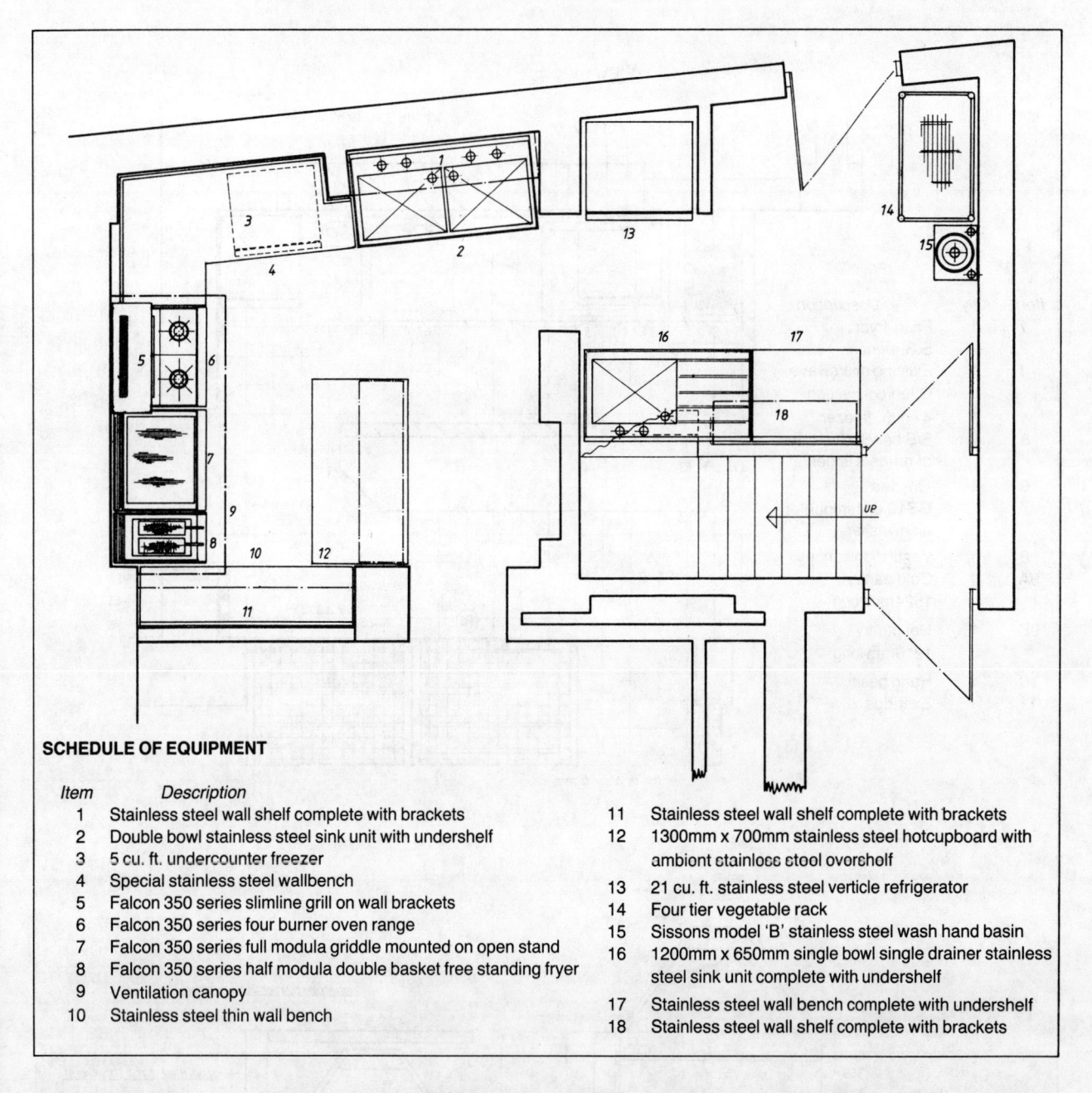

SCHEDULE OF EQUIPMENT

Item	Description
1	Stainless steel wall shelf complete with brackets
2	Double bowl stainless steel sink unit with undershelf
3	5 cu. ft. undercounter freezer
4	Special stainless steel wallbench
5	Falcon 350 series slimline grill on wall brackets
6	Falcon 350 series four burner oven range
7	Falcon 350 series full modula griddle mounted on open stand
8	Falcon 350 series half modula double basket free standing fryer
9	Ventilation canopy
10	Stainless steel thin wall bench
11	Stainless steel wall shelf complete with brackets
12	1300mm x 700mm stainless steel hotcupboard with ambiont stainlocc ctool ovorcholf
13	21 cu. ft. stainless steel verticle refrigerator
14	Four tier vegetable rack
15	Sissons model 'B' stainless steel wash hand basin
16	1200mm x 650mm single bowl single drainer stainless steel sink unit complete with undershelf
17	Stainless steel wall bench complete with undershelf
18	Stainless steel wall shelf complete with brackets

Figure 6 *Here two oddly-shaped rooms, each too small on its own, and separated by a supporting wall, have been combined to create a neat, tight work unit with a minimum of structural change and hence cost. Note the tidy grouping under the extract hood*

be too heavy for the floor loading capability. A choice must then be made. Is the menu changed to some more modest style? Is alternative plant available? Should the floor be strengthened? Or is the scheme to be abandoned altogether? Choices will need to be made, but the package must remain coherent. The costs of new equipment and building work are not the only ones. Retraining, recruiting, printing and loss of trade during work are among the others. All these have to be considered and compromise decisions reached.

All the constraints can be viewed as challenges. A difficulty may at first appear insuperable, but there will invariably be a way out, even if it calls for a radical change in accepted practice. A shortage of space or ventilation

Meeting Market Demand

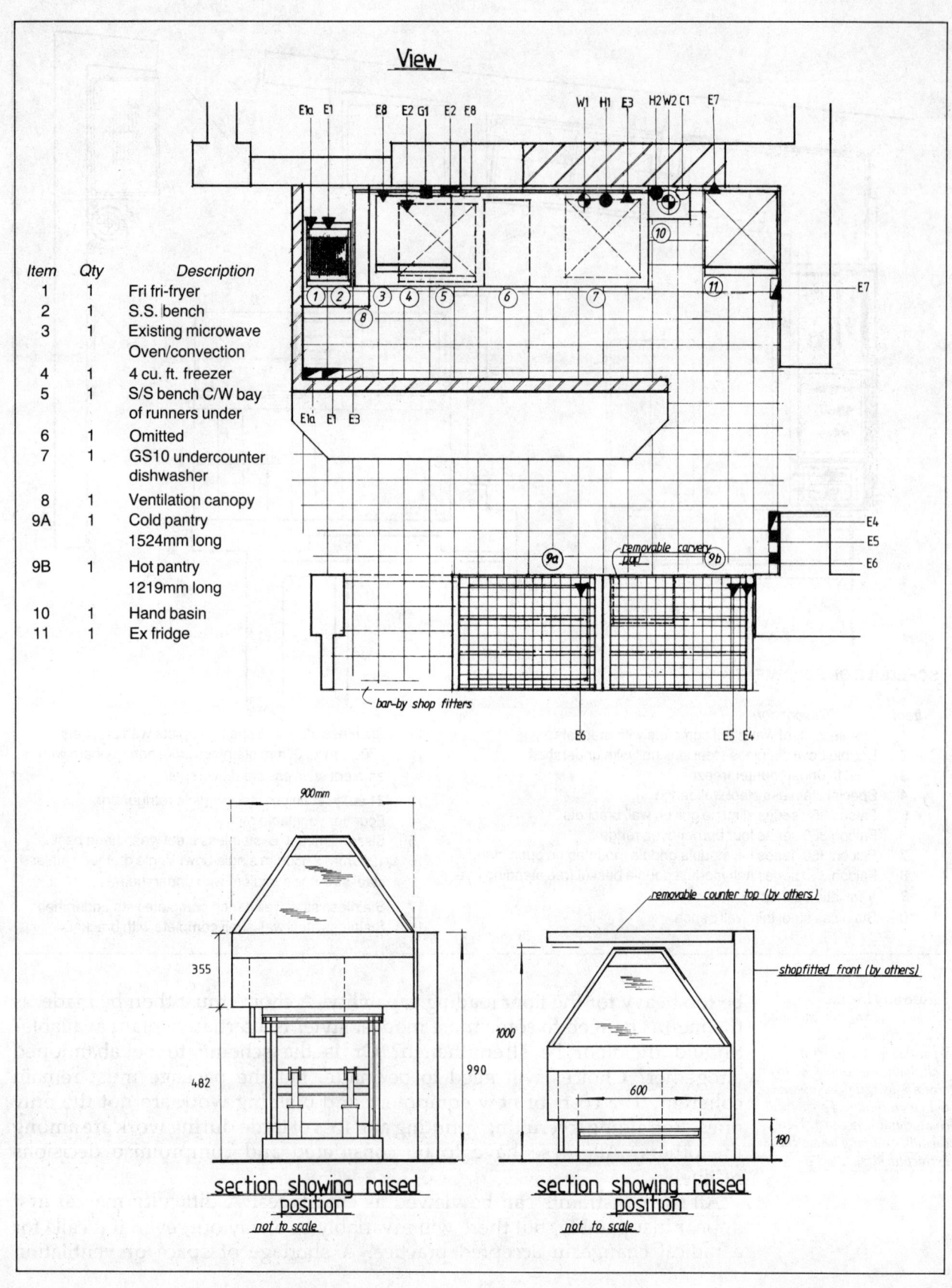

View

Item	Qty	Description
1	1	Fri fri-fryer
2	1	S.S. bench
3	1	Existing microwave Oven/convection
4	1	4 cu. ft. freezer
5	1	S/S bench C/W bay of runners under
6	1	Omitted
7	1	GS10 undercounter dishwasher
8	1	Ventilation canopy
9A	1	Cold pantry 1524mm long
9B	1	Hot pantry 1219mm long
10	1	Hand basin
11	1	Ex fridge

section showing raised position
not to scale

section showing raised position
not to scale

58

Factors in layout and planning

Figure 7 *Units such as these, which can be raised and lowered, enable dual use of the counter. A lunchtime food counter can be quickly transferred into an evening bar. Note the very limited range of kitchen equipment minimizing capital cost consistent with a modest catering plan, at least to start with*

difficulties might be overcome by abandoning traditional cooking methods such as frying, boiling and grilling in the kitchen and changing to a microwave or 'Mealstream' oven-based system.

Severe curtailment of the space available for washing up caused by the enlargement of the cooking or drinking area, could be avoided by use of disposable ware instead of china. If the kitchen and the eating area are a long distance apart, then cold food could be emphasized and kitchen staffing problems may be reduced by purchasing ready prepared fresh or frozen dishes. Grilling or griddling can be carried out to good effect on public view in a restaurant if kitchen space is inadequate, and even a poor local greengrocer may be turned to advantage by emphasis on home-grown produce (see Figure 7).

Practical steps

Once the plan has been devised, the costs analysed and the compromises chosen, the dream can be turned into reality. This, too, is best done step by step.

Plan timetable Timing is vital. If minimum cost and disruption are to be combined with maximum efficiency, every significant step must be meticulously charted. This is probably best done in plan form on a weekly calendar. There will be gaps in the information required to complete this, but approximations can be made. When a cash flow analysis is required by a bank or other source of funds, then this timetable document can form a useful basis. Establishing accurate lead times is important. Large and sophisticated pieces of equipment, and those which are partly or wholly tailored to individual requirements, can take a long time to produce, and foreign imports can be delayed in transit. Probably the longest lead times will relate to obtaining consents, especially planning consent and that of the licensing justices where required. Delay is unpredictable, and can frustrate an apparently impeccable timetable. Other requirements such as purpose-made stainless steel benching or decorative tiles can also interrupt progress if they are not ordered at the right time.

Calculate pay-back From a provisional timetable of work and a rough estimate of costs related to the trading of the enterprise may be assessed the time expected for repayment of the original investment, or the rate of return expected on the investment. This estimate will be approximate at this stage, but it should be made so that a rough figure is known, and so that the formula for its calculation is established and can then be applied when more accurate costings or a timetable revision is to hand.

At this point it may become clear that the project is not economic, that it will never provide an adequate return to justify borrowing the money required or to directing surplus funds into it. If this is the outcome of the calculations then it is better to abandon the scheme at this stage before any further expense is incurred. However, it should be remembered that this is an analysis based on estimated costs and work times, and although such estimates are seldom over-pessimistic it may still be worth obtaining firm price and timing commitments before taking a final decision on whether to proceed or not.

Obtain finance At this time, if not before, a provisional indication of support should be obtained, if required, from a suitable source of funds. The information so far collected and recorded will prove a helpful basis for such an application, although other facts or figures may also be called for. If a customer is financially worth while, then his bank manager will probably prove no more difficult to convince.

Draw plans Detailed plans, to appropriate scales for consent applications and for working drawings (1:100 and 1:20), should now be prepared to a professional standard. A licensee who eschews professional help for this should know that it is a time-consuming job for which, unless he has training, he is unlikely to be technically qualified.

To accompany these plans, and to be read in conjunction with them, a detailed work specification should also be drawn up. For a project of some size the drawing up of this specification also calls for considerable expertise, and takes a good deal of time and energy. This document details all the items of work to be carried out, and cross-refers as necessary to the relevant drawing. It is advisable to seek individual pricing by item in any tender, since this aids comparison, and also makes the omission of individual items easier.

Seek tenders The drawings and specification, together with a suitable standard form of tender document indicating the conditions applicable and the submission date, should now be dispatched to selected contractors. The size of the project determines the number of contractors who are asked to tender, but this would seldom exceed four or perhaps five if the job were sizeable. Three to four weeks later, on the closing date, the tenders will be opened and compared and the contractor can then be selected.

It is now possible to revise the financial appraisal document, and this should be done. The total sum required for the scheme and its source can be fixed. The programme of work may also be amended as appropriate.

Obtain consents Certain permissions can be difficult to obtain quickly and it is sometimes prudent to submit drawings and applications at an earlier stage in the proceedings than this, and at least before going out to tender. The ideal project should be planned well in advance of the intended starting date. In such circumstances the application for and granting of consent to carry out work which, when its exact cost were known, would be abandoned, should be avoided. This is especially advisable when the proposed work includes substantial improvements to toilet accommodation, for example, since the abandonment of such a scheme can cause some embarrassment with the consenting authority. Consents are generally sought before or at the same time as tenders, for practical reasons such as the risk of contractors' prices rising as time passes.

Factors in layout and planning

Order of work This task also may need to be phased. Furniture, carpets, stainless steel benching and shelving, gas or electricity supplies, display cabinets, specialist cooking equipment, and many other specific items may have long ordering lead times. If work is to proceed smoothly, such items should be ordered before the main contract is placed, then it is as well to check cancellation terms, especially if the item is to be made to measure and if the customer will have no alternative use for it. Once consents have been granted, finance is secured, and all other preliminaries have been dealt with, the main contract should be placed so that the starting date which has been agreed as most suitable for the business, and possible for the contractor, can be achieved.

The next few days or weeks will afford a little time to attend to all other arrangements, such as notification of customers, arrangements for staff holidays or lay-off, advising suppliers, running down stocks, planning reopening advertising, and clearing areas which will be affected.

Carry out work The work will require constant supervision, both to ensure that agreed standards are met, and so that any questions which arise can be answered on the spot. It is vital to take note of any extra work which is authorized under such circumstances, since it will invariably become the subject of an extra charge in the account.

Reopen and run in Staff should be trained in the use of any new equipment in advance of the reopening, and preferably by a representative of the supplier. This is usually best arranged at the time that the decision to purchase is reached.

Equipment suitable for public house kitchens

The assessment of the best equipment for any given house depends on factors such as menu style, fuel available, volume of business, finance available, level of skills to be employed and space allocated, as well as special factors in some individual cases, such as availability of servicing in remote areas, floor loading capabilities on upper floors, staircase widths and so forth. All these and similar questions should be considered, with the following general principles.

Quality Since quality and price generally change in direct ratio, the two factors cannot be considered separately. There is little point in buying much lightweight domestic equipment for a busy catering house, since it will prove to be money wasted. Lightweight pots, pans and kitchen utensils will quickly burn out or break in commercial use with rough handling. On the other hand, if the staff are local housewives doing a little part-time work it may not be appropriate to ask them to use very heavy commercial plant.

Stoves, fryers, grills, salamanders and other main cooking plant should generally be of medium duty grade, which is a suitable compromise between being of reasonable cost and durability and not too daunting for unprofessional staff.

Lighter plant such as mixers, mincers, peelers, waste disposal units, coffee-making equipment, juice pressers and microwaves should all be of commercial quality. The domestic versions of this kind of equipment are invariably designed to a standard appropriate only for use at home by their owner, although often they are cheaper to buy than their commercial cousins.

Standard equipment will usually prove cheaper to buy, maintain and replace than tailor-made items, and wherever possible it should therefore be favoured.

Materials Walls, ceilings, floors, cupboards, shelving and all working surfaces must be finished to Food Hygiene (General) Regulations standards, the objective being the achievement of an easily cleaned, impervious finish. They should be durable and appropriate to the circumstances, and the floor should not become too slippery in the event of spillage.

A gloss paint finish is regarded as satisfactory for ceilings and walls above about 2 metres, provided it is applied to sound and smooth plaster. Below this height glazed ceramic tiles are favoured in kitchens, although gloss paint would usually be acceptable in ancillary areas. Heavy-duty linoleum is still sometimes used for floors but a composition floor covering incorporating a non-slip grit, and capable of being heat bonded along its joints, is more suitable. Attention should be paid to ensuring a good fit and a sealed bond with a coved skirting around the edges. On solid or rigid floors, quarry or similar tiles are a favoured alternative, although these can be slippery and cold, and are fairly expensive when laying them is taken into account.

Tiling will ease kitchen cleaning. It should be at least 1.8 m (6 ft) in height from the floor. Where there is an extraction canopy, tiling should be extended to meet its back fitting. Place as much of your cooking equipment as possible under these canopies, whether against a wall or under a central island scheme.

Benching and worktops may be of stainless steel, or timber with a plastic or laminate finish. The former is more expensive but durable, indeed will last almost forever, but can form a somewhat slippery work surface and creates a cold clinical atmosphere. Laminated wooden units are available in stock modular form, and this can make them cheaper and also easily replaced piecemeal if necessary.

Plumbing should not be in plastic as a rule, although for well-protected short runs it is acceptable. Copper, in spite of being expensive, is usually the ideal material. Sinks should be stainless steel, wash hand basins may be stainless or china, and plate racks should be plastic-coated wire or stainless steel.

Cupboards and shelving must be impervious and, although a laminated finish is probably best, gloss-painted wood is quite adequate. Chopping boards must be used and should be of one of the patent composition materials which are available, not of wood.

Fuels Gas is liked for commercial cooking, being quick to respond, relatively cheap and visible. Gas appliances are, on the whole, less susceptible to water damage than electrical ones. Certainly where mains gas is available it is

Factors in layout and planning

usually best for fuelling a conventional stove, grill, salamander or steamer and, in conjunction with electricity, for a convection oven.

Electrical deep fryers are widely preferred to others because of the standard of their thermostatic controls, and electricity is the only fuel for equipment such as microwaves, mixers, mincers and so on. Consider alternative uses of gas or electricity, as running costs can be high.

In remote areas away from the mains, LPG is a useful alternative to gas. It is distributed in bulk by private companies and also by some of the gas boards. Solid fuel is not recommended for commercial kitchens, although a stand-by alternative to electricity may be desirable in case of power cuts.

Ancillary areas

Storage of equipment and utensils Kitchen and restaurant equipment will usually be stored in its area of use. When there is separate storage for such items, the standard of finishes must enable cleanliness to be maintained.

Washing up Facilities for washing up pots, cutlery, crockery and even glassware may be provided in the kitchen or in a nearby area. The standard of finish should be similar to those in the kitchen, and adequate ventilation must be installed. For larger installations there is some washing-up machinery which incorporates its own heat recovery system, and thus not only uses fuel economically but also discharges little or no heat or steam. When machines are used, provision for the storage of trays for both dirty and clean crockery must be made.

Dry goods storage A separate dry goods store is desirable. There is a view that 'closed' food, that is food sealed in an approved container (as defined in the Food Hygiene Regulations) need not be kept under conditions as demanding as those for 'open' food, but it is safest to apply to a dry goods store the same standard as for a kitchen, except that the walls do not need to be tiled. Surfaces should be easily cleaned, and the shelves, which should range between 0.25 m and 2 m in height, should allow adequate air circulation. The store itself should have permanent air vents allowing about two air changes per hour. The ideal temperature is about 12–14 °C (see Figure 8).

Cold storage This should be available as near to the point of use as possible, without being in too hot a part of the premises. Fridges or freezers which have to be sited in a hot place may be fitted with 'tropicalized' units which will run in high temperatures; otherwise deep freezers should be sited outside the kitchen where possible.

Cleaning materials These must be stored away from food, preferably in their own cupboard. All stores should be made secure against casual pilferage.

Meeting Market Demand

Figure 8 *A careful look at this drawing suggests a very well designed kitchen, complete with as much space as might be desired, good layout and all the kit, but excessive for the available trading area. Only one lavatory, no cellarage or changing room, and half the total area designated kitchen: the importance of keeping any scheme in proportion cannot be overstressed, especially to the expert kitchen planner!*

Item	Qty	Description
1	1	Worktop, deep freeze under
2	1	Twin pan deep fat fryer
3	1	Purpose built worktop infill/extension
4	1	Worktop, cut out in top to accept containers, refrigerated cabinet under
5	1	Purpose built expeditor shelf
6	1	Twin infra red heat lamp gantry over
7	1	Purpose built worktop infill/extension
8	1	Worktop shelf and drawer under
9	2	Griddle plate units
10	1	Low level ventilation extract system
11	1	Low level ventilation extract system
12	1	Worktop, sink inset shelf under
13	1	Wall mounted shelf over
14	2	Three tier storage racks
15	1	Double bowl sink units
16	1	'L' shaped wall shelf over
17	1	Worktop shelf and drawer under
18	1	General purpose preparation machine
19	1	30 cu. ft. Deep Freeze Cabinet
20	1	Worktop, shelf under
21	1	Wall mounted wash hand basin and taps
22	1	Shaped service base counter sink and wash hand, shelf under
23	1	Stainless steel top service shelf bar
24	1	Cash registers (by others)
25	11	Swivel bar stools/chairs on pedestal base
26	28	Swivel chairs on pedestal base
27	10	Dining tables
28	2	Planters (by others)
29	1	Run of divider screens (by others)
30	1	Dumb waiter station
31	1	Worktop cupboard under, two cup tubes inset
32	1	Milk pack dispensing machine
33	1	Pour on hot beverage machine
34	1	Hot chocolate machine (by others)
35	1	Set of post mix machinery (by others)

Hazards and prevention

Fire Precautions against fire are of the first importance, and fall into a number of areas.

Equipment All equipment should be appropriate to its use. Electrical plant should not be overloaded, adaptors should never be used, and fryers in particular must always be fitted with emergency overheat cutout devices in case of thermostat failure. The fryer most commonly used in public houses lacks the standard fitting of this device. Worn salamander radiants must be replaced, leaky gas valves serviced, and, above all, the equipment and its surroundings must be kept clean.

Ventilation The ventilation system represents the second largest fire risk in public house kitchens after deep fryers. Especially where there are hoods and ducting it is vital that the system is constructed with access panels of suitable size so that it can be kept clean without difficulty. Grease filters must be incorporated in the hoods, and regularly cleaned and kept in place at all times when the ventila-

Factors in layout and planning

tion is operating. Too often a costly installation is rendered imbalanced, dangerously susceptible to fire, and far more difficult to clean in the end, by a kitchen worker's removing of filters and setting them aside merely to gain a temporarily increased air flow on a hot day. Ducting should also be fitted with fire dampers, which should be held open by 'fusible links'. These are hinged panels which will drop closed when heat in the duct melts the links, and which thereby hinder the rapid spread of fire along ducting.

Extinguishers The local Fire Officer will advise on suitable fire fighting appliances and their best siting, but advice may also be sought from the suppliers of extinguishers, who will usually survey premises and provide their recommendations free of charge. Every house must be considered individually, but the following general notes may be useful.

Water extinguishers are not now recommended for kitchens because of the risk of their being used by mistake on fat or electrical fires. Thus a combination of appropriate equipment is generally chosen from carbon dioxide, foam and dry powder extinguishers, and asbestos or man-made fibre blankets. The last, although suitable for domestic use, are not as a rule of adequate weight where there is a commercial deep fryer fire risk. The traditional heavy asbestos blankets are preferred in such cases.

All extinguishers should be painted in the standard colour code (red for water, black for carbon dioxide, blue for dry powder etc.). Any old extinguishers which do not conform should be repainted or replaced.

A clear notice explaining the colours and uses of all extinguishers, and indicating the location of all fire appliances, should then be displayed in a suitable place, and the attention of all staff and new recruits should be drawn to it. This training responsibility on a licensee is not only common sense; it is also a legal obligation under the Health and Safety at Work Act.

Electrical layout Just as the usual advice is that an extinguisher provided in case of a fat fire is not likely to be of much use if it is sited beside the fryer, so the siting of emergency isolating switches for kitchen equipment is important. These switches must be so placed that they are likely to be within easy reach in the event of the appliances which they control being on fire.

Notices In addition to the colour code and location chart mentioned, special instructions relating, for example, to the operation of a hosereel, and emergency exit and related signs in the correct format and size, must be displayed in any required locations. They should be visible and maintained in good order.

Exits All emergency exits must be kept clear of obstructions, and doors must be kept locked or unlocked, as the case may be, during trading hours if that is required. A licensee must train his staff to establish the necessary routine, and himself check from time to time that it is observed.

Injuries Injuries likely to occur in licensed premises fall into two broad categories. One is that of accidents arising out of carelessness, and the other is that associated with specialist equipment likely to be found in such premises.

In almost all cases, accidents can be prevented by thorough training and adequate supervision. However meticulous a licensee may be, some accidents will inevitably occur, and then his other responsibility, that of dealing with the results as efficiently as possible, will arise.

Careless accidents are especially likely to be related to a number of particular risks, some of which are as follows:

The use of knives
Wet or greasy floors
Wet rubber mats
Worn floor coverings
Spillage of hot liquids
Loading and unloading lifts
Lifting heavy objects
Kitchen overcrowding

In training and supervision, these and similar risks must carry particular emphasis.

High-risk equipment which is often or increasingly found in licensed premises includes the following:

Deep fat fryers
Slicers
Mincers, grinders, liquidizers
Fresh orange crushers
Microwave ovens
Lifts and hoists
Refrigeration plant
Waste disposal units
Potato peelers
Mixers
Beer kegs, carbon dioxide bottles and pressure mains.

The special risks associated with this sort of equipment must be emphasized to the staff, and they should be thoroughly trained in its use. Fryers, for example, must never be left unattended, guards must never be removed, and no equipment should ever be misused. The fundamental need is to instil staff awareness of, and respect for, the dangers implicit in both misuse and momentary forgetfulness. When accidents do occur, first aid must be readily available. A properly filled first aid box has to be provided and the staff must know where it is. It is even better to have a trained 'first aider' on the staff.

If the accident is more serious, then someone competent to do so should be on hand to make all necessary arrangements. There is a statutory duty to report to the local authority any industrial injury or accident on the premises which results in more than three days' absence from work.

Maintenance

The counterpart to training is the proper maintenance of equipment, and especially of the particularly hazardous equipment listed earlier. Some favour maintenance contracts with suitable firms, whereas others are sceptical of their value.

Table 1 Equipment schedule and inspection checklist

House: **The Dog and Duck, Upper Benwell**   Licensee: **Ken Fleet**

Item of plant	Details	Location	Inspection by	Frequency	Actual dates	Maintenance by	Frequency	Actual dates
Manual service lift	Not known	Kitchen to bar	Globe Assurance	Annual	3.4.82 28.3.83 22.3.84 30.3.85	Raisewell Lifts	As required	6.4.83 15.4.84
Crate hoist	Raisewell Lifts (installed 1979)	Cellar to bar	Globe Assurance	Annual	3.4.82 28.3.83 22.3.84 30.3.85	Raisewell Lifts	As required	6.4.83 15.4.84
Fire appliances	Quench	See schedule	Quench	Annual	4.81 4.82 6.83 5.84 5.85	Quench	As necessary	
Deep fryers (2)	Electric Fryers Model K2	Kitchen	KF	Monthly (oil etc.)	First of each month	JB Electrical	As necessary	22.11.84 thermostat split
Ventilation filters	—	Kitchen hoods	KF	Monthly	First of each month			
Microwave oven	Bagasaki model 2000 (purchased 1984)	Kitchen	KF (with patent tester)	Test for leaks six-monthly	1.6 and 1.1	JB Electrical	As necessary	
Stoves, salamander	Therm	Kitchen	—	—		Gas Board	Annual clean and service (contract)	4.8.83 5.10.84 30.9.85
Boiler	Hotair	Boilerhouse	—	—				
Flues, chimneys	Boiler	Boilerhouse	—	—		John Brush	Annual sweep	6.83 7.84 7.85
	Two open fires	Saloon bar Restaurant	—	—				

At least the obligation to remember to arrange regular inspection where there is a specific statutory duty to do so can be passed on in this way. Falling into this category are non-passenger lifts and hoists, which must be the subject of a form F54 report made to the local authority by an insurance inspector annually, and pressure vessels such as steam boilers, which also have to be inspected annually.

On the other hand, there is a general health and safety obligation on the licensee to ensure that all the equipment on his premises is maintained in a safe working condition. For this reason alone, it is desirable to arrange regular inspection and maintenance of some items by professional contractors, and regular inspection by the licensee himself of others.

A suggested layout for an equipment schedule and inspection and maintenance checklist is given in Table 1.

Further reading

The Electricity Council, *Finishing Kitchen Planning Guide*, 1977.
The Food Hygiene (General) Regulations, HMSO, 1970.
Fuller, John, *Professional Kitchen Management*, Batsford, 1981.
Lawson, Fred, *Principles of Catering Design*, 2nd edn, The Architectural Press, 1978.
Parker Morris Report, *Tomorrow*, Ministry of Housing and Local Government, HMSO, 1961.

6 Equipment for catering
Anthony Milson and David Kirk

The rapid development and diversification of catering operations in recent years has been equalled by a similar advance in equipment and techniques in preparing food. The needs of the fast food caterer in particular have resulted in the development of equipment well suited to any likely pub catering operation, from that run by the licensee to more ambitious restaurant projects.

Changes in the nature of commodities have also brought a response from equipment manufacturers. Microwave and forced convection ovens and refrigerated equipment are relevant to the use of, for example, frozen foods. The publican who uses new forms of food on his fast food counter and in conventional meal service should be aware of developments which will make his job easier and help his business to be more efficient and profitable.

Design considerations

The design and performance of equipment has an important influence over the overall performance of a catering establishment, whether measured in terms of customer satisfaction, profitability or job satisfaction for manager and staff. On the other hand, the operators of catering businesses, anxious to meet a set of customer and company needs, impose on the equipment designer a number of constraints.

Other factors to be taken into account by designers include the nature of raw food materials, energy costs and the equipment needs of other sectors of the catering industry. To identify the major factors influencing the design of catering equipment affords some criteria by which we can judge any new designs.

Factors influencing equipment designs

Equipment should provide a product acceptable to the customer, who will also expect consistency of quality. The equipment must be reliable, in these terms, over its lifetime.

The kitchen should be as small as possible so as to leave more space for the dining area. This means using as few items of equipment as possible. This is important for most pubs where kitchens may be cramped and less than ideal.

Meeting Market Demand

Each item should be in use for as long as possible and food should be prepared as rapidly as can be. This will make the maximum use of available floor space.

The food sold should require the minimum of skill and effort to prepare, so as to reduce labour and space requirements. This implies that food at a high level of previous preparation will normally be used (i.e. much preparation taking place in a food factory or in a centralized catering production unit).

The equipment must be capable of preparing the food to the customers' satisfaction. Where food must be fully prepared in the pub kitchen, labour-saving devices should be used where possible.

A pub supplies food for relatively short periods of the day; thus equipment is often used for shorter periods than elsewhere. The capital cost must be written off on short production runs. Seek to minimize the cost of equipment, otherwise the capital charges per unit of output becomes too high.

The pub catering market is fickle in that menus and concepts may need to change rapidly compared with less dynamic catering outlets. The life of equipment is likely to be determined not so much by age but by the need to restyle the concept of the operation. It is necessary then to write off equipment in a relatively short period or to try to make it fit a revamped operation. In the former case capital costs must be minimized; in the latter the versatility of the equipment becomes more important.

The equipment should be reliable over its planned production life. This will reduce maintenance costs and the loss of goodwill due to interruption in smooth food production. Thus, equipment should be purchased with a clear idea of its intended lifetime and the intensity of its use.

If an extensive menu is offered then the equipment needs to be versatile to cope with the range of products. When specialized equipment is used the proportion of time it is in use could be low and hence the capital charges per unit of output high. On the other hand, if the operation is specialized then it is possible to make use of these special items.

Safety

All foods deteriorate in quality if held for any length of time. Correct storage is therefore important. Deterioration can be minimized (not avoided) by keeping the food frozen ($-20\,°C$) or chilled (less than $5\,°C$). Hot foods deteriorate rapidly and in general should be served as soon as ready. In any event, food will always be better if it is cooked to order and served straight away.

Rapid cooking or heating is desirable since it minimizes customer waiting time and increases the turnaround of customers. This requires equipment designed to heat food rapidly in small batches.

The equipment should be designed to provide a safe and acceptable working environment for the operator. This is important in terms of health and safety legislation. Both the British Gas Corporation and the Electricity Council have schemes for testing and approving catering equipment which are aimed at the safety aspects in particular, and anyone purchasing equipment should ensure that it has the appropriate approval. The Gas Corporation scheme also includes cooking tests. Cleaning equipment is time consuming but essential for the hygienic preparation of food.

Energy costs

The running costs of equipment attributable to energy consumption are relatively small but increasing attention is being paid to economy. Automatic ignition of gas-fired equipment, good temperature control, rapid heating and good insulation are features which lead to improvements in energy use. The caterer can also help by not switching on equipment until needed, by using the full capacity of the equipment, by not leaving doors open and by maintaining his plant in good order.

Such factors need to be taken into account when buying equipment. In addition, the caterer must decide whether to use gas-fired equipment or electricity. He will need to use electricity for lighting and for kitchen machinery. Discuss with electricity and gas boards how to minimize energy costs.

Heat transfer

To understand the advantages and disadvantages of new equipment designs the licensee should look at the four basic methods by which heat can be transferred to food:

Direct contact with a hot solid surface, as on a griddle plate

Convection of heat from hot gases (combustion products, air or steam) to the food surface

Radiation from a hot surface with penetration of the energy to 1 or 2 mm from the surface

Microwave heating with much deeper penetration than in radiation.

In the first three methods, the energy is conducted into the food from the surface. As the temperature of the food changes, the process is one of unsteady state conduction. In this process, heat is conducted from the surface to the centre of the food and heat is stored in the food so as to raise its temperature.

If food is frozen then the heat required to thaw the ice is of the same order as that required to raise its temperature. This additional heat must also be conducted inwards from the surface. Conduction of heat in food is a slow process (and heating frozen food is obviously much slower than with unfrozen food). To speed up the rate of heat penetration we can do a number of things.

It is possible to increase the heat flow to the food surface, although there is a limit to this determined by unfavourable surface effects. We can decrease the thickness of the food, but this is limited by customer expectations with regard to food size and shape. Alternatively, heat can be generated inside the food itself: in pub catering microwaves are often used and food can be heated quickly by this method.

Many new types of equipment make use of one method of heat transfer, whereas others attempt to harness more than one. The problem with the latter is that it increases the capital cost of the equipment considerably, despite its significant benefit in terms of reducing heating or cooking time.

Cooking and heating methods

Griddles/fry plates Solid food materials are heated on griddles and fry plates. In the contact grill (griddle grill), the food is sandwiched between two hot surfaces so heat is applied directly on both sides. Small double-sided contact griddles remove the necessity of turning food but are of limited surface area so that only a few items can be cooked at one time.

Griddle or fry plates heat food on one side only. Food must therefore be turned to heat the other side. Heated surfaces can be flat or grooved, the latter leaving a pattern on the meat. Griddle plates are heated by gas or electricity whereas contact (two-plate) grills are electrically heated. A drainage channel and collection tray must be fitted to collect cooking juices.

Steaks, hamburgers, eggs, bacon, chops, liver, pancakes, mushrooms, tomatoes etc. can be cooked by this method. The griddle grill is suitable for thicker food items such as steaks or hamburgers. Rapid heating and even temperature distribution over the whole plate are required by the British Standard Specification. To minimize energy use, griddle plates should be switched on only when needed and the surface should be completely covered with food as soon as possible and maintained in a shiny condition. Thickness affects the heating time of, say, a steak on a griddle or contact grill. The correct heating time for each thickness of product can be calculated and if adhered to, will result in a consistent product.

Under-fired grill This type of grill utilizes a heat source below the food. It usually consists of pieces of volcanic lava or synthetic material heated by gas or electricity. These glow red when hot and cause the heat to be radiated to the food.

Food is placed on bars above the heat and fat droplets fall on to the hot pieces of rock causing flares (hence they are sometimes called flare grills). The flame, and smoke accompanying it, give food a characteristic taste and appearance. The under-fired grill was originally charcoal fired.

A requirement of this type of grill is good ventilation, otherwise smoke and smells drift into the dining area. It is a speciality item and not to all customers' taste. It is limited to grilling, unlike the more traditional over-fired grill which can be used for gratinating, toasting and browning. The pieces of rock are cleaned automatically by the high temperatures involved. Temperature is regulated by the rate of heat input and the height of the bars above the rock.

Over-fired grill This grill has its heat sources situated above the food. The electrically-heated types may have two or three separate element circuits to permit a number of different heat outputs. The output is uneven because the elements are of finite size and this may cause uneven heating at low total outputs.

Gas-heated types may have open flames heating a metal fret to generate radiant heat. Flames vary in length, and hence the evenness of heat output varies when the gas is turned up or down. This can result in uneven heating of the food.

The latest type of gas over-fired grill is fitted with a porous plate burner. Turning the burner up or down is effected over the whole surface and this avoids uneven heating.

Equipment for catering

Figure 9 *A selection of pub catering equipment*
(a)–(d) Courtesy R V Rutland Ltd
(e) Barbecue King Ltd

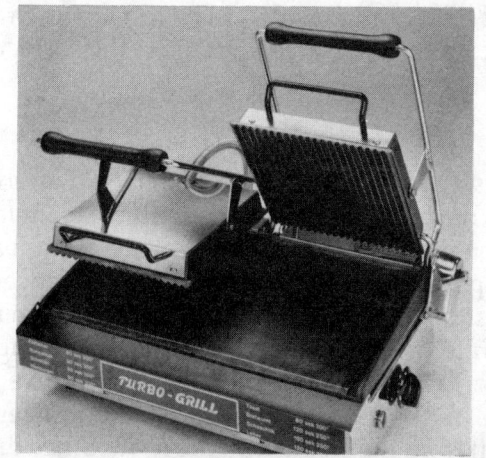

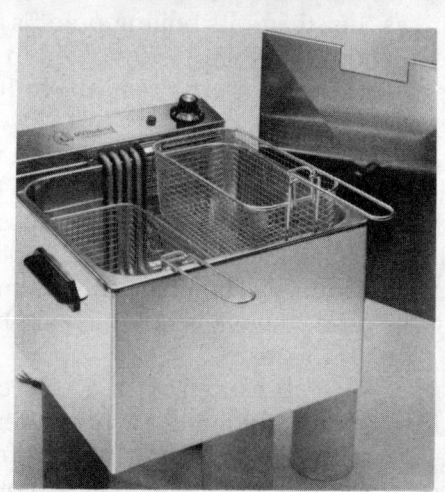

In over-fired grills, food is held on an open metal grid or on a solid metal plate so that the distance between the food and the heating surface may be varied, thus controlling the intensity of heat. The solid metal plate can be preheated and will act as a contact heat source at the start of cooking. These grills may be fitted to a cooker or be independent units for placing on a counter.

Forced convection ovens

In a forced convection oven, air is made to flow over the food more quickly than in a conventional one. This speeds the transfer of heat. This type may be either gas fired or electrically heated and comes in a wide range of sizes and designs. Some just generally stir and are less effective than those designed to make air flow rapidly over the food. In the latter case, baffle plates are fitted inside the oven to try to predetermine the direction of air flow.

Forced convection ovens designed correctly for frozen foods enable them to be heated rapidly and to hold more food than a normal oven and still give evenness of heating. They have a higher throughput for less floor space.

Some newer designs provide for the injection of water into the cooking space. This keeps the atmosphere moist and reduces the amount of water lost from the food when it is heated. In all designs the more rapid the rate of air flow over the food surface the faster will be the heating rate. Designs differ in their abilities and care should be taken to select the correct oven for the heating time required.

Steamers These use steam as a means of transferring heat. At atmospheric pressure the steam is at 100 °C. In those operating above this, steam temperature depends on the pressure generated in the unit and can be as high as 120 °C. The higher pressure and temperature produce a greater difference between steam and food surface so that heat arrives at the food surface at an increased rate. Some steam may penetrate the food, causing internal heating.

Steam in contact with the colder food will also give rise to heat transfer when it condenses on the food. This type of heat transfer enhances the rate at which heat is taken from the steam into the food. Since the water in the food is at the same pressure as the steam, its boiling point is also raised. This in turn accelerates the rate of chemical reactions involved in cooking. Drying out of food will not occur even if the temperature is above 100 °C because the steam atmosphere is 'wet'.

The trend is towards steamers of small capacity but with rapid heating rates – in some cases only a few minutes. This means that a large number of batches can be processed, linking food production more closely with the rate of food ordering and service. In small steamers, either a separate steam generator is situated underneath the unit's cabinet or the water is sprayed inside the cylinder containing the food, the walls of which are heated. When the water hits this surface it turns into steam.

Some small steamers are also fitted with a row of steam jets which are directed on to the food surface, blowing away condensed moisture and thus improving the rate of heat transfer. Similarly, if air from the steam and food builds up on the food surface, heat transfer will be slowed. The steam jets also remove this air layer and reduce heating time. The more recent atmospheric pressure steamer is fitted with a fan and has many of the advantages of convection ovens in evenness of cooking and lower cooking times.

Steamers operating above atmospheric pressure require compulsory inspection and insurance. Pressure steamers should be fitted with a safety device which locks the door when the steam is turned on: this prevents the operatives being scalded. Doors must be sealed to prevent a leak which could cause a deterioration in working conditions and waste energy.

Pressure fryer This combines features of the deep fat fryer with those of the pressure steamer. It enables food to be fried rapidly because the temperature of water in the food is increased as it is in a steamer. The pressure fryer consists of a deep pan of oil heated by electrical immersion heaters. The food is placed in the hot oil and the fryer lid is fastened down. Evolution of steam from food on its immersion in oil causes pressure inside the fryer to build up. A valve allows steam to escape and yet maintain a preset pressure in the fryer. The evolution of steam is suppressed by the higher pressure and this causes better contact between the oil and the food, thus increasing the rate of heating; less moisture is lost.

Turbulence is created in the fat; this tends to roll the food around and can

Equipment for catering

cause problems because batter and small particles of food are deposited in the oil during cooking, causing the quality of the oil to deteriorate more quickly.

The condensed water is removed through a valve and must not be allowed to mix back with the oil. If it does, the quality of the oil will deteriorate rapidly. Safety valves are required with this type of equipment. The pressure fryer can be used for rapidly frying items such as portions of chicken. It is not suitable, however, for items such as raw chips which contain a high proportion of water.

Microwave ovens These heat food quickly, but unless a special device is fitted over the food they cannot brown it. The microwaves are generated from the normal electrical current by means of a magnetron and waveguide and they enter the oven cavity. In order to disperse them evenly within the cavity it is normal to use a mode stirrer which deflects them in various directions.

Dangers of microwaves Since microwaves are dangerous if they come into contact with the body, the oven door must be designed to ensure that any leakage is kept to a safe level. This is achieved with a door seal and safety switch cut-out which operates when the door is open. Often the door of the oven incorporates a perforated plate so that it is possible to see inside. The British Standard requires that the perforated screen is covered by glass to prevent food spitting outwards on to the face of the operator. The glass door itself does not prevent leakage of microwaves because glass is transparent to them.

The oven variety is cubical or rectangular and is constructed of stainless steel or aluminium. When microwave radiation comes into contact with the metal surface it is reflected back on to the food. The walls themselves do not heat up and therefore the oven only uses heat when it is actually in operation and is more efficient than other forms of heating. It is important not to place metal containers inside the oven otherwise they will reflect the microwave radiation back to the waveguide and damage it; it is expensive to replace.

Advantages and disadvantages of microwave ovens The main advantage of microwave ovens is that they cause internal heating of the food since the waves penetrate below the surface. The rate at which the energy is absorbed from the surface inwards depends on the food's properties. However, in all cases, more energy is absorbed on the surface than inside. This means that there is still a temperature difference between the surface of the food and its centre and therefore some conduction from the higher temperatures on the surface will still need to take place.

Another problem arises when frozen foods are heated. Because of the difference in the properties of the ice and the food compared with water, if spots of ice melt then their temperature will accelerate rapidly causing a problem known as runaway heating. One means of overcoming this is to use microwaves which alternate between being switched on and off. These are known as pulsed microwave ovens and they allow the temperature in the food to even up when there is no microwave power. This prevents uneven heating in frozen foods and therefore the overcooking of parts of the food.

The microwaves penetrate the food and cause some of the molecules to vibrate rapidly. This vibration causes heat to be generated. Some conduction of heat also takes place locally within the food. Thus the slow heat transfer process involved in unsteady state conduction is not involved to the same extent as in conventional equipment, and so microwaves heat food rapidly.

Microwave ovens should be checked regularly (a) to make sure there is no accumulation of dirt on the hinges and oven door seals and (b) for microwave leakage, at programmed service intervals.

The principal advantage of microwave ovens in pub catering is that they heat food rapidly. Food production and service can be matched more closely than with other methods. They prepare efficiently small batches of food at a time. They are easy to use and do not require skilled operatives, having simple dials for presetting the time of treatment for different kinds of food.

Multisource heating units One disadvantage of virtually all types of equipment is that each offers heat transfer by one means only. This means that heat arriving at the surface of food takes a long time to be conducted to its centre, or in the case of microwave, heat penetration is obtained but surface reactions do not take place. It is possible to combine both these modes of heat transfer, thus eliminating the disadvantages of each. Some method of applying heat by radiation or convection is used in conjunction with microwave energy which penetrates below the surface.

One way of doing this combines the principles of a forced convection oven with that of a microwave cooker. On the one hand the hot air passing over causes the surface of the food to rise in temperature so that browning reactions take place; on the other hand microwaves penetrate the food making sure that its inner layers are raised quickly to a high temperature. A problem is that such equipment is expensive. However, it is appreciated by chefs and where sufficient money exists and circumstances warrant its adoption, it should be used.

Fridges and freezers

Frozen and chilled foods are increasingly used and therefore caterers need adequate means of storing them at the correct temperature. On the other hand, excessive storage capacity is wasteful in terms of capital cost, space and the cost of retaining larger stocks than are necessary with regular deliveries. Fridges are suitable for keeping food for a few days at temperatures between 0 °C and 5 °C (i.e. without the food being frozen). Freezers keep frozen food at temperatures of about −20 °C and this means that food can be kept longer, but the cost is higher than keeping it chilled in a refrigerator.

The main advantages of using frozen storage are for products which are used very little or for vegetables out of season. Further, in pub catering, the purchase of high-quality frozen dishes will enhance the menu. Normally these would be too difficult and expensive for a licensee to consider producing himself. Turnaround of freezer stock must be maintained or quality deterioration is likely to occur.

In order to minimize changes in freezer temperature, doors must be closed as much as possible. Opening and shutting causes increases in temperature and can cause quality deterioration. To maintain their efficiency, freezers need to be defrosted regularly according to the manufacturers' instructions. Once a

Equipment for catering

layer of ice has built up on freezer walls then heat removal to keep the temperature at −20°C becomes more difficult and costly in electrical consumption.

Most fridges now have automatic deicing equipment which reduces the problem. Most efficient is the chest freezer with a top lid opening, allowing less warm air to infiltrate. The front door type makes it easier to find foodstuffs because of the many trays or racks to which there is easy access. For efficient use fridges and freezers should be kept away from any warm influence such as ovens.

Chilled foods Chilled food systems are significant because of the expensive energy requirements of frozen food and meals. These systems do not freeze food but maintain it at about 3°C, and therefore less heat needs to be abstracted from the food or put back. Operating and capital equipment costs are also lower.

The major problem is keeping the chilled food at the correct temperature. Care is needed to ensure that food reaches the required temperature during the chilling process and that it is not allowed to creep up during storage and transport. If it does rise then there is a danger of microbiological growth and food poisoning. However, with care this system is cheaper in operating costs than frozen systems, but food cannot be kept for such a long time. If a pub group has a central production system based on chilled foods it needs to make deliveries every few days to keep stocks fresh and prevent storage periods from becoming too long.

Accurate ordering and monitoring is needed of the different items used. Frozen food systems are more flexible in that replacement times need not be so near together and food can be kept for several weeks before there is noticeable deterioration. Both systems are helpful in minimizing kitchen space in a small pub operation. By freezing and chilling prepared food well away from the actual point of service, a pub caterer can concentrate on food service to the customer rather than become involved in its production.

However, a licensee must be careful when reheating frozen and chilled foods, and must have strict control over heating times and the maintenance of temperature of his equipment. A small deviation from the desired norm will harm food quality and lead to dissatisfied customers.

Mechanical preparation equipment

Mechanical kitchen aids aim to simplify labour-intensive activities such as vegetable peeling and dicing. With the trend towards the use of prepared foods, these activities are not so costly and time consuming as before and the need for vegetable preparation equipment is diminishing. Much preparation equipment available is both sophisticated and expensive and is unlikely to be justified by the low-volume caterer such as a licensee.

Mixing machines are widely used because of their versatility; they have a range of attachments for mixing, whisking and blending as well as for vegetable preparation and mincing. Small machines are available for operations which use quantities of fresh salad and cooked vegetables. These have a range of interchangeable blades for slicing, dicing and shredding. They produce

Meeting Market Demand

many variations of thicknesses, sizes and shreds and operate on a range of fruit and vegetable products as well as cheese, hard-boiled eggs etc.

Many specialized food preparation machines are available, ranging from extruders which produce chips from mashed potato powder to automatic ice cream makers. Most are expensive and are unlikely to be useful to pub caterers.

One executive involved in pub catering has stressed the following points in buying kitchen equipment:

Satisfy yourself that equipment will have maximum use.

Do not be baffled by technical data.

Ensure that the right deal is completed by inviting tenders from various equipment manufacturers based upon detailed specification.

Thus, bypass the more expensive wholesalers whenever this is possible and convenient.

Check at time of purchase that equipment has the usual guarantee periods and can be serviced and maintained regularly without hidden cost, i.e. do not fall into the trap of buying heavy-duty equipment only to find later that there are financially burdensome but essential service agreements.

Keep an up-to-date inventory of your equipment and list purchase date, service agreements and replacements where necessary.

Disposable materials

These can be used in food preparation and service. The reasons for their use are various, the most common being to reduce the cost of dish and pot washing and also, in the restaurant, to reduce laundry costs. With personalized printing, disposables can be used as promotional material.

Aluminium foil, plastic cling film and polythene bags have long been used in kitchens. Foil containers for cooking, holding, storing and serving food can reduce food handling and eliminate labour-intensive and unpleasant container washing.

Plastic-coated board containers are also available and these withstand cold ($-20\,°C$) and hot conditions. Caterers use plastic film for their own boil-in-the-bag dishes. Plastic bags, made of high-density polythene, nylon or laminates, are filled with hot foods sealed on a portable heat sealer (with the elimination of as much air as possible) and frozen. These can be treated in the same way as the commercial products.

Disposables in restaurants initially met with some resistance. The poor acceptability of paper plates and plastic cutlery mitigated against their use at all but the most basic levels of catering. Now the quality has been improved through the introduction of plastic-coated plates, printing and embossing. The advent of fork-food and take-away catering has reduced customer resistance to disposable materials. From the range of disposable cups, plates and cutlery made from paper, plastic, plastic-coated paper and foamed polystyrene, the individual licensee can assess which suit his establishment.

Disposable products may also replace napkins, place mats and tablecloths, and their quality can be high. Printed and/or embossed tablecloths reproduce the appearance and feel of damask and linen. Place mats and napkins can be printed to suit individual establishment needs. Disposables also enter restaurants in the form of portion-controlled foods.

Give proper consideration to the means of disposal; for large quantities of disposables, a waste compactor may prove desirable.

To sum up, the majority of pubs will have a minimum of kitchen space and may need to offer a relatively limited menu. Equipment will accordingly be limited to one or two units only, and these will need to be operated by unskilled staff. If the pub caterer bears this in mind he will not go far wrong and should find equipment to match his requirements with little difficulty, but there is plenty of choice among sophisticated methods for the more ambitious.

Further reading

Fuller, John, *Professional Kitchen Management*, Batsford, 1983.
Gladwell, Derek, *Practical Maintenance and Equipment for Hoteliers and Licensees*, Hutchinson, 1981.
Johnson, R. H., *Running your own Restaurant*, Hutchinson, 1981.
Milson, A. and Kirk, D., *Principles of Design and Operation of Catering Equipment*, Ellis Horwood and Avi, 1981.

7 Design and decor for dining

Bruce Braham

The design and decor of a licensed house depends upon the image that is to be created, and there are many variations (see Figures 10–13). The licensee may have preconceived ideas of what he wants to create, but this chapter aims to act as a memory aid so that important considerations are not overlooked. Where structural alterations or major works in specialized areas are contemplated expert help should be sought, and where equipment purchase is planned a number of competitive suppliers should be approached. In all cases the relevant legislation must be observed.

Design for function

The design of any licensed house will depend on the level of personal service offered; a silver service restaurant will require a different approach from a self-service food area.

The chosen scheme will depend first on the composition and cost of the menu. The type and quantity of customers will have to be researched so that the desired service is given to the required number of guests within the confines of available space. It may be found after research that the only alternative in a particular scheme is to extend the licensed premises. This involves complications such as liaison with the local authority over planning.

Many licensed houses will have a number of differing service areas under the same roof so that formal meals and snacks can both be served to complement the liquor. This complicates the overall scheme. Therefore the licensee must investigate all possible solutions and especially the financial consequences of the potential design and decor before a scheme is agreed. The licensee who is allied to a brewery may be able to draw upon the recommendation of experts at his head office.

The idea behind the scheme might initially come from the type of menu. If it is to be French bistro style then typical French tables with their distinctive turned wooden legs might be used; they would be covered with gingham linen. A silver service restaurant would use traditional tables with crisp white linen. A pizzeria scheme might involve terrazzo surfaces with vine draperies. A food service area specializing in English dishes might be of Tudor style. The variations are limitless.

Influence of the site

The site of the pub itself might prompt a theme, as in many railway inns where bars and restaurants may create the feeling of a railway carriage and achieve the effect of booth seating. Children's restaurants may be laid out to resemble the compartments of a carriage. Both may be complemented by items of railway regalia.

The Old Mill Inn might feature a working water wheel around which the bars and restaurant are built, and a typical riverside pub could spotlight fishing spoils in glass cases. Many licensed houses build their own themes around collections ranging from common horse brasses to foreign coins or dolls.

Many public houses are named after local historical events or characters, and this theme may be researched. If an inn is known as the Duke of Wellington or the Mountbatten Arms for example, material concerning the famous person can be collected and displayed.

Any theme in pub interior should carry it through as the customer will have formed an idea of what the decoration will be like. Care must be taken that the exterior catches the notice of passing customers. At night floodlighting or coloured lights may transform an otherwise unremarkable building.

Decor and market

Whatever the scheme, it should give customers an impression of the establishment's standard and an idea as to whether it is expensive or cheap before he enters. A decor that conveys dignity gives an impression of expense and quality, whereas a gaudy decor could indicate a less exclusive one of popular price. The former tells the customer that he is able to drink and eat at leisure, whereas the latter conveys a business expecting a high turnover of customers. The licensee bears in mind such psychological factors when planning his scheme.

The customer seeks a pleasant atmosphere in which to obtain refreshment, whether he requires a leisurely or a brief stay. He will select the establishment that is comfortable and attractive and which may give his desired level of privacy. The designer should aim, therefore, towards a particular market sector and not dilute his efforts in a vain attempt to please everyone.

Materials and layout

Where possible the publican should select materials that require minimum maintenance in a specific environment. Although space should be used carefully, materials contained in the existing building should be exploited. Even metal girders, beams and exposed bricks may be built into a successful scheme. Any views or aspects that the building might enjoy will be a primary attraction.

All schemes should also be built around the catering business as a place of work. There should be an organized workflow for speedy service to the customers. There should be adequate aisle space, which generally means a

Meeting Market Demand

minimum of 0.9 m (3 ft) between groups of furniture. The layout will depend upon the average size of a group of customers and the physical divisions of the floor plan. The more sophisticated the menu, the more restaurant floor space will be needed. As an illustration, in a bar where only drinks and basket snacks are consumed the tables may be close together, but in a full-service restaurant trolleys need to be wheeled between the tables. In the latter, spare space may be used for waiters' sideboards and hotplates.

Figure 10   (a) *At the King Charles Inn, Poole, a new bar has been built into the roof. A mock window is a vital feature*
(b) *A gas fire and a false minstrel's gallery make interesting features at the King Charles*
Photographs by Frank Cowburn

Colour and lighting

To convey the required atmosphere a designer will use warm colours and dim lights to give a luxurious image. Gold, yellow, brown and orange are used to warm a room, whereas green and blue are essentially cold colours.

A major trick of interior design is to use lighting to convey atmosphere. Care must be taken with the colour, and a fine balance is achieved by positioning light sources to avoid spotty illuminations, glare and shadows. Wide rooms usually use light better than small or narrow ones. The type of business will again affect illumination. A high level will be required where fast eating is the norm, and a low level where customers require a leisurely meal or drink. Lighting levels will vary throughout the establishment, but dimmer switches allow an infinite variation. A dimly lit bar can be flooded with light at cleaning times. A sudden increase in light is useful to reinforce closing time when customers linger for an excessive drinking-up period.

Typical levels of illumination may be as follows:

Low level:	restaurant	400 lux (lumen/m²) (or 37 lumen/ft²)
	bar	300 lux (lumen/m²) (or 28 lumen/ft²)
High level:	cafeteria	600 lux (lumen/m²) (or 56 lumen/ft²)

Where food is served, quartz lamps may be useful to light and warm the food where candlelight would normally be ideal. Red incandescent light is flattering to food and will help to achieve a primary aim of lighting – eye comfort for the customer.

Fluorescent light will change skin and food colours. This could be a problem near a food display. Fluorescent lighting may be attractive on cost grounds as it is the cheapest illumination (apart from natural light, which should never be discounted). Use natural light where possible but be careful to be able to screen out excessive sunlight.

Acoustics

Noise is often a problem in licensed houses. Acoustics are important to atmosphere and the interior design should avoid surfaces such as terrazzo, stone or concrete which may act as magnifiers for noise. In the luxurious surroundings of a restaurant, good quality carpet deadens sound. However, some customers feel insecure unless there is some noise.

Furnishings

It takes time to ensure that the furnishings are correct. There are a multitude of manufacturers and types, but several basic principles should be followed as the commercial situation differs from the domestic one. Commercial furnishings are used much more than those in the home and therefore the prime consideration is to use the best quality for durability.

Antique chairs can be obtained cheaply as single chairs. They must be carefully chosen for strength. Some pubs have even made a theme of using old commodes and bidets as seating.

Furnishings should blend with the decor to form a part of the whole image; all the internal fittings, coverings and furniture should co-ordinate with each other. Furnishings will be chosen for their function, appearance and cost. If specifications for these are combined to apply to the eventual purchases, hopefully no compromise will be needed. Extensive comparisons, costings and samples should be examined before coming to a decision.

All the furnishings selected should be easy to clean. They should have smooth, hygienic, non-absorbent surfaces and thus resist attack by liquids, particularly those containing alcohol. They should be durable enough not to be affected by soiling or by continuous cleaning. Materials should ideally be resistant to heat and in no way so fragile that they are easily damaged.

Damage will happen even with the best furniture but it should be easy to repair. With the Health and Safety at Work Act in mind, furnishings should be safe, i.e. free from jagged edges on which staff or guests cut themselves. They should be non-slip. Most importantly, colour, pattern and texture should be correct for the furnishings' purpose and should integrate readily into the surrounding decor.

Carpet

An important item of furnishing in public areas is the carpet. This has to be of outstanding quality to cope with customers' assaults on it. Alcohol, cigarette ends, food and general grime all fall on to the carpet and are ground in. Materials used in its manufacture must withstand all of these without suffering permanent damage.

It is not worth cutting corners where carpet quality is concerned, and the licensee should not be tempted into purchasing the cheapest alternative. A patterned carpet may be chosen as not showing stains as much as a plain one. Whatever the design, the carpet must have a secure backing and pile fixing and a close resilient pile. Industrial carpet tiles may be appropriate as individual tiles can be replaced or swapped. Carpets invariably investigated include Wilton and Axminster, both used extensively in licensed houses. Carpets sustain extra wear around doors and along aisles in bars and restaurants. A plain carpet is prone to show this up, but does have the advantage of making a room look larger. To last as long as possible, carpets should be expertly laid on a level floor on an underlay of felt or rubber. Should the pub's design and decor include stairs, the carpet will have to be securely attached by grippers, whether foam or material backed.

Possibly the most popular carpet material is wool. Although the most expensive, it will probably give the best service in most applications. Wool may be used alone or blended with another material, but it has the advantage of being warm, resilient to mechanical wear and notably less inflammable than many of its synthetic competitors. The latter advantage is important in a licensed house where the fire hazard is always present. Should the price of a wool carpet prove too high, acrylic ones are a good alternative as they are particularly stain resistant. Some heavy-duty polypropylene carpets now on the market are virtually indestructible and have a plain coloured, pleasant ribbed effect. However, take care in colour choice as this type tends to show dusty footprints.

Decor and design for dining

Carpets give warmth to a room and also reduce noise, but they are inappropriate in some areas. A problem area is that around the counters or bars where floor suffer the heaviest use, and abuse, with constant spillage etc. For a set area around bars it is probably sensible to consider using asphalt thermoplastic, resin rubber or composition tiles as they are more resilient to constant heavy use.

Figure 11 (a) *The feeling of being in someone's lounge works well at the Fisherman's Haunt, Christchurch*
(b) *A compact, yet functional food servery at the Fisherman's Haunt. Note the extensive menu display*
(c) *Family groupings around small tables are encouraged at the Fisherman's Haunt*
Photographs by Frank Cowburn

Curtains, safety and quality

The important contribution of soft furnishings to an overall scheme should never be underestimated. Curtains have several applications in pubs apart from their night-time function of providing privacy to room occupants. Blank brick walls or walls without windows may be transformed by curtains as wall coverings and add interest to an uninteresting or ugly decor.

A heavy-duty lining material should be used to minimize draught, and there is a metallic lining (Millium) on the market that is good from the point of view of insulation and light exclusion.

Curtain heading tapes in numerous varieties create different curtain styles. When ordering curtains, allow double the window width for best effect. One and a half the window width is the absolute minimum.

Although the exact design and handling of the curtains will depend upon their location, one should know the range of materials available. The occupants' safety in an emergency should be the uppermost factor. Materials selected should be chosen partly for their ability to stand up to fire and heat. The tragic Summerland fire, which prompted the Fire Precautions Act, was worsened because melting curtains spread the flames. Always consult manufacturers about the fire resistance of materials and consider special curtains both to protect and to match the decor. Materials are available which will help to minimize the effect of blast from an explosion and contain flying debris. Again, seek expert advice.

In public rooms, the setting will determine the quality of curtain material. The best quality will normally last longest. Brocade, damask, printed linen or velvet may be among the final selection, but choice is determined by the application.

The specification of furniture for bars and restaurants in a licensed house is vital to atmosphere creation. The scheme must form one co-ordinated package. A customer may not remember the decor details but an impression of luxury will remain with him, as will the comfort or otherwise of the furniture he has used.

Comfort and durability

Furniture in a department store window, though beautiful, may last only a few months in commercial use. The furniture selected must conform with the style of establishment. Although comfortable, the degree of this will depend on the type of business. In luxury operations, where customers linger over their drinks and meals, the greatest possible comfort should be built into it. Where a business requires customers to pass quickly through, furniture should be comfortable only for a relatively short time. For examples of this last type, look in department store and other fast food operations where psychological and ergonomic research has gone into design and selection of fittings. The crucial factor in the comfort of chairs is the shape of the back and seat width. Generally size increases with the improvement in luxury.

The British Standards Institute label indicates quality and extensive research into the design. Most furniture is made of wood but metal, plastic and fibreglass are used in an increasing number of applications. For padding, foam rubber has largely replaced traditional metal springing.

In covering chairs, seek a material resistant to heat and food droppings, with a smooth finish to ease cleaning and prevent harbouring of bacteria. Plastics are becoming popular owing to their ease of cleaning and their comparatively low cost.

Tables

The table is an important item of furniture, certainly in the food service area, as is its relationship with the accompanying chairs. The table will be approximately 0.7 m (28 in) high and the matching chair 0.43 m (17 in) high in order to comfortably seat the average customer.

When selecting an appropriate table, the material for the top is important. If not covered, a table top must be of a substance to withstand heat, water and alcohol and be non-scratch for hygiene. Varnished wood, formica or even marbled tops are commonly used in pubs. When covered by a cloth the top is not so vital, though it should be impervious to spillage and possibly covered by baize to cut down the wear on linen. For banqueting, it is useful if the tables can be linked together to enable long tables or top table and 'sprigs' to be created.

Tables and chairs that do not match cause discomfort. A table should be 0.8 m (30 in) across to allow sufficient room for customers to face each other and eat from their *couvert*. To increase the number of customers in the food service area, a licensee may try rectangular and circular tables, which may cope with unusual numbers in a party while economizing on space. Psychologically, designers use small tables where customers are required to eat quickly, and larger tables or booths for privacy and leisurely eating.

Booths

Booths are popular in exclusive restaurants because each party of customers may be screened from their neighbours and can converse without interruption or fear of eavesdropping. Booths can pose problems. Waiters may have to lean across customers to serve those against the wall.

Booths can also be used effectively in a self-service area. In the latter, tables will be lower so that conversation is not encumbered by a high table between. Plain wood booths suitable in a country inn could be upholstered for a luxury feeling.

Heating and ventilation

Comfortable pub seating is of minor importance to a customer if the atmosphere is too cold or humid. Efficient ventilation should be designed so as not to cause draught. Doors should also be designed to reduce draughts to the minimum with the constant flow of customers into and out of the pub.

Heating is an important design consideration. A major problem is that the temperatures vary during the day owing to intermittent use of facilities.

Figure 12 (a) *Recent 'Pub of the year', the Baker's Arms, Poole, features collections of butterflies, army badges, holograms, birds' eggs, a near complete set of English stamps, coins and notes, and a display of comparative statistics 1900–81. Note a modern gas fire adding atmosphere*
(b) *An ingenious use for redundant casks and kegs at the Baker's Arms*
(c) *Food servery at the Baker's Arms. Carvery roasts are displayed on the left while other main meals and snacks are collected from the servery on the right. Customers view their meal ticket numbers on televisions throughout the pub and then come to collect their meal*
Photographs by Frank Cowburn

Decor and design for dining

Whatever the type of heating, it must be controlled via sensors and thermostats to ensure that energy is not wasted in heating empty rooms. Customers themselves contribute to the heat, so the main consideration is to raise the temperature of rooms shortly before they arrive. If good control is exercised, coupled with adequate insulation, the aim will be achieved of making the customers feel at ease and avoiding temperature variations which might make them insecure.

Open wood-burning fires add atmosphere, but take care that they do not smoke or become a fire hazard.

Fume extraction There could be build-ups in restaurant and bar of steam and smells as well as fumes, moisture and heat, all of which annoy customers and staff alike. Beware of excessive frying. Customers can be put off if the smell of cooking fat lingers, especially if it remains on their clothes after leaving.

The first approach to ventilation will be to use the kitchen extractors to assist in a flow of polluted air from the eating area towards the kitchen where it will be sucked out above the cooking equipment. In the bars and restaurant themselves there may be ceiling inlets positioned around the perimeters of the rooms so that new or recycled air may be injected. The ventilation system will aim to recirculate the air in a balanced manner to reduce draughts, noises and vibration.

A major problem is build-up of smoke from cigarettes. To cope with this there must be at least four to six air changes an hour. Avoid concentrated extraction, for build-up of fumes is undesirable. Increase air changes in proportion to the number of customers so that there is no increase in smells, heat or humidity to disturb them or staff. Clean air will help to reduce the amount and the consequent cost of cleaning.

Tableware

Tableware and crockery are often forgotten, but they also must fit into the overall package.

Customers form an impression from tableware of a pub's hygiene standards. The type and quality should be considered at the time of purchase, as a mistake can be costly.

Silverware Silverware is a major cost in establishing a catering business, and what initially appears a bargain may be the most expensive in the long run. The exact specification depends largely on the theme desired, but there are several rules.

Different grades and qualities of silverware offered and described by manufacturers may prove confusing. Items may be described as lasting for a number of years, usually twenty or thirty, and the longer lasting grades contain the most silver and are the heaviest. Length of life depends on care in its use and storage.

For a restaurant, purchase a design that is complementary to decor and function. Elaborate designs prove an ideal harbour for bacteria, whereas a plain design invariably proves suitable and easier to clean.

Cutlery Cutlery comes in many sizes and prices. Plan carefully against your budget requirements to ensure that it does not become an expensive replacement. Total amounts depend on your anticipated sales per session, and that should be for your busiest period, not your norm or average. Nothing infuriates a customer more than finding that he can obtain food but nothing (clean) to eat it with. Do not let good business be your excuse for poor service. Care should be taken to buy cutlery with secure handles (or all-metal styles) as this is usually the weakest point.

Choice of material Stainless steel resists scratching. It is probably the most hygienic alternative in tableware and may be obtained with varying degrees of 'shine'. It is likely to be the most economic choice.

There are several terms which may confuse the licensee. 'Flatware' is used to describe spoons and forks, 'cutlery' for knives and cutting implements and 'hollow-ware' for other silver items such as bowls or teapots. The use of incorrect terms may result in mistakes. When making a choice, consider quality but also check future availability of supplies.

In a full silver service restaurant the list of basic items is as follows:

Flatware	*Cutlery*	*Hollow-ware*
soup spoon	table knife	vegetable dish and lid
dessert spoon	dessert knife	entrée dish and lid
teaspoon	carving knife	soup bowl and lid
salt spoon	butter knife	salvers
mustard spoon	fish knife	ice bucket
table spoon	fruit knife	finger bowl
service spoon	tea knife	bread basket
dinner fork		cake stand
dessert fork		flower vase
fish fork		egg stand
ladles		coffee pot
		tea pot
		water jug
		toast rack
		sauce boat

This range may be reduced for simple forms of catering.

The silver is subjected to hard use and should be inspected frequently. It will not be uncommon to find fork prongs bent and pots with defects such as ill-fitting lids. All these should be rectified. The silverware should be stored in drawers lined with baize and ideally under lock and key as losses can be expensive.

Disposables Many licensed houses equip snack bars with plastic knives and forks of dubious quality. These may be attractively priced but often cause annoyance to customers owing to frequent breakages. Ideally plastic should be avoided. Disposable cutlery has its place for pubs catering in gardens where cutlery can be lost or stolen more easily. Check for good quality plastic ware.

Decor and design for dining

Figure 13 (a) *The main feature of the Beehive Hotel, Poole, is the large family room and terrace built onto the rear of the original pub. The barbecue is especially popular*
(b) *At the Beehive Hotel, Eldridge Pope has converted a traditional Victorian pub into a mock Swiss atmosphere with clever use of timber*
(c) *The Beehive features a popular chef-assisted barbecue grill in the main eating area. The succulent odour of steak sizzling is guaranteed to increase food turnover*
Photographs by Frank Cowburn

Crockery

Crockery or china should be economical and practical, blend with the decor of the establishment, and complement the surroundings and the menu. If possible, the design should be colourful and cheerful.

Different types of food service require different designs and qualities of china. The most desirable type is the finest quality, but this cannot be recommended because of its great expense and the care it requires. Earthenware is universally accepted these days because it is cheaper as well as being extremely durable.

When purchasing china, check samples for a complete glaze and see that there are no imperfections. Look for a design that has a rolled edge which reduces chipping which harbour bacteria. The glaze should cover the pattern entirely to avoid uneven wear.

Vitrified earthenware is recommended for its low cost and because many standard colours and designs are available. When purchasing ensure that hotel weight, rather than domestic, is bought. The latter will not stand up to the heavy work in a commercial operation. Ensure that the china is capable of withstanding great heat, as many of the items may be subjected to periods in oven or grills. Also ensure that the design is going to continue for an indefinite period, thus enabling replacements to be bought.

The basic items which may be required are as follows;

hors-d'oeuvre dish	tea cup and saucer
hors-d'oeuvre plate	coffee cup and saucer
soup plate	tea pot
fish plate	sugar basin
joint plate	milk jug
sweet plate	butter dish
side plate	cruets

In less sophisticated operations, reductions to this range may be made.

Purchase an adequate amount of china to provide for a reserve for replacing inevitable breakages. Check the china at regular intervals and remove chipped or cracked items from service. Crockery with minor defects might be utilized in staff areas; otherwise it should be disposed of.

Washing up and storage

Keep china in a secure place where it is unlikely to be accidentally broken. Items regularly used for service and which have to be kept hot are commonly stored in the hotplate in the kitchen ready for use. Staff should wipe down all china immediately before placing it in front of the customer.

Often a design afterthought, the area allocated for washing must be adequate for an organized workflow. A mechanical washing-up machine is needed in all but the smallest establishment, with a conveyor or rack system so that items being washed are securely held while being sprayed with jets of hot water. Ensure that there is plenty of room for a closely defined place where dirty items may be left by the restaurant staff. Many breakages occur because the dropping-off facilities are too small, leading to great piles of crockery which fall over. Allow similar space for washed-up items.

All equipment should be stored in an hygienic manner and arranged so as to reduce losses. Most catering establishments have lockable china, linen and silver stores.

Keep in contact with your suppliers to ensure the correct use of cleaning and washing-up materials. See that these are carefully controlled, as they are expensive and often wasted. It is folly to throw valuable money down your kitchen sink.

Fast food operations

The traditional pub restaurant may have a menu based on French or hotel cuisine. In many establishments, the service and food will be aimed at a fast-moving clientele who do not linger over a lengthy meal. Such a fast food operation may not be quite at a cafeteria level but can incorporate many of its better points.

In many licensed houses a restaurant incorporating a counter has become popular. The typical layout is a stand-up counter, frequently U-shaped, and this is faced by stools with booths and tables around the perimeter. This type of menu and service has long been common in hotel coffee shops and butteries. The standard of service will go a long way to satisfying customers desiring a fast food meal.

The design must be geared to speed the menu peculiar to this type of operation. Normally the range of dishes will be limited and the kitchen will incorporate a minimum amount of storage space for deep freezers and refrigerators. All equipment must be proven to be used non-stop so that there is no wastage of capital or space. The staff must be given quick and easy access to the counter (and consequently the customers) and the kitchen must be close to the service area, if not actually within it.

A constraint on the efficiency and therefore the profitability of fast food restaurants is the shape of the counter. This is determined by the space available, which tells the designer how many seats he may provide for. The aim is to accommodate as many customers as possible within the constraints.

There must be room for the counter, stools, an aisle and space behind the bar. For a width of approximately 9 m (30 ft) it should be possible to install a U-shaped counter; this will create extra seats, although the complicated design will cost more.

Eye-catching themes

Incorporating an eye-catching feature enables customers to identify a particular theme. For example, a restaurant might feature narrow boats by having a lifesize model of the side of a boat along one wall of the restaurant, or might show a medieval scene in which the ceiling could be in the form of a tournament tent. Hot air balloons are another possible theme, or a stable setting such as might be found in a country inn.

From this chapter a licensee should gain some understanding of the pitfalls that it is possible to encounter when trying to create a catering package. However, by no means every problem has been dealt with in depth. If uncertainty exists about a particular snag, refer to a professional or expert for advice.

Further reading

Smith, D., *Hotel and Restaurant Design*, Design Council Publications, 1978.

Part Two

Policy and Operations

8 Menus and their compilation

J. J. Morel

Food and its service is sold through the menu, and we should first look at the pub catering market, the pubs and their customers.

Pubs now have an exciting image, particularly for young people. They come in many shapes and sizes, some traditional others modern. The new style of public house which embodies a full catering service is a mini-hotel with bars, a restaurant and overnight accommodation. Two basic types emerge: the town house, and those in residential and rural areas. Earlier chapters have indicated how these may be themed.

Just as there are different types of pub in cities, towns and villages, so there are various types of customer. They are either regulars or chance visitors. They may be on a fixed income or have a disposable income. There are wage and salary earners, business executives on allowance or entertaining on expense accounts, local residents and overseas tourists and holiday-makers. These all have to be considered when planning a menu at a price to meet the needs of the market.

Pub catering

It is easier to dispense a drink than to provide food service, a specialized operation needing knowledge, flair and attention to detail.

Pub catering falls into two basic types: the pub restaurant offering a table service, and the bar serving food over the counter. The former is a conventional catering activity and the latter a fast food operation.

A number of houses, especially those in residential and rural areas, offer both types of service. The busy town house with an ongoing trade may concentrate upon a fast food service. Business in residential and country areas may be concentrated in the evening and at weekends, whereas in towns there is the lunch trade.

The town house is usually frequented by regulars and the country pub by a passing trade plus a hard core of local residents. Regulars are well known and their tastes in food are usually conservative. Chance customers may call only once, but might return next time they pass if they liked the atmosphere of the house, its menu, if they were made welcome and were satisfied with service and price.

Depending on its location, a pub can either build up a good regular trade or rely on a passing one. A regular trade is the bread and butter of any business and it is worth cultivating since regulars look upon the local as their own pub.

Policy and Operations

Some publicans consider them too 'sensitive' and prefer a passing or non-residential trade in a town location.

The chance customers from a passing trade may be more appreciative and more interesting in their variety but it could be risky to rely on them, particularly at holiday times; factors such as weather or even the political and economic climate can affect their habits.

Initially the chance customer has to discover the pub. A country house may increase trade with a roadside sign a short distance from the pub. The motorist seeking somewhere to eat has time to stop. Parking space is important and a number of cars parked outside is an indication of a good pub. Catering can be speculative; so to set and maintain good standards is essential to secure a constant trade.

Menu planning

The menu aims to inform people what is available to eat. There are common factors in all menu planning but in dealing with two defined operations, pub restaurants and bar food, each must be looked at separately.

Planning a restaurant menu requires practical knowledge of catering. Drawing up a pub bill of fare consisting of a selection of popular selling lines is more straightforward. Care should be taken with typing or printing, layout and presentation. Dog-eared, soiled or defaced menus are an indication of careless management.

There should be sufficient menus to go round so that customers do not have to queue to catch a glimpse of what is available. A large and neatly chalked bill of fare on a blackboard is a clear and personalized method of presenting a fast food menu.

Menus should be displayed outside the premises. This is a requirement under the Price Marking (Food and Drink on Premises) Order 1979, but it should be seen as an opportunity to demonstrate. A passing customer decides whether or not to come in by the exterior appearance *and* the menu on display. Therefore menus should promote interest and be easy to read and understand.

The restaurant menu

A menu is not so much written as composed; it is a creative affair. There are three kinds: the table d'hôte (the host's table), a set menu at a fixed price; the á la carte, which consists of a choice of dishes and prices; and a third type which combines the table d'hôte with the à la carte. This is known as a 'liner' menu where the main dish price indicates the price of the full meal. This is the type of menu pioneered by steak houses.

The set price table d'hôte and the liner menu are normally made up of three courses – starter, main dish, sweet or cheese – and there is a choice at each course. Coffee is usually charged extra.

A steak house menu is usually a two-course meal, i.e. main dish and a sweet or cheese. Starters are listed and there is an extra charge for these. Examples of the three types of menu are shown in Figures 14–16.

Menus and their compilation

Which type? The best type of menu to feature – the set meal, an à la carte or a liner – depends on the market. Where customers consider price to be of secondary importance to quality, such as in expense account business or in celebrating an occasion, it would be the à la carte. Where customers want a good idea of the meal's cost, or for a special function ordered in advance and where a fair number of covers are involved, feature a set price meal, the table d'hôte. As a happy medium and for a fairly regular trade, the liner, which combines features of both, would be acceptable. Liner menus are characteristic in steak houses, since there is a choice of grills at charges varying according to meat cut and the other items listed. In comparatively small restaurants it is not always advisable to put on a set meal *and* an à la carte as this could confuse and embarrass customers and, unless carefully devised, lead to waste. When both are offered, customers will go for the set price meal, not trusting or feeling able to afford to eat from an open-ended à la carte menu. If variety is thought necessary, one or more dishes of the day may be featured.

There are guidelines in menu planning. The three prime considerations are price, type of customer and numbers. Naturally, the menu should be well within the capabilities of the kitchen staff and equipment.

Imagination and balance Menus should be imaginative, weatherwise and topical. Imagination means avoiding getting into a rut of predictably ordinary menus: customers should not be able to guess what is on without even seeing the menu. Taking a chance on the weather calls for a flexibility, not always easy with sudden changes. It means giving preference to lighter and cold fare in warm weather and more substantial hot dishes when it is cold outside. Topicality indicates pancakes on Shrove Tuesday, traditional festive fare during the Christmas period, fish on Friday, as well as taking advantage of fresh vegetables and fruit as they come into season.

Menus should be balanced, and repetition of foodstuffs and colours should be avoided. Chicken soup should not be followed by poached chicken in white sauce, rice by rice pudding as a sweet, steak and kidney pie by apple pie, and so on.

Terminology Pay attention to terminology and culinary terms. Customers are often knowledgeable and should be able to recognize dishes they have ordered. This does not suggest that kitchen creativity should be discouraged, but a house speciality or creation of the chef should be so named and not named after a standard dish to which it bears no resemblance. Where a brief description or translation of dishes is given on the menu, this should be in simple terms and not in flowery language.

Menus must not misinform lest the Trade Descriptions Act 1968 be contravened. If salmon is frozen and comes from Norway, it should not appear on the menu as fresh Scotch, and if fresh vegetables are stated they should not come out of a can or from the freezer.

Mainly for economic reasons the tendency is for shorter and more standard menus, but there should always be adequate choice. The main course should offer meat, poultry, fish and a cold dish. Variety is achieved by a frequent change of menu or by including dishes of the day. A good selection of starters,

Policy and Operations

Table d'hôte menu   £4.50

Grapefruit cocktail cerisette
Pâté maison
Crème St Germain with golden crôutons

■

Choice of:

Fillet of plaice Mornay
Roast sirloin of beef
Yorkshire pudding and horseradish sauce
Fried chicken Maryland
Served with two varieties of potatoes and a selection of vegetables
The chef's cold collation

■

Apple and blackberry pie à la mode
Fresh fruit salad and double cream
Peach Melba
or
Cheese tray

■

Coffee (extra)   20p

Prices are inclusive of VAT but not service

Figure 14 *Table d'hôte menus*

Table d'hôte menu £7.50

Hors-d'oeuvre
Orange and grapefruit cocktail
Consommé Célestine
Crème vichyssoise
Spaghetti à la bolonaise

●

Poached fillet of turbot in shrimp sauce
Roast dressed turkey with grilled frankfurters and bacon
Cranberry preserve
Sauté of beef Stroganoff and pilaff of rice
Chicken Kiev
Served with two styles of potatoes and a selection of vegetables
Game pie and assorted salads

●

A selection of sweets from the trolley
Chocolate nut sundae
Ice cream: vanilla strawberry coffee
or
Cheese board

●

Coffee and after dinner mints

Price inclusive of coffee
Prices are inclusive of VAT but not service

Policy and Operations

a sweet trolley and a cheese board (British and imported cheeses) should also be offered.

Pay attention to the quality and service of coffee. A large cup (not those tiny ones) of real coffee rounds off a perfect meal. A feature could be made of special coffees; Irish coffee, for example, is popular.

Variety is the spice of catering. The average customer may not be adventurous in his food choice; regulars are often known to staff not by their name but by their order. Nevertheless, people do like to have a choice, just in case they wish to change.

Portions and service
Portions should never be mean; this needs careful evaluation when drawing up a portions chart. Customers' appetites should be gauged carefully. Give thought to the way in which the food is served – silver or plate service? If the latter, it should be neatly arranged for eye appeal.

Hot food must be served hot not lukewarm, and cold fare cold not tepid. Food which arrives cold when it should be hot is one of the two most common complaints in restaurants; the other is that of slow service. Pay attention to detail. Offer the recognized accompaniments to dishes; customers should not have to ask for toast and lemon wedges with pâté, or tartare sauce with fish, and so on.

English and French menus
Should the menu be composed in French or English? Since the pub is a British institution, English menus are more in character; but there are certain culinary French terms which should not be translated. Only a restaurant catering for an up-market clientele and featuring an exclusive à la carte service might attempt to complete the ambience with a French menu. This needs care since French is a difficult language. Blunders in spelling, grammar and idiom could bring the restaurant into disrepute. Figure 17 shows an example of an à la carte menu in French. It is sometimes the practice to write the lunch menu in English and the dinner one in French.

Fashion and trends
A British fare menu could be a winner because it is encouraged and publicized by the tourist boards, particularly when local dishes are listed. Menu planning is an exacting task. As with all things, proficiency comes with practice. One way to learn is to see what others do. Keep an eye on the trade press. The *Caterer and Hotelkeeper*, with its weekly menu feature file is a useful guide.

Collecting menus is a hobby which can be put to practical use. There are trends and fashions in food. This means remaining abreast of the market and putting on dishes which are in vogue. Current examples are vichysoisse, pâté, seafood cocktail, scampi and Black Forest gâteau.

Bookings
Mention has been made of the speculative nature of catering. In a well-patronized restaurant where seating is restricted, encourage customers to book in advance. Some pub restaurants make it known that they take advance bookings only. In taking a booking it might be possible to discuss the menu at the same time, and this is often the case with special parties.

Menus and their compilation

Figure 15 *A la carte menus*

À la carte menu

French onion soup	50p
Cream of chicken	60p
Smoked trout	£1.00
Honey dew melon	75p
Avocado pear and prawns	£1.20
Liver pâté	80p
Lemon sole à la bonne femme	£2.50
Scampi à la meunière	£3.00
Gammon steak Hawaiian	£2.75
Coq au vin	£3.25
Minute steak à la hôtelière	£4.00
Escalope of veal cordon bleu	£4.50

Potatoes: parisienne   duchesse   allumettes
Vegetables: minted garden peas   baby carrots
                broccoli   braised celery hearts

Compote of green figs	75p
Fresh fruit salad	75p
Charlotte russe	75p
Assorted ice creams	50p
Cheese tray	80p
Welsh rarebit	60p
Coffee	25p

Prices are inclusive of VAT but not service

À la carte menu

Florida cocktail	50p
Soup of the day with golden croûtons	50p
Fruit juices: orange tomato grapefruit	25p
Fried fillet of plaice à la tartare French fried potatoes and green peas	£2.00
Half a roast chicken Sage and onion dressing Grilled chipolatas and bacon rolls Fried potatoes Brussels sprouts	£2.25
Steak, kidney and mushroom pie Whipped potatoes Green peas and baby carrots	£2.50
Cold chicken and ham platter	£2.25
Baked jam roll and custard	50p
Strawberry gâteau	60p
Crème caramel and ice cream	50p
Cheese board	60p
Coffee	25p

Prices are inclusive of VAT but not service

Menus and their compilation

Other menus In pubs with overnight accommodation, catering for a residential bed and breakfast trade, menus are needed other than for main meals. These can be standardized. It is usual to provide a choice between a light continental and a full breakfast. Most bed and breakfast guests opt for that British institution, the full breakfast. The light one may consist of cereal or fruit juice, toast and marmalade, tea or coffee. The full one is more elaborate and provides a better opportunity to impress the customer, as Figure 18 shows.

Breakfast, being the first meal of the day, is generally agreed to be the most difficult. People are not always at their best first thing in the morning, and this is all the more reason to pay attention to breakfast preparation and service.

For residential guests, and sometimes for passing trade, high tea is provided. This is an afternoon tea augmented by a hot or cold main dish. Figure 19 shows a high tea menu.

Another possibility is an all-British liner menu. An example is shown in Figure 20.

There should be no need to extol the virtues of a good cup of tea, particularly the early morning cuppa. Loose tea is not often used now; the tea bag is almost universal because of its convenience and ease of portion control.

Whereas other meals may be prepared with convenience foods, breakfasts and most high teas should be prepared to order. These menus should be drawn up with as much thought as those for lunch and dinner.

Pub food

The words 'food' or 'hot foot' in bold lettering seen outside pubs proclaim that food, as well as drink, is served inside. Variously described as 'eats' or 'pub grub', pub food is representative of pub catering. Here is a market that few, if any, pubs can afford to ignore. Pub catering has made a contribution to culinary literature: who had heard of a ploughman's lunch, in the basket, or king-sized sausages before the advent of pub catering?

Much of what has been said about the pub restaurant applies to pub food in general. However, the menu is more straightforward; it is à la carte in that it provides a choice of dishes and prices.

The term 'bar snack' is probably a misnomer implying something rather light. People may not want a full meal but often require something fairly substantial. There should be a choice of hot and cold dishes, cold being more acceptable at midday and hot food in the evenings. A sit-down restaurant meal takes time to prepare and serve. Pub food should be made more readily available by a quick (or fast food) service. In many houses food service is too slow and this frustrates the customer who probably drops into a pub (rather than elsewhere) for a quick meal.

Premises One drawback to a fast service is likely to be the premises. It may be difficult to introduce food service into an old pub originally intended only for drinking, and it will almost certainly have to be modified to cope with food service.

Where there are space and structural problems, the bill of fare will have to be planned accordingly. Better just a few lines which can be prepared and served well, than an unwieldy menu which is impractical to carry out and

Figure 16 *'Liner' menus*

Liner menu

Egg mayonnaise
Cream of asparagus
Smoked mackerel pâté
Tomato juice cocktail

Rainbow trout amandine	£3.50
Roast best end of lamb à la boulangère	£4.75
Duckling à l'orange	£5.00
Escalope of veal Holstein	£3.75
Fondant and sauté potatoes French beans	
Broccoli Mornay Sliced carrots Vichy	
Cold chicken and ham with dressed salads	£3.50

Black Forest gâteau
Meringue glacée à la napolitaine
Rum baba Chantilly
or
Cheese board
or
Sardines on toast

Coffee   25p

The price of the main dish denotes the price of the meal
Prices are inclusive of VAT but not service

maintain at a good standard. Brewery companies are aware of the problems and invest substantially in adapting old premises to modern requirements. New pubs are larger in size than hitherto and may embody full catering facilities with well-equipped kitchens, restaurants and bars where the service of food can be kept separate from that of drink. The trend is towards a layout

Menus and their compilation

Liner steak house menu

Prawn cocktail
Cream of tomato
Chef's pâté

Fried scampi à la tartare	£3.75
Grilled rump steak	£4.00
Grilled sirloin steak	£4.25
Grilled fillet steak	£5.50

Served with French fried potatoes, grilled whole tomatoes and salad bowl

---

Coupe Jacques
Chocolate profiteroles
Blackcurrant cheesecake
or
Cheese and biscuits

Coffee   25p

Price of the main dish indicates the price of the meal
Prices are inclusive of VAT but not service

---

design widely applicable but capable of individual character, and where customers recognize that they can get food in one place and drink in another.

Most older houses differ in design, size and procedures. Unless the customers are regulars and know the ropes, getting something to eat is not always easy. Bar and counter staff should be aware of this and anticipate the needs of those wanting food. Eating is personal, and social skills on the part of

À la carte menu in French

Truite fumée au raifort	£1.50
Avocat à la vinaigrette aux crevettes	£1.50
Crème à la vichyssoise	80p
Bisque d'homard	£1.00
Consommé double en tasse	80p
Scampi frits ou belle-meunière	£3.00
Filets de sole à la caprice ou à la florentine	£3.50
Tournedos Rossini	£4.50
Entrecôte grillée	£5.00
Suprême de volaille pané aux pointes d'asperges	£4.00
Caneton à la bigarade	£5.00

Pommes:　　frites　　croquettes　　sautées　　mouseline
Légumes:　　haricots verts　　petits pois　　épinards en branches
　　　　　　　choux de Bruxelles
Assiette anglaise　　Salade panachée　　　　　　　　　　£3.50

Entremets de la voiture	£1.50
Glaces au choix	80p
Fraises Melba	£1.00
Plateau de fromages	£1.25
Café	40p

Prices include VAT but not service

Figure 17　*A la carte menu in French*

Menus and their compilation

those dealing with food are essential. This can do much to alleviate the difficulties in outmoded premises with improvised facilities.

Once served, customers want somewhere to sit down and eat. Strangely this elementary point is often neglected. Assess the number of customers requiring food at any one time and provide the necessary seating and tables. If space precludes this, 'stand-up' eating facilities could be the answer.

A catering service must be organized effectively and, except possibly for food served from a counter display, orders for food from the kitchen should be written on a check pad and a copy handed to the kitchen.

Pub food menu Ideas on the type of food can be illustrated by three specimen menus. One offers a choice between hot and cold dishes (Figure 21), the second features hot ones (Figure 22) and the third is for an up-market operation (Figure 23).

These menus are made from dishes popularly found in pubs. In houses patronized by young people a variety of pizzas, quiches and other 'fun foods', all of which can be bought in, may also be an alternative to more traditional lines. In fast food service it is advisable to keep menus short but with a choice between hot and cold dishes.

Figure 18 *Full breakfast menu*

Full breakfast menu

Choice of cereals
Stewed prunes   Orange juice   Grapefruit cocktail
Porridge

Grilled kippers   Poached haddock fillet
Eggs: fried   poached   boiled   scrambled
Grilled bacon   Sausage   Mushrooms   Tomato
Cold ham

Toast   Oven rolls
Jam   Marmalade   Honey
Tea or coffee

Policy and Operations

Figure 19 *High tea menu*

High tea menu

Choice of:
Egg, bacon, and fried potatoes
Fried fillet of fish and fried potatoes
Grilled sausage, bacon and fried potatoes
Salmon mayonnaise

Rolls and butter
or
Brown or white bread and butter
Preserves

Biscuits
Cake

Pot of tea

Presentation Drawing up a menu is one thing; presenting it is another. The operation must be well organized, supervised and followed through by the management. The aim should be to make your food the most attractive and generous of any pub in the area.

Experience will tell which are the best-selling lines. Groups of customers often emulate others' eating habits and order what they see other people eating.

Menus and their compilation

Figure 20 *British fare 'liner' menu*

British fare 'liner' menu

Potted shrimps
Curried egg and rice
Scotch broth
Oxtail soup

Grilled turbot and anchovy butter   £5.50
Parsley new potatoes   Cornish broccoli

Steak, kidney, mushroom and oyster pudding   £6.50
Mashed potatoes and mushy peas

Roast rib of beef and Yorkshire pudding   £7.50
Horseradish relish
Baked jacket potatoes and buttered cabbage

Game pie and salads   £5.00

Baked marmalade roll and preserve sauce
Mincemeat tart and custard
Royal trifle
or
A selection of farmhouse cheeses
or
Sardines on toast

Coffee   25p

Price of main dish denotes price of a three-course meal
Price includes value added tax but not service

Figure 21 *Pub catering menu*

Pub catering menu

Prawn sandwich	85p
Ham sandwich	75p
Chicken sandwich	75p
Roast beef sandwich	85p
Toasted bacon sandwich	75p
Ploughman's lunch	85p
Liver pâté and toast	85p
Veal and ham pie salad platter	£1.00
In the basket:	
Fried scampi and chips	£1.50
Fried fish and chips	£1.50
Grilled sausages and chips	£1.00
Fried chicken and chips	£1.50
Steak pie and chips	85p
Egg, bacon, sausage and chips	£1.00
Welsh rarebit	75p
Buck rarebit	85p
Coffee	30p

Prices are inclusive of VAT

The kitchen   The kitchen must be equipped to deal with menus featured. It should be adjacent to the food service area. The menu should be planned before fitting out the kitchen. In old premises space for food preparation and cooking is often a restricting factor.

Where there is a simple pub food service, apart from preparation and storage space, a deep freeze cabinet of suitable size and a refrigerator, com-

Menus and their compilation

Figure 22   *Hot bar dishes*

Hot bar dishes

Cottage pie	80p
Cornish pastie	60p
Fisherman's pie	80p
Lancashire hot-pot	£1.00
Curried beef and rice	£1.00
Grilled sausages and mashed potatoes	90p
Faggots and mashed potatoes	90p
Toad in the hole	90p
Steak, kidney and mushroom pie and mashed potatoes	£1.00
Sausage roll	60p
Baked beans	50p
Bubble and squeak	50p

Prices are inclusive of VAT

paratively little other equipment is needed. This will consist of a gas stove, twin deep fryer, salamander grill or automatic toaster and a microwave oven. Where there is also a restaurant, larger plant may be required – certainly a bigger stove or cooking range and a brander for grills. Other plant includes coffee-making equipment and possibly a boiler. (Chapter 6 provides further guidance.)

Charges   Money taken for food should be kept separate from that taken for drink. This practice is generally recognized by the customers, who know what they have to pay separately for each. Prices should include VAT at the current rate, and a note to this effect should be clearly printed on all menus and price lists. There should be *no small print*. If charges include service this must also be stated. Food consumption off the premises does not attract VAT. Remember that VAT does not represent revenue but must be paid to HM Customs and Excise.

Policy and Operations

Figure 23 *Up-market pub food menu*

Up-market pub food menu

Sandwiches
Smoked salmon	£1.00
Prawn	£1.00
Chicken	75p
Ham	75p

Toasted sandwiches
Gammon	£1.00
Cheese	75p
Club	£1.25
Bookmaker's	£1.50

Platters (served with French fried potatoes)
Pâté	£1.00
Ploughman's lunch	80p
Veal and ham pie	80p

In the basket (served with French fried potatoes)
Jumbo scampi	£1.25
Wing of chicken	£1.00
Fried fish	£1.00
Sausages	80p

Coffee	30p

Prices include VAT

Menus and their compilation

Catering should be carefully correlated to charges. Menus must be costed and portions calculated in budgeting for a certain return on food. Food is expensive and must be properly accounted for; otherwise it is possible to run a seemingly lucrative business at a loss. Charges should be constantly reviewed in these inflationary times.

When pricing menus, take care not to undersell or price yourself out of the market. Remember that staff must also be fed and that this costs money. Pub food charges are generally competitive in order to attract business and help sell drink. If in kitchen terms the gross profit sought is 50 per cent, so the cost of the food is multiplied by two. Because of higher payroll costs and overheads a greater profit yield will be required from the pub restaurant. The usual gross on food is 60–66 per cent (but see Chapter 13 for further details of costing and pricing). Maintain a daily record of takings, costs and estimated profit, thus keeping your hand on the pulse of the business.

Further reading

Coombes, S., *Dictionary of Cuisine French*, Hutchinson, 1980.
Coombes, S., *Restaurant French*, Barrie & Jenkins, 1977.
Fuller, John, *Professional Kitchen Management*, Batsford, 1983.
Morel, J. J., *The Caterers' Companion*, Pitman, 1973.

9 Purchasing food for pubs

J. J. Morel
Material from Eric Ellmes is included in this chapter.

Purchasing is the first and most important function in the food management cycle. Unlike the speculative aspects inherent in day-to-day catering, buying supplies is more responsive to planning and control. Therefore it should not be left to any odd member of staff to order supplies in a haphazard manner. It requires the personal attention of the licensee for, in purchasing more than anywhere, money can be wasted or saved. Delegate buying only to staff who are competent and understand the operation. Even then ensure that there are adequate checks on, for example, quantities and use.

The publican sets his charges to keep them competitive within his chosen market yet give him an acceptable margin of profit. He also budgets his expenditure and this requires a knowledge of market trends and prices.

When buying, the publican becomes the customer and should be able to keep the initiative. However, a buyer relies on his suppliers in supply matters, and the publican's and the supplier's objective should be to build mutual trust and respect so that both can function effectively. Seek consistency in quality and price from suppliers who can guarantee an adequate delivery service. Although useful in establishing standards, buying out may be time consuming. Take care in deciding a policy most convenient for your operation. Consistency is the key as recosting and repricing are time consuming. Constant switching of suppliers because goods seem cheaper may prove unproductive. Suppliers who specialize in particular categories of foods can help diversity and in establishing uniqueness.

Specifying requirements

Food purchasing depends on the menu and the composition of its dishes and responds to planning. First the publican needs to set out a shopping list showing the items required for each dish on the menu with a detailed specification for each. Experienced buyers are aware that you only get what you pay for and that, important though price may be, service and quality must also be considered. Continuity of supply (without delays or disappointments) as well as quality maintenance should be brought into your specifications. The best is neither necessarily nor usually the cheapest.

Specifications should tell suppliers exactly what you are looking for and willing to accept. The simplest specification will be a brand name with a pack

Purchasing food for pubs

size. This may well cover most items required. A more detailed specification will be needed for others, for example meat. The *Meat Buyers' Guide* is a useful reference for a full range. For other items, talk to various suppliers to see what is available and then decide on what you want and write your specification with the help of your suppliers. A guide to market prices and availability is the trade press, for example the weekly *Caterer and Hotelkeeper*.

How much to order depends on whether supplies are processed or fresh. Processed or convenience foods (canned, frozen or dried) bought in bulk and stored and used as required present little problem. Fresh foods, with shorter shelf life, need more accurate estimation.

Keep a portions chart showing gross (or unprepared) and net (plated) portions to assist in determining quantity needed. Then multiply the individual commodity portion by the estimated number of covers over a given period. Allow for a small margin of error; it is better slightly to overestimate. With meat, allow for cutting up. Experience will tell a licensee which are popular lines, as opposed to those less demanded but which are listed on menus to give customers an adequate choice.

Sources of supply

How to select from several sources of supply, and where and how to buy, depend upon the type of business and size of the account. Size is measured by what an account is worth to a supplier in hard cash. There is a difference between retail and wholesale buying, one being for housewives and the other for caterers. In general, deal with suppliers who specialize in supplying caterers except when only small quantities of certain products are needed. Specialist suppliers understand the catering industry and, indeed, are part of it.

There are three sources of supply in broad terms: wholesale, retail, and cash and carry.

Retailers Retailers may be of use for small requirements of a commodity or where local shops can give a service that wholesalers cannot, as can be true of bakers, greengrocers and dairies. (Small grocers may combine in co-operative buying groups under a brand name. In addition to their main retail side the co-operative may offer a service to caterers.) In all cases it is to your advantage to arrange at least weekly accounts. In this way you should have sold most of what you have purchased before you have to pay for it.

Publicans do have responsibility towards the community where they trade and will consider supporting their local traders, many of whom will be their own customers. Dairy produce, bakery goods, meat, fresh fruit and vegetables and particular local specialities can all be bought from local traders who can offer a prompt, as well as a competitive, service in terms of quality.

Where you use local retail suppliers, ensure that you still use your specifications and meet them. It is short sighted to use local retail suppliers if they are not supplying goods to your specifications at competitive prices.

Policy and Operations

Wholesalers Wholesalers sell goods by the entire piece or in large quantities. They are usually geared to delivering to your door on a regular basis. Frequency of delivery will, of course, depend on the volume of business placed with them. As a guide the following can be taken as the level of service most wholesalers will offer:

Grocery suppliers	once a week
Frozen foods	once or twice a week
Greengrocery	two or three times a week
Meat and fish	two or three times a week
Dairy and bread	five or six times a week.

If your volume warrants it they may adjust this to suit your needs.

Most wholesalers will be pleased to supply on credit terms. Usually they require a bank and two trade references. On occasions you may be able to improve the terms you receive by ordering in a larger quantity than you need; but look at this carefully as it may cost more in overdraft interest than is saved in price.

Some wholesalers may want to supply you cash on delivery; if possible avoid this, because you should be able to sell most goods bought on account before you have to pay for them.

Cash and carry This is the third purchasing option. These are, in effect, supermarket-style wholesalers supplying traders who pay cash and themselves carry the goods away. They often have a section devoted to catering and carry catering pack sizes.

Publicans may have to register with their local cash and carry before they can be supplied. The prices charged are 'middle market', between retail and wholesale.

Dealing direct with manufacturers Large operators may deal directly with big food manufacturers. In direct purchasing, the bigger the account the more advantageous the terms; however, so high is the cost of transport that there could also be delivery charges to be added. All large manufacturers and suppliers offer an advisory service in support of their products.

Decision and control

When comparing suppliers, bear in mind that purchasing must balance services, price and quality. If every company you approach quotes against a copy of your specification, you can compare prices. If they accept your specifications, you must assume that they will meet the qualities your specifications demand. This leaves service. The cheapest may not be the best buy if they can only deliver once a week. So if a supplier meets your specifications and offers competitive prices, judge service for yourself. Good service to one may not suit another. Talk to your competitors about the service they receive from companies quoting for your business.

Having set specifications and agreed suppliers, we seek the most effective control of food purchasing. Get to know your suppliers. A visit to his premises often helps in discussing mutual problems. Integrity is respected in business. Loyalty is appreciated and pays off when shortages occur. Look after your accounts and they will look after you.

Managed houses and tenancies

In managed houses purchasing is comparatively straightforward when suppliers are nominated by head office. The group's chief catering executive issues a list of approved suppliers to each house with instructions on policy and procedure, quality standards, a portions chart and other information. This is usually contained in a manual, updated and revised as required. It is usual to give managers some freedom to shop around for the best buy from nominated suppliers.

Tenders and contracts for such commodities as frozen foods and groceries are generally negotiated and controlled by head office which in steak houses, for example, monitor meat suppliers for price and quality. Some groups have their own central food processing plants for the supply of hot and cold foods to their pubs.

Tenancies and, of course, free houses have freedom in operating their catering and in purchasing; but tenants may take advantage of their brewer's group purchasing and the services of the group's catering advisers.

Stocks and orders

Food stock should never need to exceed fourteen days stock in hand. This means that at a cost price the value of the stock equals two weeks' trading. To help achieve this, set stock levels for each item to be purchased.

First, estimate the usage of each item. From this can be determined the minimum stock wanted of any one line to ensure you do not run out between ordering and receipt of goods. This should then be noted and becomes the reorder level. This is always linked to the level of service received from suppliers. If the supply is daily, you only need stock for a day; if the supply is weekly, for a week. This reorder quantity (the lowest to bring stock up to the target) needs to be linked to the packaging of the items and the frequency of delivery that a supplier offers. High-volume items will in many cases have a lower stock level in terms of days than a low-volume item. In this way the overall stock level will be held at the target of fourteen days.

Having done all this for all items there are two main ways of recording the information. One is to enter each item in a looseleaf stock book showing the reorder level. This system is necessary if you wish to check movement of goods from more than one outlet using the same items. Then make up orders from the book after entering the day's issues and receipts. Check the book against actual stock regularly – at least once a week.

The other method is to label the storage space for each item with the reorder level. It is then obvious at the time of being used when an item needs to be reordered.

Policy and Operations

Keep a written record of all orders to enable you to check goods received. In the stock book system, compile the orders from the book; if using the other method, walk round the storage area.

Orders should now be placed with the supplier. In most cases these can be telephoned. Many suppliers will have set days for your delivery and this will determine the order days. Make use of the supplier's telesales department and get them to telephone you. Efficient suppliers will, after a time, know your purchase record and may remind you of anything overlooked. Getting the supplier to telephone you also builds in the discipline to check your stocks to ensure that your orders are ready on time.

When the goods are delivered, check them to ensure that they agree with details on the delivery note/invoice. If they do, sign the delivery note/invoice and the supplier will forward the invoice if required. If they do not agree, the discrepancies should be noted on the delivery note/invoice and signed by you and the driver. A credit note should then be raised by the supplier for the discrepancy.

Any goods returned because they do not match your specifications or were not ordered should also be noted on the delivery note/invoice and signed by both you and the driver. Again, the supplier should raise the necessary credit.

The delivery note/invoice should then be checked against the order. Any items not supplied or not as ordered should be queried with the supplier and reordered if necessary.

The goods should then be stored in their appropriate space. The goods should always be used on the FIFO (first in, first out) system.

Paying

It saves office work for the small buyer to pay cash for goods. It should also ensure the keenest price and enables the buyer to shop around, but receipts should always be obtained and a record of expenditure kept. Where accounts are opened for certain regular supplies, do not allow them to run on unchecked; all accounts need regular supervision. It is not good policy to open too many accounts which can mean much unproductive office work.

Carefully check deliveries against written orders and check purchases for quality and quantity, for costly errors can occur here. Pay attention to the clerical accounting side of purchasing and to the inspection of all deliveries.

Publicans have their problems, as do suppliers: both have a living to make. The buyer wants the best possible deal, but it is not sensible to screw suppliers down or to play one account against another. Fast deals, like bad debts, are not appreciated, and it is not unknown for suppliers to gang up on a devious buyer.

Selecting supplies

In dealing with the choice of commodities for pub catering, only some of the features of interest to licensees can be included from what is a wide body of knowledge. Further reading is listed at the end of the chapter.

Purchasing food for pubs

Meat Meat is variable and should be purchased with care. We rely upon the source of supply. Wholesale firms provide a service to caterers. In the London area many are around Smithfield market. In the country, many pubs are able to purchase from a local butcher. The publican should discuss and specify his requirements with the meat supplier. He must be guaranteed continuity. Terms are negotiated and enable the publican to price his bill of fare.

Beef The main grades of beef are: Scotch, English, Irish, cow and imported. Scotch is usually considered to be the best and often commands a premium price. English/Irish is generally accepted as a good standard catering quality in steak bars. Imported can be good but tends to vary widely in quality. Imported is only as boneless cuts; be guided by the butcher as to its quality. Cow beef is normally used by manufacturers but some is offered to the general trade. It is generally unusable in pub catering.

All meat should have been aged by the butcher and be ready to use. With developments in vacuum packing there is less need to purchase frozen meats. Vacuum-packed meat, stored correctly, will have a shelf life of three weeks. If buying in vacuum pack keep the meat in the pack under refrigeration until one half to one hour before it is needed. Then open the pack and tray up the meat as usual. This gives time to disperse the confinement smell.

If buying in fresh meat, tray up steaks using peach paper or equivalent. Tray or hang large joints to ensure that they do not stand in their own blood.

Steaks Unless you are an expert butcher or have one on your staff, it is sensible to buy meat cut by the suppliers into portions rather than as large joints to be cut. Certainly the T-bone (and the prime T-bone, also known as the Porterhouse steak) is more conveniently bought portioned. Another way is to buy steak meat in the trimmed piece, e.g. trimmed boneless striploins, boned-out rump and the long fillet. Steaks can then be cut to order.

Cutting steaks to size without undue wastage of an expensive commodity requires skill. There can be waste in cutting a striploin into steaks; by buying ready-to-use cuts you also buy butchery expertise. The price per pound may appear more expensive, but the price per portion may work out less.

In a steak house where grilled steaks are the main feature, these are usually sirloin, rump, fillet and T-bone, raw weight being 225 g (8 oz) for the sirloin, rump and fillet steak and 340 to 450 g (12 to 16 oz) for the T-bone. Everything depends upon quality; business is ruined by a reputation for tough, flavourless or badly grilled or undersized steaks.

Accompaniments affect buying Good meat carefully purchased can be spoilt by bad cooking. Steaks are grilled to order to a customer's individual taste and commonly served on a platter with a portion of fried potatoes, grilled mushrooms and a tomato with a small bunch of watercress garnish. A mixed dressed salad on a side plate or in a small bowl may be featured; also a baked jacket potato with a dressing can be offered as an alternative to fried potatoes. These accompaniments have to be purchased in appropriate quantities.

Lamb The two main sources of lamb are New Zealand and the UK. All New Zealand lamb is imported frozen and should, therefore, be delivered to you frozen. It

Policy and Operations

should never be refrozen. UK lamb is always fresh and is considered better quality than New Zealand during the spring season. New Zealand lamb has the advantage of all year round availability, and if handled correctly is more than adequate for the pub trade.

The main items used are chops or cutlets and legs for roasting (a better buy for caterers than shoulders) (see Figure 24).

Lamb chops 225 g (8 oz) and cutlets may be bought ready portioned, fresh or frozen. Cutlets are either raw trimmed 120 g (4 oz) or French trimmed 75 to 90 g (2½ to 3 oz).

Veal Most veal tends to be Dutch, supplied fresh or defrosted by your butcher. Veal is still not popular in the UK and is generally used as escalopes. These from the leg or the cushion may be bought in prepared portions at 120 to 175 g (4 to 6 oz).

Pork Most pork is home produced and should always be fresh. The main items will be chops, leg or loin for roasting, and pork escalopes are also acceptable.

Offal Hearts, liver or kidneys are the main items, although one can include brains and sweetbreads. Lamb and pig liver are acceptable for grilling or frying, but usually ox kidneys are bought only for steak and kidney pies and puddings. Generally the larger the animal, the stronger the offal taste. Most offal is supplied defrosted and should never be refrozen. All of these can be used to make inexpensive and interesting additions to the menu.

Meat products Delicatessen and meat products include bacon, gammon, ham, tongue, brisket, various slicing sausages, frankfurters, pâtés and individually wrapped and large pies. Back and streaky bacon is purchased ready sliced in catering packs, gammon steaks in 150 to 175 g (5 to 6 oz) portions. Depending upon whether they are for sandwich fillings or for sliced plate portions, ham, tongue and brisket are purchased in large cans or in the whole piece. Frankfur-

Figure 24 Henry Telfer *New Zealand Lamb, a new range of meat cuts for caterers, featuring specially graded lamb, available for the first time*
Courtesy Henry Telfer

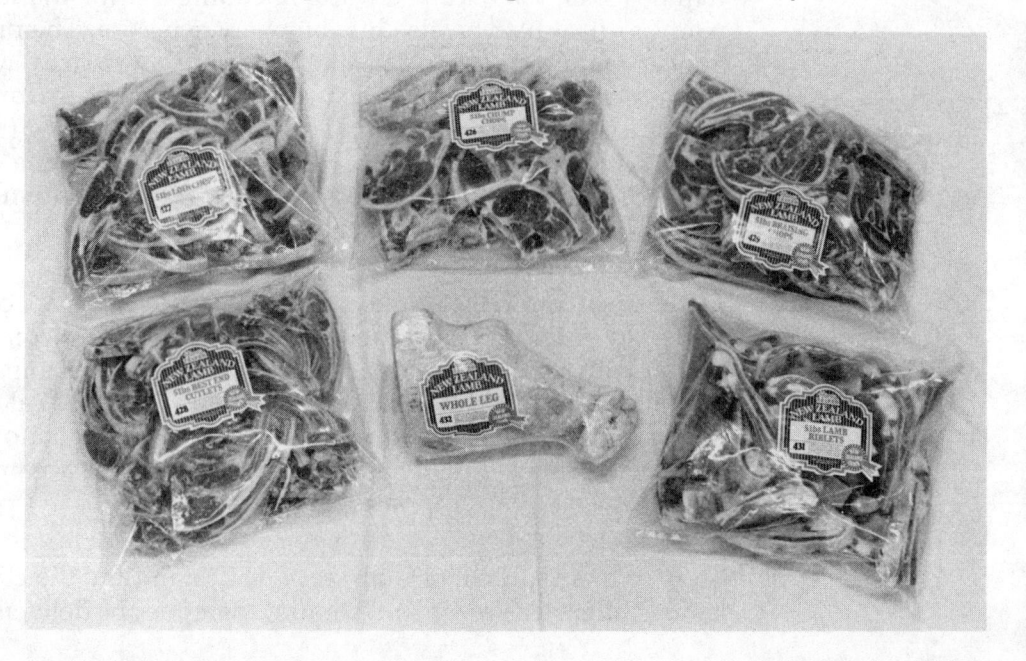

Purchasing food for pubs

ters are usually bought by loose weight but are available canned in brine. There is a choice of pâtés and pies include gala, pork, veal and ham, and game. When buying delicatessen and charcuterie products, select branded goods through reliable suppliers or from cash and carry depots lest the can should contain surplus unusable fat or inferior meat.

Butchers also supply hamburgers and sausages of their own manufacture and stewing meat, braising steaks and minced beef for cottage pies.

Poultry

Chickens   When comparing prices for poultry, ensure that you use the same specifications. Buy poultry eviscerated; thus you only pay for what you receive. Even then, check to see if their weight includes the giblets. If you have no use for giblets, why buy them?

Chickens are bought as whole birds and in portions. As with beef, buy poultry as you need it rather than cut your own portions. According to the type of trade, recommended whole bird sizes are the two-portion 450 to 510 g (16 to 18 oz) poussin or the 566 to 679 g (20 to 24 oz) broiler. Two-portioned birds make for good portion control and costing.

Chicken portions   Chicken portions consist of the suprême or breast and the leg/thigh piece each at an average weight of 225 to 340 g (8 to 12 oz). Most butchers will supply chicken portions. These are often cut into quarters from frozen birds with a band saw. If your butcher has a large trade in suprêmes (fillets), he may be prepared to offer you chicken legs at a competitive price. These will usually be fresh, as most suprêmes have to be cut from fresh birds. Chicken pieces can be purchased 'convenienced', i.e. prepared in a similar manner to scampi and fish for featuring in the basket with chips and garnished with salad (lettuce, sliced cucumber and quarters of tomato).

Storage and defrosting   Frozen chickens offer good value. However, a percentage of the frozen weight is water and fresh chicken is considered to have more taste. The fewer phosphates that have been added in the freezing process, the more expensive the product but the better the taste. If using frozen, ensure that birds are stored correctly and that before cooking are fully defrosted. This is best done overnight in the fridge. Failure to defrost before cooking can greatly increase the risk of food poisoning.

Owing to their small size, cooked chicken products tend to be of a poorer quality and no substitute for whole chicken, even in sandwiches.

Turkey and duck   Follow the same rules for other poultry items such as turkey or duck. An alternative to whole turkey is to purchase ready cooked turkey breast. These products are ideal for sandwiches and can be purchased frozen or chilled. If frozen, ensure correct storage until required then correct defrosting. If chilled, store in a suitable refrigerator.

Fish   Unless you specialize in fish, frozen fish will meet your demands and offers several advantages over fresh. The main three are ease of storage, availability of range and portioning. Fish freezes and handles well, so quality is ensured.

Policy and Operations

A general rule is to deal with a national multiple supplier either directly or through an appointed local agent. Their monthly price list gives information about availability, price, pack and portion size.

Range available Flatfish fillets, scampi and other shellfish are marketed, prepared for cooking and also ready coated and precooked for heating. Coated precooked fish and shellfish may or may not require defrosting prior to reheating. It is important to follow the instructions on the packet.

The most widely used fish products include:

Prawns North Atlantic individually quick frozen (IQF) are best and are usually used for prawn salads and cocktails. Any other cold water prawn can also be used. Free-flowing peeled prawns for sandwich fillings and seafood cocktails are sold averaged at so many to 450 g (1 lb). Warm water prawns, although cheaper, are often block frozen and are best used only for cooking.

Scampi Scampi are usually graded by size based on number to the pound. Normally IQF, they are available plain, in breadcrumbs or in batter. Free-flowing scampi are available in four graded sizes, the usual portion size averaging four to six 450 g (1 lb).

Crab A wide variety is now available in the UK, allowing you to serve crab all year round without any of the problems which fresh present. Crab claws make an alternative to plain dressed crab.

Potted shrimps Shrimps covered with lightly spiced butter. Often in short supply owing to overfishing of the shrimps.

Cod Readily available in its natural fillet or in preportioned battered or breaded portions.

Plaice fillets Plaice fillets are in several graded portion sizes: the usual fish and chips size is 165 to 176 g (5½ to 6 oz), and 227 g (8 oz) is normal for the à la carte portion.

Fish alternatives As alternatives to plaice, turbot fillets and roundfish fillets of haddock, cod and whiting are all size graded. These freeze so well that when defrosted in a brine solution they regain their sea freshness.

Whole fish with recommended size portions include 227 g (8 oz) rainbow trout and 340 to 397 g (12 to 14 oz) Dover sole.

Salmon and halibut portioned steaks at 170 to 227 g (6 to 8 oz) are also available.

Smoked fish Smoked fish include salmon, trout, mackerel fillets, eel, kippers and haddock. Poorly prepared smoked mackerel can cause food poisoning so buy brand names only.

Other lines include whitebait, rollmops, fishburgers and a range of ready-cooked fish entrées.

Potatoes Fried chipped potatoes are the mainstay of most pub catering operations. Thought is needed in purchasing the right quality in sufficient quantities. Straight-sided chipped potatoes ready for frying and in bulk bags are available in most areas; being economic they are commonly used. Alternatively, oil-blanched frozen chips in 4.5 kg (10 lb) cartons are marketed by frozen food

Purchasing food for pubs

suppliers. All these chipped potatoes may be deep fried to order. Some pubs prefer to make their own chips and they can be cut to any required size. Most large potatoes can be fried, although preference is given to 'whites'. The usual portion of chips is 113 to 170 g (4 to 6 oz).

For jacket baking, select large unblemished potatoes. For mash a complete potato mix may be used. The best quality is the potato granule which reconstitutes quickly when boiling water is added. Canned new potatoes are labour saving.

Fruits and vegetables For an up-market restaurant trade, customers prefer vegetables that are fresh, in season and locally grown. Fresh vegetables, fruit and salad materials are perishable and daily deliveries may be needed from a local greengrocer. Items used in large quantities and which need special attention are tomatoes, lemons and lettuce. For the latter, the iceberg variety is recommended. Should tomato supply be difficult, canned whole tomatoes are a standby. Melons and avocado pears require special care in buying to ensure ripeness and good condition for service.

Convenience vegetables frozen, canned or quick dried offer advantages in ease of handling and storage. Green peas, French beans and carrots are among those which freeze and can well. There is a good range of quick-dried vegetables which include fine peas, sliced green beans, diced carrots, mixed vegetables, the popular mushy peas and savoury rices. These are available in catering packs. Mushrooms for the grill trade are bought canned or fresh according to demand. Vegetables are frozen in free-flowing packs and the canned product is packed in brine or, as for baked beans, in sauce.

The seasonal availability of fruit and vegetables is now less restricted. Modern farming techniques and overseas produce flown in by air mean that most fruit and vegetables are available, at a price, all the year round. There is also an ample variety of canned fruit in syrup, and various fruit juices in catering packs.

Bakery and confectionery goods Bread and rolls are purchased from the local baker, usually on a contract basis. For sandwiches, large sliced and wrapped loaves are needed. Since bread freezes well, a supply of loaves may be kept in the deep freeze cabinet. Bread rolls, bap and finger types for hamburgers and hot dogs, and also French bread, are needed daily. Pubs featuring French bread or the crispy cottage loaf in their ploughman's lunch may obtain them in individual sizes as well as larger loaves for cutting into portions.

Pastry mixes, short and puff, sold in catering packs are also included here. Gâteaux, pastries and similar confections for the sweet trolley or the sweet course are available in attractive variety from a frozen food company, a big concern or a local supplier; the last ensures freshness and quality.

Dairy produce
Milk Fresh milk is packed in quantities from the half litre, litre or pint and quart to larger bulk quantities. Homogenized (red cap) is the caterer's milk. Disposable cartons are preferable to bottles, which have to be washed and returned.

Policy and Operations

Cream Three grades of fresh cream are generally used in catering, single (18 per cent), whipping (38 or 40 per cent) and double (48 per cent); the last is used for speciality coffees. Ultra heat treated (UHT) cream is available in unit jigger packs. Milk and cream supplies are usually negotiated with the dairy which supplies the locality, and payment for supplies may be on a weekly or monthly account; records should be kept.

Cheese Farmhouse and imported cheeses are available in the piece or in portioned packs. Most cheeses are packed in individual portions. For a pub trade, preference is usually given to British cheeses.

Eggs All eggs, except those going directly from producer to consumer, must be marketed according to weight. The former five imperial grades have yielded to seven metric ones. The usual catering egg size is 4, at 55 to 60 g (approximately 2 oz).

Groceries and dry goods Groceries are likely to be almost exclusively proprietary brands, for the brand name is an indication of quality. Again, catering packs can be purchased directly from manufacturers, wholesalers or the cash and carry. Apart from the more obvious lines used in quantities, many groceries are only needed in small amounts and these can be purchased from the local grocer.

Soup: canned and dry mix Soup is the original convenience food. Different soups can be created by mixing varieties. Some licensees may make their own soup but otherwise the decision is between dry mix or canned or frozen soup.

Soup mixes are packed for caterers under proprietary brand labels and end-result packs. The metric pack is 5 litres (8¾ pints). The average yield per end result is between 25 and 29 servings of reconstituted soup. Most manufacturers market a standard quality and a de luxe one. Varieties include asparagus, celery, chicken, chicken noodle, French onion, green pea, kidney, minestrone, mushroom, oxtail, scotch broth, spring vegetable, thick vegetable, tomato, vichysoisse and white onion. In addtion, most suppliers have one or more special lines of soup.

Canned soup, either condensed or in standard form, are usually selected for an up-market restaurant trade, and include soups such as consommé, vichysoisse, turtle and seafood bisques and game soups. A limited range of frozen de luxe soups offer a 'fresher' taste.

Sauces and gravy Sauce and gravy mixes are labour saving. Curry sauce, brown espagnole, tomato, béchamel, white and others are packed for catering purposes. Where quantities are concerned, frozen and dried mix products should be more economical than canned. Price, quality and convenience are the considerations when selecting soups and sauces.

Steak and kidney, fish, cottage and other pies can be bought ready for heating or assembled on the premises from convenience items and then cooked.

Batter mixes Batter for coating fish, scampi and other deep fries prior to frying (unless purchased ready coated) are available. Convenience batter mixes sell under proprietary brand labels in various qualities and types in catering packs and can be made up in a mixer with the addition of water.

Another popular alternative for chicken pieces is the shake and bake type; the chicken pieces are dredged in the mix and oven baked.

Coffee and tea   The type of coffee required will depend on how the beverage is made. There are instant and ground coffees of various roasts and blends, packed in single and multiportion and end-product sachets. Instant coffee in powder form and in granules is convenient, though for a good class trade a freshly ground blend is advisable. However, the tea bag is now universally adopted in catering. People are critical about coffee and tea; so purchase quality and ensure that beverages are freshly and correctly made.

Other groceries, dry goods and sundries   Sugar is packed in wrapped cubes and in sachets of quick dissolving sugar. Sweet and cheese biscuits are also best handled in unit packets. Condiments, sauces, relishes and preserves previously mentioned in unit packs are available in larger catering packs. Butter and soft margarine are also marketed in both unit and bulk packs.

Sweet and dessert mixes packed for catering include custard, crème caramel, mousses and jelly crystals in a variety of flavours, sweet toppings and lemon pie filling with meringue.

Other 'dry goods' used in catering are breakfast cereals, cereal grains and pasta. Bulk packs are available but breakfast cereals in individuals are favoured.

Sundries for bar counter sales such as potato crisps, savoury snacks and nuts and raisins are bought wholesale or direct from manufacturers who may deliver.

Frying oils   As fried foods are so prominent, the selection of frying media merits attention. Various types and qualities of oils for deep frying are available in 5, 10 and 20 litre drums. Oil temperature performances vary considerably. The three important temperatures are the ones for the actual frying, the smoke and the flash points. Foods rarely need a temperature over 194°C (380°F), the average frying temperature being 184°C (360°F). In theory oil should be selected which has a high flash and smoke point. The following table gives some idea of these temperatures:

	Flash point		Smoke point	
	°C	°F	°C	°F
Vegetable oil blend	324	615	221	425
Groundnut oil	324	615	243	470
Maize oil	324	615	221	425
Olive oil	285	545	169	335

When a special type or brand of oil is used the supplier will provide information regarding the flash and smoke points and the frying temperatures.

Where frying predominates in an operation, consider a long-life frying medium. Correct use can more than double the life no matter what oil is chosen. Ask for a manufacturer's instruction pack on how to look after your oil.

Policy and Operations

Convenience foods

Buying convenience

The term convenience foods covers all processed food but is strongly associated with frozen food (see Figures 25 and 26). They are expensive but pub catering relies on them heavily. In purchasing convenience foods you buy not only food but also a proportion of the processor's labour costs, overheads and possibly storage and transport, as well as a contribution to the supplier's margin of profit. This is true of canned, dried and any ready prepared fresh and frozen cooked foods.

The variety of bulk and individual portion made-up dishes is considerable. Dried foods include soups and other mixes. Fruit, vegetables and pie fillings are usually canned, as are many soups.

Fresh convenience foods may appear to be a contradiction in terms but they include peeled potatoes, chips ready for deep frying, washed and prepared vegetables for the pot and unfrozen oven-ready poultry and butchered meats.

Figure 25 (below)
Easy-to-serve, portion cost salmon steaks. The packs eliminate wastage and enable precise portion costing
Courtesy Olaf Foods Ltd

Figure 26 (right, above right) *A new à la carte range by Henry Telfer developed exclusively for the pub trade*
Courtesy Henry Telfer

Purchasing food for pubs

Costing Being either wholly or partially prepared, convenience foods are almost 100 per cent usable; there is no initial waste, less storage space is needed and laborious kitchen preparation is eliminated. Prepared foods, as initial preparation waste has been removed, are more readily portioned and costed than bulk unprepared food.

The comparative costs between the gross weight of unprepared fresh commodities and the net prepared weight of convenience products should be understood. Take account of the wastage in the preparation of unprepared items together with the labour and general handling. Convenience foods are produced by factory methods. Volume of throughput and bulk buying raw materials proportionally reduce manufacturer's costs compared with a caterer purchasing unprepared commodities and carrying out his own preparation.

To facilitate accurate costings, the net weight or yield from convenience food is printed on the container by the manufacturer together with handling instructions, which should be closely followed to get the best results. Convenience food does not eliminate staff and must be used with care.

Though only sound commodities are selected for processing, quality is commensurate with price. The user selects the items best suited to his particular need, and the products should be quality sampled before buying.

Many manufacturers supply the catering industry with a wide range of lines. The large firms' advisory service is available and caterers should keep in touch with what is on offer from manufacturers' price lists, the trade press and exhibitions such as the biannual Hotelympia.

A pub caterer must bear in mind ready food costs, volume and type of business, kitchen space, skills and standards of the establishment before deciding what he can achieve on the premises and what to buy in.

Usage What are the disadvantages of these foods? Customer acceptance can be critical. Ready foods are as well known on the retail market as they are on the wholesale one. It may not do to feature lines identical to those of your competitors any more than to offer people what they can use at home. Use imagination. Preparing instructions should be followed closely, but the food can be individualized for service by personal finishing touches such as adding chopped parsley or passing croûtons with soup.

In restaurants, convenience foods are looked upon as commodities prepared in advance. Even where fresh foods predominate they are supported by such ready lines as sauces, vegetables, potato, pastry and other mixes. Where these score is with desserts: gâteaux, flans, cheesecakes, tortes etc.

Many individual products of fish, meat, poultry and potatoes have already been mentioned. There is also a variety of boil-in-the-bag entrées, individual or multiportioned lines, easy to store, simple to handle and widely used in hotels and restaurants.

Choosing processed goods Frozen, canned and other packaged commodities are generally available in three sizes: retail, individual and catering packs. Retail packs are seldom of use to caterers who usually select individual and bulk catering packs at trade

Policy and Operations

prices. Individual portion packs of certain canned and frozen de luxe and exotic foods are useful for restaurants featuring an à la carte service with an ample selection. Individual packs of popular lines are used by fast food units and in pub catering. The wide range packed in individual units includes sauces, salad cream, mayonnaise, sweet pickle, salt, pepper, vinegar, mustards and a range of preserves. They aid portion control and accurate costing.

Frozen convenience foods such as entrées are packed in individual and recommended numbers of portions. Other lines are packed in bulk or end-product packs. Where the number of portions is suggested, they probably need testing since manufacturers may have a different idea of portion size from caterers.

Labelling and warranty Labelling food is the subject of much legislation. Labels must truly state pack contents and, with made-up foods and dishes, provide a detailed statement of ingredients. Further legislation may require additional information such as gross and net contents with foods in sauce, brine or syrup and also warranty dates. Most packs provide instructions as to handling the contents. This is of interest and assistance to purchasers who should read labels properly.

Canned goods have a warranty and should be used before the expiry date. Inspect them for dents and rust. Always reject blown cans. Dried goods should be packed in airtight and moisture-proof containers.

Ice cream A delivery service is usually required from a local manufacturer or from one of the big firms that provide a service for caterers; but for the comparatively small business a local supplier may provide the best service. There are three kinds of ice cream: bulk in 2.25 litres and 4.5 litres (0.5 and 1 gallon) packs; packeted iced cream; and iced confections such as bombes, puddings, parfaits, sorbets, cassatas and gâteaux, some available in single portions.

Metrication and the buyer

Conversion from imperial to metric weights and measures continues. All packaged goods are now available in metric packs and, until full metrication becomes accepted, packets will carry both measures. Complications may arise during this transition stage, not just in weight and volume but also in prices. Straight conversion is impossible. Loose ends and odd quantities must be rounded off.

A practical view should be taken. Textbooks are in advance of the actual situation, for the general public has not yet fully accepted metrication. For this reason, where weights are given on menus, the 8 oz steak may still be listed as such and not as 250 g. (Note that the weight has been rounded up; this is good marketing, implying that the customer gets more, not less, with metrication.) The main advantage of metrication is simplicity in calculations. The British Standards Institution has produced a slide rule, Readimetric Conversion, a useful aid for those unfamiliar with the subject.

Keeping in touch

As catering becomes more specialized, more outside factors affect supplies. Those which can disturb a business in unstable times include industrial troubles, fuel crises or even abnormal weather conditions. For supplies vital to a catering operation, it is not advisable to live from hand to mouth. A well-stocked store cupboard and freezer guards against unforeseen circumstances.

Keep in touch with new products and developments in convenience foods such as vacuum-packed cooked dishes and canned multiportioned entrées. They have the advantage of keeping quality and are not dependent on deep freeze equipment. In selecting supplies, especially frozen, canned and dried products, customer acceptance must not be overlooked. Test quality by sampling for any permanent menu feature.

Most reputable suppliers give thought to the allocation of their products so that restaurants in a particular locality do not all offer the same dishes.

Frozen foods must be stored at 0°F or −18°C, and at these temperatures they will usually keep for up to three months. There should be adequate storage space; manufacturers often comment that caterers do not have sufficiently large deep freeze storage facilities.

The rule with all convenience products and especially with frozen entrées is that they must be better in flavour and appearance than you could make yourself at the same price. Comparative costings between items made on the premises and convenience products are usually at break-even point. For the licensee and the small restaurateur the scales are tipped in favour of the bought-in item on the score of convenience and because they offer the opportunity to widen the menu scope.

Standards and profits

Food supplies come from many trades, and each is specialized. Food purchasing is a big subject and a management responsibility. Once menus are devised, standards set and sources of supply selected, publicans should not trust to memory alone but should get information down on paper. A looseleaf book for reference as a purchasing file or manual should be maintained and kept up to date with information from the trade press and from suppliers' price lists. Reliefs and others concerned will thus be informed of procedures, how and where to buy and in what quality and quantity. Standards of quality differ according to the type of business, whether bar food or restaurant. Aim to set and maintain a good even standard of supplies and one which will turn in an acceptable profit.

Maintain a balance between food expenditure and revenue. The difference between what you buy and sell represents the profit margin. When food costs rise consider ways to offset this other than by lowering standards, reducing portions or immediately increasing charges. The publican should know his market and how to judge whether or not or by how much to raise prices. Costs can be held down by using standard recipes, in portioning and in dish presentation.

Planning and controlling are keys to efficient buying, which is indicative of a well-managed and profitable pub.

Policy and Operations

Acknowledgement

The editor is grateful for the assistance of Eric Ellmes (who is responsible for purchasing for Imperial Inns and Taverns) in preparing this chapter.

Further reading

Davies, B., *Food Commodities*, Heinemann, 1978.
Fuller, John, *Professional Kitchen Management*, Batsford, 1983.

10 Receiving, storing and issuing food

James Steel

Although caterers all operate in the same general way, there are different sizes and types of operation involved in producing food for the public. The scale of catering within a licensed house will therefore dictate the extent to which a formal stewardship system is called for. In many cases the licensee will carry out all the duties. However, irrespective of the degree to which a system is deployed, the concept of custodianship is important in catering management because of the volume and value of food used in the business, and the principles discussed in this chapter will hold good for all operations.

Food is the principal working asset of a catering operation and will be purchased, stored and utilized in considerable quantity. Neglect and carelessness would quickly result in losses which, in the light of the trade's narrow net profit margins, become significant.

This chapter aims to inform the reader about theoretical aspects of food stock control so that decisions as to how best to control will be more easily reached.

Supervising

Formalized control systems use administrative labour and thus form a non-productive wage expense. As there is no flow of revenue from such labour, it is difficult to judge its value to the organization. Only if the alternative were to be evaluated – the cost of any loss incurred because the system did not function – could a judgement be made as to whether or not it is worthwhile to incur the expense of the system. Where a system operates successfully, the losses do not happen and thus the alternative is never evaluated.

Fear of this unknown quantity makes management become involved in instigating and carrying out receiving, storing and issuing procedures. In small establishments this might be done directly by management, but in larger operations labour could become involved to varying degrees. Nevertheless, even in the absence of formal records and procedures, the need to supervise the functions of stewardship is self-evident.

Receiving delivery of food

The objective in managing the receipt of food supplies is to verify that the goods delivered are precisely those that were ordered. It is thus essential to

Policy and Operations

Figure 27 *Details by which to check delivery*

> **Details by which to check delivery**
>
> From the order duplicate
>
> 1 *Quantity* Numerical measurement of the units, weight or volume of goods requested.
>
> 2 *Unit* The trade pack of the goods in terms of outer container pack, single container, unit of weight or unit of volume.
>
> 3 *Description* Qualification of the nature and quality of the goods, such as a trade brand name.
>
> 4 *Price* The unit cost value at which it was desired to purchase the commodity.

have a detailed note of the order, usually available in the form of a copy of the purchase specification sent by the orderer to the supplier. This should conform with the sample shown in Figure 27.

The purchasing considerations to be applied are discussed in Chapter 9. Applying them in clear and unambiguous terms is important in the receipt of goods. Without such a means to check in the supplies delivered, a receiver would simply have either to accept the delivery on trust or to summon the orderer to come and inspect the goods for accuracy. In practice, neither of these courses of action make sense. However, it can happen that orders for meat, fish and vegetables are placed by telephone and not noted, as they ought to be, on order confirmations. In the absence of a duplicate order confirmation the situation described would arise.

Follow-up Another advantage in having a duplicate copy of an order with which to check the delivery is that any delay in receiving the supplies can be monitored. Suppliers require varying periods of notice to make up and deliver an order. This is referred to as a firm's 'lead time' and may vary from firm to firm from between a few hours to a fortnight or longer. Delays arising for this and other reasons can obviously occur, and so it is an important function of the receiver of goods to watch for undue delay in the delivery of supplies and follow them up in good time. Dated order copies provide just such a facility.

An internal control which should be applied at this time is for the receiver to check that all duplicate order copies bear the initials of the member of the management delegated to authorize the placing of orders. It is a recognized aspect of management that orders are not transmitted to suppliers without having been inspected, and duly initialled, by the manager as a control against irrational and excessive ordering.

Checking in This is straightforward as the actual goods are checked against the order copy with close attention being paid to the details of weight and quality. Where the data match, the delivery note, which usually accompanies the goods, may be

Receiving, storing and issuing food

verified and endorsed as correct. As in many cases the duplicate of the delivery note is retained by the deliverer; the endorsing signature is taken as acceptance of title to the goods. The consideration – the value – then becomes due to the supplier. Naturally, a signature should not be given for faulty or incorrect goods without an appropriate qualification accompanying it on the delivery note.

Returns note The sort of errors which can occur include delivery of the wrong items or of damaged or spoiled goods (in the case of food, items may not be fresh). When goods are not acceptable they should be rejected with an appropriate returns note made out in duplicate, giving details of the reason for the return of the goods and acknowledged by the signature of the delivery man; one copy is taken away by him with the goods.

A brief record could be made in a returns daybook or diary and the copy note passed to the bookkeeper to await due credit in the supplier's statement of account. Sometimes, in resolving dissatisfaction, telephone agreements are made whereby allowances may be granted without the necessity of actually returning the goods in dispute, and a confirmation note should be made out to cover this situation.

From this it can be seen that a receiver should not only be sharp witted but also have a good working knowledge of the commodities used by way of trade in order to scrutinize the deliveries effectively. (He should be capable of telling the difference between haddock and whiting, for example.) However, although it might be excusable for him to err in the detection of quality, it would not be acceptable for him to omit weighing bulk goods, counting quantities, and checking ostensible quality by means of brand names and label descriptions.

A return of a different nature is that of the chargeable container. Although disposable packs are in extensive use, the odd incidence of returnables might have to be dealt with. It is usual to treat such containers as goods, checking them in and out via the returns note procedure. Suppliers who make a habit of using chargeable containers often provide for their redemption in a special section of the delivery note (and subsequent invoice), and the procedure is thus simplified. Care should be taken to avoid charging container values as food costs. If in stock, they are assets; if lost, they are an expense of the business and not a food cost.

Documentary evidence Obviously, documentary evidence (delivery notes etc.) is a vital part of the accounting process, and care should be taken of these documents during processing and for several years afterwards. Sometimes order copies attached to delivery notes are kept, but alternatively the order copies may be destroyed by this time because the delivery note itself will carry an appropriate reference to it, thus dispensing with the need to retain a copy.

In the majority of instances the original person making up the order never becomes involved with the receiving process except in the investigation of apparent error. This is in accord with control theory, which aims to separate the functions of purchasing and storing in order to avoid fraud.

Policy and Operations

Recording goods received

This is a customary action at this stage in the receiving procedure. Although the delivery note forms a lasting record of the transaction for accounting purposes, many firms require the receiver of the goods to maintain an accurate diary of the details of all deliveries. This usually takes the form of a simple daybook in which the supplier, order reference and details of the units received are listed. It is also customary to record the unit value charged for the goods. The latter serves two purposes: (a) to provide an up-to-date reference to the prices of commodities, and (b) to give, by extension and summation, the total cost value of the goods delivered which, in turn, may be used to verify the subsequent invoice when it arrives. Figure 28 shows a typical form of this record.

As will be seen later, the total value figures for deliveries of perishable food received directly into the kitchen area (as distinct from dry stores, or other types of purchase) greatly facilitate the calculation of food consumption for a period of operation. The record thus forms a valuable aid to other control procedures besides that of receiving goods.

This is all worth while, because the labour involved in accurately maintaining the record could well be deemed unproductive if the information were not put to good use. Its real value is not, therefore, in providing a back reference for documentation, but in being a source of practical knowledge of use in indicating current prices and in operating further controls.

Malpractices These include simple theft, substitution and fictitious transactions. Goods may be checked in correctly, but when empty containers are being removed, or simply when delivery men are leaving the premises, goods may be stolen.

Secondly, where deliveries of fresh commodities are being made, a proportion of the items may be less fresh, included in the hope that they will not be noticed.

Thirdly, where collusion exists between the receiver of goods and the delivery men, fictitious supplies of certain commodities may be booked in to a department in the expectation that a short delivery will not be noticed, thus enabling the participants to split the proceeds from the subsequent sale of the items. The sum involved could be small compared with the food production cost for the appropriate period and the loss might not be noticed.

The management of smaller operations may consider it convenient to buy goods on a regular basis from roundsmen, thereby buying just the right

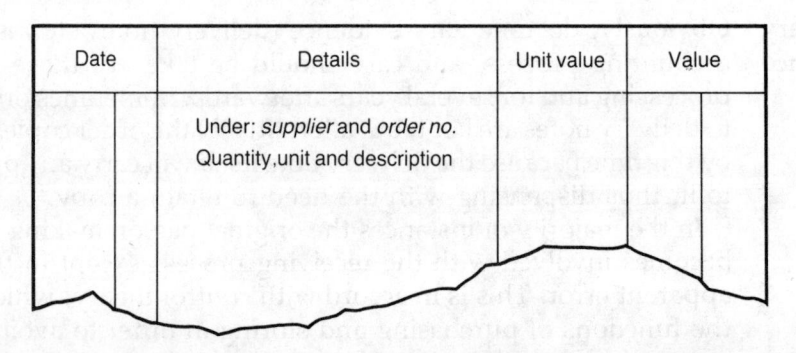

Figure 28 *Goods received book*

Date	Details	Unit value	Value
	Under: *supplier* and *order no.* Quantity, unit and description		

amount of fresh supplies to last for a short period. In such cases it is strongly advised that the purchase should be on a credit basis for settlement by monthly cheque rather than by paying cash on the evidence of sales slips processed by subordinates. Such a situation obviously opens the door to collusion and fraud and so should be avoided. Where deliveries take place at times when the operation is lightly manned and staff are under pressure, management should be particularly vigilant in having the documents and supplies checked.

Procedure The outcome of the checking-in process is that the vouched delivery note is held in the bookkeeping system pending the due arrival of the corresponding invoice from the supplier. Some firms combine the function of the invoice with the details of the delivery note, thus making it serve both functions. The more traditional approach is to forward the invoice separately.

In either instance the total arising from the extension and summation of the data is verified following a matching of the details with that of the actual deliveries. The total is then entered in the accounts of the business, usually by means of a purchases daybook, whereby the account of the supplier is credited with the sum now liable to be paid and the account representing the appropriate food purchase is charged. The latter would normally be a food purchases account, but could be a food stores account were it decided by management to control the latter separately from food trading. For returns, the process is the other way about.

Once these postings have taken place the receiving procedure is complete: the accounts show the financial position; documentary evidence is to hand; a permanent record of the details is available; and every item forming the delivery had been checked and vouched.

Where the supplies are perishable they are usually taken straight into production, either immediately on to the work table or placed in refrigerators, pantries or lockers. Where they are more durable and not immediately in need of protection they are placed in the stores.

Storing food

Two criteria govern the management of stored food: it should be in the best possible condition, and the stores should be scrupulously clean. The guiding principle for good management is stock rotation, that is to say, the older items should be the first to be used and the most recent supplies should therefore be placed to the rear so that the older stock is to hand when issues are called for. By this means, shelf life is minimized.

Vermin protection Although stored items may be well protected by the packaging, dust, dirt and spilled food can encourage vermin. These will seek to forage for food, penetrate packages and, apart from unspeakable direct effects, aggravate the situation! On the basis that prevention is better than cure, the use of a suitable bait containing poison should safeguard against, and give early warning of,

Policy and Operations

infestation by rodents. In the event of an infestation, private pest control firms or the local authority will assist in dealing with it.

Contaminated foodstuffs lead to illness and should be avoided at all costs. Smaller pests may be less gruesome than rats and mice but can, by sheer persistence, be a serious risk to health and should be rigorously exterminated.

Deterioration Quite apart from direct contamination, foodstuffs decay at varying rates. Loss of freshness is to be regretted and so, where food is still edible, natural deterioration should be avoided. Canned food may be expected to have a shelf life of a couple of years, but stock rotation should have drawn stocks of food into consumption long before that time had elapsed. To aid this objective the outer packaging of items should be broached and the individual cans etc. shelved or binned. Outward evidence of ageing, such as faded labels and rust marks, should stimulate close inspection and, given acceptability, early use.

Perishable goods in stores should be inspected daily as their unpreserved state will lead to rapid deterioration. If foodstuffs are not used in the freshest possible condition the policy of buying fresh goods will be a futile exercise, as the discernible qualities of wholesome freshness will be lacking on presentation. Furthermore, the opportunity cost of a lower material cost in such food when compared with ready-prepared commodities would be lost because of the high wastage resulting from neglect.

Bacteria Perhaps of greater importance is the danger of food spoilage arising from the action of bacteria on the food. Once a natural food has been taken from its live state, the life forces can no longer systematically maintain the material in its healthy state. Chemical and physical changes occur in the material and bacteria from the environment are able to reproduce and extend their influence on the material uninhibited by any natural defence processes. Strange and repugnant odours will manifest themselves and visually unattractive changes take place in the food.

Refrigeration Refrigeration is the holding of food at a temperature within the range of 0 to 4 °C, thereby sufficiently inhibiting bacterial action to preserve the food in an acceptable state for a day or two longer than might be the case in the normal environment. For foodstuffs in the 'work in progress' category there is no better place for them to be stored than in a refrigerated atmosphere, including storage on display at the point of sale in the usual glass compartments. Although the latter type may not achieve a temperature as low as the range indicated, nevertheless their low working temperature is preferable to that of an operating environment of say 17 °C.

The hygienic condition of such storage compartments is of great importance. Bacteria can be active at low temperatures. Frequent attacks on their presence should be made through defrosting and cleaning cabinets on a weekly or, at the longest, fortnightly basis. Refrigerated display cabinets should be cleaned at least once a day between service periods. Additionally, the defrosting of cabinets not equipped with modern self-defrosting mechanisms is a necessary aid to the proper functioning of the machine.

Receiving, storing and issuing food

Freezing Where the freezing technique has been applied to food for storage over a period, then much lower holding temperatures are called for. At leat −20 °C should be reached. Even at that level the temperature cannot be relied upon to destroy bacteria. It is important, therefore, not to permit the temperature to fluctuate in case some of the hardier types of bacteria increase their numbers. For the same reason, food taken out of a deep freeze and not used should not be returned to the cabinet. Different commodities have different freezer lives, but a general rule could be to limit the period of storage to one year and certainly not more than a year and a half.

There are three basic forms of cold holding cabinet. For large establishments the walk-in refrigerator or deep freeze is popular because of the handling facility this offers. In the case of smaller houses, the choice will be between upright and chest cabinets. The former is preferable in that it gives better access and avoids the need to lift out the topmost layers in order to reach the stock at the bottom of the chest. An upright cabinet can provide some fifteen cubic feet of storage space and, for the smallest houses, this can be divided into deep freeze and refrigerated sections.

Where fresh fish forms part of the refrigerated stock, it is preferable to have a separate fish compartment in order to avoid cross-contamination of odour. As bacteria notably multiply on the skin of fish, deliveries should be washed in cold water to minimize this effect.

Planning and layout of stores

The planning and layout of stores makes an important contribution to the good management of the establishment. There will be cases where a licensed house is so small and such full use has to be made of existing space that conformity with an idealized layout would be out of the question. However, even with such restricted circumstances, a systematic use of space would offer advantages and thus general principles should apply. These arise from basic elements in the flow of materials through the organization:

Receiving and checking in supplies
Unpacking and storage of these supplies with an attendant discharge of packaging waste
Issuing of commodities for inclusion in food production.

Ideally all of these functions should be on one floor and as close as possible to a rear roadway and the rubbish area. They should be in close relationship to each other and with reasonable one-level access to the kitchen.

Delivery area A recognized delivery bay, even if little more than a specific area in a corridor, should be set apart for the receipt and inspection of supplies. A small table would provide a helpful means of sorting out and facilitating the procedure. If space does not permit this then the doorway area of the storeroom will suffice. It is particularly advantageous to have the management offices located at this point in order to have ready supervision over the process as well as providing for rear door security and staff observation.

Policy and Operations

Storerooms These will vary in size and shape from cupboards to quite large areas. The anxiety of running out of stock coupled with the need to carry a surprisingly large range of items engenders an almost obsessive desire for large storerooms. Just what size the area should be depends on such factors as the availability of supplies, the range of food on the menu, the variability of the menu and so on. However, a tough-minded management often deliberately minimizes the storage provision so that investment in stock is sufficient only for immediate needs.

In the case of smaller houses, a rule of thumb would be to provide for some 5.66 cubic metres (200 cubic feet) of space in a basic 1.83 m × 1.83 m (6 ft × 6 ft) store. Where a level of operation of over 100 meals per day exists, one third of a cubic foot per additional meal would provide enough extra space. These are only average guidelines for a dry stores provision, and naturally individual circumstances affect the basis upon which a storage area is allocated.

Rubbish disposal Movement of materials is minimized if the store is near the receipt and issue points. The first thing to do in good storage practice is to unpack the items from their outer cases. Cardboard rubbish should immediately be got rid of in bunkers or skips so designed or positioned that the wind and rain do not scatter the contents about or make its subsequent removal unnecessarily difficult. Where paper rubbish is not salvaged, incineration could be contemplated as an effective way of disposing of it as long as this does not create a public nuisance.

Shelves The shelving in a store should be sufficiently compact to make full use of the space and should also be designed so as to permit smaller people to gain access to all the stored items. With main shelving at a level of about 0.9 m (3 ft), the space underneath could provide an area for the storage of larger items such as sacks and the A10 size of can. The main shelf will be the deepest at some 0.5 m (20 in) and the shelving above that level normally narrows in to some 0.3 m (14 in). No shelf should be higher than 1.7 m (5 ft 6 in). Wire shelving will trap the least dust.

The main criterion for a store is dryness and so care should be taken to avoid condensation arising through uncontrolled humidity and temperature. Heating of space is not normally a problem in storerooms, but care should be taken to avoid having central service pipes passing through the room as heat loss may adversely affect butter and cheese if they are kept in the dry store. Some storerooms might contain a small refrigerator to hold such items, the heat from the refrigerator engine not adversely affecting the storeroom temperature.

Where a storeroom is sufficiently large it can be a good idea to use available space for the overnight parking of a trolley bearing items such as sugar, condiments etc. in daily use in the kitchen During the day the trolley provides handy access to such commodities and, by being locked away each night, dispenses with the need for kitchen cupboards or shelves with their attendant security problems, particularly in relation to unsupervised early morning cleaning staff.

Receiving, storing and issuing food

Vegetables and fruit These cause storage problems because of their tendency to deteriorate. A well-ventilated cool room may be used to house these items, with shelving which is both shallower and deeper than normal. By such means the vegetables and fruit may be conveniently set out in single layers, thus avoiding the bruising and cross-contamination which so often arises when items are piled on top of one another. Preferably located on an outside wall, ventilators then provide for good air circulation and mosquito netting set over these will stop the intrusion of flies.

As licensed houses are likely to have salad material associated with the food items, much care may be needed to ensure that the vegetables are in the freshest condition for service. Regular daily inspection should ensure early detection of rotting stock. Where unpeeled potatoes are used the sacks should be stored on raised slats or duckboards to allow circulation of air; ready-peeled potatoes need not be stored in such a way since air circulation is not so important. Smaller houses without the benefits of vegetable storage areas may use refrigerator capacity for this purpose, although such space may well be at a premium.

Stock levels

As the cycle of receipt, storage and issue of supplies continues over time, the quantity of any item in stock varies. Management should aim to control the cycle in such a way that the average stock is sufficient to meet likely requirements; stock should never be allowed to run out, but an excessively large quantity on hand at any time is equally undesirable. To calculate the average, minimum and maximum levels of stock for any item, the factors to be considered are

Average rate of consumption of the items
Frequency of delivery from suppliers
Amount of time required by a supplier for notification of a delivery prior to the delivery date.

For example, let us suppose that a caterer uses six units of an item per day on average. The unit is an A1 size can; thus there are forty-eight cans to a trade pack of one 'outer'. The supplier delivers on a fortnightly basis and requires five days' notice to ensure inclusion in a delivery cycle. If a three-day stock is estimated to be adequate as a buffer in case a delivery is not on time, the stock levels would be computed thus:

Minimum stock
Buffer holding (6 cans × 3 days)   18 units
Maximum stock
Between-drop consumption (6 cans × 14 days)   84
Rounded up to two trade packs (48 × 2)   96
Add buffer stock   18   114 units
Reorder level
Five days' notice of consumption (6 × 5)   30
Add the buffer stock   18   48 units

141

This may be used as a method when evaluating sensible stock levels. In the overall sense of a total value of stock held, there are common yardsticks. One measure is that of the average value of stock in the stores as a factor of the average daily consumption, i.e. x days' consumption. Once x has been established, the stock value may be consistently verified as being in accord with it. To calculate the value, the cost of sales of food for a year (estimated or actual) is divided by the number of operating days in the year. This will give an average day's cost of food consumed.

In the trade, from about ten days' to one month's consumption of stored items is held to be an average stock. Therefore thirty times the average daily consumption will yield a maximum objective stores stock value. For example, if the cost of food sold in a year were £30,000 and there were 300 full operating days of food sales in the year, then

$$\frac{£30{,}000}{300} = £100 \text{ per day} \times 30 \text{ days} = £3000 \text{ maximum stock holding}$$

Of course, the measure was for an overall stock. Perishable food stocks in the kitchen could have specific yardsticks applied to them; stocks of say two days for fish, three days for vegetables, seven days for meat. It would thus be that an overall stock of dry and perishable food stocks comprises a value resulting from applying different average day's consumption factors to specific classes of stock.

Such measures may be used to assess the efficiency of stockholding. Clearly, when stock is 'turned', i.e. sold out, gross profit attaches to the exchange and comes in with revenue from the sale. As the objective of business is to make gross and the resulting net profit, the stock has to be turned, and the more frequently the better. A value of thirty days' consumption held in stock on average is equal to turning the stock ten times in a 300 day operating year. Slower turnovers than that could be deemed inefficient in terms of stockholding. Faster turnovers, up to twenty-five times in a year, could be deemed efficient.

Stock security

Stock security in most licensed houses would probably be centred on management supervision of the assets in the stores. This involves having the storeroom securely protected by lock and key with management being available to supervise the receipt and checking in of deliveries and, in turn, supervising the issue of items from stock to each department.

Should the work be carried out by employees, management might operate some sort of paper system for reference. The theoretical system in such a case is based on a series of bin cards upon which transactions for every single item are noted. Although the name suggests that the cards should be located on the bins or shelves and be maintained by the employee who looks after the stock, it is better to have them maintained by a separate bookkeeping assistant from evidence submitted by the various departments. The system thus becomes that of a stock ledger comprising stock record cards.

The significance of having the set of record cards for the items in store maintained separately from the stores themselves lies in the obvious point

Receiving, storing and issuing food

that it is not the commodities themselves that need control, but the work of the person in charge of them. If malpractice on the part of that person results in loss through goods being unaccounted for, then the system should show this up. Naturally, if the stores person is allowed to maintain the records of stock, then such losses from malpractice can be covered up by means of fraudulent entries which may never be detected. Therefore, the theory suggests that an assistant to the management should maintain the stock record cards from data which has not been altered by false entries and adjustments. Provided that this is the case and that no collusion exists between the recordkeeper and others associated with the system, then the management should be satisfied that the agreement of actual balances of stock on the shelves with those on the cards means that the stock movements have been accounted for.

Stock card An example of a common form of record card is shown in Figure 29. For any movement a reference notation, such as the supplier from whom the incoming stock was received or the receiver to whom the outgoing stock was issued, will pinpoint the movement to delivery data or requisition data. The progressive movements in and out of stock will lead to a continuous note of the balance of stock of any item. Thus the originating data may be audited by inspection in the case of query. The shelf balances may be subjected to a continuous form of audit whereby, every so often, a few item balances may be verified.

The sources of posting would be: for in entries the delivery notes concerning the items with the receiver's signature endorsed on them; for out entries a copy of the stores requisition with the storekeeper's and drawer's signatures. The latter should pass directly to the recordkeeper from the drawer of the goods in order to avoid fraudulent adjustments to the data made by the storekeeper. Further information which may usefully be included on a stock card for control purposes would be the maximum, reorder and minimum stock levels. Where, as is now common, there are frequent cost price changes for the unit of stock, the provision of a suitable space on the card can facilitate the balances for old and new stock to be shown on the card over the time, and number of entries, it takes to exhaust the old price stock.

Figure 29 *Stock card*

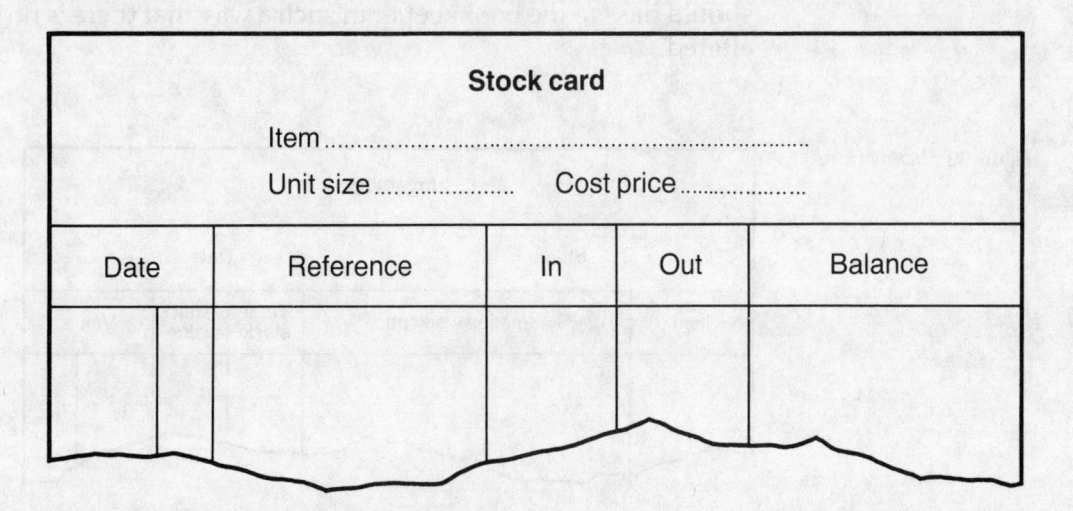

Stock card				
Item				
Unit size .... Cost price				
Date	Reference	In	Out	Balance

143

Policy and Operations

Stocktaking

Mention has been made of a continuous form of stocktaking whereby a few stock balances are confirmed as correct over a series of almost daily stock checks. This is the simplest and easiest form of stocktaking. Other methods set out to achieve different objectives.

It may be necessary to take an inventory (a statement of assets) valued at cost price on a weekly, fortnightly or quarterly basis in order to adjust purchase figures to a value for consumption of food in the appropriate period for management trading account information. Alternatively a similarly valued inventory may be required in order to verify a balance on a food stores account for management control purposes.

A similar inventory value is required in order to value the stores stock in hand for balance sheet purposes at the end of the financial year.

Thus the aim of a stocktake may be various; none of the aims should be confused with the others, although several or all of the outcomes may result from the taking of a single inventory.

A common form of the inventory used at such times is shown in Figure 30. It may be preprinted to include the most common stock items but, as these will perhaps not always be located in one specific place in the stores, it is often found more convenient simply to enter the items by hand as they present themselves on the shelves. For stocktaking purposes it is best to commence on one spot and work progressively round the room rather than dart about noting items. Care should be taken to differentiate between items of stock at different cost prices.

The stores account hinted at in relation to stocktaking can serve as a useful substitute for a stock record card system if the time and labour cost of maintaining the latter is unacceptable. Based simply on the notion that if a food stores account was charged with the values of all invoices for deliveries received into stores and if it was credited with the values of all requisitions drawn from stores, then the balance on the account should, at any time, represent the actual value of stock left in the store. An inventory would confirm this to an acceptably accurate degree. Therefore the management could rely on a regular verification of a stores account balance to act as a reassurance that the department is operating as it should. Again, the data should pass to the bookkeeper in such a way that there is no chance of it being altered.

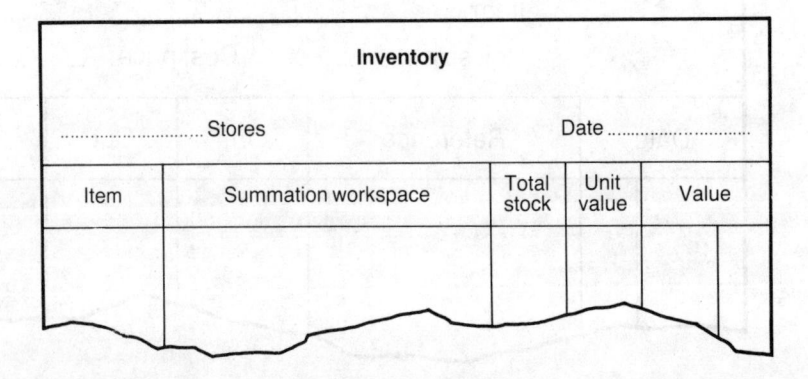

Figure 30 *Inventory*

Receiving, storing and issuing food

Pilferage   This is the evil against which stock control systems are directed. Theft from stores and other areas should, if possible, be controlled at its roots by means of a close visual supervision of operators and by back door security checks when workers go off duty. Although the latter control might actually be carried out only infrequently, the threat of its implementation should be an effective prevention of theft. Needless to say workers should be notified of such precautionary measures when they are recruited.

Control of pilferage lies in taking precautionary measures to inhibit the act rather than after-the-event disclosures. Certain obvious precautions should be taken.

1. Do not allow deliveries of supplies to lie unattended in corridors or work areas, but have them placed immediately under lock and key or else directly into the charge of the employees responsible for their care.
2. Broach all packing case outers and shelve items so that there can be no use of the cases to cover the theft of their contents.
3. Be continuously on guard to ensure than cans and bottles etc. contain their true contents and are not lying empty, upturned, or holding some substitute contents.
4. Survey the memoranda on the evidence of which goods have been moved between departments in order to make sure that they have not been altered or items moved without authorization.
5. Ensure that items issued to a department did in fact arrive and were used for finished goods for sale.
6. Ensure that certain small-bulk high-value items such as fresh fruit are not left in open positions where employees may be tempted to help themselves with impunity.

For overnight security it is advisable to have locks on cupboards, freezers and refrigerators and, despite the fact that wet stock in licensed houses offers a greater attraction to intruders, an alarm bell system in the storeroom could prevent theft.

Issuing food

When food is issued from the store, no matter how small the operation and regardless of whether or not a systematic control system operates, it is accepted as good practice that a requisition should be submitted in exchange for the items. The simplest of duplicate books may be used for this, with the original being retained in the stores. An illustration of a common form is shown in Figure 31.

This form is laid out in the way one normally speaks, e.g. 'two kilos or five pounds of such and such'. The more precisely a unit is described the better. For example, it is insufficient to request a 'can' of a particular item. Several can sizes are in common use and a commodity may be stocked in one or two sizes to accommodate different requirements. Apart from the potential waste of receiving the issue of a can size which is too large for the task in hand, confusion may arise in the stock control system because the actual issue is different from the size noted. Further, different qualities of a commodity may

Policy and Operations

Figure 31 *Duplicate book*

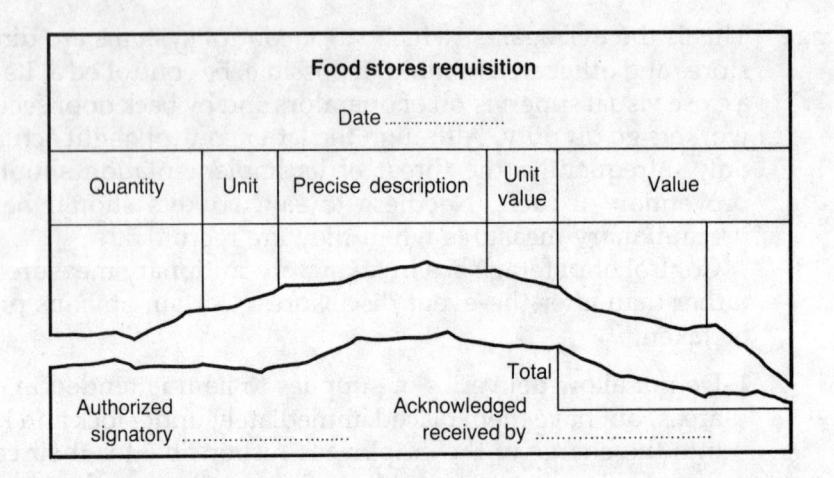

Food stores requisition
Date ....

Quantity	Unit	Precise description	Unit value	Value
				Total

Authorized signatory .... Acknowledged received by ....

be stocked because of varying uses; thus the preferred brand should also be stated.

Through precise description of the item to be drawn from the store, error, frustration and waste are minimized. Furthermore, it may be that the precision of thought thus demanded could have a spin-off in the actual efficiency of food production.

Stores requisitions   All stores requisitions should bear the endorsing signature of the employee who authorized the withdrawal of the stock and the employee who actually received an issue of stock from the stores. The former should take care, when signing the document, to put a line through any unused space on the form so that no further entries can be inserted as a means of obtaining unauthorized issues by other people. Equally, as items are checked out, the receiver of the stock should tick the entries on the form as a reference mark that the commodities were actually received. Three copies of the form would provide evidence of the transaction to the storeperson, the employee taking responsibility for the goods in production, and the original orderer of the goods from the store. A store record card system could make use of the last mentioned copy as the source of information for posting the 'out' entries on the appropriate stock cards. Needless to say, the accuracy of the stock control system is dependent upon the receiver of an issue from the stores checking to ensure, particularly in the case of broken bulk commodities, that the full weight, quantity and quality are given.

Cost control   For cost control purposes the financial extension and summation columns would provide information necessary for the maintenance of a stock account, were it to be operated as a control over stores and also for charging consumption to a regular food cost control process (see Chapter 13). The unit cost value would be obtained from the item's stock record card or from the relevant entry in the goods received book.

However, in the smaller licensed house, stores control might not be separated from the food operation control and in such a case there would be no need to cost the stores requisitions. The consumption of food from the stores

Receiving, storing and issuing food

would be taken into account through the stores stock being regarded as part of the kitchen stock. Thus the value of a closing inventory subtracted from the addition of opening inventory and purchases during a period would provide the equivalent information. A choice on whether or not to value requisitions from stores depends upon the exclusion or inclusion of stores stock in kitchen stock for control purposes.

Non-food items such as cleaning materials may be processed in exactly the same way, but usually it is sufficient to control them simply by having them under lock and key. Of course, where requisitions are used for such purposes, care must be taken not to include the information in charges to the food operation cost. It is not advisable to keep soaps and the like with food commodities which may pick up the taint of these items.

Management should regularly inspect the stores and the documentation connected with it, particularly requisitions. These should be scrutinized to question both the need for an item's consumption and the quantity of it withdrawn. For instance, comparing quantities regularly withdrawn in correlation with the probable and actual consumption by customers may lead to a realization that there has been an excessive use of certain items which may have alternative domestic uses!

Management internal control

To summarize, the management of receiving, storing and issuing food is divided into two aims. One is to have an effective system of internal check operating on the goods; the other is to have a sufficiently reassuring system of internal audit of transactions. Internal check is an automatic process carried out by employees as a matter of job routine. Internal audit is an intrusive probe operation carried out with sufficient frequency to monitor the operation.

The internal check   The internal check control depends upon workers in a continuous process checking before acting on the output of previous workers in the process. That is to say, errors are spotted and the work sent for correction before being accepted further into the system. Obviously such a process can be applied to what goes on in the stewardship functions previously described:

1. The orderer's work is checked by the receiver of the supplies through order verification.
2. The receiver's work is checked by the bookkeeper through delivery note verification.
3. The storeman's work may be checked by a bookkeeper through delivery note and requisition postings, either to a stock ledger system or to a stores account.
4. The bookkeeper's work is checked by an accountant or by management through a verification of the accounts according to suppliers' statements.
5. The accountant's or management's accounting work is checked by professional auditors through verification of the cash payments made to the suppliers and posted to their accounts.

Policy and Operations

From this, it will be appreciated that the chances of accidental or deliberate errors passing through the system undetected are indeed remote. The efficiency of the system is effected through the imposition of its own operational controls, and this is the concept of internal check.

The internal audit On the other hand the internal audit is not implemented as a routine of the business. It is instead a management probe operated from time to time as is deemed necessary. This may be on a regular basis or applied at irregular intervals. Where errors are detected by audits, their frequency would be expected to increase until the causes had been brought under control.

Applied to the receiving, storing and issuing process, internal audit would include snap inspections of the documentation involved to see that it conformed with expectations. A similar process is carried out for stock balances on shelves, either through the stock record card system or by a total value through a stores account balance. In the course of this, ancillary unsatisfactory aspects such as excessively long waiting times for supplies and variations from predetermined stock levels would be identified and corrective action could be taken.

The operation of internal control associated with a close visual supervision of the physical aspects of stewardship must inevitably lead to an efficient system of operation in receiving, storing and issuing food.

Further reading

Fuller, John, *Professional Kitchen Management*, Batsford, 1983.
Johnson, R. H., *Running your own Restaurant*, Hutchinson, 1982.
Steel, James, *Control in Catering*, Hutchinson, 1980.

11 Selling functions
James Fuller

The next chapter deals with planning and organizing functions; but first, bookings have to be secured from customers. Irrespective of the style or size of function that can be accommodated, the same principles of selling apply.

The need to sell is simply illustrated. A written or telephoned enquiry to local competitors about holding a fictional function will often show how poor their selling skills are. Response is often slow, sales literature is of poor quality and the person handling the enquiry is ill equipped to respond to detailed questions or give advice.

Having established the 'strength' of his competitors' selling skills, the caterer can then set out to beat him.

A publican as salesman must know his product. The obvious products are the menu, the wine list, table plans and available dates. Not so obvious products are expertise, experience and professionalism. For the organizer – such as a social secretary, or the mother of a bride – the function will be all important, and in some cases the only function he or she will ever organize. The organizer will look to the caterer for help, guidance and reassurance. Function selling should only be entrusted to those staff – normally management – who are totally familiar with this full product range. The easy part of function selling is that the client usually comes to the caterer which, in itself, indicates an intention to buy the product. If the size, type and date of the function can be accommodated then the booking should never be lost.

Brochures

Any publican who has (or who is trying to establish) a regular, efficient and profitable function trade should produce a brochure summarizing the services which he can offer and the type of food which he can provide. This brochure should be carefully aimed at his potential clientele (see Figure 32).

It is essential to include a range of menus so that the client can have his or her ideas formulated by what the caterer has to offer. If the client can think, 'Ah! That's exactly what I had in mind' the caterer is halfway to making a sale. For this reason, the range of price and style should be as wide as is practicable.

The menus should, however, not be priced in the brochure itself, because any change in price would involve altering the price printed, which would mar the appearance of the brochure and arouse suspicion in the reader. Small typed or printed inserts containing the tariff overcome this difficulty and facilitate up-to-the-minute quotations.

Figure 32 *A function brochure*

The White Swan

We specialize in wedding receptions and our function room makes an ideal setting for your wedding day. We can:
- Order your wedding cake
- Order bouquets and other floral requirements
- Select a menu to suit your needs

Menu
3 course meals, including sherry, wine, champagne and coffee, from £7.00 per person

Bar and drinks
Private bar facilities can be made available and drinks can either be charged to account or served on a cash basis.

Table plan
We will arrange table and place cards to your requirements.

Entertainment
A disco can be made available to you at additional cost.

For further details telephone or write to:
The White Swan, Canal Street, Cheddington.   Tel: 6489

Apart from specimen menus the brochure might also contain a map showing the location of the house; photographs of the function room; details of parking facilities; and any other information which may help to turn an enquiry into a sale.

The sale and layout of the brochure are important in creating the general image, and most general printers are pleased to advise and supply samples of their work.

Function enquiries

Enquiries come in three forms: telephone, written and personal.

Telephone Often a major source of potential business, it is vital that salesmen are available to handle telephone enquiries throughout the day. In the licensed trade, where often no business is conducted during the afternoon, the telephone is unmanned and bookings are lost. If the enquirer gets no reply he is more likely to call the next establishment on his list than call back later. If an enquiry cannot be dealt with correctly at the time, take the client's name, number and address and call him back. Do not ask the client to call back at a convenient time. He probably won't, and the booking is lost.

Written When a written enquiry is received the response must be by telephone in case competitors have also had the same enquiry. Clients' requirements cannot be 'discussed' by letter. If the enquirer lives locally and is not on the telephone then a personal call by the manager is required, particularly if the potential business is significant.

Personal This is probably the easiest of enquiries to convert to a firm booking as the facilities can be viewed, dates, menus and other arrangements can be discussed and the right impression given to the customer to instil a feeling of confidence in the manager's ability to create a successful function. The opposite can easily occur, however, if the enquirer is kept waiting because he has called at an inconvenient time or he is shown facilities uncleared from a previous function which show them in a poor light. Staff must, therefore, be aware of the correct routine when dealing with personal enquiries to ensure that the best possible impression is made.

Wherever possible the manager should arrange to meet prospective clients to discuss their requirements. It is only when the detailed requirements are known that the manager can accurately quote for the business. The customer may be flexible on dates, and a keen quotation may persuade him to accept a date less favourable to him but better for the business. It is also easy to underquote where a little persuasive discussion could have resulted in a higher-price menu being sold.

With any enquiry, it is essential that the customer is 'chased' until the booking is either secured or cancelled. All details agreed should be confirmed in writing to the client to ensure that nothing is overlooked.

It is only with meticulous selling that you can have meticulous planning and, hence, successful functions.

Providing a total service

In addition to providing food and drink, the caterer is often asked to arrange entertainment, floral decoration, menu printing, photographer etc. The cost of such arrangements is often passed on to the client with the addition of a handling charge. Although this total package approach may help in securing business, the caterer is entering areas out of his control. If the band fails to turn up, or they do not play well, the caterer gets the blame. It may be preferable to give the client a list of contacts so that he can book the service required direct.

Further reading

Taylor, Derek, *How to Sell Banquets*, Northwood, 1979.

12 Functions and outside catering

Michael R. Small

Catering in licensed houses varies widely from a modest range of bar snacks up to a point where turnover on food is greater than that on drink. In those houses which have facilities to undertake functions, the importance of this trade fluctuates. At one end of the scale, function trade may be as little as 5 per cent of food turnover and the approach to the occasional function may be more akin to that of enthusiastic amateur. At the other end, function business may be substantial and handled with professionalism.

There is also a diversity of operation since the factors to be considered vary according to whether the establishment is a managed house, a tenanted house or a free house. The proprietor of a free house with a large function trade will be concerned that each event carries its share of the general overheads of the house. The licensee of a managed house may only be required to consider gross profit on food, though accountability for controllable costs, particularly wages, is increasing.

This chapter deals with functions in a general way. Thus each reader will need to adapt its general principles to suit his own circumstances.

Function catering can be challenging, rewarding and profitable, and can form an important part of annual turnover. However, neither the satisfaction of a successful event nor its anticipated profit will materialize without adequate premises, suitable equipment and meticulous organization.

Premises and profit

The ideal situation is where there is a separate, self-contained function suite with its own entrance, cloakrooms and toilets, ante-room, bar and servery. Where such a suite exists, the volume of function trade must be sufficient to offset the overheads involved and give an adequate return on capital employed. The volume of business required will also be linked to the realizable gross profits on food and drink. These are dependent on the market segment being served. A greater volume of low margin business will be required than of high margin business to yield the same bottom line profit.

In any event, the break-even point below which it is not profitable to operate the function facilities should be calculated. This is normally expressed to the customer in terms of minimum numbers, minimum spend per head or a combination of the two.

Another situation where function business is relatively simple is where the establishment has a restaurant which is only used for weekday lunches (often

Functions and outside catering

the case in city business areas) and can be used for functions during evenings and weekends. In these circumstances a lower volume of function trade is viable, since overheads are at least partially covered by the restaurant operation. Again, a break-even point should be calculated to ensure that direct controllable costs are covered, notably wages.

A restaurant which would normally be open to the general public should not be closed in order to hold a function without careful thought. Regular customers may be offended and the opportunity to turn chance trade into regular custom lost. This danger is alleviated if the establishment has more than one restaurant or if a substantial and well-served meal can be offered in the bar to would-be diners.

A further alternative is where one room (a bar or a lounge) can be closed to the general public without upsetting regular trade. This is less simple because a room designed and furnished for one purpose may not be suitable for an alternative use. However, the use of space in quiet trading periods (such as early in the week) for (simple) meetings without food can yield (a) a room hire charge which is virtually pure profit, and (b) spin off bar trade.

There are two other possibilities: catering in other premises (dealt with later) and utilizing a room (bar or restaurant) outside its customary opening hours. The latter alternative, which almost always means an afternoon function, can be worrying because the function may overrun its time or guests may linger on and disrupt regular trade. Again, this problem is alleviated if there is more than one bar or restaurant. An occasional licence will be needed if alcohol is to be served outside normal hours.

Space requirements These vary according to the type of function, the table plan and the shape of the room. In general terms, however, 1.2–1.4 m² (13–15 ft²) per guest are required for a dinner, 1.5–1.6 m² (16–17 ft²) for a dinner dance and not less than 0.9 m² (10 ft²) for a fork buffet or reception. Do not try to accommodate too many people since cramped conditions are annoying for guests and difficult for staff.

Table plans Table plans can be determined by trial and error, i.e. by physically moving tables around, but this is expensive in terms of time and labour, not always convenient and far from efficient. A more professional approach is to prepare a scale plan of the room showing all entrances, alcoves, pillars etc. and make a set of cardboard templates to the same scale using these to set out the plan. This is essential if a variety of plans are called for or if a function is close to the maximum capacity of the room.

A minimum of 1.829 m (6 ft) is needed between tables to allow for chairs and passageway. It is useful to include this in the templates, as shown in Figure 34, in order to avoid the danger of producing a plan on paper which will not fit in reality. This system enables the production of plans which show the maximum numbers of the various seating arrangements that can be accommodated within the passageway for service.

There are three basic types of table plan. These can be termed formal, informal and cabaret, and are illustrated to scale in the following figures. Figure 33 shows a typical formal layout with a top table and five sprigs. This layout, using twenty-five tables 1.829 m (6 ft) × 0.760 m (2 ft 6 in) would

Policy and Operations

Figure 33 *Formal layout with top table and five sprigs*

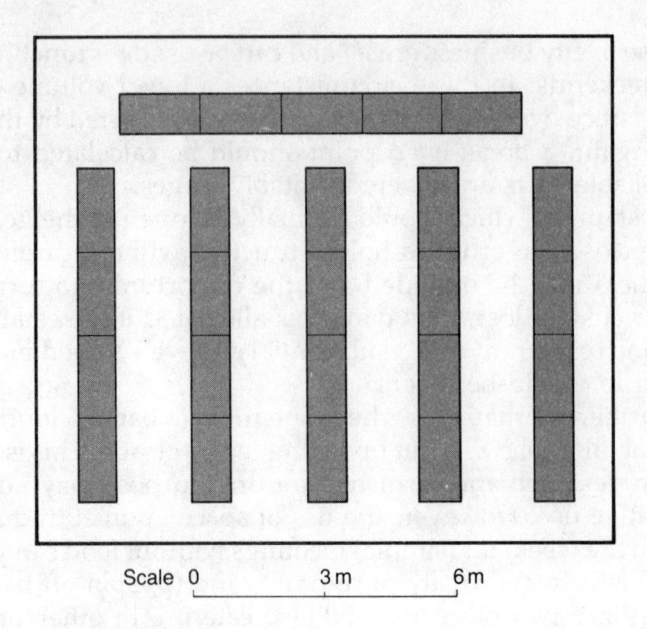

seat 135 covers, i.e. fifteen on the top table and twelve on each side of each sprig. This type is suitable for occasions when the after-dinner speeches are important, since all the guests are facing towards the speakers. (It is not usual to seat guests on the inward side of the top table.)

A formal plan can also have the sprig touching the top table, like the teeth of a comb. This minimizes the 'them and us' aspect between guests seated on the sprigs because of the restricted access to the top of the sprigs.

Figure 34 shows a typical informal layout with a straight top table of five 1.829 m (6 ft) tables and eleven 1.524 m (5 ft) round tables. This plan seats 125 people.

A cabaret layout is where tables are grouped round an empty area of the floor which is later used for dancing. Figure 35(a) and (b) shows two typical examples seating ninety-six people and ninety-two people respectively.

Staff requirements A banquet waiter or waitress will serve ten to twelve covers at a silver service function and if one or two wines are included will normally serve these also. However, if wines are ordered and paid for by guests, separate wine waiters or waitresses will be required, each able to serve about four tables of ten or twelve covers.

An alternative to wine waiters taking orders at the table is to arrange for pre-ordering of the wines in the reception area, placing bottles on the appropriate table or cover before the guests sit. (Obviously a table plan is required.) Each host then pours the wine for his guests.

Most reputable staff agencies can supply a brigade of banquet staff and they are usually competent, but many pubs build up their own team of reliable temps possibly augmented by agency staff for extra large events.

The same applies to kitchen, bar and washing-up staff, but if a large volume of wine sales is anticipated it is best if the cellar or dispense bar is under the control of a reliable member of the permanent staff.

The calibre of available staff in both service and production, and the style of service offered, are closely linked. It is pointless setting silver service as the

Functions and outside catering

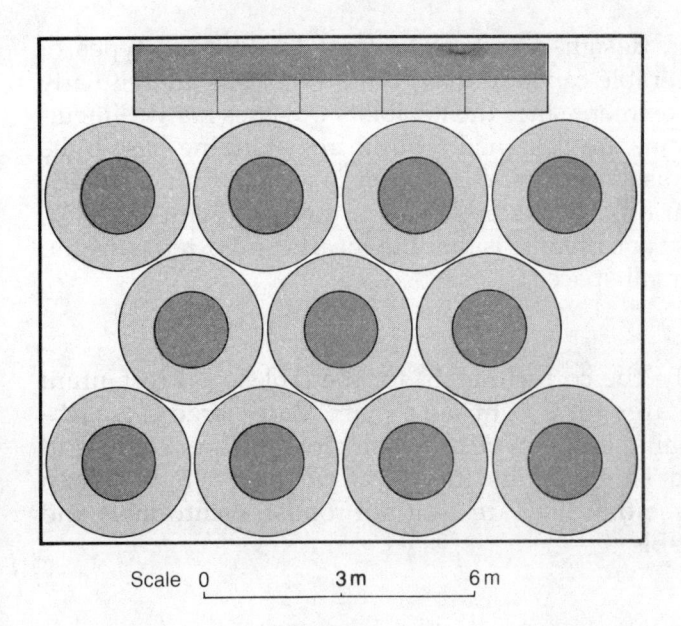

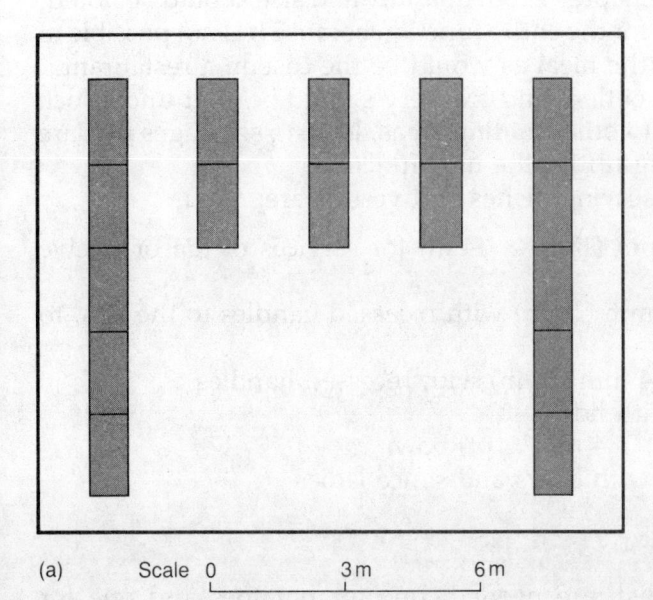

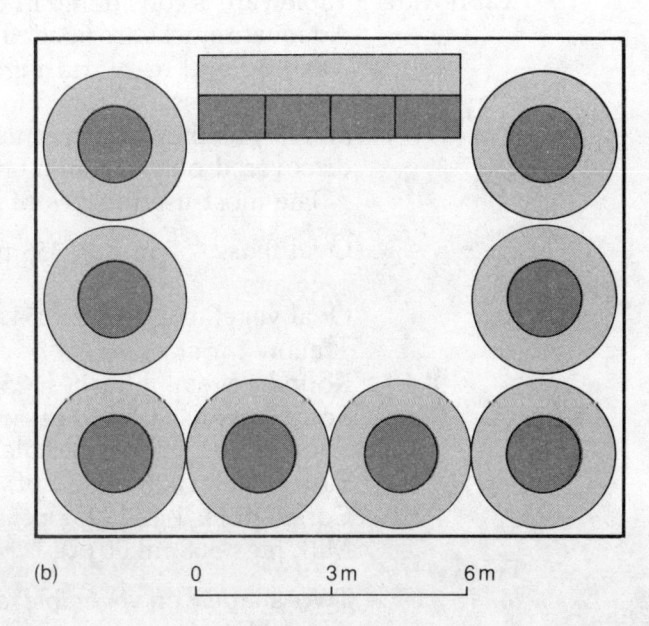

Scale 0   3 m   6 m

(a) Scale 0   3 m   6 m

(b) 0   3 m   6 m

Figure 34   *Informal layout*

Figure 35   *Typical examples of seating plans*
(a) *Ninety-six people*
(b) *Ninety-two people*

standard if functions are only held occasionally and available staff are unpractised and clumsy simply because of the low volume of business. A pub rarely has sufficient volume to justify full-time service staff adequately trained to this level.

Equipment

Tables   Not all restaurant tables are suitable for banquet use. Rectangular tables with legs at the corners give rise to the problem of 'double legging' when placed end to end to make a sprig, and two rectangular tables each seating six people will only seat eight when placed side by side.

Policy and Operations

Special banquet tabling, designed to be adaptable to different types of layout, represent a considerable capital outlay, but if functions are regularly undertaken it is a wise investment since the flexibility obviates many difficulties. Generally these systems are designed around free-standing base units which can be used by themselves, can be linked by inserts to form sprigs or can take larger tops of various shapes and sizes to form individual tables. Another advantage of this type of table is that the inserts and extensions can be stored in a relatively small space.

Chairs Obviously these need to be the correct height for the tables, but restaurant chairs are sometimes too large for a tight table plan. Many large establishments have two sets of chairs, carver type armchairs for small functions and top table use and standard 'banquet gilts' for use when space is tight. When chairs are being selected see that they are light but robust, comfortable and either collapsible or stackable.

Tableware Tableware is considered in Chapter 7, but quantity and size should be noted. Adequate stocks are needed for the entire function because it is not possible to wash up and re-lay during the meal as would be the case in a restaurant.

Where possible, function cutlery and crockery should be kept under lock and key as they can stray into other trading areas, leaving shortages that are discovered only when laying up for the next function.

The most useful sizes of serving dishes and vessels are:

Oval flats: 457 mm × 356 mm (18 in × 14 in) for services of ten or twelve covers
Oval vegetable dishes: 254 mm (10 in) with recessed handles to the lids, to allow for stacking
Round vegetable dishes: 254 mm (10 in) with recessed handles
Soup tureens: 4.5 l (8 pt) with lid
Soup ladles: curved handle, 284 ml (½ pt) bowl
Sauce boats: 426 ml (¾ pt) with bases and sauce ladles
Coffee pots: 1.42 l (2½ pt)
Milk jugs 568 ml (1 pt).

Two shapes of vegetable dish are needed, one for potatoes and one for vegetables, to avoid a waitress inadvertently taking two of the same item.

Disposables Not all functions are to de luxe standards on generous budgets, and for more modest occasions modern disposable banquet roll and table napkins may be appropriate. The more expensive of these are available in attractive colours and can enhance the appearance of the room and form the basis for a colour scheme.

Hire Virtually anything required for a function, from tables to teaspoons, can be hired, but this adds to running expenses. If functions are regularly held, the capital outlay on purchasing adequate stocks must be considered.

However, items may need to be hired for an extra large event or for an outside event if the house equipment is not suitable for transportation. The following points should be noted:

Adequate notice is essential, particularly in June, July and December when hired equipment is in great demand.
Extra staff time is required to sort, count and repack hired items.
Hired china rarely matches the house pattern. If extra china is required, hire the items needed for all or some of the tables from the same source to avoid serving some courses on one type and the rest on a different pattern.

Planning and organizing

Planning and organization are important in any catering, but in functions they are essential. Alternative arrangements to alleviate errors or problems are not usually possible. The caterer cannot close one waiter's station if a member of staff is sick; cannot change the menu if food production (or delivery) goes wrong; cannot ask customers to wait because their table is not ready. In short, any failures are obvious and cannot be disguised. Therefore, ensure that these things cannot happen. This can only be achieved by effective, meticulous and 'failsafe' planning.

This failsafe aspect is unique to function catering. The caterer must have contingency plans for almost all eventualities or the resources to cope effectively at the time. (In the event of a major change in circumstances – a fire, a national strike, a complete freeze-up – all customers are co-operative and sympathetic, but this most emphatically does not apply if the chef has flu.)

Every aspect of the function must be written down, and kept in a file. Writing 'roll and butter' on the draft menu reminds the caterer to order rolls and to think if the budget will allow the use of seeded knots from a specialist baker or only crusty dinner rolls from a multiple baker. The written note 'flowers' is a reminder that he must also order and organize these.

Function form The basic document for planning a function is the 'function form'. If functions are undertaken regularly this form can be printed or duplicated, and many breweries provide such forms in triplicate sets (Figure 36). If functions are relatively rare, a typed form (Figure 37; see also Figures 38 and 39) will serve equally well. In addition to being the basis for planning the function and compiling the bill, these forms should be indexed and filed thus enabling enquiries for similar events to be handled quickly.

Function bookings diary A function bookings diary is essential; it should be used only for function bookings and not as a general diary. A day to a page A4 diary is preferable, ruled off to show the various lettable areas, e.g. function suite, restaurant, lounge bar. It should be kept in one place, usually an office, by the telephone and with the appropriate back-up information to hand, i.e. menus, wine lists, room hire tariff and customer files. Therefore in the event of a call the publican

Policy and Operations

Figure 36 *A typical function form*

TRUMAN TAVERNS
FUNCTION BOOKING / ENQUIRY

No. **A   0076**

1. HOUSE:
2. DATE OF BOOKING:
3. DAY AND DATE OF FUNCTION:

4. PARTICULARS OF CLIENT
   (a) Name ....
   (b) Address ....
   (c) Address for A/c ....
   (d) Telephone ....
   (e) Organiser's Name ....

5. No. OF COVERS:
   (a) Deposit (if any): ....
   (b) Extension requirement: ....

6. PARTICULARS OF FUNCTION:
   (a) Type of Function ....
   (b) Actual room(s) reserved ....
   (c) Provisional number .... @ ....
   (d) Menu

7. ESTIMATE OF COSTS:
   Hors d'Oeuvres ....
   Buffet ....
   Dinner ....
   Cake ....
   Beverages ....
   Wines ....
   Flowers ....
   Miscellaneous ....
   ....
   ....
   ....
   Gratuities ....
   ....
   ....
   ....
   Miscellaneous ....

   ESTIMATED TOTAL

8. DRINKS:
   Before Meal: ....
                                                              Cash / A/c
   During Meal:
   (a) Aperitifs ....
                                                              Cash / A/c
   (b) Table Wines ....
                                                              Cash / A/c
   (c) Liqueurs and Cigarettes ....
   ....
                                                              Cash / A/c

10. SIGNATURE OF CLIENT:

9. SPECIAL REQUIREMENTS:
   (a) Room Charge ....
   (b) Music ....
   (c) Flowers ....
   (d) Menu Printing ....
   (e) Wedding Cake ....
   (f)   "   " Stand and Knife ....
   (g) Toastmaster ....
   (h) Photographer ....
   (j) Cloakroom Attendants ....
   (k) ....

11. FOR OFFICE USE ONLY:
    (a) Date of Diary Entry ....
    (b) Total A/c Rendered ....
    (c) Date of Rendering ....
    (d) Date of Payment

TRUMAN TAVERNS, THE BREWERY, 91 BRICK LANE, LONDON E1 6QN Telephone 01-377 0020

Functions and outside catering

Figure 37 *Function form for a dinner dance*

Function:	Briggs & Co. Dinner Dance Host: John Newby (MD) Organizer: Richard Parker (Personnel)
Date:	Sat. 12 December 1986
Time:	7.00–12.00 (dinner 8.00)
Covers:	150 ∓ 5
Cost:	£7.50 per cover (£1125) ex VAT
Reception:	7.00–7.45 in foyer. Usual drinks, cash only
Menu:	Plan E plus biscuits and cheese
Wines:	Lutomer Riesling, two glasses per head inclusive (top table – Pouilly-Fuissé)
Liqueurs:	Top table to be billed, rest cash only
Speeches:	Two, brief
Toastmaster:	No
Band:	Sid Daventry booked 8.00–12.00, to be billed
Cloaks:	Usual, in foyer. Mrs Peacock and Winnie to see in and out
Flowers:	Mimosa – ordered
Notes:	1 Extension to 11.30 – granted 11/10/86 2 Menus Hardwick Press, to be billed 3 Top of 20; 13 × 10 rounds 4 Russet banquet roll, yellow four-ply napkins
Staff:	Bar: Tom Jenkins + four Service: Mrs Ives + fifteen Washing-up: Mrs Downey, Winnie and Bill Kitchen: Chef + Anne + Harry

can respond efficiently. The function diary should not contain great detail of the function booked, and entries should be in pencil. It should state whether the booking is provisional or confirmed, the name, address and contact telephone number of the customer, and the type and the starting and finishing times of the function. This is important so that an enquiry for an evening function is not turned away because the room is shown as booked when, in fact, the booking in the diary is for a luncheon only. The full function details

Figure 38 *Menu for dinner dance*

Briggs & Co Dinner Dance   Saturday 12 December 1986

MENU

Prawn cocktail   *Home-made sauce, well garnished*
Brown bread and butter

**

Roast turkey   *White and dark meat per portion*
Stuffing
Chipolata
Glazed carrots
Brussels sprouts
Roast potatoes
Giblet gravy

**

Black Forest gâteau
Whipped cream

**

Cheese and biscuits   *Cheddar, Danish Blue, Caerphilly*

**

Coffee
After dinner mints

**

Lutomer Riesling   *Two glasses per head, lightly chilled*

---

should be kept separately in the customer's file. In the event of a cancellation or failure to confirm a provisional booking, the entry can be easily erased.

A 'chase' system is extremely useful as a reminder to chase provisional bookings. A simple date order card index box, checked daily, reminds a publican to call a client who made a provisional booking a week earlier to secure the business. A booking is not a booking until it is confirmed in writing by the client. A functions diary full of provisional bookings may look good but

Functions and outside catering

Figure 39 *Quantity sheet for dinner dance*

Briggs & Co Dinner Dance　　　　Saturday 12 December 1986

Prawn cocktail		
13 × 1 kg Norwegian prawns		Brooks
4.5 l sauce		Chef
6 Webbs Wonderful		Pavitt
3 cucumber		Pavitt
14 lemons		Pavitt
Turkey	2 × 20 kg (balance for bar salads)	Halse
Stuffing	3 × 2 kg loaves	Chef
Chipolatas	4.5 kg pork chips	Halse
Carrots	19 kg	Pavitt
Sprouts	14 × 1 kg button	Brooks
Potatoes	27 kg	Stores
Gravy	6 l	Chef
Gâteaux	10 in no.	Brooks
Cream	3.5 l bakers cream	UD
Cheese	16 × 250 g each	Fitch
Biscuits	3 kg cracker }	Stores
	5 kg digestive }	
Butter	2.5 kg	Stores
Coffee	3 × 4.5 l	Stores
Milk	2 × 4.5 l	Stores
Mints	3 kg After Eight	Fitch
Cover	160 seeded knot	Glynn
	2.5 kg butter	Stores

---

if they do not materialize other business may have been lost in the interim. Once the function is over, the forms in Figures 37–39 have several uses.

The bill　Always send the bill for a function promptly while the enjoyment of the event and details of the arrangements are fresh in the client's mind. The bill for the function illustrated in Figures 37–39 might appear as in Figure 40.

Policy and Operations

Figure 40 *Bill for dinner dance*

```
Annual Dinner Dance on 12/12/1986

To:   148 covers @ £7.50                                        1110.00

To:   Top table liqueurs as per enclosed list                     12.85

To:   Sid Daventry Quintet 8.00–12.00              110.00
      Meals for above, as agreed                    12.50
      Two rounds of drinks, as ordered by
      Mr Parker                                      5.00         127.50

To:   Printing of menus                                            50.00

To:   Presentation bouquet                                         12.00
                                                                ───────
                                                                 1312.35
      V.A.T. 15 per cent                                          196.85
                                                                ───────
                                                                £1509.20
```

Costings

Like all catering activities, functions are undertaken to make a profit. However, unless thorough and accurate costings are available, profit may be less than anticipated. Many individual caterers dislike paperwork and rely upon their instinct and experience when determining selling price. In many instances this works well but the selling price of a function menu will have been quoted in advance, and cannot be changed if costs increase meanwhile; furthermore, a miscalculation of the cost price of a function for 250 covers could be multiplied 250 fold, which is a sobering thought.

If a function is booked well in advance, such as a wedding or a repeat annual dinner, it is best not to quote on a particular menu, although the contents may be agreed, until nearer the date of the function. Drink prices in these cases can be quoted but subject to changes in duty.

Food cost The food cost of a function is more controllable than is the case with the ordinary trade of the house because the numbers to be fed are known in advance, thereby removing the element of chance.

The food cost is calculated in the usual way, either by reference to existing costings if the dishes are normally available or, if not, by pricing, extending and totalling the quantity sheet shown in Figure 39. If all the costings are filed then, as the file grows, the need to undertake costings from scratch diminishes. Care should be taken to include all recipe items when

Functions and outside catering

costing, such as oil for frying (an expensive commodity), garnishes and accompaniments.

Some wastage may occur if there is a last-minute shortfall in numbers or if guests ask for an alternative dish for reasons of diet. Wastage risk can be reduced by (a) the common practice of requiring customers to guarantee payment for an agreed number of guests, and (b) by enquiring when arranging the function if any special meals are likely.

Labour costs In many businesses management is expected to contain labour costs within a predetermined percentage of turnover (like food costs), and these percentages are used to calculate selling prices and to monitor financial performance. The labour costs for a function, however, may differ considerably from those of the usual trade and therefore need to be specifically calculated.

Direct labour costs are easily ascertainable, since these are wages which would not have been incurred without the function, but agency fees or taxi fares should be included where applicable. Extra hours worked by permanent staff are also to be taken into account and if paid at overtime rates they must be costed at that rate.

Indirect labour costs are less easy to calculate since they represent work done towards the function by permanent staff within their normal time of work. The chef, for example, may have done a considerable amount of preparation on the previous day and the cleaning may be partly undertaken on the following day. It is tempting to ignore this extra labour since no extra costs are directly incurred, but it is nevertheless part of the cost of providing the function and to omit it would show an artificially high level of profit. Management and clerical costs are more easily treated as part of indirect overheads.

The cost of bar labour may be omitted as this will be reflected in increased takings in the normal ratio of cost to turnover. However, extra bar labour may be required to cope with peak demand such as a premeal reception requiring coverage for only half an hour or so, although the extra staff may need to be paid for a longer period (possibly the whole night) in order to ensure coverage of that critical period.

Overheads Direct overheads, those costs other than food and labour directly incurred because of the function, are readily identifiable. Such items as laundry, table decorations or the hire of equipment come into this category. Some additional costs such as table decorations, place cards etc. ordered on the customer's behalf can be passed to him direct by adding a 'handling' charge (unless they form part of the house standard, in which case they should be reflected in the menu price). This can be calculated as cost per cover.

Indirect overheads such as insurance, advertising, depreciation and so on can only be estimated as a percentage of turnover as in the normal business of the house, but indirect overheads may not concern the individual manager.

Profit The profit level on functions is usually sufficient to make the extra effort worth while. The actual net profit (when all costs are taken into account both

Policy and Operations

controllable and fixed) may not be known to the unit manager who may simply be required to show an operating profit by control of food, liquor, wage and controllable costs. In these circumstances the incentive to the manager to seek function business is generally in the form of increased commission on profit arising from the provision of the function and the extra sales engendered.

Any profit depends upon the selling price as well as the costs involved and a considered decision needs to be taken when determining the price to be quoted. It is perfectly reasonable to vary the percentage profit required according to the type of event and the value to the house of regular business from the same source. Thus, if a company regularly uses the restaurant for entertaining visiting businessmen a licensee or manager might accept a lower profit margin on their annual dinner as opposed to that required for a 'one-off' special event such as a wedding breakfast. This is normal commerical judgement used by any intelligent vendor of goods or services, and is not unique to selling and quoting for functions.

Formal functions

Of the various types of functions, perhaps the basic is a formal meal, i.e. a meal preceded by a reception and concluding with a speech or speeches with no other entertainment required. Business luncheons and dinners and many wedding receptions come into this category.

Seating at formal meals The main requirements are ample space for guests to assemble before the meal and take aperitifs; punctuality; smooth and efficient service; and silence for the speeches. A sprig layout is the most suitable, but tables of eight or ten are also frequently used.

The caterer will discuss the table plan with the client, for only the client can determine who sits where and with whom. This can be problematical for him, and the caterer should be as flexible as his circumstances allow even though uniform tables of ten are preferable from his point of view. Although the seating plan is the responsibility of the client, the caterer should try to ensure that every guest knows where he or she will sit. Each table or sprig will require a letter or number, boldly displayed and readily visible on entry. One or two copies of the guest list, in alphabetical order, should be displayed in the anteroom with the table numbers appended. For large functions, a copy of the plan should also be displayed.

Dinner dance A dinner dance is not necessarily an entirely informal affair; indeed, at many such events there are speeches after the meal before dancing commences. If the room is large enough to contain the table plan and the dance floor, insist that waitresses do not cross the dance floor during service to avoid any spillage marring the dancing surface. If, however, the tables need to be rearranged after the meal in order to provide dancing space (a 'strip job'), several factors need to be taken into consideration.

Functions and outside catering

Floor covering   Those areas of the dance floor needed for seating guests during the service of the meal should, if possible, be protected with a carpet or drugget until the tables are rearranged. This covering should lie flat and flush, with no upturned edges or corners to trip guests or staff. Arrange to have it speedily removed and neatly stored once the strip is completed.

Table arrangements   Either some tables will need to be collapsed and removed or most tables reduced in size in order to provide the extra space. When necessary to remove tables, it is better to merge two tables into one rather than three tables into two since the latter alternative involves splitting up groups of guests.

Staff   All tables need to be stripped, rearranged and relaid with cloths and ashtrays. Be sure to have enough male staff to handle tables and removal of the drugget (if used). Ensure that the anteroom bar is well stocked and staffed.

As well as being offered in measures, spirits and fortified wines can be sold by the bottle at a modest discount against nip price. This can ease pressure on the bar, reducing labour costs, and can increase bar takings with a negligible reduction in gross margin.

Guests   Guests need to vacate the room during the operation; at the end of an enjoyable meal they are often reluctant to do so. Polite persistence by the head waiter or toastmaster may be required.

Buffets

Buffets are popular with both caterers and customers because of their relative informality. However, the term 'buffet' can embrace everything from an elaborate display carved on demand to a small selection of finger food offered from trays. The three main types of buffet are: full buffet, fork buffet and finger buffet.

Full buffet   A full buffet is virtually a normal banquet meal except that guests collect their own food. Cold foods predominate, but hot dishes such as curry and rice, goulash and noodles and soups served from table-top hot-plates on the buffet counter can also be served.

The appearance of the buffet and dishes are important, but dishes should not be over-decorated because, once the decoration is destroyed by serving the first few customers, the appearance can deteriorate rapidly to a point where it looks downright messy for the last people. Simple elegant garnishes are best.

Have each dish on display served to the guests by a member of staff, otherwise service tends to become drawn out. Carving whole joints at the buffet is pleasing to guests, but should only be contemplated when sufficient skilled carvers are available to ensure that no delay occurs; even then, have presliced portions available before service starts.

Policy and Operations

Guests will require normal banquet tables and chairs for a full buffet (so no floor space is saved) and where possible these should be fully laid up in advance. If the tables are being used prior to the buffet service, individual sets of cutlery, each wrapped in a table napkin, can be put on the tables in advance.

Try to stagger the arrival of guests at the buffet counter to avoid a cafeteria-like queue. If the starter cannot be in place on the tables in advance, then it is helpful if this can be served from a separate point.

Fewer dining room staff will be required when a buffet is being served, but remember to have staff to collect used plates and cutlery from the tables.

Fork buffets When the food can be eaten standing up with a plate in one hand and a fork in the other, then more people can be accommodated; but provide as many tables as possible for guests' glasses and empty plates. (Plastic clips are available that allow a wine glass to be attached to the rim of a plate.)

Ensure that the food really *can* be eaten easily using only a fork. Salmon mayonnaise is preferable to portions of salmon, for example, and a diced chicken dish more suitable than portions of chicken.

Fork buffets are popular for wedding receptions as they enable guests (who may not meet often) to mingle more freely than at a sit-down meal, but can also be sufficiently substantial to count as a main meal.

Finger buffets Again, provide as many chairs and tables as possible, although easy chairs and occasional tables are adequate. Choose food with ease of eating in mind; crumbly items such as bouchées and vol-au-vents should be bite sized. Finger buffets are not normally as substantial as a main meal and should not be offered at times when guests would normally be eating more substantial fare.

Wedding receptions

A wedding reception can take any form from a light finger buffet to a seven-course meal. A luncheon is often called the 'wedding breakfast'!

Although arrangements may vary widely, as can the type of food provided, some standard procedures are frequently adopted. The caterer should be familiar with these and with other aspects of wedding etiquette, since the bride's parents frequently seek his advice.

Wedding breakfast If it is a sit-down meal the other guests enter the dining room first then rise (and usually applaud) at the entry of the bride, 'groom and bridesmaids. The table plan can be in any style but seats on the top table are arranged as in Figure 41. The cake is displayed between the bride and 'groom.

Figure 41 *Wedding table top*

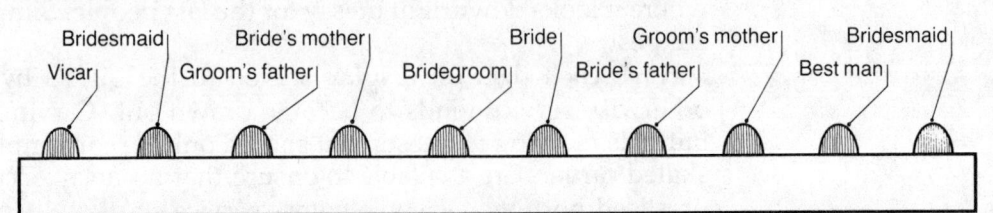

Bridesmaid | Bride's mother | Bride | Groom's mother | Bridesmaid
Vicar | Groom's father | Bridegroom | Bride's father | Best man

Functions and outside catering

Other points
1. Many caterers ban confetti on their premises.
2. Photographs taken at the reception are good publicity and the caterer should ensure a pleasant background.
3. The host may need reminding to provide a meal for chauffeurs (of hired cars).
4. Wedding table napkins (and book matches) can be obtained with the bride's and bridegroom's initials printed on them.
5. A pleasant custom is to split one of the champagne corks and insert a 10p or 50p piece of the current date and present it to the bride.
6. The wedding party often arrive late for the reception particularly in fine weather when photographs outside the church linger on. If a hot meal is being served, prereception arrangement and timing should be discussed with the host.
7. The bride can be presented with the cake knife by the manager – an effective and inexpensive public relations exercise in front of guests.
8. Non-residential establishments should note that bride and 'groom may require changing facilities.

Rotary and other business lunches

These are useful because many guests may be in a position to order further functions on their own behalf. The menu is usually a simple two- or three-course meal, speedily served, because most of those attending will be anxious not to be late for their afternoon's work. It is usual to serve the coffee with the sweet in the interests of speed, and usually little alcohol is consumed at these events.

Such lunches are all too often marginally profitable, and detailed costings may show no profit at all. Unless there is spin-off business from such lunches they may not be worth holding. Indeed, there is no guarantee that the society will hold its major annual function at the same venue as it holds its business lunches.

Menus for functions

A set meal, served to a group simultaneously, has its own requirements. Gastronomically the whole meal is planned as an entity rather than as a succession of courses, since guests have no choice. Clients occasionally want to offer options to their guests, but this is difficult and should be avoided in all but the most unusual circumstances.

Contrast of colour and ingredients are important in a function menu, but perhaps the most important, and all too frequently overlooked, factor is texture. Tomato soup, poached salmon and strawberry ice-cream, although similar in colour, would be more acceptable than, say, oxtail soup, chicken fricassee and rice, and strawberry mousse because the soft moist texture of each dish would have a cumulative cloying effect upon palate and stomach.

The question of menu acceptability is difficult. There are, at any social level, adventurous caterers and those who are suspicious of and unhappy with any dish they do not know well. Of course, the menu choice is that of the host but,

Policy and Operations

in general, well-tried paths are safer, if less exciting, than excursions into the little-known byways of unusual dishes when the need is to cater for a cross-section of the public with a set menu. (Diners clubs or gourmet societies are an obvious exception.)

In ordinary circumstances the location and ambience of the establishment determine the type of client and hence the type of menu likely to be popular. The wise caterer will evaluate this potential demand carefully, and by serving menus suited to the needs of his clientele can save work and worry.

The practical aspects of function menu planning also need consideration. A function meal inevitably involves elements of bulk food production and service, and the kitchens of many pubs, even those with function rooms, are often designed and equipped to produce a continuous flow of meals and snacks over a period.

Adequate hot cupboards and hot-plates are important when hot meals are being served, but a hot-plate with sufficient capacity to serve 150 covers between 12.30 p.m. and 2.00 p.m. will not be large enough to serve 150 covers simultaneously. This difficulty is aggravated if the function requires the food to be dressed in services of ten rather than being at least partly plated. Bulk production involves different work methods and the caterer must evaluate the ability of both equipment and staff before planning the menu. Both can be supplemented when needed: temporary staff can be engaged and portable plug-in hot plates can be bought or hired, but identifying and costing both before the menu is agreed is essential.

In general, do not include dishes which will deteriorate if held for any length of time (soup is easy; fried whitebait almost impossible) or dishes which require more last minute garnishing than is practical (sole bonne femme is easy; Wiener Schnitzel could be difficult).

Avoid dishes poor at retaining heat such as cauliflower and courgettes, and dishes difficult to serve (depending on style of service, e.g. silver, serving whole lemon sole), as well as those leaving a lot of debris on the plate such as poussin, whole fish etc. that make clearing difficult and increase the risk of spillage.

Take into account the need to overprovide for a function meal; for the caterer *must* have a reserve of food which can be utilized almost instantly should numbers go up or should accidents occur. Hold the reserves at such a point of preparedness that they can be quickly produced if needed but will not deteriorate if not needed. It is also necessary to be able to sell them (at a reasonable profit) if they are not used. The restaurant, buttery or bar snack menu are obvious outlets for such reserves provided they are in a suitable condition for reuse.

This aspect of economical menu planning is particularly relevant when the meal is a full buffet. This almost inevitably involves an element of choice and hence a higher proportion of unused food, which is not wasted if it can be resold.

Convenience food for menus When the usual restaurant or bar menu differs greatly from the function menu demanded, the skills of the kitchen staff or the standard kitchen equipment may be inadequate to service the function menu.

Convenience foods such as preportioned pâtés, smoked salmon, tinned soups, ready cooked meats, multiportion entrées, frozen vegetables, desserts etc. can be used to offer a variety of choice with minimal kitchen skills and equipment.

One advantage is an immediate cost saving on labour. Although convenience food costs more than home prepared, it is far more controllable. In addition, the product is consistent, prices do not fluctuate as much as fresh, back-up supplies can be held without deterioration if numbers decrease, and reserves can be held if numbers increase. Short-notice bookings such as coach parties can be accommodated. Costing of menus is easier and thus more accurate.

Food service The type of service required depends upon the style and price of the event. Full silver service normally associated with a function may not be appropriate for all events. Alternatives are frequently used. Silver service has the advantage of style and is fast and efficient for serving a roomful of guests at the same time. For these reasons it should be used whenever circumstances and budget allow; but it requires skilled waiting staff and more hot-cupboard space and serving dishes than other forms of service.

Family service, where the meat is plated and vegetables are placed on the tables in dishes for guests to serve themselves, tends to be slower (because waitresses need to make more trips to the servery) but fewer skilled staff can be used.

Plated service, where the complete meal is plated, is not recommended except in special circumstances. It is slow but does not require skilled staff.

Patterns of menu It is unusual nowadays to serve meals of many courses. Starter/fish/main/pudding/cheese/coffee is the usual maximum, with the possible addition of a sorbet between the fish and the main course (although this is not classically correct since a sorbet should come between the two meat courses).

If the wine is playing an important part in the meal, then many people prefer to have the cheese before the pudding in order to continue drinking the wine served with the main course.

The menu card itself makes useful publicity for the house, as many guests take them as souvenirs. It should be written in English or French but not a mixture of both.

Drinks at receptions

If reception drinks are for cash, their provision and service is no different from the ordinary bar service which is the stock in trade of every licensee. To cope with demand, popular spirits can be prepoured and trayed up behind the bar.

Occasionally, however, reception drinks are inclusive, usually at private parties such as weddings or for company promotions, and difficulties can arise if the estimated quantity proves insufficient. Guests will, in these circumstances, average one drink every fifteen minutes; if a normal range is offered, check on the value of drinks consumed. This can be done by clearing a till and ringing up the value of each drink dispensed even though no cash is

Policy and Operations

taken. At any time, the till can be read to give the cumulative total. An adding machine can be used but a pocket calculator is risky since the total is not printed and consequently is easily cancelled.

If the bar is not in the reception room, waiters or waitresses circulating with trays of drinks afford an easy way to limit consumption without offending guests.

Wine with meals   When possible, the caterer should persuade the host to include the wines. This is easy and less expensive because wine waiters, dispense bars and cash handling are not required. In this case, the wines should conform with the standard practice, i.e.

A dry white wine with hors-d'oeuvre
Dry or medium white wine with fish
Medium white wine, a rosé or a light red with poultry or white meat
Full-bodied red wine with red meat or game
Sweet white wine with sweets or puddings
Port (or red wine) with cheese

In general, inclusive wines should be sound, palatable wines – 'standard' wines, as L. W. Marrison has termed them. Ordinary wines ('plonk') are somewhat down-market for function work, and fine wines would not normally be appreciated.

Service waiters and waitresses can serve the wines, which must be at the correct temperature for service. If two or more wines are served in succession, more of the first wine will be required than of the subsequent ones. A choice of red or white wine can be offered, and this neither slows the service nor increases the total amount consumed.

Cash wines   Almost everyone takes wine at a function, so the sales organization must be fast and efficient. A good wine waiter can usually serve four tables of ten covers under favourable circumstances. The wine list should be short – no more than eight or ten well-chosen still wines plus two or three sparkling ones. Give a brief description of each. Include some of the well-known, heavily advertised wines because guests who do not normally drink wine will go for the familiar name. Hold the wines at the appropriate serving temperature.

Organize and staff the dispense bar to avoid discrepancies and delays. This involves keeping a record of what wines (or other drinks) are issued to each waiter for settlement at the end of the function. The use of duplicate check pads is obvious. Although waiters should be aware that they will not be held responsible for bad debts incurred by guests leaving before settling their wine bill, they should be trained to prevent this.

Speed is important because a frequent complaint of function guests is that they did not get their wine until halfway through the meal. This grievance is aggravated if a party has ordered two different wines to be drunk with successive courses, and each wine arrives one course too late.

Accuracy is important to ensure that every bottle issued is accounted for when the function is over. One way is to insist that wine waiters pay cash with

Functions and outside catering

order at the dispense bar, using either their own money or a float provided by the house. In this method wine waiters act as semi-independent salesmen which gives them the incentive to increase sales (particularly if they 'buy' their wines at a slight discount). No wine is issued on credit, so the pub will not lose. However, there are disadvantages. One is the need for cash handling and cash control *during* the service, rather than a settling-up period after the rush is over. The other is that, because of the monetary incentive, wine waiters may be tempted to indulge in sharp practice.

Function etiquette

Whenever the style of a function requires it, engage the services of a toast-master. These gentlemen are listed in the yellow pages or can be recommended by a satisfied customer. Their knowledge is encyclopaedic, their presence is inimitable and their tact legendary. No licensee should try to emulate the skills of a toastmaster.

Staff instructions

Adequate instructions to staff involved in the function are essential, partly because a function is likely to be a non-routine event and partly because extra staff are usually required. Even when frequent, functions differ from each other in their details. Even a regular team of banquet staff needs to be reminded of procedures.

Kitchen staff The menu and the number of covers and services are obviously vital information. Use a blackboard for the latter two items so that any changes can be easily made and the numbers shown are always up to the minute. Depending upon the respective roles of the caterer and the chef, the following may also be required:

1 A quantity list denoting precisely how much of each item is to be prepared. This may also include delivery details, e.g.
roast sirloin, three strip loins, Woodhouse Hume, Monday 4th
Brussels sprouts, 25 × 900 g (25 × 2 lb) frozen buttons, Brooks, Tuesday 5th.
2 A timetable denoting the starting time of each operation and the time by which it must be completed, e.g.
3.30 chickens into ovens
4.30–5.00 chickens cut into portions and trayed up in twenties
7.00 chickens returned to oven
7.15 chickens dressed on flats, sauced and into hot-plate by 7.30.

If kitchen staff are inexperienced this detail is important since otherwise too many tasks will be left to the last minute or food will be prepared too early and suffer from being kept hot.

Policy and Operations

The kitchen staff should also be ready to produce an omelette and plain ice cream should any guest be unable to eat any dish on the menu.

Food service staff All food service staff must know the menu and be able to describe the dishes in simple but accurate terms if requested.

They must also be certain of their station. Tables of ten are useful because as well as being one kitchen service they allow the station allocation of one waiter per table. When there is an uneven number of covers per table no waiter or waitress should have more than twelve covers, less than eight covers or covers on more than two tables. This calls for precise and detailed allocation of stations, and a second copy of the table plan may be required. On a sprig layout, if the sprigs are not multiples of ten covers, the stations start at the top end of the first sprig and go successively up and down each one.

Staff should collect their food in a specific order – those serving the top table first, then those whose stations are furthest from the servery, and so on – so that those with the nearest stations collect last. The order of service is obvious from the menu, but specific instructions are required as to the time of clearing such items as sauce boats and condiments (and serving items, if family service is used).

Supervise both guests and staff to ensure a smooth running function, e.g. usher guests from bar to dining area on time so that food does not deteriorate. Staff should act as one, serving and clearing in unison on signals given by the supervisor. Warn kitchen staff when one course is being cleared to allow them to finish off the next course prior to service. Delays due to unexpected speeches during a meal must be communicated to the kitchen.

Cloakroom staff At a private function (a wedding or twenty-first birthday party) with a small number of guests, all personally known to the host, it may not be necessary to supervise the cloakrooms, but for other events it is advisable to do so. Use cloakroom tickets (remember the pins) and ensure that articles deposited are stored in strict numerical order for speedy retrieval. If there are two staff, one should receive the articles and give out the receipts, the other should store the items.

Staff in general The need for courtesy should be impressed upon all staff, particularly under pressure, for functions can be hard and worrying work. All staff must understand the need for silence during the speeches; this is often hard to enforce.

All staff should be aware of their terms of work:

Will the banquet staff be required to lay up on arrival?
Are they paid by the hour, or a lump sum for the function? If the latter, until what time must they stay?
Are service staff also expected to serve wine?
If the function finishes late, is a taxi fare home part of the bargain?
Will they be provided with a meal?

Settle these details in advance to prevent misunderstandings during or after the event.

Outside catering

Outside catering for functions is perhaps the most difficult of all branches of catering and affords most opportunities to make mistakes. No caterer should contemplate undertaking one, other than on his own premises, without plentiful experience of in-house function catering and a tried, trusted and enthusiastic team of banquet staff. Given these resources, an ambitious caterer may well be tempted to undertake outside functions and, in spite of the difficulties, it can be a profitable market if assessed and organized correctly.

Costings and quotations The only logical way for a caterer to quote for an outside function is to inspect the site; agree the menu and service required; establish what the cost and selling price would be if the event were held in his own establishment; and then add on the extra costs incurred by providing the same food and service at a different venue. The problems and costs incurred by the change of location are peculiar to outside catering, and these are analysed briefly below.

The venue The venue is the key. If it were not vital to the client he or she would hold the function at the caterer's own premises; the extra costs incurred by catering elsewhere will determine the price quoted by the caterer.

If it is an indoor venue – a church hall, a school hall, a sports club pavilion or some similar building – the caterer must check the facilities for cooking and washing up, which are usually inadequate. He must also ascertain when the premises will be free for setting up; how soon they must be vacated for other use; what security is provided if some items must remain overnight; whether rubbish can be left (suitably bagged) or must be removed; and many other important details. These can only be settled by a personal visit and direct discussion with the relevant person.

An 'outdoor' venue usually means a marquee on the lawn of the bride's father's house, and if the publican has the best reputation in the area for food and service he may well be the host's first choice to 'provide the catering'.

The tenting contractor will hire, deliver, erect, dismantle and collect the marquee, and often the host will handle this account himself. If not, it should be passed direct to him for payment. Drugget is usually included with the marquee but the caterer may want to hire tables and chairs from the same source, on the same bill, in order to reduce his own transport costs.

The need for 'catering space' for dressing food, receiving dirties and similar operations should not be overlooked. The size and availability of the host's kitchen and the ease of access to the marquee site must be verified by a personal visit before deciding upon what food and service can be offered, and before estimating the costs and giving a quotation.

Occasional licence If any liquor is to be *sold* at an outside function, an occasional licence is required, which should be displayed at the point of sale. This requirement would obviously not apply to a wedding reception, but fund-raising activities (such as a cheese and wine party for a local society) where drinks are given out against prepurchased tickets should be treated with caution, as a licence may be required.

Equipment Existing cooking equipment can be supplemented, and if no equipment is available it can be provided. The range of Calor gas items available for hire is extensive and covers all needs from hot cupboards to barbecues. It is possible to hire tables, chairs, linen, mobile bars and virtually everything needed to provide a full service.

Cooking equipment needs to be sited with care in view of its potential fire risk. Trestle tables are generally used, but they must be firm and stable.

In many cases it is possible to arrange for the hired equipment to be delivered direct to the site, and also collected from there. Most breweries will provide the equipment needed for a service of drinks, often without charge, if a substantial drink order is also involved.

Food The menu decided upon determines the equipment required at the site (or vice versa, depending upon the priorities). In general restrict the number of hot items on the menu to one hot dish and coffee; the hot dish should be in the nature of a casserole or 'wet cooked' item.

As much preparation as possible should be undertaken at base, so that only portioning, dressing and garnishing takes place on site. The food can then be transported in bulk, as can the serving dishes. Cold meats can be sliced, salads washed and cans opened in the caterer's own kitchen, which is easier for staff than trying to perform basic tasks in unfamiliar surroundings.

Clearing up Whatever the site, it must be left clean. This involves the collection and bagging up of all rubbish (and possibly its removal). Washing up can be undertaken on site if facilities are available; however, if machine washing up is available at base, an operation is saved if dirties are returned there.

General organization The essential requirement here is for written lists of everything needed for the event: equipment, foodstuffs and liquor. The lists need to be exhaustive, including every minor item, since it is these items which are most easily overlooked. The absence of lemon slices or ice behind the bar; of parsley or watercress for garnish; of a bowl and whisk to whip the cream; or of a block and gavel to announce the toasts are all potential sources of embarrassment to the inexperienced. The lists are also necessary for checking that everything is loaded on to the transport and also that everything is returned after the function.

Conclusion

Catering for a function might be thought of as 'catering in microcosm' because all aspects of catering – food, drink, service, staff, equipment, costings, profitability and so on – are involved in one single event. For this reason, all the contents of this book are relevant to a licensee undertaking function work, and this chapter can only highlight how some of these aspects affect function trade.

The successful function caterer must be an all-rounder, proficient in every aspect of his trade with, in addition, a flair for organization, a strong entrepreneurial streak and more than a dash of showmanship.

Further reading

Small, M. R., *Catering for Functions*, Hutchinson, 1983.
Small, M. R. (ed.), *Buffets and Receptions*, Virtue, 1984.
Taylor, Derek, *How to Sell Banquets*, Northwood, 1979.
The weekly *Caterer and Hotelkeeper* (for function menus).

13 Costing, pricing and control

James Steel

Associated with the vocation of providing food and drink is the science of arithmetic. Those who earn their living by trade owe any success to the adequate recovery of the cost of materials and overheads. No matter how subjective the feelings which inspire a venture, it only makes commercial sense when figures express the value of the business opportunity. Thus, the pub caterer has to see his activities in terms of value as well as quality.

Costing

Costing – the allocation of financial values to materials and services – is arguably the businessman's prime skill. Applying correct values to all a business's components leads to a satisfactory net profit on its statement of account. The three methodical steps to take towards this are to cost, to price and to control.

Although formal means of calculating costs common to catering will be explored, businessmen might only infrequently use actual paper forms. Rather, quick mental calculations might suffice to deal with situations as they arise. Whereas this will be on a regular pattern, there may be little need to fill in forms. Costing should therefore be seen as an essential process and not as a tedious desk task.

Many aspects of catering call for costing, but this does not involve grandiose theoretical application; it is a matter of using common sense in obvious areas. The aim is to facilitate good trading at keen prices and prevent stupid transactions.

To cost, one identifies the components of any activity and, by evaluating them, arrives at a financial expression of the activity so that it may be judged economically.

Pocket calculators relieve the burden of this job, and it does not take much business acumen to identify the elements which form the subject of costing. In the catering trade the main object of concern is the cost of the materials used, i.e. food. Although other aspects of the operation will also be costed, it is this area which most concerns management.

A fundamental notion in costing is that the outcome is expressed as 'per' connotation, e.g. per portion, per batch, per customer and so on. Business expenditure, on the other hand, is reported in the form of expenses: wages, stationery etc. By continuously reporting the costs of units of activity, costing aims to provide management with expenditure information in its most man-

Costing, pricing and control

Figure 42 *Gross profit sheets*

Detail	£	%
Price (sales)		100
Food cost		
Gross profit		

ageable form so that something may be done about specifically identified units comprising an expense.

Gross profit and price

The relationship of food cost to both gross profit and price (and thus sales) should be clearly understood. The gross profit is the balance left from price (or sales) after the cost of materials (i.e. food) has been deducted. The gross profit must therefore be sufficiently large to pay all the operating expenses of the business and leave a net profit adequate to satisfy the capital investment. The gross profit and the food cost are thus complementary, i.e. they both add up to the price (or sales). Further, the price is always taken to be 100 per cent. Therefore the food cost and gross profit can be measured relative to 100 per cent and will complement one another in adding to that figure. Figure 42 is a simple matrix to illustrate the point.

Since the price (or sales) is always 100 per cent, knowledge of any other two aspects of the situation leads to completion of the matrix. For example, if an item has a food cost of 80p and a 66 per cent gross profit is desired from this sale, the complementary nature of the information quickly leads to 33 per cent being associated with the 80p and 100 per cent being calculated as £2.40 and 66 per cent as £1.60 (see Figure 43(a) and (b))

Obviously, as the framework applies to individual dishes, so it may apply to aggregate amounts. By analogy, it can easily be seen that if a day's food cost has been evaluated at £80 and a 66 per cent profit is desired, the sales should amount to £240 and the gross profit would be £160. It is most important that these relationships are understood.

A few minutes' practice with some matrices will quickly consolidate the relationships in the mind. Notice particularly that both food cost and gross profit are expressed relative to the income from price (or sales), and this is the way these components are described in business. Thus one should never claim 200 per cent profit because, of course, that would be impossible; 100 per cent would be the most that could ever be earned. Such a remark is attempting to describe the percentage 'mark-up' of gross profit on material cost.

Figure 43

Detail	£	%
Price (sales)		100
Food cost	80p	
Gross profit		66

(a)

Detail	£	%
Price (sales)	2.40 ←	100
Food cost	80p	33
Gross profit	1.60 ←	66

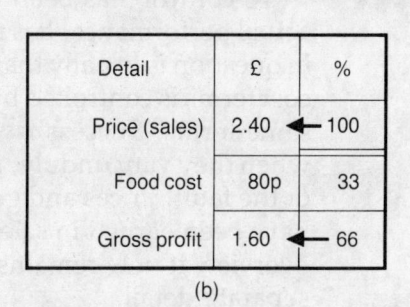

(b)

Policy and Operations

Mark-up Mark-up is the term used to describe a rule-of-thumb which may be used to link both gross profit and price with a known material cost. It is used quite commonly in retailing but can lead to confusion if it is mixed with the complementary relationship discussed earlier. So that it might be understood within the context where it is used, two methods of marking up will be described.

The first is where, given that a food cost is known, the gross profit to be added on to make up the selling price may be evaluated as a percentage of the food cost. Taking the matrix example in Figure 43(a), a gross profit of 200 per cent, i.e. twice, of the cost added to the food cost would result in the selling price of £2.40. Thus the gross profit could validly be described as 200 per cent of the food cost but not of the price, of which it is only 66 per cent. As has been pointed out, the latter is the customary way of expressing the profit percentage.

The second method is where, given that the food cost is known, the selling price may be marked up to either a percentage of the price or by a simple factor. Taking again Figure 43(a), the selling price of £2.40 may be described as 300 per cent of the food cost of 80p. Alternatively, as 300 per cent of something is simply three times it, an arithmetic factor of 3 by which to multiply the 80p food cost would result in a price of £2.40.

Thus there are three different approaches to marking up, two of which involve an expression of percentages of food cost. If the customary proportion-of-price way of expressing gross profit is included then it can be appreciated how confusing the scene can be.

Since businessmen are likely to make use of all four methods, the reader should become conversant with each approach and understand when each is being used. This is all the more so when, as at the time of writing, a popular way of arriving at a selling price is to declare 'three times cost, and two-thirds off'. This simply reflects the example used; the selling price is three times the food cost, and so the resulting profit is two-thirds (66 per cent) of that price. This approach is generally referred to as cost-based pricing. Although somewhat arbitrary and crude because not all dishes can bear the same relative proportion of gross profit (some can bear much higher proportions), nevertheless it is now a common guideline for price fixing.

Control Having established that costs are measures of the input values (notably of food material) of manageable activities such as the production of dishes, and that prices and gross profits are output values associated with these costs, we next consider the control of costs.

'To control' has been defined as the comparison of the planned with the actual performance. It is thus a simple monitoring of events. The performance in question is usually that of cost. A catering activity planned and evaluated in cost terms is controlled by a comparison with the actual event evaluated in the same terms. Success is where the two results agree within tolerable limits; when they vary unduly, management action is called for to correct a repetition of the fault. Prices and gross profits are 'costed' aspects, and so prices should have been earned in sales and the gross profit achieved as a result. From this overview it now remains to examine costing, pricing and control for profit in separate detail.

Costing, pricing and control

Budgeting

Costing may be divided into two types of activity: that which is carried out before the event takes place, and that which is undertaken afterwards.

Costing carried out prior to the event is called budgeting. Budgeting for day-to-day operations is a regular practice of management, and perhaps its most important aspect is to determine the food costs per portion of the dishes to be sold. Formerly, the outcome could be left as a standard cost for a reasonable period. Nowadays inflation forces caterers continually to update costings in tune with the market. The method employed is that of unit costing.

Unit costs These are the cost values of the food sold in units to the customers as portions, either as components of a dish or as the complete dish in itself. An illustrative pro forma is perhaps the easiest way to outline the method, and that shown in Figure 44 is a common version.

Whether the costing is of a single unit (such as a steak) or a portion to be 'cut out' from a batch produced (as in the case of a stew), a simple writing down of the quantities of ingredients used, their extension at cost price and summation to a total enables a portion to be valued. If a single item is being costed then the total will be the unit material cost of the dish. If a batch is being costed, for example a stew or curry, then a division of the total by the estimated number of portions in the batch will result in a unit material cost of a portion of the dish. These unit material costs then become standard costs for the items as long as the present circumstances affecting the items do not change. Snap tests of future production should result in costs which are significantly the same as those standards. Should any test reveal an unacceptable variance from the standards, then review the circumstances as this would be an instance where the actual costs do not match the planned ones. Naturally, this is a constant job for management who should be alert to such deviations at all times.

The bottom two lines of the unit cost pro forma (Figure 44) illustrate the application of the mark-up process through, in this instance, a factor by which to multiply the unit cost. The outcome would be the unit selling price of the item. Further, the subtraction of unit cost from unit price gives the gross profit to be earned from selling the item. A percentage column serves to show the relative proportion that each of the ingredients bears to the total food cost, and would also be used to show the percentage gross profit relative to price.

Profit It is the work of only a few minutes to cost the items on a menu. Having done so, management knows the profit to be made from their sales. Obviously, the best items to sell are those within the comparative classes of starting, main and finishing courses which yield the greatest 'penny profit'.

Although some dishes might yield high relative profits from their selling prices, such prices could be low in penny terms. Other things being equal, it is preferable to receive, say 60 per cent gross profit from a £2.00 sale than 80 per cent gross profit from a 30p sale; £1.20 is a much more attractive receipt to a businessman by way of profit than 24p!

One should not, therefore, get carried away with the prospect of high

Policy and Operations

Figure 44 *Unit cost pro forma*

| Item .... |
| Date of costing ..../........../ 19...... |

Quantity	Unit	Commodity	Unit value	Value	%

Total unit or batch cost

Divide by .... portions = unit cost

Multiply by .... factor = unit price

Difference = gross profit

relative (percentage) profits. Concentrate instead on selling for the highest penny profit; but constantly check that this stays in its due proportion to the item's price.

Inspection of the gross profits expected from a range of dishes on a bill of fare will no doubt lead to the conclusion that the greatest penny profits are to be earned from dishes made on the premises from raw materials, as opposed to ready or semi-ready foods purchased from outside producers.

Economically speaking, catering staff should be fully worked to prescribed limits in order to maximize the output from their labour. This could mean engaging them in preparation and production when they might otherwise be idle.

It is almost inevitable that the food cost of items thus produced will be less than the food cost of equivalent items bought in. Maximum gross profit therefore lies in the sale of self-produced items, and this should be the aim of management.

Of course, where there is a small staff and no spare time to put to good use in production, then the trading of foods ready made by others might fit the bill. The smaller staff would place less demand on the gross profit and so a reduced gross profit flow, because of smaller penny profits, could be quite adequate to pay the wages, meet the overheads, and leave a satisfactory return from catering. In this case the resources are balanced. The earlier point is that it is easy in catering to overlook unbalanced resources by having heavy manning on one hand and poor profit-making items being sold on the other.

Prime cost Caterers often ask, in relation to unit costing, why it is that the labour and other expenses associated with producing dishes are not included in the unit cost computation. The simple answer is that it is usually too difficult a task, involving work study, to calculate and evaluate the time spent on producing specific items. This applies similarly to expenses such as fuel etc., but this is not to say that it cannot be done. Some of the larger catering companies have indeed practised this.

Their method has been to allocate reasonable estimates of work and expenses to dish costings based upon tests, allowing for the absorption of idle or indirect time not directly devoted to cooking. The effect is that by charging in the labour and direct expenses to the cost of a dish, the unit cost is no longer a material cost but a prime cost.

This is the term applied to any cost which includes the three primary elements: materials, labour and direct expenses. As may be imagined, these would comprise a considerable proportion of the selling price, perhaps in the order of 60 or 70 per cent of the price. Firms using this approach could then assess their trading through the margin of profit to be earned by comparative dishes after prime costs have been met. As a refinement to costing, it is perhaps beyond the management aims of licensed house caterers.

The key to successful trading in food lies in a continual examination of unit costs and prices. The portions actually being served should be monitored to make sure that they agree with the underlying specifications of the portion cost, no more and no less than determined, and that at current prices the unit costs would yield the required profit.

Since the perishables markets and the commodity markets in general suffer both varying and increasing unit costs of materials, it is becoming more important for management frequently to review the unit costs and prices of dishes, with the objective of either modifying ingredients to match a constantly held selling price or raising the price according to the costs.

Multiple costs As the name implies multiple costing means taking more than one unit into account when finding out the cost of something. It is no more difficult than unit costing but uses a broader framework to examine the business. Generally it is used in catering in two ways; one to investigate the revenue emanating from sales and the other to appraise the trading position after a short period of operation.

Costing to check revenue

Once unit costs have been calculated they should be fully utilized. It is common for management to utilize their information to check up on the business done after each service or day's operation. Because the number of portions of each dish which is produced are known, and similarly the number of portions left over as unconsumed, it is simple to subtract the latter from the former to find the number of portions of each dish sold.

If this information is evaluated at the selling price of each dish, the outcome is a notional figure of sales revenue which should, of course, be in evidence in the takings. Secondly, if the information is evaluated at the unit cost of each dish, the sum total subtracted from the takings would give a notional value of gross profit earned on the service. This would allow the caterer to assess whether or not the trading has been worthwhile as a means of covering the

Policy and Operations

Figure 45 *Service sales check pro forma*

Menu item	Portions produced	Portions unsold	Therefore portions sold	Unit selling price	Sales value	Unit cost price	Cost value
					Total		

Sales : Cash
Credit

Therefore : surplus (deficit) ... Gross profit
(%)   (%)

expenses of the operation and that it leaves a sufficiently adequate balance to justify the activity.

Figure 45 is a common type of form used to produce this information. It takes account of the credit aspects of food sales which may affect some licensed house operators, so that between cash and credit sales the revenue therefrom should match the notional value of the total units sold under the various categories of dishes. Even bread and butter sold according to individual prices may be accounted for in the form.

One would normally expect the notional value of the sales to equate with the actual sales returned via the cash register and any notes of credit sales, but life does not work quite so accurately. Therefore there would be an expected variance, either a small surplus or a small deficit.

Where the variance is not acceptably small, then further action would be called for to investigate the cause and to stop the same thing recurring in the future. A measure of tolerance in the variance would be its relative magnitude to the notional sales value, i.e. its value as a percentage of it. Up to 1 per cent might be considered tolerable as a surplus or deficit. The overall gross profit percentage would also serve to inform management as to a satisfactory level of profit-taking. This percentage would be the outcome of the mix of sales at various gross profit margins. With the sales check and gross profit information to hand at the end of every service, or day's trading, management would clearly have the operation firmly in hand thanks to a few moments' costing.

Costing to monitor consumption

An extension of the gross profit assessment of a food service period is to undertake a more accurate costing of the materials consumed over a longer period, taking stocks of unused purchases into account. This routine is commonly carried out weekly or monthly by catering firms and is considered an

Costing, pricing and control

essential audit of the catering activity. The aim is to assess the gross profit earned from food sales in a given period. Expressed relative to food sales, the result is known as 'the food percentage' and is the measure against which the business is tested week after week. (Americanized companies prefer to express the food *cost*, rather than the food gross profit, as the percentage of sales for this control.)

In theory the following is the method. Take an inventory of all the food stock in the house and evaluate the component parts of the stock at cost price. Add up the cost value of all the supplies delivered to the kitchen and stores during the course of the ensuing period, e.g. a week. Take a further inventory of all the food stock in the house at the end of the period. By adding the first two values and subtracting the last, arrive at the cost of food actually consumed in the period.

The difference between the cost of the food consumed and food sales in the period is the gross profit from food sales and is expressed as a percentage of it. Given that trading continues on a constant pattern, the food gross profit percentage should be constant. If it varies in any given period, then this is an alarm signal to the management who will take investigative action.

The following is an example:

		£
	Stock of food at start of period	500
(+)	Food purchased during period	1000
	Total available to sell	1500
(−)	Stock of food at end of period	600
	Cost of food consumed	900
	Food sales in the period	2700
	Therefore, gross profit in period (66 per cent)	1800

The difference between this approach and that of finding the gross profit on sales by way of the sales check is that the latter was based upon assumed costs (standard unit cost of items), whereas the gross profit computed as a result of stocktaking and the summation of purchase invoices is based upon reality although the sales check gross profit results are acceptable as tests of performance, they are no more than that. It takes the computation based upon actual consumption to produce a true statement of the case. However, like anyone who works towards an objective, management is all the better informed through the sales check profit measure.

Classification For greater information the purchases figure in the computation may be broken down into a classification which will provide more meaningful information to management. For example, by such means the proportion of meat in total food sales may be monitored with a view to ensuring that it remains at an established level for the type of business transacted. This is illustrated in the example that follows. Furthermore, because the staff of catering houses are customarily fed from the food produced in the establishment, due allowance should be made for this by deduction of an amount estimated to cover the cost of this food.

As it would be unreasonable to expect accurate costings of such staff food to be made, an estimate is used instead, based upon the kind of food eaten by those authorized to do so. The computation in the example shows the effect of

Policy and Operations

this in calculating the gross profit from the actual cost of sales. In the accounts of the business, the amount deducted from the food consumption would be added to the wage expense in recognition of the fact that it is really a form of remuneration.

In the example the classification of purchases into types of food material follows simple lines. In practice, this could be broken down further to accommodate the particular wishes of individual management. For instance, a poultry heading could be separated from that of meat. Also, the closing stock value of one period of operation naturally becomes the opening stock value of the succeeding period, thus minimizing what might appear to be a rather laborious sequence of events.

Included with staff food is entertainment food cost incurred in the course of promoting business. The corresponding accounting charge for this would be the sales advertising account. By removing such non-revenue recovering expenditure from the food consumption, the balance left represents the food actually sold for profit.

Putting all those ideas together, the framework in Figure 46 shows the kind of report management should seek to receive on a regular basis over short periods. Should staff resources not stretch to undertaking the work, the customer audits department of a brewery firm or a trade accountant may carry out the procedure for a reasonable fee.

Closing stock The effects of three aspects of the operation should be noted within the example. First, the effect of having a larger closing stock than that at the beginning of the period results in the purchases figure being trimmed down by the £100 involved. Thus the relationship of total purchases, and indeed each component, is overstated. Therefore proportionate percentages of meat,

Figure 46 *Food percentage report*

Detail		£	%
Purchases in the period:			
Meat		550	26.2
Fish		110	5.2
Vegetables		150	7.1
Dairy and bread		110	5.2
Dry stores items		80	3.8
Total		1000	47.6
Add: opening stock at cost value		500	
		1500	
Less: closing stock at cost value		600	
= Cost of food consumed		900	42.8
Less: staff food estimate	190		
entertainment food at cost	10	200	9.5
= Cost of food sold		700	33.3
Food sales in the period		2100	100.0
Therefore gross profit in the period		1400	66.6

Costing, pricing and control

fish etc. as purchases relative to sales can be misleading because of the stock adjustment aspect.

Appropriately classified inventories of stock would, of course, allow for adjustments to be made to each class and thus give more accurate figures, but this is not widely practised. The crude purchases percentages are read with this in mind. As stock variances will probably be slight, the percentages could act as useful guidelines in the long run.

Staff and entertainment food Second, staff and entertainment food has a considerable effect on the computation. It reduces an apparent cost of food consumed by way of trade to a dramatically different percentage – from 42.8 per cent of sales to 33.3 per cent. Correspondingly, the gross profit percentage has increased by a like amount. Therefore, without this adjustment having been made, the measure of gross profit taken from the customers has been severely distorted. The hiding of real profit could lead to a raising of prices, which might be such a poor exchange for value that customers would resist paying it and take their patronage elsewhere. It is strongly recommended that where there is a significant element of staff food in an operation, the adjustment should be allowed for in the computation.

Short cuts Third, the procedure of taking stock can be so boring that some alleviation of the work can be achieved by (a) assuming that stock levels are constant from period to period, e.g. by taking the time point as Monday morning when stocks could well be at their lowest levels; (b) assuming that some stock is constantly of the same value and taking stock only of those commodities which are liable to fluctuate to a significant degree (e.g. meats etc. in refrigerators) and taking these minimized values into account; or (c) removing dry stores stock from the inventory and treating it as an internal 'shop' supplying the kitchen, with daily requisitions of items being treated as invoices and costed as 'purchases' in the period. Management must decide which, if any, of the above savings in effort would be worth the foregoing of accuracy in the computation.

The inventory

The inventory should be taken at a quiet time when the stock is fairly static. The method is to commence notation at one point in the department and then work systematically round the stock, thus avoiding the pursuit of specific items around the department. The pro forma illustration (Figure 47) provides for a notation space to allow for the sequential noting of stock (such as eggs) which might be held in several places. The inclusion of recurring items on the form cuts down on writing. Classified headings in line with the commodity analysis illustrated in the food percentage report provide for appropriate adjustments to the purchases figures to convert them to those of consumption.

It is unlikely that a series of food percentage reports will present constant figures. Variances call for attention and it is up to management to find their

Policy and Operations

Figure 47 *Food stock inventory pro forma*

Food stock inventory Date ...../...../.....				
Item	Notation	Total	Unit value	Value
Meat Beef: fillet sirloin rump shoulder Lamb: loin shoulder etc.				

causes. When the faults are remedied, the position of future trading will be restored. The technique applied is variance analysis.

Variance analysis The approach is to break down the error into its two main causal parts, those of usage and price. Obviously, if expenditure has been more than that anticipated, it could have been caused either by more of an item being used than is necessary, or else by the anticipated quantity being used but at a higher unit price. To know the former, a planned performance, the usage allowance would have been set according to the recipe for a particular dish. Thus, given the number of portions of that dish sold in the period, the quantity of an ingredient allowed per portion would provide a figure for the total allowance, which may then be compared with the actual quantity consumed and the error detected for future correction.

Similarly, with the price, the unit material cost for the dish would have been calculated on a standard unit cost for the ingredient; therefore an increase in the unit cost charged by the supplier would account for a measure of unanticipated expenditure.

As an example, suppose that the meat component of the commodity analysis in the food percentage report had jumped out of proportion to the extent which aroused the interest of management. An audit of the meat-associated production in the period would lead to a series of analyses along the following lines. The sales checks carried out in the period would provide information about the number of each dish produced during that time. The unit cost of each dish can then be used to produce data to explain the variance.

Example Dish: Cottage pie: meat ingredient, minced beef.
                Usage allowance: 85 g per portion
                Standard cost price: 80p per 450 g
Numbers produced, per the sales check, reported to be 300

Costing, pricing and control

1 *The material usage variance*

Usage allowance = 85 g × 300 portions	25.5 kg
Actual quantity consumed in period per invoices and inventories	27 kg
Therefore	
Multiplied by the standard cost price	80p
Gives the mateiral usage variance	£3.00

2 *The material price variance*

Actual quantity consumed in period	27 kg
Multiplied by the standard cost price	80p
Gives the purchase cost allowance	£48.00
Less: actual cost (say, 27 kg @ 82p)	49.20
Gives the material price variance	£1.20

Therefore the total variance, made up of the usage variance and the price variance, will be:

	£
The effect of consuming extra material	3.00
The effect of paying a higher cost price	1.20
	£4.20

This may be verified by considering that the planned expenditure should have been:

25.5 kg @ 80p = £45

and the actual expenditure assumed in the example:

27 kg @ 82p = £49.20

a difference, being extra expenditure, of £4.20, i.e. the total variance computed and analysed into the two components of £3 usage variance and £1.20 price variance. As the total variance of £4.20 is 9.3 per cent of the planned expenditure, obviously deviations of this magnitude would have serious effects on profitability if they were allowed to continue.

Just as the example dish would be used to show up excess expenditure so would all the meat dishes be investigated in order to produce an aggregate variance. This would account for the deviation which instigated the audit. The information thus provided would be sufficient for management to take corrective action in future production.

In the example case, closer attention to portion weights would be called for in order to correct for the £3 element, but the 2p per kg market price fluctuation might have to be absorbed in the short term. Should the price variance persist or indeed increase, respecification of the dish or a review of the price charged would have to be undertaken.

Variance analysis is not confined to food cost. It can be applied to any aspect of the operation. Management simply notes an intolerable variance from a standard or budget, and then analyses the error so that corrective action may be taken. As usage and cost are the interacting causes of a variance, their separate effects must be identified and assessed for management action. Variance analysis is the uniform method of achieving this.

Policy and Operations

To summarize the technique, costing in catering is carried out to determine the food cost of dishes; to reconcile consumption with sales on a service-by-service basis; to compute the gross profit earned from food sales on a weekly or monthly basis; and to investigate the causes of a variance from planned expenditure in food, wages and other aspects of the operation.

Pricing

Although in many ways a form of costing, pricing relies so heavily on economics that it may be regarded as a separate procedure. The relationship between cost (and its complement, gross profit) and price in the general field of catering was discussed earlier. The approach there was in the form of cost-based pricing whereby knowledge of the cost of an item led, through mark-up rules of thumb, to an evaluation of the selling price. Whereas this approach is simple and, because of widespread use, apparently effective, another form of pricing – consumer based – is worthy of consideration.

Cost-based pricing   This somewhat arbitrary approach depends on average behaviour in the marketplace. Recognized dishes marked up by constant yardsticks are expected to evoke a demand from a sufficient number of customers to yield a satisfactory profit to the entrepreneur. Thus the mark-up produces a price whose supply/demand interaction results in a sufficient volume of trade. Experience and a study of the prices of competitors would lead to the adoption of successful mark-up yardsticks. Although a mark-up factor of three was suggested earlier, thus producing a 66 per cent gross profit rate, this was an overall figure by which to generalize the concept. Various categories of catering items have noticeably different mark-ups which result in different gross profit rates. Some examples might be as follows:

Category	*Factor*	*Gross profit (per cent)*
Starting and finishing courses	5	80
Lighter main meal items	3	66
Heavier main meal items	2.5	60
Vegetables	6	83
Beverages	6	83

These are not suggested either as average figures or as guidelines, but are examples of the different values which could be found in the catering trade. The individual licensed house caterers should ascertain by enquiry the factors and rates of resulting gross profit which apply to the various categories of food in his or her own particular market sectors. Despite an overall gross profit reported in the food percentage costing, several separate factors rather than one blanket one are applied to food costs in the course of pricing. The objective is to establish a series of 'times' factors to give 'off' sales gross profit rates, e.g. from the above:

Five times cost gives 80 per cent off.
Three times cost gives 66 per cent off.

and so on.

Costing, pricing and control

Average price and indifference

The aim of all pricing is to fix a price for an item which will appeal to the average section of the market sector in which it will be sold. An average is usually taken to be a point estimate representing the exact middle of a dispersion. However, it is more realistic to consider the average as representing the middle two-thirds of a market section, expressive of the central tendency to respond to a particular price.

A good price might be considered one to which the average customer responds willingly and to which fellow customers in the market, although evaluating the items slightly differently, are sufficiently indifferent to the margin between to place their custom.

For example, the price of a cup of coffee may be fixed at 18p, to the satisfaction of most of the middle of the market. Although some might value it from, say 15p to 20p, they are sufficiently indifferent to the alternative price to be willing customers. Only if the price were raised to 25p might they take their custom elsewhere.

From this it may be seen that, whereas cost-based pricing is simple to carry out because of the ease of applying fixed mark-ups to specific classes of commodity, it could be too crude a method. There may be more value in a trade-off than the price resulting from a mark-up calculation would yield because of a continuing capacity to be indifferent to an increased price and, as clearly a continuing value exists in such a case, it could be a pity not to take advantage of it. As value is conceived in the mind of the customer, an alternative form of pricing is the consumer-based approach.

Consumer-based pricing

A classic approach to this is by insight probes, questionnaires and other forms of sampling to ascertain the maximum price that could be borne for a product. Such an opportunity is rarely given to licensed house operators and so the alternative could be one of trial and error against a background of the comparative price charged by competitors. In arriving at a balance, to take optimum advantage of a trading situation does not necessarily mean maximizing sales revenue. As the principal business objective is to earn the highest profit from an opportunity, maximized profits are usually more important than maximized sales.

The aim of selling is often associated with low-priced items yielding low rates of profit sold to a great many people. This could result in high revenue but with only a modest proportion of profit. Another entrepreneur might choose to sell for a higher price, bearing a higher rate of profit, to fewer people. The lower comparative revenue could yield much greater profit. As fewer resources by way of labour etc. might be required in the latter case, the net profit resulting could be significantly better and the whole undertaking less hectic than the former.

To demonstrate this point (which is often overlooked or ignored) let us take an example of a dish with a unit food cost of 20p priced to sell at 60p. At that price, a trade of 1000 units is foreseen in a given period. Alternatively, were the dish to be priced at 80p, a trade of 800 units could result. The question is: which of these two prices, or indeed any other price, would give the greatest gross (and by assumption net) profit?

It is therefore suggested that the aim of price fixing is to achieve an economic balance in the operation rather than to sell the greatest number of units to the

Policy and Operations

greatest number of customers. Having said that, once a price has been fixed, all-out selling to the limit of the resources should then be the aim in order to achieve the budgeted number of customers.

Although rules of thumb common to the catering trade may be applied to unit food costs when undertaking pricing, this could be too crude an approach for some managements. Recognition of a degree of indifference in the customer and an interpretation of the likely price elasticity of demand (the extent to which custom will shrink in numbers as prices are raised) could lead to prices which would maximize profit as opposed to revenue.

Control

Control – the monitoring of operations to check that actual performance matches planned performance – has been an underlying aspect of much which has already been discussed. However, systematic control is something which should be a separate function in its own right in catering. Internal control is made up of two elements, check and audit. There is a modicum of the former in the exchange between a table waiter and the cook, where the former checks that the issued food accords with the menu description and the latter checks that the written note customarily associated with such circumstances agrees with the food issued. However, catering control lies mostly in the audit function (an audit is where transactions are verified by review).

In bar catering food is normally exchanged for cash, thus avoiding the need for documentary notes (the waiter's 'check'). The audit would consist of the sales check whereby the consumption of each type of item sold would be translated into selling price terms and summed for reconciliation with cash takings from food per cash register totals or a separate cash drawer. Where food and liquor takings are merged in cash without separate records being kept, cash per the sales check would be abstracted and the residual liquor takings controlled by means of the usual periodic liquor stocktake.

Where licensed house catering is carried out in a dining room or restaurant, the dishes issued should be reconciled with sales by matching food checks with duplicate bills. If paper checks are not employed in this situation then other means, such as the consumption of plates from counted stacks, should be used. If the process is not carried out there is an obvious danger that profit will be lost because issues are not being accounted for.

In turn, duplicate bills should be used to draw up a summary of business according to food, liquor and other sales in the dining room so that appropriate sales accounts may be credited. At this time, analysis into service charge (if applicable) and value added tax would take place in order that the liabilities under these accounts could be recorded. In cash sales circumstances such as bar catering an appropriate deduction from revenue (e.g. 13.04347 per cent in the case of a 15 per cent tax), or divide total sales by 115 and multiply by 15, would separate value added tax from sales income for due recording in separate accounts.

Internal audit Thus the initial internal audit should be practised as soon after service as possible and at a point as close to the actual transaction as possible. As a

Costing, pricing and control

matter of principle, as soon as a contract is entered into (e.g. a food sales order) it should be noted for future audit. As soon as a cash sale is made, it should be recorded on a cash register. After service, this information should be used to verify sales, all items sold having been accounted for in revenue. Each day, the dishes prepared for sale should be reviewed with the object of verifying that their portion dimensions and costs are in line with prices. Especial note should be taken of items whose nature means that their food cost is susceptible to fluctuation because of the market price. If variances are not noticed, profit will be lost.

Periodically the total cost of sales should be related to sales to test that the planned gross profit margins have materialized in actual gross profit. Variances within commodities should be detected through a suitable analysis of raw materials, and variances beyond tolerances set by management should be analysed in order to ascertain if the fault arose through a mismanagement of materials or because of changes in raw material prices.

Statements of account At slightly longer periods, statements of account should be presented for appraisal by management so that planned (budgeted) figures may be compared with actual results. Indeed this is a useful initial exercise for anyone contemplating catering in licensed houses.

Every businessman must make some prognosis of what will happen. By applying average trade statistics to the outcome the volume of business at the evaluated prices may be tested to see if the trade which is deemed feasible would indeed be viable. Overleaf is a pro froma within which the types of dish forming a bill of fare may be listed, associated with the probable unit sales in a period (e.g. a year) and quantified through the selling price in terms of revenue and gross profit. The result is subjected to overhead expense norms evaluated as percentages of total sales. The norms included in Figure 48 as percentages of total sales are intended only to indicate the kind of structure catering has in this context, but it may be that they reasonably represent the business of licensed house catering.

Net profit The food net profit resulting from such a forecast should, of course, be sufficiently attractive to warrant proceeding with the venture. In licensed houses, some might consider it to be simply a contribution profit to the general profit pool of the house and therefore at significantly large figures, worth operating. Others might, through the commitment of capital to the undertaking, want a satisfactory return on capital judged in terms of a percentage of it, for example 20 per cent per annum. In this particular instance a correlation emerges between the capital and the anticipated sales. For a given profit before tax to be 13 per cent of sales on one hand and 20 per cent of capital on the other, the relationship between the two would be that capital is 65 per cent of sales. This kind of correlation is evident in the purchase prices asked in the trade press for licensed houses. Inviting offers at approximately 80 per cent of annual sales, those selling the houses are obviously using correlations whereby the 13 per cent food net profit would satisfy a 16 per cent return on capital under these terms. Where, as is normal in such undertakings, an amount of loan capital is borrowed, then care should be taken to test that the

Policy and Operations

Figure 48 *Budget pro forma with indicative norms*

Menu items	Probable unit sales	Price	Probable sales	Total food cost	Probable gross profit	%
		p	£	£	£	
Total			(100%)			66
Less: Wages						27
Net margin						
Direct expenses						7
Food income						
Administration						4
Heat, light and power						3
Advertising						–
General expenses						3
Food profit						
Repair and maintenance						3
Plant depreciation						3
Property expenses						3
Food net profit (before interest and taxation)						13

net food profit is sufficient to satisfy the interest payment, meet tax levied on the balance and fulfil arrangements regarding the annual repayment of the loan.

Taxation

This feature of commerce has two aspects; profits tax and value added tax. Whereas in practice the caterer relies on professional accountants in relation to tax matters, nevertheless there are broad generalizations which may be applied in relation to an operation.

Profits tax This is levied under Inland Revenue Schedule D on profits from businesses. The inspectorate examines the accounts of the business to ensure that all expenses charged against profit were wholly necessary for the running of the business. If this is not judged to be so, the expenses, or proportions of them, are added back for tax purposes, thereby making the profit greater for taxing at the appropriate rate. The appropriate tax will depend on the nature of the ownership. The catering trade is unique in being allowed to charge all business entertaining (not just that pertaining to foreign customers) against profit.

To stop businessmen minimizing taxable profit by allowing unrestricted depreciation values on plant and equipment against profit, the tax inspector adds back depreciation which has been charged and, instead, capital allowances on plant and equipment may be claimed according to set rates. Light equipment may escape this process (after its initial value has been agreed) through charging annual replacement costs against profit. Buildings do not enjoy depreciation through capital allowances unless they are hotels and offer accommodation involving ten or more rooms, and also satisfy other conditions such as provision of certain meals and opening periods.

Value added tax This is collected on behalf of the Excise at rates prevailing upon specified goods and services. Food, generally, is zero rated and so most invoices would be paid without being subject to tax. Exceptions would be certain items of confectionary. However, sales carry the tax and should be taxed by the caterer at the existing rate.

The income from the tax is separated from sales revenue and accounted for to the Excise authorities on a three-month basis. The time point of the tax is at the moment of sale, and within the three-month period all tax levied is summed. Tax paid on certain food invoices and invoices for overhead expenses is summed and deducted from the incoming tax, and the balance is remitted to the Collector of Excise. Meticulous records should be maintained of these transactions for approval by visiting inspectors.

Increased familiarity with the tax has led businessmen to dispense with the original, rather laborious, method of adding up the sales value of a purchase, perhaps levying a service charge on the total, and then taxing the outcome at the appropriate value added tax rate. Instead, where the nature of sales is such that the value added rate is common, the modern approach is to sell the product inclusive of all taxes. This gives the customer the benefit of knowing exactly the value of the purchase without levies being added and, further, cuts out the need for minute calculations to be made every time there is a sale.

Instead, blanket sums are deducted from aggregate totals so that one calculation stands in the shoes of many. For example, as already mentioned, 13.0437 per cent (or divide by 115 and multiply by 15) deducted from an inclusive total would provide the amount due at a 15 per cent (or divide by 110 and multiply by 10) value added rate; 9.0909 per cent of the balance would provide the amount due to staff for service charge levied at a 10 per cent rate; and the residual balance would be the actual sales revenue. The first two amounts would be credits to the liability accounts of the Excise authorities and staff respectively, and the residual balance would be a credit to the sales account.

In conclusion a sound management policy should be founded on consumer-based pricing supported by frequent unit costings and controlled by daily sales checks, weekly gross profit percentage checks and interim summary operating statements prepared from the accounts of the business.

Further reading

Kotas, R., *An Approach to Food Costing*, Hutchinson, 1980.
National Economic Development Organization, *A Standard System of Catering Accounts*, HMSO, 1978.
Neil, A., *Running your own Hotel*, Hutchinson, 1982.
Steel, James, *Control in Catering*, Hutchinson, 1980.
Walton, Peter, *Modern Financial Accounting in the Hospitality Industry*, Hutchinson, 1983.

… Part Three

Meal Service

14 Snackbars, counter and informal service

Brian Cheesman

Material from G. A. Cromack, Peter Hime and Nigel Pullan is included in this chapter.

Food service can be divided into:

Service provided at table or counter: examples include restaurants, steak bars, grill and griddle bars, pizza and fast food operations and counter service buffets.

Self-service: examples include hot and/or cold buffet and cafeteria services.

Choice of service depends on local demand, speed of customer turnover, available space, the initial cost of installing equipment and local staff availability. Many houses find that two types of food service complement each other, particularly at lunchtime where customers with limited time use counter service and others seek restaurant service.

Pubs usually choose one of the following three approaches:

Counter service Counter service for snacks and sandwiches ordered and collected by customers from the bar (see Figure 49). Many pubs maintain a separate food bar to avoid congestion with drinks service. There may be a seating area for customers wishing to eat.

Simple waiting service Food is ordered at the bar. The customer's seat position is noted so that the food and cutlery can be brought when ready. This informal service is often thought preferable to issuing a numbered ticket when the customer pays for his food (this number being called out when the order is ready for collection).

Separate restaurant Some up-market pubs may seek the style of top class restaurants with full waiter/waitress service. This is considered further in the next chapter.

Informal service

A restaurant may not be suitable for a licensed house, which may find it impossible to provide the appropriate space. Also, the pool of local staff may not yield qualified or skilled employees. High investment in equipment and an increased wage bill for the larger number of skilled staff often indicate an alternative method of food service.

Licensed houses realize how food sales add to profit and few establishments ignore such sales. Most pubs opt for informal food service either from a counter or to tables occupied by customers already drinking.

Tables in the bar itself may be used for this service, or a separate area may be

Meal Service

Figure 49 A typical pub food display in a Charrington pub
Courtesy Charrington & Co. Ltd, Brewers. Photograph by LPA International Photo Services Ltd

cordoned off from the bar for the consumption of food. The aim is to avoid the formality of a restaurant and to give customers a value for money meal in a pub atmosphere.

Traditional public houses or coaching inns make ideal surroundings with their wooden beams and low ceilings. This type of effect is created in many newer public houses; but informal service can be offered in almost any public house.

'Informal service' may call to mind sandwiches or a ploughman's lunch, but the possibilities are endless. Many licensed houses operate steak bars, grill and griddle bars, pizza and fast food counters as well as those for snacks and buffets (see Figure 50).

Steak bars

Steak bars offer a good percentage return, especially as the number of staff involved is low when measured against the number of customers who can be served. A couple of waitresses can serve sixty or more customers during a service period, thus keeping the wage bill down. The type of service is usually plated with a menu tailored to suit.

Snackbars, counter and informal service

Steak bar menus A steak bar's restricted menu (to avoid carrying a large food stock) might be: soup or prawn cocktail; rump, sirloin, T-bone steaks; fried plaice; chips, two salads; apple pie, cheesecake and coffee. The following is a more extended example:

Starters
- Selection of fruit juices
- Chicken, mushroom or tomato soup
- Prawn cocktail
- Chilled melon

Grills
- Entrecôte steak
- Rump steak
- Lamb cutlets
- Gammon steak and pineapple

All grills are accompanied by French fried or baked jacket potatoes, grilled tomato, mushrooms, peas, and/or salad.

Sweets
- Choice of ice cream
- Peach Melba
- Pear Belle Helene

Cheese and biscuits
Coffee

Such a standard menu could also allow for house specialities if applicable. One touch is to vary dish names to suit the establishment, as at a Devon pub where the vegetable soup is called 'Nobody Inn Soup'; however, in these cases describe the dish to avoid confusion.

Figure 50 *Barnaby's at The Telegraph, Putney Heath*
Courtesy London Hosts

Meal Service

From the service point of view, this type of menu is easy for staff to master with only minimal training. With the addition of simple starters and sweets, financial return may be improved easily.

Controlling simplified operations Payment may be made while ordering (but this is not popular with customers), or drinks and food may be paid for separately. Menu variety may be enhanced by set speciality menus as is done for functions. This increases trade and reduces cost because no menu reprinting or redesigning is necessary except when prices increase. Christmas is a time when daily customers accept a range of specialized menus as they find themselves incorporated into a 'function' atmosphere.

Further customer incentives are discounts and wine and food vouchers.

Steaks are already portion controlled to exact sizes by specification. Tills itemize all food and liquor commodities. Other items may be controlled by equipment of standard size so that staff find it difficult to be careless. Some service aspects (which also apply to other operations) include:

Exploring with an experienced equipment supplier the kind of utensils to help control size and presentation

Plates of uniform size so they are neither overfilled nor appear disappointingly meagre

Fostering wine sales, as customers tend to accompany a steak with wine

Cooking in front of customers; and although issues are made before service begins, most items go to a secondary refrigeration area so that they appear and taste fresh

An intentionally compact kitchen area to minimize movement by preparation staff

Regarding a well-run steak bar as almost a fast food operation

Maintaining an informal but well-themed eating area for a well-established identity

Minimal general training because planning has so ensured outlines that aids control

Cutting out variation so that the operation will not be queried or jeopardized.

Accompaniments In the small eating area needed for a steak bar, the limited number of accompaniments may be included in the table lay-up so that separate sideboards are not required. As plated items go straight to table, all reserves of china and cutlery may be kept behind the scenes.

Accompaniments such as brown bread and butter for the prawn cocktail form part of the presentation of the dish, so that the only service equipment needed is a tray to carry the food from kitchen to dining room. Preparation of the room consists of cleaning and laying up of tables.

Disposables Disposables like plastic utensils and attractive paper plates and napkins can be used in pubs. Wicker baskets for disposables are retrievable but should be kept clean and replaced when they start to look shabby.

Condiments and sauces Tartare, tomato and brown sauces and salad cream in individual sachets are useful in pub trade, as are wrapped portions of butter, biscuits and various cheeses. However, a generous portion of *fresh* cheese should always be served for a ploughman's lunch together with sweet pickle or pickled onions, French bread or cottage rolls. Bread and rolls should be served hot.

Grill and griddle bar

Many licensees and breweries may decide that the steak bar market in a particular area is fully catered for and may offer an alternative type of menu. Many customers may prefer a wider selection. Care must be taken not to be over-optimistic and make menus too comprehensive and complicated to cook and serve easily. A typical menu of dishes might be:

Starters
    Selection of fruit juices
    Chicken, mushroom or tomato soup

Fish
    Fried cod in batter
    Fried plaice

Grills
    Mixed grill
    Grilled lamb chops
    Grilled gammon and egg
    Grilled pork chop
    Bacon, egg and sausage
    Grilled minute steak
    Grilled chicken and bacon
    Hamburger

    All grills are accompanied by French fried or baked jacket potatoes, grilled tomato, mushrooms, peas and/or salad

Sweets
    Selection of ice creams

Coffee

Cold buffet

A cold table and a salad bar encourage impulse buying. If there is a space for a generous visual display of cold fare then it should become a popular attraction. A slection of roast beef, turkey, chicken, ham and tongue, carved to order, and cold pies (steak and kidney, veal and ham, game and gala), with customers helping themselves to a well-displayed variety of salads, gives people something to talk about and enjoy.

The following, each dressed appropriately, are suitable for a salad bar:

Potato	Savoury rice
Mixed vegetables	Egg mayonnaise
Coleslaw	Mustard pickles
Pickled red cabbage	Sweet pickles

Meal Service

Cubed beetroot
Baked beans
Sliced mushrooms
Mandarin segments
Cucumber
Shredded cheese
Sliced red and green peppers
Sweetcorn

Plumped currants and raisins
Grated raw beetroot and carrot
Tomato
Sliced frankfurter sausage
Potato and chopped fried bacon
Butter beans
Lettuce

If space does not permit a full table display the pub can still make a speciality of cold platters.

Snacks

The pub service of snacks is important. They may be brought to the table or served over a special counter. Merchandising by using a display cabinet is considered later in this chapter. The top of the display might form part of the counter, allowing staff plenty of work room.

Bar counter food service falls into three main categories: cold items, hot items or a mixture of both. The simplest cold snack is a sandwich, sausage roll or filled roll. Even these must be well displayed, look fresh and attractive and be served on a paper napkin and plate together with a knife. Pickles, cruets and accompaniments such as mustard should be available.

The greater the variety of snacks, the more need for a display sited on the bar or at the back. For cold buffets and salads, plates can be made up for the customer with meat and poultry being preportioned or carved to order. As space is at a premium on the counter, separate salad plates may be unsuitable and the whole meal should be plated and passed to the customer.

Hot buffets

Using special equipment, hot food can also be put on display. Overhead infrared lamps enhance the appearance of the dishes, as well as keeping them hot.

Eye appeal is a potent force, and it is always preferable to display bulk dishes of such lines as steak pies, hot pots, cottage and fish pies, curries and rice, sausages and mash, faggots and bubble and squeak from which customers can make their choice.

For hot food, hot plates may need to be carried on trays. Plastic cutlery is sometimes supplied for cold food but this should be avoided for hot food which usually requires something more substantial. If space is at a premium, meals may be plated in a rear kitchen; but food then needs greater advertising since there is no display.

Self-service

Several different forms of self-service may be introduced where volume of trade demands it. Cafeteria self-service could be employed in a snack bar or similar situation within a public house, for example, which deals with travellers from a busy main road. Only limited numbers of staff are required behind the counter and the customer may select hot or cold dishes for himself. There is little service needed other than providing trays and cutlery.

An important feature in cafeteria self-service is cleanliness of the eating area. Tables must be cleaned regularly and cleared of used cutlery and crockery; the trays should be neatly stacked or returned to the pick-up point. Keep the floor clean and ashtrays emptied.

Self-service can also be effectively applied up-market as a buffet from which customers help themselves at lunchtimes. Also, in the evening, daily buffet specialities may be served. The customer might help himself for an inclusive price or a member of staff may carve and plate meat. A strict watch needs to be kept on portions.

With all types of self-service, any food servers must be clean and tidy and use the correct, clean equipment for handling the food. Presentation of dishes should be appetizing and attractive.

Fast food competition

The pub snack market presents a challenge for enhancing your reputation and increasing profits as food and drink retailers. The pub food market is fast growing and many pub sites are envied by other entrepreneurs. To maintain or increase our place in food retailing, we must compare favourably with our competitors.

The success in our high streets of fast food retailers, many from overseas franchise operations, is partly due to identifying and fulfilling a market need – catering for those with little time during their lunch break or any other time. It offers attractively decorated establishments with fast, efficient service in a congenial atmosphere.

Presentation and product quality are important. No matter how attractive the premises, if food does not look and taste good, customers hesitate to come back.

Pubs have several advantages in competing with these other operations. Your premises are licensed; the majority of high street operations are not. Take advantage of this. Stricter legislation governing the dispensing of food and beverages has ended the days of simply displaying items of food on hot trays on counter tops or the curled up sandwich heaped on a china plate. Take advantage of these new laws when designing your snack bars, bearing presentation in mind.

Siting the service

Peter Hime has pointed out:

If you locate either the restaurant or the snack bar in a second-rate position, you will get second-rate revenue and profit. Have the courage of your convictions and site them to make it easy for customers to buy. Check that customers know what price they are going to pay, and that the environment is right for eating either a full meal or a snack. This includes clean cutlery, napkins, condiments and other accompaniments,

Meal Service

as distinct from one pot of salt and pepper and mustard between six tables and a snack bar. Dress the bar positively to show that you expect customers; and customers will come to you.

Packaging

Packaging aims to eliminate all negative selling aspects of any situation.

Just as there is no value in creating a product that will not sell, so there is no merit in selling a product that makes no profit. A loss leader is simply a product that makes less profit than others. It is normal that food gross profit expected in a snack bar is no higher than 50 per cent overall. This does mean that some products will be sold with no more than a 20 per cent gross profit mark-up, so that a variety of products can be created to give regular customers a choice. This also enables a more effective display on the snack bar counter to create maximum impact.

The principal concept behind the development of a snack bar trade is to create a greater volume of consistent trading revenue throughout licensing hours. The cost of good snack bar equipment is such that there is little point in equipping premises unless you are confident of achieving a bar snack revenue which shows an adequate return on the investment.

Cold display counter

Letting customers know what they are getting can be achieved by presentation within a cold display counter. The best type is a delicatessen case – a glass-fronted display case on the customer side, with an open back to the rear. This allows access for the operator, with a good quality cutting surface at the back. Many counters come with no base, and need to be sited on a pedestal; some are free standing with refrigeration below. This alleviates the operator's need to keep returning to the kitchen to top up various dishes.

Display case siting needs study. Ideally, it should be in a part of the counter on full view to customers entering the pub, and so positioned that it does not interfere with liquor sales. For example, food service from a display case in the middle of a counter could get interference from a cross-flow of liquor service staff at the rear of the counter. An ideal position is at the end of a counter. Which end is determined by, for example, allowing:

Customers a better view of the cabinet on entering the pub.
Staff ease of access to the kitchen
Customers' access to service point without bottlenecks.

Display factors   A bar area can be as little as 1.828 m (6 ft) in length for display and service. Limited but good food is obviously imperative; so pay attention to work flow and menu sequence. Starters should be followed by the main course and then sweets. It is unwise to display starters and sweets together in one area followed by main course items. Ensure an adequate area for the service of cutlery, serviettes, plates and condiments.

Snackbars, counter and informal service

To take advantage of a cabinet's display potential, it must be kept full. Pay attention to colour. Half empty cabinets can be a disaster. Operators complain of a lack of foodstuffs to present within their cabinet because, among many causes, they have been let down by their food supplier not turning up on time, or they have had a busy weekend with no delivery until Tuesday.

Seek to keep the cabinet attractively filled. It is an efficient form of refrigeration, and your back-up fridges can often yield items to make all the difference to a stark display. Lettuces, oranges, apples, tomatoes, lemons, cucumbers, whole cauliflowers, carrots, courgettes, marrows or any greengrocery items help create colour whether or not they are for consumption.

Requirements may vary from area to area, but tasks are becoming 'internationalized' through the influence of fast food operations and travel abroad.

Meat Many contend that no pub cold food operation would be complete without cold meat salad. But should you buy meat presliced or whole? On or off the bone? Too many cold meat products take up much space in the cold cabinet and are not easy to control in terms of portions. Concentrate on one type of meat; but vary it from week to week.

Ham and pork The ideal hams for cold counters are shaped, whole, boneless hams, glazed, breaded or plain, displayed on a ham stand on an oval platter. Preslice a quantity, arrange in overlapping slices around the base of the ham stand, garnish with a little lettuce, a piece of tomato or wedge of lemon, rather than remove the whole ham every time a ham salad is required. Any whole joint can be metal skewered with a number of colourful vegetable items including lemon wedges, whole tomatoes, radishes, cucumber barrels etc.

Beef Probably the next most popular joint is beef, especially forerib and topside. Topside is cost effective for it is easier to slice and cheaper to buy. Forerib makes for better presentation but is generally more expensive and presents a harder portioning task. For either of these, apply the presentation previously described.

Pork Leg pork is the ideal joint for counters, purchased as either a half or a whole leg or cut into even smaller joints.

Pies, flans and pâtés
Pies Several companies specialize in this product. The ideal is the traditional hand-raised pie, approximately 178 mm (7 in) in diameter and 102 mm (4 in) deep. This, if you have the facilities, is relatively easy to produce home-made in different combinations.

Hand-raised pies from wholesalers include chicken and ham, turkey and game. Cut them into twelve good wedge-shaped portions, but do not preslice until you know your trade potential. If you do preslice for ease of service, a good selling technique is to withdraw one slice and display it on top of the pie towards customers who can thus see the content. Remaining slices, if presliced, should be kept tightly packed within the pie to avoid drying. The first

Meal Service

slice served should be the presentation one, then another withdrawn for presentation and so on.

Savoury flans or quiches   The many varieties now available are excellent for display. The ideal quiche is 305 mm (12 in) in diameter, generally yielding a good sixteen portions when served with a full salad. This popular pub snack can also be served hot. Under refrigeration it should last three to four days.

Pâté   The most common of different purchasable styles is the terrine, i.e. the round or oblong earthenware container in which the glazed pâté is topped with some form of decoration. Others can be purchased in cryovac, i.e. a block of pâté vacuum packed without the terrine; this facilitates service and portion control. Pâté can be served in different styles:

Simply with a salad
With hot toast or hot garlic bread
With French bread with a salad garnish.

Seafood   Some licensees specialize in seafood, devoting their cold cabinet to this one product.

A simple seafood platter, or fisherman's platter, may be a round or oval plate, garnished with lettuce and cucumber and offering a variety of seafood. Platters can consist of flaked, smoked mackerel, a rollmop herring, a small quantity of prawns, three or four mussels and a scoop of fish mousse or a smoked fish pâté. To prompt impulse purchase, make up one platter only to display in your cabinet, detailing its content and its price on a nearby blackboard or menu card. Serve the item on display first and then replace each time with a new one. Other seafood items (popular with the weight conscious) are smoked salmon mousse, taramosalata, smoked mackerel fillets and smoked fish pâté.

Charcuterie   As far as possible leave continental sausages whole and cut to order. This avoids drying up of precut slices. Popular types of salami used in public houses include Italian, Danish and French, square, round and peppered (there is a vast range). Liver sausages may have a white fat skin that is edible or a man-made skin which needs to be peeled off. A mixed sausage platter made up with a choice from the above, and Mortadella sausage and numerous others, can be offered. Space permitting, make up a plate prior to service for cabinet display.

Other snacks   Other items for cabinet display include gala pie, Scotch eggs, cold pasties, hard-boiled eggs, cold pizza pie, brawn and made-up meat salads, i.e. strips or cubes of cold ham and cold beef that have been trimmed from a cold joint. These can be mixed with celery cubes, peanuts, cheese, apple and onion dressed with a vinaigrette dressing, and make an excellent way of disposing of leftover meats.

Snackbars, counter and informal service

Salads Cabinet display items need salad support. Many made-up salads can be purchased, but if you have time and facilities they can be home assembled as well if not better. They also help dispose of surplus foodstuffs. Two favourites, i.e. potato salad and coleslaw, can be home-made more cheaply than if purchased outside; potato salad in particular is invariably superior, if homemade.

To ease service, preplate and stack salads in advance by using plastic plate rings. A basic salad may consist of lettuce, tomato, cucumber, coleslaw and potato salad. Avoid beetroot, for its colouring may spread into other salad items and mar display. As plating each salad individually at a peak period causes delay, keep these preplated salads in refrigerated storage beneath a chilled cabinet until required. When a customer asks at the counter for a piece of pie or slice of quiche, remove a salad from beneath the cabinet and plate the portion to hand to the customer.

Any other salads in your cabinet can be at an extra price per portion over and above the cost of the basic salad, i.e. the salad plus the main item. Although they add colour, avoid stocking too many alternative salads as this could be wasteful.

Alternative salads, of many types made on the premises, could include: rice and fruit; corn and mayonnaise; pepperoni salad with red and green peppers in a vinaigrette dressing; Russian salad; and pasta salad, i.e. a salad from macaroni or the shell pastas bound in mayonnaise with finely chopped onion.

Overall presentation When you get to know products that sell well, place them for ready replacement and easy service. Place slower selling items deeper into the cabinet as access to them is not so frequent.

Do not leave bare spaces in cabinets but fill them with vegetables and salad items as indicated earlier. When dressing your cabinet, come to the other side of the bar and see from a customer's point of view how your display is developing.

Pubs with a busy lunchtime snack trade use their cabinet as a selling aid. If you have plenty of worktop and extra refrigeration, consider stocking a second item under the counter. This maintains an attractive display throughout the service period; however, the customer prefers an item that he has ordered to come fresh from your refrigerated display.

Hot snacks

Hot items may not be so extensive as cold but a pub should consider having three hot dishes each day. If you specialize in a particular hot dish, one may well be on every day.

Pizza Pizzas are an example of a common feature and only require a microwave oven for rapid cooking. An infinite number of garnishes may be added to the base and make an excellent speciality.

Hot foods may be bought in multiportion frozen entrée or home-made. If you or your cook has flair you may produce your own, but for ease of service and

Meal Service

cost control it is hard to beat the multiportion entrées now available. If going down the frozen road, here are a few tips:

Never present in original foil containers. Remove from the container while the product is frozen and place in an earthenware dish. These dishes are available from most frozen food manufacturers or catering utensil suppliers. Do not put this earthenware container straight into a hot oven, as the cold product inside and heat on the outside can crack the dish. Let it stand for one or two hours before placing in the oven.

Decide beforehand how many portions to get from each of these dishes and cost your menu accordingly. If you can score the top of the pie prior to cooking, this forms a guide to exact portion control.

Decorate the product. For example, garnish shepherd's pie round the edges with layers of sliced tomato with a sprig of parsley in the middle. Decorate a fish dish with slices of lemon and so on.

Consider the use of microwave heating for frozen and non-frozen food.

Home-made food   Correctly cost each of your own hot food dishes prior to cooking and decide how many portions you are able to get from it. Divide this number of portions into the overall cost to get a cost price per portion. Then calculate selling price to achieve the required gross profit. Do not forget to add on VAT, or to include all sundry items in your cost such as salt, pepper, brown sauce, ketchups, mustard etc. (Perhaps allow a fixed amount per portion to cover sundries.)

Are you going to display hot food in front of the customer or call it up from the kitchen? The former helps the eye sell the product. You must, however, consider hygiene and health. Products must be thoroughly heated and protected from the public, i.e. by a sneeze screen, to stop contamination from ash, smoke etc. Invariably this is a stainless steel hot tray with a sneeze glass in front of it and two infrared lamps suspended over the food. Food will then be heated from below and above, maintaining the required temperature.

Try to serve a selection of vegetables. However, if space does not permit, try individual bowls of mixed salad, especially with casserole dishes or even hot rice dishes.

Price display

Display equipment in itself is a selling aid, but you still need to price and display prices of available dishes. Do this with neatly printed menus around the bar area and a sign-written display board positioned near the food. This can list items that appear daily and can incorporate a blackboard for specials to be chalked in as they change (see Figure 51).

Small plastic flags within cold cabinets identify what is available and speed service by obviating the need for enquiries about items and causing a queue.

Sandwich guidance

Sandwiches should be freshly made; frozen or chilled ones are not successful. In advance, fillings can be prepared, butter softened for spreading, bread

Snackbars, counter and informal service

Figure 51
Courtesy Charrington &
Co. Ltd, Brewers.
Photograph by LPA
International Photo
Services Ltd

sliced and rolls cut; then sandwiches can be made to order. Chicken and turkey sandwiches should not be made from chicken or turkey roll but from the real item. Smoked salmon and prawn sandwiches should be prepared with brown bread. (See Chapter 21 for further suggestions.)

To avoid wastage, which can be high, encourage methodical work. Specifically:

Determine your range of sandwiches, i.e. maximum number in variety and actually made.

Pay attention to season; determine the range of bread/rolls; check your selling price limit.

Establish daily orders for bread, rolls and portioned packs for sandwich filling requirements.

Monitor durability carefully by adequate refrigeration and cooled display units.

Determine the equipment required for display purposes. Limited service gear is needed: sideplates, knives, forks, condiments and serviettes.

Determine each cost item by defining quantities required in grams or ounces.

Bring in staff prior to peak selling times to minimize delay in actual cash sales.

Establish control by till receipts.

Food in wine bars

Nigel Pullan points out:

One reason for the success of wine bars is that they set out to attract people by offering a good choice of well-cooked, well-presented food, served in a friendly informal atmosphere. It is doubtful if wine bars could succeed on the scale they do unless good food was also available.

Meal Service

His notes on wine bar food follow.

The style of food can vary from simple but well-made home-cooked dishes such as pâtés, quiches, cheeses and salads collected and paid for at a counter, to full-scale restaurant type meals with a choice of hot or cold food served at the table.

Variations depend upon location, space, kitchen facilities and local demand together with the particular skills and inclinations of those running the wine bar. In the simpler format with limitations of space and therefore staff, the selection might include:

A choice of three pâtés: perhaps chicken liver pâté, a terrine and a fish pâté
Smoked mackerel or kipper fillets
Two quiches: perhaps a quiche Lorraine and a spinach quiche
Cold ham
Cold turkey
An additional interesting cold dish such as a home-made **meat** loaf or chicken in aspic
A range of salads served by the portion, at least some of which might include the more interesting flavours and textures such as celery, apples, nuts, peppers etc.
A selection of English and continental cheeses, French bread. Good French bread is perhaps the single most essential item to be served apart from the wine itself.

Additionally, if space allows, a hot fork dish is always popular; examples include moussaka, lasagne, coq au vin, meat balls, fish pie etc.

Figure 52 shows sample wine bar menus. This type of menu could easily be prepared daily by two experienced and enthusiastic people using fresh food, with all the cooking being done on the premises. If lack of staff or space demands, then many items can be bought in including pâtés, cooked hams, quiches and even salads. Though the quality of food available for buying in has improved and there are a number of small caterers specializing in supplying wine bars, delicatessens and other semi-specialist outlets, there is never the same appeal as there is with food that can genuinely claim to be made on the premises.

Some wine bars with greater space and, in particular, those situated in city centres where there is a high business population, run a more elaborate food operation, probably employing a chef and assistant and various other kitchen staff. Here food and service is on restaurant lines with the food and wine served at the table. Such places, though called wine bars, usually have a 'full' licence to serve drinks other than wine, but the drink emphasis would still be on wine with perhaps a real ale or lager offered as the only beer.

For the business community, many larger wine bars have made a speciality of steaks and grills. Steaks introduce the controversial issue of chips, which are an obvious accompaniment but are alien to the wine bar image. Jacket potatoes can be a viable and popular alternative.

Concludes Nigel Pullan:

A larger type of wine bar might have two distinct areas. A bar or counter would serve wine and food, and in another separate part, perhaps on a different floor, there would be a restaurant serving a choice of hot food as well as cold. This affords an opportunity to sell a bigger selection of wines including some more expensive ones.

Snackbars, counter and informal service

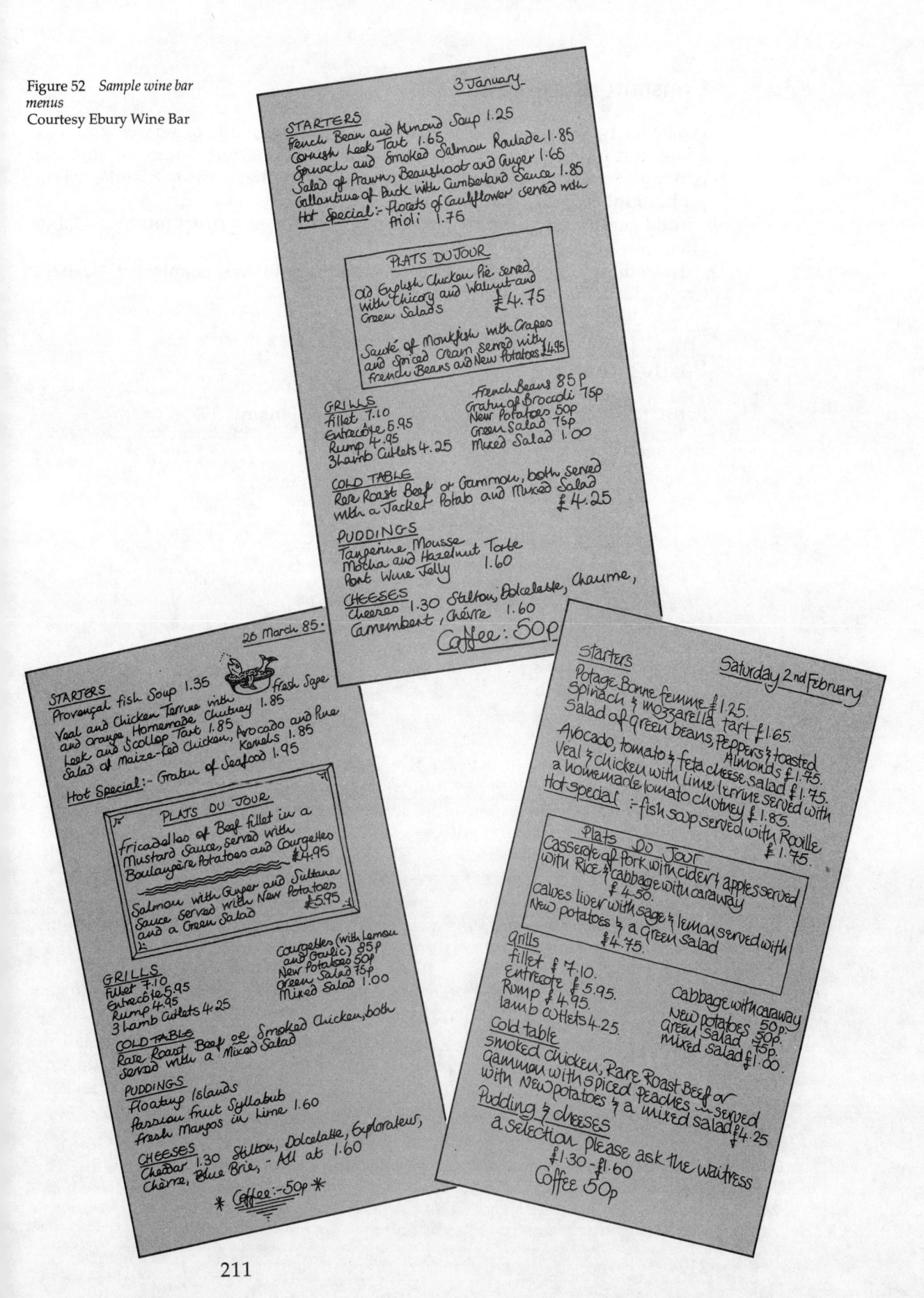

Figure 52 *Sample wine bar menus*
Courtesy Ebury Wine Bar

3 January

STARTERS
French Bean and Almond Soup 1.25
Cornish Leek Tart 1.65
Spinach and Smoked Salmon Roulade 1.85
Salad of Prawn, Beanshoot and Ginger 1.65
Galantine of Duck with Cumberland Sauce 1.85
Hot Special:- Florets of Cauliflower served with Aioli 1.75

PLATS DU JOUR
Old English Chicken Pie served with Chicory and Walnut and Green Salads £4.75
Sauté of Monkfish with Grapes and Spiced Cream served with French Beans and New Potatoes £4.95

GRILLS
Fillet 7.10
Entrecôte 5.95
Rump 4.95
3 Lamb Cutlets 4.25
French Beans 85p
Gratin of Broccoli 75p
New Potatoes 50p
Green Salad 75p
Mixed Salad 1.00

COLD TABLE
Rare Roast Beef or Gammon, both served with a Jacket Potato and Mixed Salad £4.25

PUDDINGS
Tangerine Mousse
Mocha and Hazelnut Torte
Port Wine Jelly 1.60

CHEESES
Cheeses 1.30 Stilton, Dolcelatte, Chaume, Camembert, Chèvre 1.60

Coffee: 50p

26 March 85

STARTERS
Provençal fish Soup 1.35
Veal and Chicken Terrine with fresh Sage and orange Homemade Chutney 1.85
Leek and Scallop Tart 1.85
Salad of Maize-fed Chicken, Avocado and Pine Kernels 1.95
Hot Special:- Gratin of Seafood 1.95

PLATS DU JOUR
Fricadelles of Beef fillet in a Mustard Sauce, served with Boulangère Potatoes and Courgettes £4.95
Salmon with Ginger and Sultana Sauce served with New Potatoes and a Green Salad £5.95

GRILLS
Fillet 7.10
Entrecôte 5.95
Rump 4.95
3 Lamb Cutlets 4.25
Courgettes (with lemon and Garlic) 95p
New Potatoes 50p
Green Salad 75p
Mixed Salad 1.00

COLD TABLE
Rare Roast Beef or Smoked Chicken, both served with a Mixed Salad

PUDDINGS
Floating Islands
Passion fruit Syllabub
Fresh Mangos in Lime 1.60

CHEESES
Cheddar 1.30 Stilton, Dolcelatte, Explorateur, Chèvre, Blue Brie, - All at 1.60

* Coffee:- 50p *

Saturday 2nd February

Starters
Potage Bonne femme £1.25
Spinach & mozzarella tart £1.65
Salad of Green beans, Peppers & toasted Almonds £1.75
Avocado, tomato & feta cheese salad £1.75
Veal & chicken with Lime Terrine served with a homemade tomato chutney £1.85
Hot special:- fish soup served with Rouille £1.75

Plats Du Jour
Casserole of Pork with cider & apples served with Rice & cabbage with caraway £4.50
Calves liver with sage & lemon served with New potatoes & a Green salad £4.75

Grills
fillet £7.10
Entrecôte £5.95
Rump £4.95
lamb cutlets 4.25
Cabbage with caraway
New potatoes 50p
Green salad 75p
Mixed salad £1.00

Cold table
Smoked Chicken, Rare Roast Beef or Gammon with Spiced Peaches - served with New potatoes & a mixed salad £4.25

Pudding & cheeses
a selection please ask the waitress
£1.30 - £1.60
Coffee 50p

211

Constant reappraisal

Whatever type of food you prepare and whatever mode of service you may adopt, it is important to analyse the results of your effort. For example, have you considered sales per unit area compared with that of the bar, and is this in proportion?

Food service must not be considered in terms of a ritual but as a tool in effectively selling your product.

The editor acknowledges the contributions to this chapter of Graham Cromack, P. Hime, J. J. Morel and Nigel Pullan.

Further reading

Bertram, Peter, *Fast Food Operations*, Barrie & Jenkins, 1975.

15 Formal dining service
Brian Cheesman

In many cases, pubs may seek to meet the needs of their market by operating a dining room or restaurant with full or partial waiter or waitress service. As pub staff often have no background in catering, they must be closely supervised and taught how and why the system and its control operates.

Staff appearance and uniforms

Clean and attractive appearance of staff is essential to create the right image. Although some licensees may believe that in a pub uniforms are unnecessary, even in a simple restaurant operation a uniform for service staff is desirable to comply with public health requirements. Moreover, attractive and comfortable uniforms for waiting staff help to achieve the desired image, and convey to customers a sense of the establishment's care in the preparation and service of food.

Uniforms do not have to be elaborate. For part-time staff they need to fit the smallest to the largest staff. A simple tabard for girls is inexpensive and fits all sizes. Jackets for men are more expensive but help create an impression of a skilled permanent employee. Uniform not only has an impact on customers but helps make staff feel part of the establishment. A more relaxed operation should still set a standard of dress for staff and try to foster a sense of belonging to the establishment. A tie for men and a scarf for women help them to identify with the operation.

Personal cleanliness is vital in handling food during food service.

Personality is important in establishing a relationship between staff and guest. There should also be rapport among members of staff. Other important attributes are the ability to work under stress in an orderly and unflustered manner, being helpful and co-operative, attention to detail and honesty.

Organizing service

Staffing for food service varies according to the establishment, type of service and menu. Tables are normally grouped in 'stations' of equal numbers of customers. The number of customers in each station depends on the type of service.

Overall responsibility rests with management. They must organize staff duties, including rotas for time off, coverage of restaurant preparation and

Meal Service

meal time service to ensure that the best use is made of staff. Other responsibilities include training in practical and social skills, employment of casual and full-time staff, upkeep of records and payment details, health, safety and hygiene, and ensuring that control, service and establishment policy are understood.

Organization involves the provision of restaurant supplies and equipment such as furnishings, condiments, accompaniments, floral decorations, linen, china, cutlery, glass, menus and drinks lists together with their upkeep and the maintenance of large items of equipment.

Customer relationship

Ensure the satisfaction of customers by greeting, supervising service and checking the food and drink.

Complaints suggest non-achievement of aims and must be dealt with promptly. First, rectify the situation, satisfy the customer and then ensure that the grounds for complaint do not recur. Any complaint, no matter how trivial, should be brought to management's attention. Staff should be aware of this, even if they have corrected the fault themselves. A word to an aggrieved guest will let him know that management have noted the complaint and are coping with the problem.

Control and standards

Management is responsible for control procedure. This includes queries on customers' bills arising from checking or human error, and control of the cash and credit takings.

Management is responsible for the maintenance of food service standards. Waiting staff responsibilities include the taking of food and drinks orders and their service. Assistants (commis) or trainees might help by fetching items from the kitchen and keep the room clear of dirty equipment, leaving more experienced staff free to remain in the restaurant attending to customers.

Room preparation and cleaning

Important to success in any food service is the customer's first impression, followed by an environment which makes him feel at ease. Much of this depends on preparation prior to service.

First clean and air the room, working down towards the floor so that dust disturbed at higher levels will eventually be vacuumed from the floor. Curtains, ledges, displays, window frames, table tops, counter surface and chairs should be checked daily. Lamps, shades, carpets and room decorations should be cleaned periodically.

Preparation tasks   In restaurants these tasks are allocated to waiters on a rota, but in a pub one person would be responsible. Cruets have to be cleaned, refilled and period-

Formal dining service

ically washed. Silverplated pots react with salt and form verdigris. Thoroughly dry them before refilling. Check other containers before service and clean the caps of sauce and pickle jars. Take care that where sauce bottles are refilled from a bulk dispenser, the containers do not age with successive topping up. Completely empty bottles and clean them periodically.

Bread rolls and butter pats (or prepacked portions) should be ready for service. Keep the latter on ice or in the refrigerator until required.

Check plates and coffee cups for cleanliness and keep hot in plate warmers or on hot-plates for service.

Tables, alignment and covering   In a restaurant, tables and chairs should be aligned and positioned to allow ease of access. When using tablecloths, they should hang about 457 mm (18 in) from the edge of the table, the corners covering the legs. Many restaurants use a slip or covering cloth to save laundry costs. This is smaller than the normal square table cloth by 915 mm (3 ft), being the length of the overhang of the tablecloth.

Similarly coloured serviettes and slip cloth to contrast with tablecloths are attractive. Disposable tablecloths, slip cloths and serviettes also cut costs and ease laundry delivery problems.

Polished wood or laminated surface tables, if used, should be clean and polished before table mats are laid.

Pubs often use easily cleaned laminated place mats instead of full table linen or tables topped with formica.

Sideboards   In the dining area, sideboards or service tables ease the work of serving staff by providing a working and stacking surface and a storage area to keep extra plates, cutlery and linen and any other items required during the meal.

Hot-plates on the sideboards help to keep food hot during service. Clean these before and after service, removing any spillage, which may cook on to the surface.

A well stocked sideboard should contain:

Check books for food and drink together with bills
Menus and drinks lists
Water jugs and spare glasses
A reserve of spare table and serving cutlery
Sweet plates for cold sweets, hors-d'oeuvre and cheese
Meat plates for cold buffet items and as underplates for soup service
Sauces, pickles and accompaniments
Coffee saucers and sugar
Service slip or tablecloths and serviettes
Service trays

This list depends on the type of service. Many establishments minimize cutlery and crockery so as not to tie up too much capital in 'plant'; therefore they have one size of plate and only one type of knife and fork.

Meal Service

Figure 53 (a) *Old English carvery at The Blue Posts, Bennett Street, London* (b) *Barnaby's at The Telegraph, Putney Heath* (c) *The carvery at Ye Olde Cock Tavern, Fleet Street, London*
Courtesy London Hosts

Dispensing points In a small dining room many items are kept at a central dispensing point and, in fast food operations, the sauces, coffee, sugar etc. are part of the table lay-up. Plated items come straight to the table; reserves of china and cutlery are held behind the scenes. Accompaniments form part of the dish presentation and the main preparation consists of general cleaning and basic table lay-up.

Types of table service

Variations in methods of presenting food have evolved through experience. Popular in pubs is plate service. This is speedy, needs only minimum equipment, service staff and skills to achieve a good standard presentation of food.

The number of customers allocated to a waitress varies according to the type

Formal dining service

and size of the menu and the concentration of business, but a figure of twenty-four would be a guide.

Private house service This buffet style requires a central table space and heaters (where appropriate) to keep dishes hot while the customer serves himself. Normally it is used for the service of main courses, an alternative being used for other courses. It is popular with businessmen at lunchtime, for a customer can take sufficient for his requirements and replenish his plate when necessary.

Semi-silver service This is a mixture of other forms of service, there being two main variations. Either the main items are plated and accompaniments are served, or the main items are served and the accompaniments are placed on the table for the customers to help themselves. It requires a higher degree of personal attention, and fewer customers are allocated to each member of the serving staff. An average of eighteen customers would probably be right.

Silver service and guéridon service This is only used in up-market restaurant operations. Items are placed on silver, stainless steel or other platters in the kitchen for service by the waiting staff. In its most popular form, food is served on to customers' plates by using a spoon and fork after presentation of the dish to them for approval.

An even more up-market extension of this type of service uses sidetables or serving trolleys called guéridons. Dishes may be plated in front of the guests from the guéridon, particularly if any portioning, filleting or finishing is required; they may be prepared and cooked, or else final adjustments made such as adding liqueur or flaming with spirit.

Guéridon service exists where customers have time to enjoy, and are prepared to pay for, the personal service and extra staff. It would be applicable only to pubs which could attract such a clientele. An average of twelve customers to each member of the service staff would be usual.

Guéridon service is highly labour intensive and is only used in top class, top price restaurants. A proportion of pubs do have such restaurants. However,

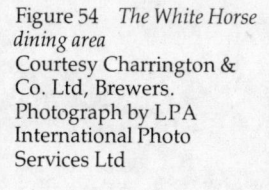

Figure 54 *The White Horse dining area*
Courtesy Charrington & Co. Ltd, Brewers.
Photograph by LPA International Photo Services Ltd

Meal Service

individual recipes are not presented here; it is suggested that you consult a specialist book.

Preparedness Whatever style of service is adopted, the pub restaurant should be ready for business at all times. If you have twelve tables in your restaurant then the dozen tables should be laid up. It is clear evidence that you do not expect to do much business if you just lay up three. Lay up all of them to a predetermined design so that each table layout is identical.

Menus

For maximum impact place menus so that their front faces customers entering the restaurant.

Two main types of menu, requiring different lay-ups, are:

Table d'hôte or a set meal at a set price
A la carte or individually chosen and priced items.

There are, as the menu chapter indicates, many variants. Many pubs have, for example, essayed steak bar and similar simplified operations with limited menus and informal service. These were considered in the previous chapter.

Otherwise, for waiting purposes (or preparation of tables and room) it is convenient to think of à la carte and table d'hôte as indicative of the main requirements.

Figure 55 *The conservatory-style dining area at The Durell Arms, Fulham Road, Fulham*
Courtesy London Hosts

Menu effect on covers For à la carte, where the customer's order is not known until he makes it, the lay-up of a cover is more simple. It usually consists of a knife and fork (with, of course, the usual side plate, napkin and other table accessories).

For a set meal with limited menu choice, all necessary cutlery can be laid in advance. A table d'hôte place setting usually consists of soup, fish and/or meat and sweet cutlery; sideplate and knife for roll and butter; and serviette, glass, cruet and ashtray.

Before considering table lay-up detail, a few points should be noted about preparing the dining area.

Laying up

In some operations this will be basic. Simply ensure that there is enough crockery and cutlery for meal service. Some pubs wrap each individual place setting – knife, fork and spoon – in a paper serviette for handing to the customer when he collects his food.

In more conventional dining rooms, when placing cutlery on the table, polish it and check for cleanliness.

A medium-sized fish plate 203 mm (8 in) centred at each setting as a 'marker', aids a symmetrical lay-up. In the set menu, lay cutlery from the inside outwards leaving space approximately 25 mm (1 in) between the

Formal dining service

handles and the table edge so that customers do not displace cutlery when they sit down.

The lay-up should look neat, with cutlery placed fairly close together and in line with the opposite place setting. Lay knives with their cutting edges facing left, with the ends of the cutlery aligned parallel with the table edge.

Serviettes Keep serviette folds simple and easy to unfold. Centre stand-up folds such as the cone and mitre at the place setting (on the marker plate). Place simple triangular folds on the side plate beneath the bread knife. Serviettes look effective when folded into a wine glass.

Glasses Glasses placed top right of the place setting may be left upside down after polishing to keep them dust free, but turn them upright just before serving starts so that they are in the positive position to receive wine. A wine glass is normally used to double for water or wine.

Service of courses

The following notes indicate the covers, accompaniments and service style in formal restaurants for selected dishes of the various courses of a meal.

Starters
A selection of hors-d'oeuvres Hors-d'oeuvres are popular for business lunches. The varieties are laid out on display dishes and plated in accordance with the customer's wishes. Separate serving spoons for each dish are essential, and it is important that the selection is attractively presented and fresh; stale dishes should be replaced.

Smoked trout The server should remove the head and tail using a service spoon and fork. A fish knife is used to loosen the skin from the belly and roll it back towards the backbone on either side of the fish. The loose skin is then cleared away from the fish, taking the back fins at the same time. The whole fish may be placed on a fish plate together with a segment of lemon and any accompanying garnish and placed before the customer, offering horseradish sauce and buttered brown bread at the same time. The pepper mill and cayenne should be placed on the table.

Smoked eel This is cut into portions and may be served in the same way as the trout.

Pâté maison This is normally presented to the customer in the pot or terrine or turned out on to a dish. A portion is cut and plated up together with any garnish and placed before the customer. Hot toast cut into fingers or triangles, with the crusts removed, is placed in a serviette on a plate to keep it hot until it is served at the table.

Melon Freshly cut segments of melon, honeydew or cantaloup, look attractive when portioned at the table. The melon should be removed from its dish of crushed

Meal Service

ice and both ends trimmed flat. Standing the melon on end, insert a carving knife through the centre of the fruit and draw it down, making a straight clean cut from end to end. Gauging the size of the portion required, repeat the operation and extract the portion, laying it on a working board.

The base of the cut portion should be trimmed flat to ensure that it will sit steadily on the plate, and the pips should be scooped away using a sweet or soup spoon. The cut portion should then be placed on a cold sweet or fish plate before being presented to the customer. Caster sugar and ground ginger should be offered. The section of melon may be cut and decorated if required.

Poached, grilled or shallow-fried sole   The whole fish should be presented to the guest for approval. Then if it is to be filleted, the head and tail are removed. The bones consist of side fins and a backbone. Using a table fork and pressing against the side fins, push away from the body of the fish and continue to do this until the fins are cleared.

Blue trout   This is readily available from trout farms. A freshly poached trout, accompanied separately by hollandaise sauce or melted butter, can be very brittle, and normally the fish is skinned but not filleted. A sharp table knife is run gently down the back and along the belly, making an incision in the skin. This can then be peeled back from belly to backbone on either side. The head and tail are removed and the fish put on a plate and garnished. If it is being served as a course prior to the main meal then a hot fish plate is used, but if it is the main course then a hot meat plate is required.

Main courses   There are four main types:

1   Dishes which need finishing before service to the customer
2   Dishes which need portioning before service
3   Dishes which are prepared and/or cooked at the table
4   Dishes which are carved in front of the customer.

Pubs seldom offer all these types, but may consider one as a special feature to attract customers.

Papilotte dishes (type 1)   These are cooked in a sealed casing of paper or foil. It is pierced in front of the customer and the contents are then plated. Breast of chicken or veal and fish fillets are commonly cooked by this method.

Sous cloche dishes (type 1)   These are cooked in a similar way to the papilotte dishes, but they are covered with a glass dome in a special dish.

Chicken breast Kiev (type 1)   Butter is inserted into a breast of chicken, and during the cooking the water in the butter turns into steam and swells the meat. A pressure has built up inside the chicken breast and it is released by piercing the meat after presentation to the customer; it is then plated.

Kebab à la grecque (type 1)   Skewered items, which are normally served with a dish of rice, are first presented to the customer. Two joint forks are then used, back to back, the first used to hook the ring of the skewer while the second is slid along the shaft of the skewer, removing the items.

Formal dining service

The rice is served on to the plate at the guéridon or table and the kebabs then served on to the rice. Worcester sauce may be offered with other accompanying sauces.

Double fillet steak (type 2) This needs to be carved into portions; for two customers the steak should be carved on the slant into four equal slices. Normally each customer would receive an outside and an inside slice per portion, but should one customer prefer his steak rarer than the other he could have both the inside portions. These are plated, garnished and placed before the customer.

There is a large selection of dishes prepared or cooked at the table. Several specialist books on flambé work are available; the main advantage and appeal of this technique is the showmanship involved.

Steak tartare (type 3) The basic ingredients are raw minced fillet steak, a raw egg yolk, gherkins, capers, parsley and shallots, but there are optional extras such as chopped anchovy fillets and garlic which may be added if the customer desires them.

The raw egg yolk is placed on the rissole of raw steak surrounded by the other items for the customer's approval. The ingredients are then mixed thoroughly in a soup plate together with seasonings such as French mustard, Worcester sauce, oil and vinegar and pepper and salt. The mixture must remain fairly firm in texture since it has to be reshaped into a rissole form. Place a cold meat plate on top of the preparation soup plate, turn the plates over, and the rissole of prepared steak tartare is ready. Garnish it with lettuce and tomato if required and place it before the customer.

Carving (type 4) Pubs may need to carve in the kitchen, at the counter or buffet, and only rarely at table. Displaying food in an eating establishment is an aid to sales, and thus items need to be carved from the display.

The general rules are to carve quickly and neatly, across the grain with most joints. The thickness of the cut will depend on the meat; for example, ham is cut more thinly than pork or lamb.

The knife is all important, and a good set of stainless steel carving knives are more presentable than standard kitchen ones and do not taint egg and fish dishes. Use thick-bladed knives for slicing and jointing and thin ones for carving and thin slicing.

A good carving fork with a circular protection guard and a steel or carborundum are also required. A selection of metal carving plates, including one with spikes for holding difficult joints, is also an asset. Always wipe sharpened knives before use to remove any metallic traces.

Salads Salads should be dressed just prior to service. Green salads should be placed in wooden or glass bowls and cut using a service spoon and fork. Sufficient dressing to coat the salad is added if required, turning the salad over until the coating is evenly applied. The salad may then be arranged neatly on crescent-shaped salad plates or sideplates.

Remove tomato and egg from mixed salads during the cutting and turning, since they break up easily, and replace in the dressed salad. Dress tomato salads on the plate by gently ladling over salad dressing.

Meal Service

French dressing or vinaigrette consists of seasoned French mustard to which one part of vinegar is mixed and then two parts of oil. For ease of service it is usually prepared beforehand, but Roquefort dressing is made to order. Mash the cheese using a table fork and cream it with a little vinaigrette. Add further vinaigrette until the dressing reaches coating consistency.

Fruit-based salads such as Waldorf (diced apple, walnut and celery) and japonaise (diced tomato, pineapple, orange and apple) are covered with a soured or acidulated cream dressing (seasoned cream spiked with lemon juice). This is normally made in the kitchen.

Sweet dishes
Pear or peach flambé

Dishes cooked at table require a chafing dish; this is a copper, silver plated or stainless steel pan that is thicker at the base than a flambé pan. The lamp which is used must have an adjustable flame since many of the items cooked at table are finished with cream and this should not be allowed to boil. Tinned or fresh fruit poached in syrup can be used. The halves of fruit and syrup are heated in the pan and lightly pricked with a fork to make heating them easier. Baste the fruit with syrup, which should be allowed to reduce to a sticky consistency, and then sprinkle the fruit with caster sugar and flame it using brandy or kirsch.

Crêpes Suzette

This dish consists of pancakes swathed in orange and lemon sauce and flamed. For ease of preparation, the basic Suzette butter can be made beforehand and consists of creamed butter, caster sugar, grated lemon and orange zest. This butter is melted in the pan and orange and lemon juice is added together with a measure of orange curaçao. The edge of each pancake is skewered on the prongs of the fork, lifted into the pan and coated on both sides with the sauce. The crêpe is folded in half, the fork is removed, the crêpe is folded into four and pushed to the side of the pan.

The process is repeated with all the pancakes, and when they are completed the pan is shaken so that the folded pancakes are arranged round it. The sauce is checked to make sure that it is at the right consistency and then the pancakes are flamed with brandy and served from the pan on to the plates at the table.

Trolley service

A vital aid to sales is to display available dishes attractively; and a sweet trolley is relatively simple and profitable. Gâteaux and flans should be cut and served using a cake slice. A serving spoon and fork is suitable for most other sweets. Trolleys should be kept clean and the portions removed so as not to mar the display.

Cheese

This ever-popular item goes with a variety of drinks. It can be served in pubs in a ploughman's lunch or in the much grander form of a cheese board.

An attractive cheese board needs a trolley or sidetable to serve it from. Each type of cheese must be known and can be labelled to aid in identification. Once the knife used for portioning the cheese has been used it should be replaced by a clean one to avoid cross-contamination with other varieties.

When the customer has made his choice, serve the portion with the rind and wrapping removed. Celery, biscuits and butter should be available. For cream cheeses, caster sugar and sweet biscuits may be required.

Formal dining service

As a dairy product, cheese needs careful storage and display. Ideally just keep it cool, but if it must be stored in a refrigerator, place in an airtight container twice its own size. Keep different varieties separate from each other.

Fresh fruit The basket of fresh fruit should be brought to the table for the customer to make his selection. The chosen fruit is plated on the trolley using a spoon and fork and then placed before the customer. Caster sugar and cream may be offered. A finger bowl, together with a serviette for drying the fingers, is necessary in up-market service for dessert fruit.

Coffee A number of pubs are now serving coffee, both as a separate service outside licensing hours and as an after-dinner drink. The publican must assess how this affects his sale of liquor.

In fast food operations coffee is prepared in the kitchen and made up in bulk before service, using machines such as the Still's coffee-maker, and served in cups or pots. Where coffee is made in the room prior to service it should be made at the last possible minute, kept at the correct heat and not allowed to boil and spoil. Ideally, coffee should be freshly made. Various filter systems give cups or pots to order.

Liqueur coffees To boost alcohol sales while retaining the coffee service, offer a range of spirit and liqueur coffees at the conclusion of the meal. Some popualr ones are:

Irish coffee	made with Irish whiskey
Gaelic coffee	made with Scotch whisky
Prince Charles coffee	made with Drambuie
French coffee	made with brandy
Russian coffee	made with vodka
Monks coffee	made with Benedictine
Calypso coffee	made with Tia Maria

The ideal presentation is in a heatproof glass, but if these are not available a coffee spoon should be placed in the glass as a precaution against it shattering.

Place demerara sugar in the glass first, followed by a measure of the required spirit or liqueur. Hot black coffee is poured in to within an inch of the rim. Stir the mixture and then float on cold double cream by pouring it gently over a spoon held just above the coffee's surface. It is possible to reduce cost by using whipped cream.

Menu items requiring special equipment

The following is only relevant to up-market locations seeking to attract customers by offering a gimmick or something different in food service.

Asparagus/artichoke Serve on a fish plate; a roll knife and sweet fork should be laid and a fingerbowl placed on the table. If it is served cold, offer vinaigrette; if hot, melted butter from the kitchen.

Meal Service

Avocado pear   Serve in a shaped avocado dish or on a fish plate. A teaspoon and sweet fork should be laid and vinaigrette offered.

Caviar/potted shrimps   Serve on a fish plate. A side knife should be laid. Offer hot toast or buttered brown bread with the pepper mill and cayenne.

Melon   Serve on a fish plate. A sweet spoon and fork should be laid and caster sugar and ground ginger offered separately or mixed together.

Oysters   Serve on an oyster or soup plate on ice (an underplate is required). Lay an oyster or fish fork on the right hand side together with a fingerbowl. Offer buttered brown bread, chilli vinegar, Tabasco sauce, the pepper mill and cayenne.

Seafood   Serve in a glass or coupe on a sideplate.

Crab cocktail   Lay a teaspoon and oyster or fish fork; offer buttered brown bread, the pepper mill and cayenne.

Smoked salmon   Serve on a fish plate. A fish knife and fork should be laid, and buttered brown bread and the pepper mill and cayenne should be offered.

Smoked eel   Serve on a fish plate. A fish knife and fork should be laid and buttered brown bread, the pepper mill, cayenne and horseradish sauce should be offered.

Fresh fruit   Serve on to a sweet plate. Lay a fruit knife and fork or roll knife and sweet fork, together with a fingerbowl.

Lay for these items can be adjusted depending on the cutlery available. Some settings may be adapted to suit a particular environment, i.e. smoked salmon sandwiches or avocado and pâté on toast.

Control

Control aims to ensure that customers pay for all items of food and drink supplied at the correct price. The main control points in a restaurant are:

Receipt of an order
Issue of food and drink
Payment.

Subsequently, the three are checked against each other and with the cash takings. To aid this process, each restaurant table should be lettered or numbered.

There are various forms of check. The triplicate system employs a carbonated pad where:

One copy of the written priced order is kept by the service staff for reference.
One copy is used to make up the bill by a separate cashier.
The third copy is handed to the issue point to obtain the food and drink.

In this system no issues are made unless a check is stamped, initialled or passed by the cashier, ensuring that all items are paid for.

Where service staff write bills, check/bill or double-bill pad systems may be used. One copy is used to obtain the orders, and the bill is presented to the customer for payment. The top check may be perforated in several sections to accommodate orders taken during stages of the meal, and the prices are added to the bill.

Various forms of machine checking exist within the control framework described, and are operated by the service staff or by the cashier in a busy establishment. A basic system requires food and drink orders to be placed in the machine and priced before issues are made. The bill copy can then be placed in the machine and added up when payment is due.

The advantage of machine checking is the availability of an immediate summary of takings and a breakdown into sectors such as food and drink, business transacted by each member of the food service staff, credit sales etc. Where prices are generally standardized, machines are available with a numbered key for each menu item which can be preset with the price, giving a further breakdown of the sales and popularity of each dish.

However, the best control system for pub catering is probably to take the cash at the time the order is placed, since people are not sitting at set tables and can easily leave the premises without paying.

Payment sales checklist

Are facilities to accept and process credit cards adequate and known to staff?
Do signs prominently indicate what cards, if any, you accept?
Can you give receipts to customers from numbered pads easily controlled by issue and including your VAT number?
Alternatively, do you issue till receipts which can also itemize food so that portions and sales can be accounted for exactly?
Will several staff act as cashier, or will one person be allocated the task?
Is the cashier aware of prices to be charged, particularly with regard to hidden extras and garnishings?

Conclusion

Food service is varied and expanding in the licensed trade, and is influenced by fast food operations. There is scope for the expansion of franchised service. However, before a publican decides to serve a large range of food, several factors must be taken into account.

Initial outlay on equipment can be high. If anything more than light snacks are to be served, considerable space must be set aside for seating and tables. The legislation governing the provision and service of food is strict and may require alterations to premises. Yet the service of food in pubs is an exciting area of profitability, full of challenge to the business- and service-oriented licensee. From many types of food service, the selection of the best depends upon the market to be served by the establishment.

Further reading

Fuller, J. and Currie, A. J., *The Waiter*, Hutchinson, 1965.
Fuller, John, *Modern Restaurant Service*, Hutchinson, 1983.
Fuller, John, *Guéridon and Lamp Cookery*, Hutchinson, 1979.

16 Sales and service of wine with food

J. G. Miles

Material from Nigel Pullan is included in this chapter.

Wine with meals

A well-presented, representative, but limited line of wines available at the bar can persuade customers to use your house in preference to others for bar snacks and, where formal eating arrangements are provided, wine must be *sold* to customers. Some eaters will continue to drink beer with their food (and this is sometimes the most suitable drink), but few will continue with spirits at the table.

These customers can usually be persuaded to buy wine, particularly by the glass or carafe, to accompany their meals. Once they are seated there is an opportunity to sell them an aperitif, provided you are not intent on a rapid changeover of customers. Regular wine drinkers know their preferences, but the less initiated should first be coaxed and then advised, and there are ground rules for this purpose.

Wine may be divided into four broad categories:

Table (beverage) wines, which have fermented right out in casks or vats so that all the carbon dioxide gas is lost in the air and the wine is still. These are the wines most usually drunk with meals.
Sparkling wines have a residue of carbon dioxide in solution which should be achieved by allowing fermentation partly to take place in the bottle which is sealed before all the gas has escaped. These wines may also be taken with meals.
Fortified wines are those where the fermentation is checked at an early or later stage by the addition of alcohol which increases the alcoholic content and at the same time leaves some of the original grape sugar unfermented. Examples are sherry, port and Madeira.
Wine-based aperitifs These include the vermouths and the many proprietary names like Dubonnet. (Note that there are also spirit-based aperitifs such as Campari.)

Choice of wines In Britain we are fortunate in the enormous range of wines available. In the major wine-producing countries it is often difficult to find wines from other countries. However, this large choice does present the buyer with problems of price, vintage and style. The everyday licensee can take advantage of the excellent material provided by the Wine and Spirit Education Trust to improve his knowledge, and there are a number of good books on the market to advise the novice. Most customers will not be experts, although some may wish to

Sales and service of wine with food

impress at table by ordering expensive wine. With the assistance of his supplier the licensee will want to provide a range of choice for his customers which fits into the market he has decided to pursue in his catering operation. For that reason he should be able to identify broadly similar types of wine, be they vintage of everyday beverage wines. This may be done by the nomenclature (including origin), the bottle and the label.

Identification

The bottle The wines of Western Europe have traditionally become associated with various shaped and coloured bottles. The claret bottle is punted with straight sides and rounded shoulders; it is green. This simple shape, easy to stack for laying down, has been copied throughout the world. Bordeaux white wines, including Sauternes and Graves, are put in similar bottles, but they are made of clear white glass. Most red and white Burgundy wines are put into punted straight green bottles with sloping shoulders. The reds are usually in dark green bottles, but sometimes the whites are in a yellowish shade of green. The same shape with lower shoulders and made of heavier glass has been adopted for Barolo and Barbera, but in brown glass.

Châteauneuf-du-Pape is an embossed and heavier version of the Burgundy bottles. Beaujolais appears, not invariably, in various forms of 'pot' bottles (i.e. the sides taper towards the bottom). Loire wines are put in the same shape bottles as Burgundy as a rule, but with a more accentuated taper and often in a paler green glass. Hocks and Moselles come in bottles with sloping sides rather than with a discernible shoulder. Hock bottles are brown, whereas those of Moselle are usually green. Alsace wine bottles are of the same shape and green, but taller and thinner than the German bottles. All these traditionally contain 72 cl of wine instead of the 75 cl in the usual French bottle.

The Champagne bottles, of whatever size, are of similar shape to the Burgundy bottles, but of a very thick glass to withstand the internal pressure of the gas. The fiasco, used for all but the best Chianti, has a rounded bottom concealed in a plaited case. A similar bottle and case is used for the sweet whites of Orvieto. The Bocksbeutal of Franconia is derived from an old drinking flagon, based on a gourd shape. It has been copied all over the world as something a bit different.

Ports are bottled in Bordeaux-shaped bottles. Traditionally vintage ports have no label, the name appearing on the capsule and cork. A blob of white paint indicates the side to keep uppermost when the bottle is taken out for decanting. Sherries have no traditional shape, but are of green glass with a long neck and broad shoulders. A dumpy looking bottle with a thick lip, called a clavelin, is used for the yellow wines of Jura, and contains 62 cl.

The arguments within the EEC surrounding permitted bottle sizes continue, with France trying to protect the traditional clavelin; the Germans and Alsatians have lost their battle to retain the 72/73 cl bottle in the long term.

The label The labelling of foodstuffs was tidied up by the Labelling of Food Regulation 1970, under section 7 of the Food and Drugs Act 1955. All intoxicating liquor, prepacked for retail sale, must bear a true statement specifying the name of the packer or labeller of the liquor and an address at which he carries on business. The statement must also specify the 'appropriate designation' of the liquor, to include a reference to the name of the country or countries of origin expressed as a noun or adjective.

A label must not imply in any way that a bottle contains wine unless it is derived wholly from grapes. If it is derived from some other fruit then it must immediately precede the word 'wine' (e.g. elderberry wine). A liquor, not being wine obtained by fermentation in the district of its origin from the juice of freshly gathered grapes, or brandy, may not be described as 'vintage'. (A minor exception is made for cider.) The regulation does not require the nominal (average) content of wine bottles to appear on the label, but EEC direction will, very soon, require the labeller to make provision for this and the size of letters to be used.

Alcoholic content   EEC directives have secured the abandonment of British proof in favour of alcoholic content by percentage volume. Similarly, they will secure a declaration of alcoholic content on the labels of liquers and aromatized wines in addition to spirits (already required by UK law). For wines and fortified wines it is intended, for the time being at least, to leave this to the decision of individual members of the Community. Since it is, more often than not, a national requirement for quality wines at least to be of a strength, it should not be surprising if those countries require it to be on the label. A finished table wine does not have a high alcoholic content: perhaps 8°–12° Gay-Lussac (GL) or 15° GL for Empire wines. Fortified wines are about 20° GL. Wine should sell on its quality, not its strength.

An 'appropriate designation' is a name that describes an EEC wine according to the law of that country. For instance, EEC quality wines should be described by the names to which they are legally entitled there and bear the designation appellation contrôlée (AC), qualitätswein etc.). Blends of quality wines may not show any higher classification than a name common to all the constituents, e.g. a blend of two AC claret districts could not be more excitingly described than Bordeaux rouge. 'Blend of wines of France' is acceptable, as is 'Mouette, produce of France'. Both show the country of origin.

The advice of a good wine merchant is invaluable, particularly for cheaper wines. For many years surplus wines from AC vineyards used to be sold by the name of a French parish or district, and were often as good as the permitted quality used for AC bottling. This wine is still available, but under some brand name.

Matching wine with food

Although people may well acquire their own preferences, advice given to customers should be based on well-tried principles of compatability between different food and wines. Wine is complementary to food and should improve its taste, and this will not be so if fish is mixed with even a light red wine or if red wine or dry white wine is taken with an acid or highly spiced dish. Also,

Sales and service of wine with food

red wine does not match egg dishes or sweet food. The broad rules are as follows:

Before the meal   Fino sherry, vermouth, branded aperitif, dry white wine, champagne, sparkling wine, dry port or Madeira.
With starter course   A dry white or rosé wine; but with hors-d'oeuvre, where there is likely to be a large element of vinegar, a medium sherry is preferable to any table wine.
With fish   A white wine, which may be progressively heavier/sweeter the richer the sauce. A light wine is best with shellfish and delicate white fish, and a more full-bodied dry wine is preferable with more oily fish.
With veal, pork and chicken   A quite full-bodied dry white wine, dry rosé wine, a light red wine.
With red meats and game   A red wine: the richer the flesh, the more full bodied the wine.
With sweets   A sweet or sparkling white wine.
With cheese   Port or other fortified wine, red wine.
With coffee   Port, red wine, Cognac, Armagnac, any liquer.
Throughout   Champagne may be drunk throughout the meal.

The question of which wine to drink with what food brings us into the realm of actively selling wine, in which this list plays its part.

Promoting wine sales

In the restaurant   There are three types of customer. The rarest is the person who knows his way about a wine list and requires no more than an intelligent anticipation of his needs and excellent service. The second type is one who is used to entertaining and knows half a dozen names which he invariably orders because he can appear knowledgeable and pronounce their names without embarrassment. He is a challenge, because you can introduce a new wine to his vocabulary for his future benefit. The last type knows practically nothing about wines, finds a wine list meaningless, but is open to suggestion. He is a distinct challenge.

All three types require a different approach, but the goal is to ensure they buy wine, and, at the end, feel happy that they did so. The right approach should ensure that at least half a bottle of wine is sold with every meal served, or at least half a carafe of wine which is offered at a price that it is difficult to refuse.

The customer must be approached as soon as he has ordered his food or at the time he is ordering his food, depending upon the style and staffing of the pub. The same considerations will apply to a decision whether to include references to wine on the menu itself or whether to depend on a separate wine list, which must be used as an aid to your conversation with the customer and not just shoved in his hand.

Establish whether the customer prefers sweet or dry, red or white wine. Make a subjective judgement of what he might want to pay and then be prepared to suggest something that you consider will suit his purse, palate and his choice of food.

In most pub restaurants you are going to serve three courses and, as mentioned, your aim is to sell at least half a bottle per person, whether by the

Meal Service

glass, carafe or bottle. It is not good tactics to endeavour to sell the more expensive wines on all occasions; some cheaper wine may encourage spending on coffee or a dessert.

If the customers choose a starter followed by fish or poultry, it is probably best to induce them to start a bottle of white wine at once. If their choice of main dish is red meat, persuade them to take a sherry or glass of suitable wine, followed by red wine. In both cases there will be an opportunity to suggest at least a glass of sweet white wine with their sweet or red or white with their cheese. If they order red meat and red wine, suggest they finish the wine with cheese to follow the meat, followed by a sweet or dessert with a suitable wine. They may enjoy this sensible French approach. If a party makes radically different choices of main course, suggest different accompanying wines, which can be accommodated by serving glasses, half bottles or carafes where necessary.

Quantity When considering selling wine by carafe you must remember that the Weights and Measures (Sale of Wine) Order 1976 requires wine to be sold in carafes of 25 cl, 50 cl, 75 cl, 1 litre, 10 fl oz or 20 fl oz. The quantities in which this unbottled wine is for sale must either be 'displayed on the premises in such a position or manner as to be readily available without special request for inspection by the buyer before the sale is made, or contained in every wine list and menu which is available to the buyer on the premises'.

The advantage of using a carafe or pichet is that large bottles of wine can be broken down for sale in various smaller quantities, which can be combined with a 'by glass' operation, and the customer may feel he is getting a bargain. A disadvantage is the lack of control over staff when breaking it down, both from your point of view and the customer's, if short (and therefore illegal) measure is given. This will be avoided if one or two 'house wines' are introduced and sold in the same price range. Most wholesalers will accept reasonably sized orders for a range of their branded wines in bottles labelled as being bottled for the house by its selection. This adds a certain cachet to the operation while facilitating control.

House wine A house wine can be important for the image of a pub. It is a mistake to select inferior wines that can be sold at low prices or to make an above average profit. The publican should aim to have his own label only on wines specially chosen for their good quality and value. Well-chosen, attractively labelled, house wines can help put across a quality image.

The house wine will usually be the least expensive, and it is highly desirable that it should be dispensed by the bottle (or glass, of course) rather than from carafes which are filled behind the scenes. Although larger bottles such as 1.5 or 2 litres are excellent value, it is preferable to dispense wine from a bottle that can be seen. This applies particularly to house wines where, in the past, the practice has often been to make false economies.

Wine lists A wine list should be useful to the customer. It is not recommended that it should be divided into 'suitable to drink with . . .' sections; on the other hand,

Sales and service of wine with food

simply dividing it up by countries is not particularly helpful to the customer or staff. The list should be divided into types of wine, e.g. sparkling whites, light red wines, full red wines, sweet white wines, etc., which provides reasonable signposts for all concerned.

In the bar It is usual to find wine sales in the bar, with or without food, confined to sales by the glass. There is no reason, if large bottles are used for the purpose, why sales by carafe should not be considered provided that the price equates exactly to 'by glass' prices. Controlled sales of wine by the bottle are also worthy of consideration, provided they are in sizes not used for serving by the glass, unless their contents can be equated to the measure and price used for sales by the glass. It is safe to assume that when selling wine linked to counter sales of food greater volume will be achieved if it is in a carafe or bottle.

Sales by the glass The Capacity Measure (Intoxicating Liquor) Regulations 1983, which amended the Weights and Measures Act 1963, stipulated eleven permitted (including three new) measures for still wine sold by the glass. The measures that a restaurant or pub may use for still wine are : 100 ml, 125 ml, 150 ml, 175 ml, 200 ml, 4 fl oz, 5 fl oz, 6 fl oz, 6⅔ fl oz and 8 fl oz.

The regulation specified that wine glasses should be stamped either by the weights and measures inspectors or by the manufacturing company if it has registered its marks with the Department of Trade, and that wine glasses with measurement marks should be tested by inspectors.

Code of practice Under a voluntary code agreed by the Brewers' Society and other trade associations, those selling wine by the glass will: specify the measure used; offer either metric *or* imperial measures; offer no more than two different measures, with a difference between them of at least 50 ml if metric or 2 fl oz if imperial; and be able to prove the advertised measure. Though the code is voluntary, the Department of Trade has indicated that if it is not followed it could be made compulsory.

A pub caterer can sell wine by the glass without advertising the measure to customers, and in this case can serve wine in any kind of glass. However, if he advertises the measure of wine sold by the glass he must be able to prove the measure. He can do this in five ways:

Pour the wine into a verified glass and then serve it in any glass.
Measure with a government-stamped spirit measure.
Use a stamped wine meter.
Pour the wine straight into a glass bearing a manufacturer's mark or a weights and measures inspector's mark.

What he can no longer do is pour the wine straight into a wine glass which just has a line on it to indicate the quantity but no stamp from a manufacturer or inspector.

Since bottles are of metric capacity and much wine by the glass is already sold from 1 or 1.5 litre bottles, it is sensible to use 5 cl measured optics (already much used in the trade for vermouths). This measure is only ¹/₁₀ fl oz more than the traditional three-out measure and apart from being compatible with bottle content, two 5 cl tots approximate to the most common sherry schooner (3⅛ fl oz) and three tots are suitable for beverage wines (i.e. 15 cl, which is equivalent to 5⅓ fl oz and ideal for the universal 6⅔ fl oz glass). If, however, the three-out measure (1⅔ fl oz, 4.7 cl) is preferred because spirit optics are available, it can be used and still provide a reasonably sized glass of wine; however, it will not be so compatible with bottle volumes.

In whatever way the wine is sold in the bar, its availability must be instantly ascertainable by customers. The cheapest solution is to have some white wine in a bottle cooler on the bar counter or a back fitting and some red wine in a rack. Many companies now provide cooled wine containers as normal mechandising material. A more expensive, but excellent, solution for white wines is a cooled wall cabinet with the bottles fitted to measured dispensers. Red wines can be on optics and held in brackets outside the cabinet, possibly on a Space Saver optic stand.

At the food service point there should be a judicious quantity of advertising material from your supplier and perhaps some display incorporating bottles, grapes, maps, posters or flags. This must stand out, and that aim will not be achieved if the whole bar is cluttered with advertising material for all sorts of products. Generally bottles should sell liquor by their arrangement and prominence. Here we are talking about reminding eaters that wine is a good choice.

Storage and service

Storage

To present wines properly at table there must be a dispense system which provides a selection of white wines held at a cool temperature and racks in or near to the restaurant to hold wines at room temperature. Where there are violent variations in temperature the purchase or hire of thermostatically controlled wine racks made of epoxy-coated tubular steel may be considered. They run off a 240 V socket (12 A fused plug) and can be supplied with a locking device to prevent theft. These wines will be drawn from the cellar or store, where they should be kept at 9–14 °C (48–57 °F). Ideally the white wines should be at the lower figure, reds at 10 °C (50 °F) and fortified wines at the higher figure. Since you are unlikely to have separate cellars the best solution is to bin the white wines low down, the reds in the centre and the fortified wines at the top. The bottles should be laid down with the cork in constant contact with the wine so that it does not dry out. They should be in darkness and all draughts excluded; sudden changes in temperature must be avoided, and vibration is harmful where wines throwing a sediment are stored.

Service at table

Having established what the customers are to drink, the wines must be presented at the right time. The bottle should be shown to the host and then opened. The waiter, standing on the host's right, should pour a small quantity of wine into his glass for approval and, once this has been given, the waiter proceeds round the table to the right, starting with the guest on the host's right and ending with the host. Do not more than half fill each glass. The bottle should then be put on the table or in a wine cooler (ice bucket). This should be not full of ice but filled with cool water with some ice added to retain its coolness. The practice of serving red wines cradled in a basket is not advocated; it is an unnecessary affectation and the basket's proper use is when decanting wine.

Decanting Ideally, a bottle for decanting should be stood upright for a day, to allow the sediment to drop to the bottom. It is then handled carefully, so as not to disturb the sediment or break up the crust. Remove the capsule or break the seal over the cork and wipe the top of the neck of the bottle. Wrap the cloth round the bottle in case it breaks, and drive the corkscrew right through the centre of the cork. Then withdraw the cork with a long, even pull – a lever-type corkscrew is ideal – and wipe the lip of the bottle. Rest your elbow on something and start pouring the wine into a decanter or clean bottle. Do not stop pouring until you can see the sediment approaching the neck. A light behind the bottle will help to do this; there will be very little waste.

Champagne To open a bottle of champagne, grip the cork with one hand (left if you are right handed) and turn the bottle with the other. If the cork breaks you will have to use a corkscrew. Before doing that, wrap the bottle in a napkin in case the neck breaks. Always sniff the bottle before pouring from it just in case it is corked.

Ideal temperatures for serving wine are:

Full-bodied red wines Chambré – 16–20 °C (60–70 °F). If possible open the bottle beforehand to let the wine breathe.
Sparkling and sweet white wines, sherries (not creams or browns) 4–10 °C (40–51 °F).
Old tawny port and light white wines Slightly chilled. Do not leave the white wines in a wine cooler.
Fuller bodied white wines and rosés Cellar temperature – 10–16 °C (50–60 °F).

Glasses There is a wide range of glasses traditionally used for different wines. These are not all necessary, but a few practical considerations should be borne in mind when ordering glasses. They should be as thin as possible, plain rather than cut, and not coloured. They should be large rather than small, and narrower at the top than the maximum width of the bowl. They should have stems, but it is not necessary to have the exaggeratedly long ones traditionally associated with hocks and Moselles.

A tulip-shaped stemmed goblet, holding 17 cl (6 fl oz), is ideal for general use with table wines. If some variety is required to improve the appearance of place settings, a slightly larger goblet may be used for red wines than white ones. Two glasses by each setting will suggest wine to the customer, or alternatively the ubiquitous Paris goblet may be used, reserving tulip goblets for sherries and ports. Champagne should be served in an uncurving narrower glass or flute – never a coupe (saucer). Brandy should be served in a small balloon glass, or an incurving glass, but not a vulgarly large balloon.

Meal Service

Any warming the customer may like should be done with his own hands round the glass, not a spirit lamp in the hands of the waiter. Port should be served in a small Paris goblet, or the smaller tulip-shaped goblet in use. Small glasses filled to the brim are institutional in origin.

Cigars and cigarettes A trolly of liqueurs, brandy and decanted ports, on which cigars may also be displayed, is convenient for the customer and staff and can, if used judiciously, promote sales. It is a management decision whether a stock of cigarettes should be held in the restaurant, or brought from the bar, but a stock of cigars is essential. Whiffs and miniatures should be treated in the same way as cigarettes. The cigars stocked for sale singly should include coronas, panatellas and cheroots.

Service in the bar

The question of measure and storage in the bar has already been dealt with. Paris goblets or stemmed tulip-shaped glasses are recommended for the bar, and the size of bottles used will depend on the volume of sales. However, if the wines are on optic they will keep better than standing on the shelf, probably with the cork out because the barman forgets or mislays it.

In the absence of legislation about measure, the size should not be put on the price list. Not only will this be a size or description not included in the Weights and Measures Act, but also it would require exact measurement. However, the 'not more than half glass full' rule should not apply since the customer may be less discerning and think he is not getting value for money. A quantity of 15 cl or 5 fl oz in a 6⅔ fl oz glass is recommended. Glasses should, of course, be sparkling clean and unchipped, and they will probably be rather thicker than those used in the restaurant. Care must be taken with washing so that no 'off' smells persist, and they should be stored upright, not on their rims.

Temperature Temperature is important, because bars are hot when in use and often very cold at night. This has a bearing on the stock levels of wine held in the bar, particularly if no temperature-controlled storage is available. It means that only a short range should be kept in the bar; other wines can be brought up from the cellar or transferred from the restaurant if a customer wishes to buy a bottle. Two whites, a rosé and one or two reds should suffice.

Lined carafes should be considered, because there are many situations in which they will reduce the workload of staff and sell more wine. Also, the customers do not have to keep returning to the bar while they eat their substantial bar snack. Carafes can be filled from large bottles of up to five litres.

Summary

In the restaurant 1 Aim to sell at least half a bottle or carafe of wine with each meal.
2 Divide your wine list into types of wine, not countries of origin. You and

Sales and service of wine with food

your staff should know what types of wine 'go' best with what food. Discuss your wines with the customer.
3 Using your list, be flexible in the suggestions you make to customers, accommodating the various choices which members of a party may have ordered. Customers will feel they have had their money's worth.
4 Serve wine at the correct temperature, including aperitifs.
5 Serve with care and grace.
6 Have a small range of glasses. They should be short stemmed, uncut, uncoloured and, ideally, tulip shaped.
7 Consider a short range of carafe wines bearing your house label. This is more easily controllable than breaking down large bottles into the legally prescribed carafe sizes.
8 Control the issue of wine from the cellar to the holding area for the restaurant.
9 Try to maximize the types of wine sold with a meal rather than selling one bottle at an inflated price. Your customers enjoy their meal better and your pocket will not suffer.
10 Customers resent paying a service charge on inflated wine prices. Buy wisely, with an open mind about the place of origin. You can lower the price levels on your list, but still earn a reasonable margin (customers will recognize well-known brand names and calculate the mark-up).
11 A trolley of liqueurs, brandies, ports and cigars is very tempting.

In the bar
1 Make it plain that wine is for sale and properly kept. Have a short range so that bottles are turned over quickly.
2 Do not put less than 15 cl or 5 fl oz in a 6⅔ fl oz glass. Optics are advised.
3 Bottles and carafes should be considered when serious bar catering is done.
4 Bottle yields can be controlled if both carafes and glasses are served in multiples of equally priced 5 cl (this also applies to the restaurant).
5 Glasses must be shiny, clean and never dried with just any old damp all-purpose cloth.
6 Do not specify the amount of wine sold by the glass, until legislation lays down required quantities.
7 Try to serve wines, including sherries, at the right temperature. Cooling cabinets should be considered.
8 Do not use very large bottles if volumes are low.
9 Have some sparkling wine or non-vintage champagne for customers wanting to celebrate an 'occasion'. It can be sold if you try.
10 There must be some visual reminder of wine at the food dispense point.
11 Do not overprice your wine. It is not a luxury item in a bar.

Wine bars

This chapter has so far dealt with full on-licensed premises and not businesses such as wine bars with restricted licences. A genuinely established wine bar, which serves the range and quality of wines associated with such specialism, has different solutions to its problems than those of public houses. The following notes are based on observations by Nigel Pullan, an experienced wine bar operator.

As people acquire the habit of drinking wine so their interest and their desire for more knowledge increases. They no longer seek the same 'safe' wine they have always bought; they want to experiment. Wine bars meet this need by offering a greater choice of wines, both by the glass and by the bottle, than is usually available.

People think of wine bars serving wine by the glass; but the overwhelming volume comes from sales by the bottle. The tendency is for two people to share a bottle of wine or a group of people to have several bottles.

Wine bars have an advantage over many pubs in serving wine because they are almost always 'free' houses and are able to buy wine from any source. They usually have lower overheads than restaurants, so they can normally sell wines at a lower margin. A successful wine bar *knows* that it will sell a great deal of wine; people come to a wine bar at least as much to drink as to eat.

Range of wines Though a restaurant wants to sell a lot of wine, customers, or some of them, may be only modest drinkers. They go to the restaurant primarily to eat and sometimes drink no wine at all. Therefore, every bottle of wine in a restaurant has to carry a mark-up appropriate to the overheads.

A wine bar has opportunity to provide variety and stimulate greater interest in wine. The UK is fortunate to be the 'wine capital' of the world, with wines for sale from virtually every wine-producing country. So as a wine bar can offer wines from many countries and, though UK wine duties mean that the less expensive wines carry a disproportionate amount of duty, a good choice is possible.

An attractively presented wine list is desirable. Each wine should be described briefly, simply and informatively, to persuade customers to try a choice of wines. An example is given in Figure 56.

Pricing and promotion A wine bar will probably include wines from several countries and in several different price categories within any country. For instance, though the sales of a château-bottled claret at £15 may not be great, its inclusion not only forms a talking point but also, more practically, makes other wines in the same category at perhaps £6 or £7 look good value.

Blackboards can be used to supplement a printed wine list with special offers. If turnover is considerable, with a number of regular customers, a blackboard showing the 'wines of the day', one red and one white, served by the bottle and glass, attract interest and help influence indecisive buyers.

In a suitable location there is an opportunity for champagne sales. Though seen by many as a luxury, champagne is more familiar to wine bar customers – if not as an everyday habit at least on a regular basis. The secret is not to overprice champagnes: offer a choice, price competitively at a below average gross profit (but higher than the average 'cash' profit per wine bottle) and they will sell. Champagne can be a catching habit. The sight of one group drinking champagne will often persuade others.

Sales and service of wine with food

The Ebury Wine Bar

139 Ebury Street, London SW1W 9QU
Telephone 01-730 5447

Wine List

Fortified Wines
All served in 5 oz. glass.
Ports — by the decanter on request.

	Glass	Whole Bottle
Sherry		
Garvey San Angelo Amontillado	1.00	
Garvey San Carlo	1.00	
La Ina, Domecq	1.20	
Tio Pepe Gonzalez Byass	1.30	
Port		
White Port	1.40	
Ruby, Smith Woodhouse	1.50	8.20
Graham's Late-bottled	1.80	9.90
Smith Woodhouse Old Lodge, Fine Old Tawny	2.00	10.80
Smith Woodhouse Crusted Port	2.20	

We always have decanted at least two fine vintage ports.

Madeira
From the long established house of Cossart Gordon

Sercial, Dry	1.50	
Rainwater, Medium Dry	1.50	
Bual, Medium Rich	1.50	
Malmsey, Full and Rich	1.50	

Aperitifs/Digestifs
All served in large measures, straight or with ice.

Punt e Mes	1.20	
Chambery	1.20	
Muscat de Beaumes de Venise A.C. Domaine de Coyeux. D.B.	2.00	5.75 (half)

Soft Drinks

Perrier	½ litre	.75
Fresh Orange Juice	Large Glass	1.00
Fresh Grapefruit Juice	Large Glass	1.00

The management reserves the right to change any vintage.

The Ebury Selection
The wines in this section are all served by the glass or bottle and are especially recommended.

		Bottle	Glass 14cl (approx. one fifth of a bottle)
White			
1	Ebury French-bottled House White	4.20	1.00
	We aim to continue to give the best House White available.		
2	Muscadet de Sèvre et Maine Cuvée du Cardinal 1983	4.95	1.10
	Dry, fresh and delicious.		
3	Niersteiner Gutes Domthal QbA 1982/83	4.95	1.10
	A good quality medium-dry hock.		
4	Château de Fayolle, A.C. Côtes de Bergerac C.B. 1983	5.50	1.20
	White Bergerac has always been an Ebury favourite. This is fresh and "grapey".		
5	Frascati Secco Superiore, Villa Catone 1982/83	5.50	1.20
	Villa Catone has come top in many recent Frascati tastings.		
6	Pinot d'Alsace. W. Gisselbrecht 1981/82	5.50	1.20
	Fruity and spicy, Alsace wines are perhaps the ideal wines to drink on their own.		
7	Château Bonnet A.C. Entre-Deux Mers C.B. 1983	5.80	1.25
	A beautifully dry perfumed wine.		
8	Mâcon Villages A.C. "Les Donzelles" 1982	6.75	1.45
	Fresh and delicious, white Burgundy.		
Sparkling			
9	Comte de Jouvance, Méthode Champenoise, Brut	6.95	1.50
	Made by the Champagne method in Saumur.		
Rosé			
10	Côtes de Provence A.C. Caves Co-opérative de Ramatuelle	5.50	1.20
	Produced near St. Tropez, dry and very à la mode.		
Red			
11	Ebury French-bottled House Red	4.20	1.00
	As with our White we aim to give the best quality and value available.		
12	Côtes de Provence A.C. Caves Co-opérative de Ramatuelle	4.95	1.00
	From the romantic hilltop village inland from St. Tropez. Full of flavour.		
13	House Claret, Bordeaux A.C. Robert Ducoudray 1982	5.00	1.00
	Genuine Claret at a reasonable price.		
14	Utrero, Bodegas, Jose Palacios 1980/81	5.50	1.20
	This Rioja Bodega makes its wines by French methods and the result is one of the best and most enjoyable Riojas.		
15	Beaujolais A.C. 1983	5.50	1.20
	Fresh, fruity, typical good Beaujolais from a vintage which produced full bodied wines.		
16	Château de Fayolle A.C. Côtes de Bergerac C.B. 1982	5.50	1.20
	Beautifully balanced and fruity with a rich ruby colour.		
17	Côtes du Rhône, A.C. Cuvée Personelle J. Pascal 1978	6.25	1.35
	A big "gutsy" Rhône that compares very favourably with most Châteauneuf-du-Pape.		
18	Château Bonnet, A.C. Bordeaux C.B. 1981	6.95	1.45
	Chosen by the well known French gastronomes Gault and Millau.		
Champagnes			
We aim to offer the widest choice of Champagnes including magnums, half bottles and vintage Champagnes — all at the keenest prices.			
19	House Champagne	11.20	2.40
	Bucks Fizz (with Champagne)		3.45
	(with Sparkling Wine)		2.60
	Kir "Royale" Cassis or Framboise (with Sparkling Wine)		1.60
	Kir		1.10

Please see back page for Ports, Sherries, etc.

Ebury, Chatham & Dover Limited
178 Ebury Street
London SW1
Telephone 01 730 4618 (24 hour Ansafone)
and 01 730 8206
VAT No. 240904779

Discount Wines By The Case
All the wines on this list may be ordered by the case at wholesale prices from the separate case price list displayed on the bar. Do please take one. — All details of opening hours at our warehouse at 178 Ebury Street, collection allowances etc., are in that list.

Figure 56 *The Ebury Wine Bar wine list*
Courtesy Ebury Wine Bar

Other ideas for creating variety and interest include Bucks Fizz (sparkling wine or champagne and orange juice), sangria, kir (crème de cassis topped up with dry, white wine) and kir royale (the same but with sparkling wine). Apart from a range of table and sparkling wines, keep a good range of fortified wines such as port, sherry and Madeira. These may be served in two sizes of glass, according to people's taste or pocket.

Variety, interest, presentation and correct serving are as all important with wines as they are with food. Wine bars will continue to attract a growing number of people while they maintain high standards of food and wine, served in attractive premises by friendly and enthusiastic people. Wine bars are as good or as bad as the people running them.

Further reading

Fuller, John, *Modern Restaurant Service*, Hutchinson, 1983.

Part Four

Recipes for Pubs

The editor acknowledges with appreciation the assistance of Daniel Stevenson in preparing this section.

Recipes have been contributed by Michael Davidson and Daniel Stevenson. Dishes suitable for cook freeze preparation have also been developed by students at the Department of Catering Management, Oxford Polytechnic. These recipes reflect the diversity of pub catering. Most are suitable for both pub restaurant or bar service meals because, whereas there is demand for the higher standards associated with restaurants, constraints of time and cost make it necessary to adapt them for bar service.

Items reflect pub catering trends; from traditional British fare such as fish and chips, Cornish pasties, steak and kidney pie etc. to other national specialities, Hungarian goulash, chilli con carne and moussaka. Vegetarian, low-fat and high-fibre dishes are also becoming popular choices. Theme pub/restaurants with a unique style and atmosphere offer dishes from one or more distinctive cuisines: Spain, France, Mexico, India or China may inspire specific meal experiences.

17 Soups, sauces and dressings

Michael Davidson and Daniel Stevenson

Soups

This regular restaurant feature is not so common at the snack bar because its low price gives rise to the fear that customers may buy soup and a roll only thus producing a low cash contribution. Some believe that soup adversely affects drink sales. But soups can be a good profit-maker on a snack menu when offered at a realistic price as an individual item. If this does not suit a specific market, one method of increasing the cash contribution of soup is to offer it in combination with other menu items e.g. soup and sandwich or soup and ploughman's lunch.

To make a good soup a stock must be used as the base. It is not practical in a small pub kitchen to maintain a stock pot, and bouillon cubes or granules can be substituted; these are available in chicken, beef, ham, mutton and fish flavours.

For fresh homely soup various vegetable cutting machines and food processors can cut a variety of shapes and reduce labour and preparation time required.

As an alternative, soups in packets or cans may be personalized for individual service.

Batch sizes of soups are important for snack service, which may operate intermittently and also cover most of the licensing hours. When this is the case, fast food soups may be the most suitable. Another alternative is to prepare fresh soups or personalized convenience soups in advance of service, then quickly chill them and hold them in a refrigerator. The soup can be quickly reheated in a microwave oven in the serving dishes, thus eliminating pots and pans.

Chilling and reheating food must be done hygienically. The DHSS recommends that food which is *quickly chilled* may be stored at a temperature of 0–3 °C up to a period not exceeding five days; this period must include the cooking and service times.

Guidance for the hygienic chilling and regenerating of food is available from the DHSS.

Convenience or ready-prepared soups

Packet mixtures may vary from instant soups requiring only the addition of boiling water, to soup powders which are blended with cold water or milk then stirred into boiling water or stock and cooked for a short period. Whatever the type of soup, observe the manufacturer's instructions.

Recipes for Pubs

Personalizing soups   Preparation and finishing (this also applies to fresh soups) may be varied to create individuality. This can be achieved as follows:

Strengthen flavour   Add seasonings or bouillons or an ingredient which produces a more distinct flavour, colour or appearance e.g. extra tomato purée to tomato, spring vegetable or minestrone soups.

Use home-made stocks for convenience soups.

Complement flavour   Add enriching ingredients, e.g. extra milk or cream to cream soups.

Add wine, fortified wine or spirit to soups, e.g. adding port or sherry to game soups or clear soups.

Hybrid soups   Soups may be a mixture of fresh soup and convenience soup. For example, prepare a thin cream chicken soup (using the recipe to follow but halving the quantities of fat and flour in the roux) then add a packet soup to produce individual flavour and correct consistency – asparagus, mushroom etc.

Garnishing   Add garnishes to soups, e.g. diced cooked meat or poultry, parsley or small onion rings etc.

Accompaniments   Serve suitable accompaniments, e.g. toasted bread flutes, croûtons, Melba toast, bread, cheese straws, grated parmesan cheese with minestrone, or lemon segments with fish and shellfish soups.

All recipes are for 10–12 portions.

Clear soups
Basic recipe for consommés

3 l	Cold brown stock/bouillon – flavour determined by type of consommé	6 pt
	Clarification	
300 g	Lean minced beef (plus any appropriate trimmings – chicken, game flesh, giblets and necks etc.)	12 oz
100 g	Onions	4 oz
100 g	Carrots	4 oz
50 g	Celery	2 oz
50 g	Leek	2 oz
	Bay leaf, sprig of thyme and parsley stalks	
4	Egg whites	4
25 g	Tomato purée	1 oz
8	Peppercorns	8
pinch	Salt	pinch

Basic method for consommés

1 Wash, peel and finely cut or mince the vegetables.
2 Prepare the clarification as follows: thoroughly mix together the vegetables, herbs, minced raw flesh, egg whites and tomato purée.
3 Place the clarification into a pot or boiler, add the cold stock and thoroughly whisk together.
4 Place on a low heat and slowly bring to the boil. Stir only at the commence-

Soups, sauces and dressings

ment of heating; do not stir when hot, i.e. when the egg whites begin to coagulate.
5 Slowly simmer, leaving the crust of the clarification undisturbed, for 1½–2 hours.
6 Carefully strain the consommé through a double-folded fine cloth or muslin into a pot or bowl. Strain the mixture with as little disturbance to the clarification as possible.
7 Remove any surface grease with a dishpaper, check the seasoning and deepen the colour with a little gravy browning if required.

Beef consommé Follow the instructions in the basic recipe and method using beef stock and lean minced beef.

Variations *Consommé Carmen* Increase the tomato purée in the basic recipe to 100 g (4 oz). Garnish the strained consommé with small pieces of tomato flesh, cooked red pimento and boiled rice.
Consommé Julienne Garnish the strained consommé with thin strips of cooked carrot, turnip, celery and leek. Also add a few cooked peas.

Figure 57 *Soup served with croûtons*
Courtesy Flour Advisory Bureau

Recipes for Pubs

Chicken consommé Follow the instructions in the basic recipe and method using chicken stock, lean minced beef and chicken trimmings or giblets.

Variations *Consommé aurore* Increase the tomato purée in the basic recipe to 100 g (4 oz). Garnish the strained consommé with a little cooked tapioca and thin strips of cooked chicken.
Consommé bouquetière Garnish the strained consommé with a little cooked tapioca, peas, carrots, turnips, green beans and asparagus.

Game consommé Follow the instructions in the basic recipe and method using game stock and any available game trimmings added to the clarification. Garnish the strained consommé with a dice of cooked game flesh and add a little Madeira wine when serving.

Basic recipe for broths

2½ l	White stock/bouillon	5 pt
500 g	Vegetables (carrots, turnips, leeks, celery and onions)	1 lb 4 oz
	Salt and pepper	
	Chopped parsley	
	See each individual recipe below.	

Chicken broth Use chicken stock/bouillon and add 60 g (2½ oz). long-grain rice to the basic recipe. A garnish of cooked chicken may also be added.
Mutton broth Use mutton stock/bouillon and add 60 g (2½ oz). pearl barley to the basic recipe. A garnish of diced cooked mutton may also be added.
Pulse broth Use white beef stock/bouillon and add 60 g (2½ oz). of pulse vegetables to the basic recipe.

Basic method for broths
1 Soak any barley or pulse vegetables for several hours in cold water.
2 Wash and peel the vegetables, then cut into a small dice.
3 Place the stock or water and bouillon into a saucepan and bring to the boil.
4 Add any barley or pulse vegetables in the recipe and simmer for about 1 hour. Skim as required.
5 Add the vegetables, then simmer till cooked.
6 Check the seasoning and consistency then sprinkle with the chopped parsley and serve.

Minestrone

2½ l	White stock/bouillon	5 pt
600 g	Vegetables (carrots, turnips, leeks, celery and onions)	1 lb 8 oz
50 g	Peas (frozen)	2 oz
50 g	French beans (frozen)	2 oz
50 g	Cabbage	2 oz
4	Tinned tomatoes, chopped	4
3	Large cloves garlic	3
50 g	Spaghetti (broken into small pieces)	2 oz
25 g	Long-grain rice	1 oz
50 g	Tomato purée	2 oz

Soups, sauces and dressings

100 g	Fat bacon	4 oz
50 g	Margarine or pork fat	2 oz
	Parsley	
	Salt and pepper	

Method
1. Wash and peel the vegetables, then cut into small pieces.
2. Melt the margarine or pork fat in a saucepan, add the vegetables then slowly cook without colouring.
3. Add the stock and bring to the boil.
4. Mince together the fat bacon, garlic and parsley.
5. Blend the fat bacon mixture through the stock (or alternatively shape into small balls) then add the tomato purée, spaghetti and rice.
6. Simmer for 15–20 min then add the peas, cut French beans and chopped tinned tomatoes.
7. Simmer till cooked.
8. Check the seasoning and consistency then sprinkle with chopped parsley.
9. Serve accompanied with grated parmesan cheese.

Spring vegetable soup Prepare the same as minestrone without using the fat bacon, paste and spaghetti. Use a selection of vegetables to suit individual taste.

Purée soups
Basic recipe for purée soups

3½ l	Ham stock/bouillon	7 pt
500 g	Pulse vegetable – see below	1 lb 4 oz
100 g	Carrots	4 oz
100 g	Onion	4 oz
50 g	Celery	2 oz
50 g	Leek	2 oz
	Sprig of thyme, bay leaf and parsley stalks	
	Salt and pepper	

Lentil soup Use lentils in the basic recipe.
Split pea soup Use split peas in the basic recipe.
Haricot bean soup Use haricot beans in the basic recipe.
Red bean soup Use red beans in the basic recipe.

Basic method for purée soups
1. Soak the pulse vegetable in cold water for several hours.
2. Wash, peel then roughly chop the vegetables. Note: leave carrots whole when preparing green pea soup.
3. Place two-thirds of the stock into a saucepan.
4. Drain the water off the soaked pulse vegetable, then add to the stock.
5. Bring to the boil, stirring occasionally to prevent burning.
6. Skim off the scum as it forms on the surface.
7. Add the vegetables, then simmer till cooked, i.e. 1½–2 hours. Top up with the remaining stock as required during cooking.
8. Pass through a soup machine or liquidizer. Note: remove the carrot before puréeing when preparing green pea soup.
9. Reboil, then check consistency and seasoning.

Recipes for Pubs

Traditional accompaniments Pulse soups which do not contain a garnish are often served with croûtons, i.e. small cubes of bread fried till crisp in a little butter or margarine.

Potato soup

2½ l	White stock/bouillon	5 pt
50 g	Margarine or butter	2 oz
200 g	Onion	8 oz
50 g	Celery	2 oz
50 g	White leek	2 oz
1.1 kg	Potatoes	2¾ lb
	Bay leaf and sprig of thyme	
pinch	Salt and white pepper	pinch

Method
1. Wash, peel and roughly chop the vegetables.
2. Wash, peel and slice the potatoes.
3. Melt the margarine in a saucepan, add the vegetables and slowly cook with a lid on for 6–8 minutes. Do not colour.
4. Add the stock and sliced potatoes and bring to the boil.
5. Simmer for approximately 30 minutes.
6. Remove the bay leaf, allow to cool slightly then pass through a sieve or liquidizer.
7. Reboil, then check seasoning and consistency.

Variations *Crème cressonnère* Prepare as potato soup but add a bunch of washed picked watercress to the soup when cooking. Garnish the soup after straining with leaves of watercress which have been blanched in boiling water. Blend in 125 ml (¼ pt) cream just prior to serving.

Vichysoisse Prepare the same as potato soup using the following ingredients:

2½ l	White chicken stock	5 pt
25 g	Margarine or butter	1 oz
200 g	Onion	8 oz
400 g	White leeks	1 lb
800 g	Potatoes	2 lb
	Bay leaf and sprig of thyme	

Chill the soup after puréeing or liquidizing. When serving, lightly whip 125 ml (¼ pt) cream and blend through the soup. Sprinkle with chopped chives and chopped parsley.

Cream soups
Basic recipe for vegetable cream soups

2½ l	White chicken stock/bouillon	5 pt
125 g	Margarine or butter	5 oz
125 g	Flour	5 oz
150 g	Onion	6 oz
50 g	Celery	2 oz
50 g	White leek	2 oz
	Sprig of thyme and bay leaf	
200 g	Appropriate vegetable – see below	8 oz
	Salt and pepper	
50–100 ml	Cream	2–5 fl oz

Soups, sauces and dressings

Cream of cauliflower Use cauliflower in the basic recipe.
Cream of celery Increase the quantity of celery to 200 g (8 oz).
Cream of onion Increase the quantity of onion to 200 g (8 oz).
Cream of leek Increase the quantity of leek to 200 g (8 oz).

Basic method for vegetable cream soups
1. Wash, peel, then roughly chop the vegetables.
2. Melt the margarine or butter in a saucepan then add the vegetables.
3. Cook for 8–10 minutes with a lid on, avoiding any colour development.
4. Add the flour and mix together.
5. Cook on a low heat for 4–5 minutes without developing any colour.
6. Slowly blend in the chicken stock, stirring smooth with each addition of stock.
7. Bring to the boil then slowly simmer till cooked, i.e. 45 minutes to 1 hour. Skim off any surplus fat and impurities.
8. Pass through a soup machine or liquidizer.
9. Reboil, then check consistency and seasoning.
10. Blend through the cream then serve.

Garnish A small quantity of the main vegetable may be cooked separately in a little salted water. The vegetable is cut into neat pieces, then added to the soup when serving.

Cream of chicken Prepare the basic recipe for a vegetable cream soup using a strong chicken stock and without any predominant vegetable flavouring.

Variations *Cream of chicken and mushroom soup* Add 50 g (2 oz) mushroom trimmings to the soup when cooking, then garnish with sliced mushrooms and a dice of cooked chicken when strained.
Cream of chicken and asparagus soup Add the liquid from a small tin of asparagus to the soup when cooking. Garnish the soup with asparagus tips and a dice of cooked chicken.

Tomato soup and cream of tomato soup

2½ l	Ham stock/bouillon	5 pt
200 g	Carrots	8 oz
200 g	Onion	8 oz
100 g	Celery	4 oz
100 g	Leek	4 oz
2 cloves	Garlic (optional)	2 cloves
	Sprig of thyme and bay leaf	
125 g	Margarine or butter	5 oz
125 g	Flour	5 oz
250 g	Tomato purée	10 oz
	Salt and pepper	
50–100 ml	Cream	2–5 fl oz

Method
1. Wash, peel, then roughly chop the vegetables.
2. Crush the garlic.
3. Melt the margarine or butter in a saucepan then add the vegetables and garlic.
4. Cook for 8–10 minutes with a lid covering the saucepan.

Recipes for Pubs

   5 Add the flour and mix together.
   6 Cook on a low heat for 4–5 minutes, then add the tomato purée.
   7 Slowly blend in the hot stock, stirring smooth with each addition of stock.
   8 Bring to the boil, then slowly simmer till cooked, i.e. approximately 1 hour. Skim off any surface fat and impurities as required.
   9 Pass through a soup machine or liquidizer.
10 Reboil, then check consistency and seasoning.
11 Blend through the cream and serve.

Note: The sweet and sharp taste of tomato soup may be adjusted by adding a little sugar and vinegar boiled together.

Variations

Barbecue tomato soup   Add 25 g (1 oz) French mustard and 50 g (2 oz) honey to the soup after straining.

Beef and tomato soup   Prepare the soup with beef stock/bouillon and garnish with diced cooked beef after straining.

Farmhouse tomato soup   Prepare the soup as stated but cut the vegetables into neat shapes and do not strain or liquidize when cooked.

Crème Portugaise   Garnish the soup after straining with cooked rice.

Sauces

Sauces are the basis of many dishes but take time to prepare and need to be ready in advance.

Recipes are included here for those with space, time and equipment to make sauces traditionally, together with hints on the incorporation of convenience products.

Sauces may be an integral part of a dish, e.g. meat, poultry or game in a wine sauce, or an important accompaniment, e.g. deep fried fish with tartare or tomato sauce.

In some instances a sauce is made during the preparation of a dish; brown stew, goulash and chilli con carne are examples. However, in most cases sauces are prepared as individual products to be used as required.

Most of the introductory comments about the preparation of soups also apply to sauces.

All recipes are for a 1 litre (2 pint) sauce

Roux-thickened sauces   The following recipes and methods are for traditionally prepared sauces. To reduce preparation time amend methods as follows:

   1 Do not use the roux ingredients or prepare a roux. Whisk a mixture of lightly creamed margarine (or butter) and flour into the very hot milk or simmering stock at the end of the cooking process, then simmer for 4–5 minutes.

      The fat and flour mixture should contain slightly more fat than flour, i.e. five parts fat to four parts flour, and may be kept ready made in the kitchen to be used when required.

Note: When using aluminium saucepans, do not strike the whisk against the sides of the pan or discolouration of the sauce may result.

Soups, sauces and dressings

2 *Low-fat recipes and method*   Do not use the roux ingredients or prepare a roux. Whisk in a cold liquid and flour paste to the very hot milk or simmering stock at the end of the cooking process, then simmer for 4–5 minutes.

The paste is made with the appropriate cold recipe liquid (milk or stock or water) and flour whisked together until smooth. It is also advisable to strain the paste to make certain that no lumps are present. Use 100 g (4 oz) flour mixed together with enough recipe liquid to form a thin paste per litre of sauce.

When preparing low-fat tomato and curry sauces etc., do not fry the vegetables.

Basic white sauce (béchamel) and derivatives

Also available in packet form.

1 l	Milk	2 pt
100 g	Margarine or butter	4 oz
100 g	Flour	4 oz
1	Studded onion (onion, bay leaf and 2–3 cloves)	1
	Salt and white pepper	

Method
1 Heat the milk with the onion until almost boiling.
2 Melt the margarine in a saucepan, add the flour, then mix together.
3 Cook on a low heat for 4–5 minutes without developing any colour.
4 Slowly blend in the milk, stirring smooth with each addition of liquid.
5 Bring to the boil then slowly simmer for 4–5 minutes. Include the studded onion.
6 Check consistency and seasoning then strain if required.

Anchovy sauce   Add anchovy essence to taste.
Uses: poached, fried or grilled fish dishes.

Cheese sauce   Add 100 g (4 oz) grated cheese into the boiling sauce on completion of cooking and stir until melted through the sauce.
Also available in packet form.
Uses: poached fish, egg and vegetable dishes.

Cream sauce   Add milk and cream to the basic sauce, adjusting the consistency to that of pouring double cream.
Uses: poached fish and boiled vegetables.

Egg sauce   Add a small dice of hard-boiled eggs, 3–4 eggs.
Uses: poached fish dishes.

Mustard sauce   Add diluted English mustard to taste.
Uses: grilled herring.

Onion sauce   Add 200 g (8 oz) of diced onions which have been lightly fried in 25 g (1 oz) margarine without colour to the basic sauce. The studded onion may also be chopped and added (cloves and bay leaf removed). Also available in packet form.
Uses: poached fish, roast mutton, egg and vegetable dishes.

Recipes for Pubs

Parsley sauce   Add chopped parsley till generously dispersed through the sauce. Also available in packet form.
Uses: poached fish, chicken, pork, egg and vegetable dishes.

Veloute sauce and derivatives   This is a basic white sauce made with stock. Use the recipe and method for béchamel but replace the milk with white stock/bouillon (chicken, fish, veal or mutton) and omit the studded onion. The traditional cooking time for this sauce is one hour. Many sauces can be made from the veloutes by adding various ingredients and garnishes.

Quantities based on 1 litre (2 pint) of veloute

Bonne femme sauce

50 g	Butter or margarine	2 oz
100 g	Finely chopped onion	4 oz
300 g	Button mushrooms	12 oz
125 ml	White wine	¼ pt
squeeze	Lemon juice	squeeze
100 ml	Whipped cream	4 fl oz
	Chopped parsley	

Method
1. Lightly fry the onions in the butter without colour.
2. Wash and slice the mushrooms then add to the onions and continue cooking for 3–4 minutes.
3. Add the parsley, lemon juice and white wine and boil down until quite thick and concentrated.
4. Add the fish veloute and simmer for 2–3 minutes.
5. Fold through the whipped cream then check seasoning and consistency.

Note: The use of whipped cream produces a good brown colour or glaze when the sauced fish dish is placed under a hot grill.
Uses: fish.

Dugléré sauce   Prepare the same as bonne femme but replace the mushrooms with roughly chopped tomato flesh. Add the tomato flesh at step 3 above.
Note: This sauce is not usually glazed, therefore the cream does not have to be whipped.
Uses: fish.

Prawn sauce   Add 100 g (4 oz) of cooked prawns into white wine sauce. Also available as a tinned product and in packet form.
Uses: poached fish and shellfish.

White wine sauce   When preparing the fish veloute, replace 200 ml (8 fl oz) of the fish stock with white wine and add a good squeeze of lemon juice. A little cayenne pepper is also added when seasoning the sauce. The sauce may be completed with cream, which should be whipped when the sauce has to be glazed (browned).
Uses: fish.

White wine sauce   Prepare as white wine sauce above using chicken veloute.
Uses: poached chicken, veal, sweetbreads, vol-au-vents etc.

Soups, sauces and dressings

Hungarian sauce   Lightly fry 200 g (8 oz) of diced onion in 50 g (2 oz) of margarine without colour then add 20 g (¾ oz) of paprika. Add 200 ml (8 fl oz) white wine and boil down to one-third of the quantity. Add the veloute sauce and simmer for 2–3 minutes.
Note: Chopped peeled tomatoes or tinned tomatoes (200 g (8 oz)) and a little cream are also sometimes added.
Uses: chicken, veal and pork dishes.

Mushroom sauce   Lightly fry 200 g (8 oz) of washed sliced mushrooms without colour, then add the veloute sauce and simmer for 2–3 minutes. The sauce may also be completed with a little cream.
Also available as a tinned product and in packet form.
Uses: poached chicken, veal, sweetbreads, vol-au-vents.

Caper sauce   Garnish the basic mutton veloute with 80 g (2½ oz) of whole capers.
Uses: boiled mutton dishes.

Tomato sauce   Also available in packet form.

1 l	Ham stock/bouillon	2 pt
100 g	Margarine or butter	4 oz
100 g	Flour	4 oz
100 g	Onion	4 oz
100 g	Carrots	4 oz
50 g	Celery	2 oz
50 g	Leeks	1 oz
1 clove	Garlic (optional)	1 clove
	Sprig of thyme, bay leaf and parsley stalks	
100 g	Tomato purée	4 oz
	Salt and white pepper	

Method
1 Wash, peel, then roughly chop the vegetables.
2 Crush the garlic.
3 Melt the margarine in a saucepan, then add the vegetables and garlic.
4 Allow to cook for 8–10 minutes with a lid covering the saucepan.
5 Add the flour and mix together.
6 Allow to cook on a low heat for 4–5 minutes, then add the tomato purée.
7 Slowly blend in the hot stock, stirring smooth with each addition of stock.
8 Bring to the boil then slowly simmer till cooked, i.e. approximately 1 hour. Skim off any surplus fat and impurities as required.
9 Strain or liquidize the sauce.
10 Reboil then check consistency and seasoning.
Uses: large variety of uses – fish, pasta, egg, meat, poultry, game and vegetable dishes.

Curry sauce   Also available as a tinned product and in packet form.

1 l	Brown stock/bouillon	2 pt
100 g	Margarine or butter	4 oz
100 g	Flour	4 oz

Recipes for Pubs

25 g	Curry powder (or to taste)	1 oz
200 g	Onions	8 oz
2 cloves	Garlic	2 cloves
20 g	Tomato purée	¾ oz
100 g	Cooking apples	4 oz
20 g	Dessicated coconut	¾ oz
60 g	Mango chutney	2½ oz
20 g	Sultanas	¾ oz

Method
1. Peel and finely chop the onions and crush the garlic.
2. Prepare the fruit base, i.e. peel and core the apples, then chop together with the sultanas, chutney and coconut. Place aside.
3. Melt the margarine in a saucepan, then add the onion and garlic.
4. Allow to cook for 3–4 minutes, then add the curry powder.
5. Allow to cook on a low heat for 2–3 minutes, then add the flour and mix together.
6. Allow to cook for a further 2–3 minutes on a low heat.
7. Add the tomato purée and mix together.
8. Slowly blend in the hot stock, stirring smooth with each addition of stock.
9. Bring to the boil then add the fruit base.
10. Slowly simmer until cooked, i.e. 45 minutes approximately. Skim as required.
11. Check consistency and seasoning.

Note: When a smooth sauce is required strain or liquidize the sauce.
Uses: large variety of uses – fish, pasta, egg, meat, poultry, game and vegetable dishes.

Brown sauce and derivatives

Also available in packet form.
Traditional brown sauce (espagnole), which is made with a brown roux, is rarely prepared nowadays because of its heavy nature and prolonged cooking time.

1½ l	Brown stock/bouillon	3 pt
75 g	Dripping, lard or oil	3 oz
100 g	Flour	4 oz
100 g	Onion	4 oz
100 g	Carrots	4 oz
50 g	Celery	2 oz
50 g	Leeks	2 oz
	Sprig of thyme, bay leaf and parsley stalks	
50 g	Tomato purée	2 oz

Method
1. Wash, peel, then roughly chop the vegetables.
2. Melt the dripping in a saucepan, then add the vegetables.
3. Fry the vegetables until brown, then add the flour and mix together.
4. Cook the mixture until lightly coloured, avoiding burning.
5. Add the tomato purée, then slowly blend in the hot stock, stirring smooth with each addition of stock.

Soups, sauces and dressings

6 Bring to the boil, then slowly simmer until cooked, i.e. approximately two hours.
7 Strain the sauce, then check the consistency and seasoning. The colour may be adjusted by adding blackjack (gravy browning).

The following brown sauces are suitable for a wide range of dishes, e.g. grilled or shallow-fried beef steaks, chicken, gammon steaks, chops or hamburgers.

Barbecue sauce

50 ml	Vinegar	2 fl oz
100 g	Diced onions	4 oz
100 g	Chopped tinned tomatoes	4 oz
50 g	Chopped pickled onions	2 oz
50 g	Chopped gherkins	2 oz
25 g	Chopped capers	1 oz
40 g	Brown sugar	1½ oz
2 tsp	Diluted English mustard	2 tsp
	Chopped parsley	
1 l	Basic brown sauce	2 pt

Method
1 Place the vinegar, onions, chopped tomatoes and sugar into a saucepan and boil down by two-thirds.
2 Add the brown sauce, gherkins, capers, pickled onions and diluted mustard, bring to the boil and simmer for 4–5 minutes.
3 Add the parsley. Check seasoning and consistency.
Note: The quantities of sugar and vinegar may be adjusted to produce a weak or strong sweet and sour taste. Alternatively, the sugar may be replaced with redcurrant jelly.

Beer sauce Boil down 250–300 ml (10–12 fl oz) beer in a saucepan. Add the brown sauce and simmer for 1 minute, then check consistency and seasoning. A little caster sugar may be added to improve flavour.
Note: Depending on how strong you like the sauce, beer from a bitter to a milk stout may be used.

Bolognaise sauce Yield: 10 portions

50 g	Margarine, butter or lard	2 oz
200 g	Finely chopped onion	8 oz
20 g	Garlic (crushed)	¾ oz
500 g	Minced beef	1 lb 4 oz
500 ml	Brown sauce	1 pt

Note: This sauce is often prepared with a tomato flavour. If this is desired add 25 g (1 oz) tomato purée.

Method
1 Heat the fat in a saucepan, then add the onion and garlic.
2 Cook for 3–4 minutes.
3 Add the minced beef and shallow fry until lightly coloured.
4 Drain off any excess fat which has been produced.
5 Add any tomato purée.
6 Add the brown sauce and bring to the boil. Check the consistency and, if too thick, thin down with a little brown beef stock/bouillon.

7 Slowly simmer until cooked – approximately 45 minutes.
8 Check seasoning and consistency.

This sauce may be prepared without the use of brown sauce. After frying off the mince, add 25 g (1 oz) flour and 25 g (1 oz) tomato purée. Also use brown stock/bouillon in place of the sauce.

Chasseur sauce

50 g	Margarine or butter	2 oz
100 g	Chopped onions	4 oz
300 g	Sliced mushrooms	12 oz
300 g	Chopped tinned tomatoes	12 oz
100 ml	White wine	4 fl oz
	Chopped parsley	
	Pinch chopped tarragon	
1 l	Basic brown sauce	2 pt

Method
1 Melt the margarine in a saucepan.
2 Add the onions and cook for 1–2 minutes without colouring.
3 Add the mushrooms and continue cooking for a further 2–3 minutes.
4 Add the wine and boil down by two-thirds.
5 Add the tomatoes and brown sauce and simmer for 4–5 minutes.
6 Add the parsley and tarragon. Check seasoning and consistency.

Note: When using dried tarragon, add the tarragon at the same time as the mushrooms.

Devil sauce (diable)

150 g	Chopped onions	6 oz
	Good pinch Mignonette pepper	
100 ml	Vinegar	4 fl oz
100 ml	White wine	4 fl oz
	Pinch cayenne pepper	
1 l	Basic brown sauce	2 pt

Method
1 Place the onions, Mignonette pepper, vinegar and wine into a saucepan.
2 Boil down by two-thirds.
3 Add the brown sauce and simmer for 10–15 minutes.
4 Strain into a clean pan then season with salt, pepper and cayenne pepper. Check consistency.

Lyonnaise sauce

50 g	Margarine or butter	2 oz
800 g	Sliced onions	2 lb
100 ml	Vinegar	4 fl oz
100 ml	White wine	4 fl oz
1 l	Basic brown sauce	2 pt

Method
1 Melt the margarine in a saucepan.
2 Add the onions and shallow fry to a light golden brown.
3 Add the vinegar and white wine and boil down by two-thirds.
4 Add the brown sauce and simmer for 4–5 minutes.
5 Check consistency and seasoning.

Soups, sauces and dressings

Mushroom sauce	Prepare the same as chasseur sauce omitting the tomatoes and chopped tarragon.	

Piquante sauce	150 g	Chopped onions	6 oz
	100 ml	Vinegar	4 fl oz
	100 ml	White wine	4 fl oz
		Pinch cayenne pepper	
	150 g	Chopped gherkins	6 oz
	75 g	Chopped capers	3 oz
		Chopped parsley (or fines herbes)	
	1 l	Brown sauce	2 pt

Method
1. Place the onions, vinegar and wine into a saucepan and boil down by two-thirds.
2. Add the brown sauce and simmer for 8–10 minutes.
3. Add the gherkins and capers and simmer for a further 2–3 minutes.
4. Add the chopped parsley and season with salt, pepper and cayenne pepper. Check consistency.

Sherry, port or Madeira sauce Boil down 150–200 ml (6–8 fl oz) of the appropriate wine in a saucepan. Add the brown sauce and simmer for one minute, then check consistency and seasoning.
Note: These sauces are sometimes enriched with butter, i.e. remove from the heat then stir 40 g (1½ oz) butter through the sauce.

Mayonnaise sauce and derivatives Cold egg and oil emulsion. Available as a ready made sauce.

	1 l	Salad oil	2 pt
	75–100 ml	Vinegar	3–4 fl oz
	5	Egg yolks	5
	½ tsp	English mustard	½ tsp
	1 tsp	Lemon juice	1 tsp
		Salt and white pepper	

Method
1. Place the yolks in a mixing bowl.
2. Add the salt, pepper, mustard and two-thirds of the vinegar and whisk together until combined.
3. Slowly add the oil in a thin stream while whisking continuously.
4. When the sauce becomes very thick, adjust the consistency with the remaining vinegar.
5. Add the lemon juice and check the seasoning.

Note: Mayonnaise sauce can be made quickly and easily in a food processor. Follow the manufacturer's instructions for the appropriate machine.

Andalusian sauce Add tomato ketchup to the mayonnaise to obtain a good pink colour (100 ml (4 fl oz) approximately). Also add a garnish of diced red peppers (100 g (4 oz)).
Uses: general cold buffet sauce.

Recipes for Pubs

Herb sauce   Blanch a selection of fresh herbs (chervil, chives, spinach, tarragon, parsley, watercress etc.) in boiling water until limp. Refresh in cold water, then squeeze to a dry mass. Place into a liquidizer with the mayonnaise sauce and liquidize to a smooth green purée.
Uses: general cold buffet sauce.

Marie-Rose sauce

1 tsp	Worcester sauce	1 tsp
100 ml	Tomato ketchup	4 fl oz
100 ml	Lightly whipped cream (optional)	4 fl oz
40 g	Finely chopped shallot or onion	1½ oz
	Chopped parsley	
1 l	Mayonnaise sauce	2 pt

Combine all the ingredients, then check the seasoning.
Uses: fish and shellfish cocktails.

Tartare sauce   Add a garnish of 150 g (6 oz) chopped gherkins, 75 g (3 oz) chopped capers and a good pinch of chopped parsley to 1 litre of mayonnaise.
Uses: deep fried fish dishes.

Salad dressings

Basic salad dressing: vinaigrette   The basic recipe for vinaigrette is oil (3 parts), vinegar (1 part), mustard, salt and pepper.

Method Whisk together the vinegar, mustard, salt and pepper. Add the oil and whisk until thoroughly combined.

Blue cheese dressing   Place 200 g (8 oz) blue cheese into a mixing bowl then mash or crumble with a fork. Slowly add 1 l (2 pt) of vinaigrette while constantly mixing with a whisk.

Chilli dressing   Flavour sour cream with chilli sauce (to taste), then season with salt and add a garnish of chopped red and green peppers.

Lemon or lime honey dressing   Place 300 ml (12 fl oz) lemon juice, 300 g (12 oz) honey, 10 g (½ oz) mustard, salt and pepper into a mixing bowl and thoroughly mix together. Add 1 l (2 pt) of salad oil and whisk together.

Roquefort dressing   Prepare the same as blue cheese dressing using Roquefort cheese.

Russian dressing   Flavour mayonnaise with chilli sauce and sweet pickle relish (to taste), then season with salt and add a garnish of chopped hard-boiled eggs.

Thousand island dressing   Add the following ingredients to 1 l (2 pt) of salad dressing (or mayonnaise): 6 chopped hard-boiled eggs, 50 g (2 oz) chopped onion, 25 g (1 oz) each of chopped red and green peppers, a good dash of Tabasco sauce, 100 g (4 oz) tomato ketchup, chopped tarragon and chopped parsley.

Plate 1 *Dressed crab, page 268*
Plate 2 *Fish pie, page 271*

Plate 3 *Seafood skewers, page 271*

Plate 4 *Coq au vin, page 277*

Plate 5   *Lancashire hot pot,*
page 278

Plate 6   *Tripe and onions,*
page 281

Plate 7 *Devilled chicken*, page 283

Plate 8 *Kebab orientale*, page 284

Plate 9   *Moussaka,*
page 287

Plate 10   *Tandoori chicken,*
page 289

Plate 11 *Chilli con carne,*
page 291

Plate 12 *Beef in ale,*
page 294

Plate 13   *Country garden ratatouille, page 295*

Plate 14   *Selection of savoury baked potatoes, page 296*

Plate 15   *Savoury vegetable quiche, page 297*

Plate 16   *Cornish pasties, page 298*

Plate 17   *Chicken pie,*
page 300

Plate 18   *Steak and kidney*
pudding, page 301

Plate 19   *Shellfish cocktail,*
page 308

Plate 20   *Avocado pear*
with crab meat, page 307

Plate 21   *Selection of pâtés, including mushroom, duck and chicken liver, page 308*

Plate 22   *Rollmops, page 308*

Plate 23 *Smoked trout, page 309*

Plate 24 *Ploughman's lunch, including Stilton, cheddar and pâté, page 316*

Plate 25   *Club toasted sandwich, page 319*

Plate 26   *Raspberry cheesecake, page 326*

Plate 27 *Caramel creams,*
page 327

Plate 28 *Fruit flan,*
page 329

Plate 29   *Lemon meringue pie, page 331*

Plate 30   *Fruit crumble, page 332*

Plate 31 *Chocolate gâteau, page 333*

Plate 32 *Selection of mousses, including raspberry, orange and pineapple, page 335*

18 Egg, pasta and fish dishes
Michael Davidson and Daniel Stevenson

Omelettes

A large variety of omelettes can be produced from a few basic ingredients with little wastage to make them one of the more profitable dishes on the menu.

Points to note when preparing omelettes

Omelettes are made in an omelette pan, which should not be used for any other purpose (with the possible exception of frying eggs). Non-stick pans are sometimes used with good results, but the non-stick coating wears off and the coating or pan has to be renewed. Iron pans have a longer life but must be treated with care to keep them in good condition and prevent the egg sticking.

An omelette pan must never be washed but should be wiped clean with a dry cloth immediately after use.

At frequent intervals the pan should be heated and cleaned with a little salt to remove burnt particles and carbon. After this a little fresh oil is heated in the pan, and then the pan is left for a short period over a gentle heat. This is known as skinning or seasoning the pan.

The temperature of the pan into which the eggs are added is a crucial factor when preparing omelettes. The foaming point of butter, or the temperature just short of the smoke point of vegetable oil, is a good guide to when to add the eggs.

The mixture must be stirred and shaken quickly and evenly across the base of the pan, especially when the eggs can be seen to be setting.

Stirring must stop immediately the egg mass is on setting point but not set.

Shaping omelettes

Traditionally folded omelettes are prepared cigar shape, although half-moon shapes are sometimes used when preparing large numbers of omelettes.

Omelettes should be prepared when required for service. However, they may be prepared in advance and kept chilled. When this is the case the omelettes must be kept underdone then reheated in a microwave cooker (the omelettes should be covered with film both during storage and reheating).

Plain omelette and variations

2–3	Eggs		2–3
pinch	Salt and pepper		pinch
10 g	Butter, margarine or oil		½ oz

Recipes for Pubs

Method
1. Break the eggs into a small bowl, add the seasoning then beat well with a fork until the yolks and whites are thoroughly combined.
2. Heat the pan then add the butter or oil as follows:
   Butter or margarine   Add to the pan and continue heating until the butter foams. Shake the pan to disperse the butter over the base of the pan but do not allow to colour.
   Oil   Add enough oil to cover the base of the pan and continue heating for a short period. Do not allow to become very hot and smoke. Pour off excess oil.
3. Add the eggs to the pan, then shake the pan while stirring the eggs with a fork until a smooth, very light set mixture is obtained.
4. Remove from the heat and loosen the outer edges of the egg by running the fork round between the egg and the pan.
5. Fold the omelette:
   Half-moon shape   Fold the egg mixture to the front of the pan producing a half-moon shape.
   Cigar shape   Tilt the pan and fold one end of the egg (end at the handle) to the centre. Tap the handle or bottom of the pan to move the mixture to the edge of the pan, then fold over the other end to resemble a cigar shape.
6. Turn out on to the plate or serving dish. Neaten the shape if required.
7. The surface of the omelette may be brushed with a little melted butter or margarine to produce a light shine and attractive appearance.

Bacon omelette   Proceed as for plain omelette but add a small dice of cooked bacon 25 g (1 oz) into the beaten egg prior to making the omelette. The omelette may also be garnished with a grilled bacon rasher.

Cheese omelette   Proceed as for plain omelette, adding 25 g (1 oz) grated cheese to the egg mixture just prior to folding. Enclose the cheese within the omelette when folding.
Note: When using parmesan cheese, mix the cheese through the egg prior to making the omelette.

Ham omelette   Add a small dice of ham 25 g (1 oz) into the beaten egg prior to making the omelette.

Mushroom omelette   Mix through the beaten eggs 25 g (1 oz) sliced mushrooms which have been cooked in a little butter. Alternatively sauté the mushroom slices in the hot omelette pan prior to adding the eggs.

Savoury omelette   Add a good pinch of chopped parsley, chives and chervil into the beaten eggs.

Stuffed omelettes   Omelettes may be stuffed with garnish in two ways:
1. The garnish is placed on to the centre of the omelette, then folded neatly inside as the omelette is shaped.

2. The omelette is prepared as a plain omelette, then split along the top after placing on the serving dish. The split is then filled with the stuffing.

Egg, pasta and fish dishes

Figure 58 *Savoury pancakes*
Courtesy Flour Advisory Bureau

Chicken omelette   Stuff the omelette with a cream chicken mixture using 40 g (1½ oz) cooked minced chicken heated and bound with a little white sauce.

Seafood omelette   Prawn, scampi, crab, lobster etc. Prepare the stuffing using 40 g (1½ oz) of cooked shellfish. Leave small shellfish whole, but cut large shellfish into a neat dice. Heat in a little margarine or butter, then bind with a spoonful of tomato sauce and a little cream (1 tsp). Check the temperature and seasoning, adding a small pinch of cayenne pepper, then fill the cavity of the omelette.

Tomato omelette Stuff the omelette with hot chopped tomato flesh, i.e. tinned tomatoes or peeled fresh tomatoes. The tomato flesh mixture is often made by lightly frying a little finely chopped onion in butter or oil then adding the roughly chopped tomato flesh and thoroughly heating.

Flat omelettes To prepare flat omelettes the following procedure is usually adopted. Proceed as for a plain omelette to stage 4. When the outer edges of the lightly set egg have been freed from the sides of the pan, brush round the edges of the pan down to the egg with a little melted butter or oil. Tap the pan and shake with a circular motion till the egg mixture slides freely. Place under a hot grill to lightly cook the surface, then turn out and serve.

Spanish omelette Add to the beaten eggs 40 g (1½ oz) finely sliced onion and 25 g (1 oz) diced pimento, both cooked in a little butter, 40 g (1½ oz) diced tomato flesh and a good pinch of chopped parsley.

Pasta dishes

Pasta dishes may be prepared with fresh pasta or dried pasta or purchased ready made as a tinned or frozen product.

It is unlikely that fresh pasta will be prepared in the pub kitchen; therefore the following recipes are for commercially made dry pasta shapes.

Basic recipe and method for cooking dry pastas

Spaghetti, nouilles, macaroni, rigatoni, shells and ribbons.
Yield: 10 main course portions.

400–600 g	Selected dry pasta	1–1½ lb
50 g	Salt	2 oz
50 ml	Oil (optional)	2 fl oz

Method
1 Place a large saucepan of water (approximately 5 l (9 pt)) on to the stove and bring to the boil.
2 Add the salt (and oil to reduce the likelihood of the pasta sticking together).
3 Add the pasta into the boiling water and stir to keep separate.
4 Cook the pasta on a rolling boil, stirring occasionally to keep separate and prevent burning.
5 When cooked, drain in a colander and test for excessive surface starch. That is, if the pasta is sticky and is required for immediate service, then wash or rinse in very hot water and drain thoroughly.
6 Refresh pasta in cold running water, then store in cold water until required for use. The pasta is reheated in very hot salty water when required for service.

Egg, pasta and fish dishes

Dishes using pastas   Any of the pastas mentioned earlier may be used with these dishes.

Spaghetti Italienne   Toss the hot drained spaghetti in a little foaming butter, and at the same time add grated parmesan cheese to flavour. Season with salt and mill pepper then serve.

Macaroni au gratin   Prepare the same as Italienne style but bind the pasta with cheese sauce. Sprinkle with parmesan cheese and gratinate under a hot grill prior to serving.

Macaroni cheese with smoked haddock   Prepare the same as macaroni au gratin, adding flaked smoked haddock which has been cooked in a little milk to the pasta when binding with the cheese sauce.

Macaroni cheese with ham   Prepare the same as macaroni au gratin, adding diced cooked ham 50 g (2 oz) per portion to the hot macaroni when tossing in the butter.

Macaroni cheese with vegetables   Prepare the same as macaroni au gratin but lightly cook or heat a selection of vegetables, e.g. sliced mushrooms, diced peppers, diced onions, crushed garlic, corn niblets and cooked beans etc., in the recipe butter prior to tossing the spaghetti and binding with sauce.

Nouilles niçoise (per portion)   Heat a little oil in a suitable pan, then add and cook 50 g (2 oz) chopped onion and 1 clove of crushed garlic. Add the hot drained pasta and toss in the onion and garlic oil. Add a little grated cheese and diced tomato flesh, then bind with tomato sauce.

Spaghetti bolognaise   Toss the hot drained pasta in foaming butter and season with salt and mill pepper. Place in the serving dish and accompany with bolognaise sauce and grated parmesan. Alternatively place the sauce into the middle of the seasoned and buttered spaghetti and sprinkle over the cheese.

Lasagne verde al forno   Cook the lasagne as stated for dry pastas, then refresh in cold running water. Drain thoroughly when required for use.

Butter an earthenware dish, then place in alternate layers the following items:

1 A layer of cooked drained lasagne.
2 A coating layer of bolognese sauce.
3 A second layer of lasagne on top.
4 A coating layer of cream sauce lightly flavoured with nutmeg.
5 Repeat steps 1–4 until the dish has been filled, finishing with a layer of lasagne topped with the cream sauce.
6 Springle with grated cheese then bake in a hot oven.

Note: Grated cheese may be sprinkled liberally on each layer of lasagne and sauce during the preparation.

Vegetarian lasagne (freeze stable) (see Plate 1)   Yield: 10 portions (main course)

375 g	Lasagne	15 oz
900 g	Spinach (frozen)	2 lb 4 oz
375 g	Onion	15 oz

Recipes for Pubs

400 g	Celery	1 lb
400 g	Carrots	1 lb
40 g	Garlic	1½ oz
200 g	Mushrooms	8 oz
1 kg	Tinned tomatoes	2½ lb
150 g	Tomato purée	6 oz
750 g	Cheddar cheese (grated)	1 lb 14 oz
3	Eggs	3
150 ml	Vegetable oil	6 fl oz
30 g	Salt	1¼ oz
5 g	Pepper	¼ oz

Method
1. Wash and prepare the vegables:
   (a) Cut the onions, celery and carrots into small pieces – 5 mm (¼ in) cubes.
   (b) Crush the garlic.
   (c) Slice the mushrooms.
2. Heat the oil in a saucepan, then lightly fry the vegetables for 2–3 minutes.
3. Cook the lasagne in plenty of boiling salted water.
4. Refresh the lasagne in cold water, then drain thoroughly.
5. Allow the spinach to defrost, then squeeze out any surplus water.
6. Mix together two-thirds of the cheese with the spinach.
7. Add the eggs to the spinach and cheese mixture and thoroughly mix together.
8. Chop the tinned tomatoes.
9. Mix together the chopped tomatoes, tomato purée and juice from the tomatoes.
10. Place alternate layers of spinach mixture, vegetables, lasagne and tomato mixture into a suitable cooking/service dish. Season each layer with salt and pepper.
11. Sprinkle over the surface with the remaining grated cheese and place in a moderate oven until thoroughly reheated.

See also boffins – wholemeal curried vegetable pasties – in Chapter 20.

Rice pilaffs and risottos

Braised rices and risottos may be used to produce interesting first course and main course dishes. They also make suitable accompaniments to kebabs, stews, sautés and sauced fish dishes,

Risotto
Basic recipe   Yield: 10 portions (main course)

600 g	Long grain rice	1½ lb
200 g	Butter or margarine	8 oz
200 g	Onions	8 oz
1½ l	Chicken stock/bouillon	3 pt
	Salt and mill pepper	

Egg, pasta and fish dishes

Method
1. Peel and finely chop the onions.
2. Melt half the butter in a saucepan.
3. Add the chopped onion and slowly cook without colour for 4–5 minutes.
4. Add the rice and slowly cook for a further 2–3 minutes, stirring frequently.
5. Add half the stock and lightly season.
6. Bring to the boil, then cook slowly over a low heat covered with a piece of buttered greaseproof paper and lid.
7. Stir frequently, adding more stock as required. Use a fork at the end of the cooking period to avoid breaking the rice. When cooked the stock should have evaporated, leaving the rice grains slightly pasty with an attractive moist eating quality.
8. Fork through the remaining butter and check seasoning and temperature.

Variations *Risotto with cheese*   Add 250 g (10 oz) grated cheese to the cooked risotto at the same time as the finishing butter.
Risotto with mushrooms   Add 400 g (1 lb) washed sliced mushrooms at step 3 when preparing the basic risotto.
Risotto Milanaise   Add to the basic risotto:
250 g (10 oz) sliced mushrooms – step 3
pinch powdered saffron – step 5
500 g (1¼ lb) roughly chopped tomato flesh/tinned – during cooking
200 g (8 oz) grated cheese – step 8.
Paella   Add to the basic risotto:
4 cloves of crushed garlic – step 3
250 g (10 oz) diced raw lean pork – step 3
250 g (10 oz) diced raw chicken – step 3
250 g (10 oz) sliced mushrooms – step 3
250 g (10 oz) diced red pimentos – step 3
pinch powdered saffron – step 5
1 kg (2½ lb) cooked shellfish, e.g. scampi, prawns and mussels etc. – during cooking
100 g (4 oz) cooked peas – step 8
100 g (4 oz) diced cooked French beans – step 8
250 g (10 oz) roughly chopped tomato flesh/tinned – during cooking.

Riz pilaffs (braised rice)   Use the basic recipe for risotto but reduce the stock to 1 l (2 pt). Also add all the stock at the same time and cook in a moderately hot oven (covered with the buttered paper and lid). When cooked the stock should have evaporated, leaving the rice grains quite dry and easily separable.

Variations   These are the same as for the risottos. Plain and garnished riz pilaffs are often used as accompaniments to dishes.

Pizzas

Available as a ready-prepared chilled or frozen product. The dough may also be purchased in frozen ball shapes ready for defrosting and shaping. Alternatively, the dough may be purchased as a packet mixture.

Recipes for Pubs

Yield: 10 × 225 mm (8.5 in) or 20 × 150 mm (6 in).

Tomato pizza	1¾ kg	Pizza dough (Chapter 22)	4½ lb
(high quality)	200 g	Onion (finely chopped)	½ lb
	15 g	Garlic (crushed)	½ oz
	200 ml	Oil	4 fl oz
	1.2 kg	Tinned tomatoes and juice	3 lb
	50 g	Tomato purée	2 oz
	5 g	Oregano	¼ oz
	500 g	Cheese (grated or sliced: traditionally mozzarella)	1 lb 4 oz
		Salt and pepper	

Method
1. Prepare the topping:
   (a) Fry the onion and garlic in the oil for 2–3 minutes.
   (b) Add the oregano and lightly fry for a further 2 minutes.
   (c) Add the remaining ingredients (not the cheese) and slowly simmer until the consistency of a thick sauce – approximately 20 minutes.
   (d) Check the seasoning, then allow to cool.
2. Divide the dough to produce the desired number of pizzas.
3. Roll out into round shapes of the appropriate size, then place on to greased baking trays.
4. Brush over the tops with oil.
5. Cover with the topping leaving a 10 mm (½ in) clear border round the pizza.
6. Sprinkle over the cheese.
7. Allow to rest (dry prove) at room temperature, i.e. 20 °C (68 °F) for 30–40 minutes.
8. Bake in a hot oven, 225 °C (435 °F), for 15–20 minutes.

Various pizzas

Calzone This is a pizza which is filled with a garnish and folded in the same manner as a turnover.

Capricciosa Basic tomato pizza adding slices of cooked ham, mushroom, artichokes and olives.

Funghi (mushroom) Basic tomato pizza, adding a good quantity of sliced mushrooms cooked in a little oil.
Note: The tomato filling may be reduced substantially or omitted.

Napoletana Basic tomato pizza.

Prosciutto (ham) Basic tomato pizza adding slices of cooked ham.

Siciliana Basic tomato pizza adding tuna fish and olives.

Deep-fried items

Deep-fried foods are popular in pub catering because they have good customer appeal and are quick and easy to produce.

A wide range of ready-prepared foods ready for frying are available as frozen products:

Egg, pasta and fish dishes

Cod, sole, plaice fillets and fish burgers – breaded and battered
Savoury croquettes, cutlets, cromesquis, rissoles and Chinese rolls
Fish cakes and Scotch eggs
Croquette and chipped potatoes.

When preparing fresh fish for frying, it is passed through seasoned flour, egg wash (or thin batter) and breadcrumbs, or alternatively passed through batter, then deep fried. Chicken portions are usually cooked and skinned prior to coating with breadcrumbs or batter (Chapter 22).

The frying medium is an important factor in the quality of deep-fried foods and is also a significant part of the production costs. To get the longest working life from a frying medium and to keep costs to a minimum, the following points should be observed:

1. *Avoid overheating the frying medium;* never exceed a maximum frying temperature of 195 °C.
2. *Avoid excessive heating and cooling of the frying medium;* set the fryer to a standby temperature of 120 °C approximately when not in use for short periods.
3. *Season foods away from the fryer* to avoid salt being added to the frying medium; this increases fat deterioration.
4. *Never overload the frying medium;* a suitable ratio of fat to food is 6 × 1 for fast recovery equipment and 8 × 1 for less efficient equipment.
5. *Dry wet foods thoroughly before frying;* this is also an important safety factor.
6. *Check the accuracy of the thermostat at regular intervals.*
7. *Strain the fat to remove food particles each day;* this may have to be done more than once a day when the fryer is used very frequently.
8. *Rinse the fryer thoroughly after cleaning to remove any cleaning material;* e.g. detergent, alkali etc.
9. *Avoid frying fatty foods* such as oily fish, gammon etc.
10. *Coat foods properly* to reduce to a minimum the transfer of fats from the foods being fried into the frying medium.

Deep-fried fish dishes

Deep-fried fish English style — This indicates that the fish has a bread coating. After frying the fish is served on the customer's plate or a service dish lined with a dishpaper and garnished with pieces of lemon and branch parsley. The usual accompaniment is tartare sauce.

Deep-fried fish French style — This indicates that the fish has been passed through seasoned milk then flour prior to frying. The garnish and accompaniments are the same as English style.
Important: This style of frying, which is usually applied to whitebait, is not very popular because it causes rapid deterioration of the frying medium.

Deep-fried fish Orly style — This indicates that the fish has been battered. The fish is garnished with lemon and branch parsley and accompanied with tomato sauce.

Goujons — These are thin strips of fish cut from fish fillets. They are usually prepared, fried and garnished English style.

Recipes for Pubs

Deep-fried shellfish
Oysters, mussels, scampi and scallops

Frozen or tinned shellfish may be used.
Basic preparation Wipe off excess liquid then coat with breadcrumbs or batter (remove the shells from scampi if appropriate). Deep fry and garnish with lemon and parsley. Accompany with a suitable sauce, e.g. tartare.

In basket Deep fry the fish or shellfish as indicated then serve in a basket lined with a napkin or dishpaper. Garnish as desired, e.g. lemon wedges, parsley, French fried potatoes or baked potato etc.

Scotch eggs Allow one hard-boiled egg and 100 g (4 oz) sausage meat (usually pork) per portion. Flour, eggwash (thin batter) and breadcrumbs.

Method
1 Lightly flour the egg then cover with the sausage meat.
2 Pass through the flour, eggwash and breadcrumbs.
3 Deep fry in moderately hot fat allowing sufficient time to cook the sausage meat and reheat the egg – approximately 6 minutes.
4 *Hot service* Serve garnished with branch parsley and accompany with a suitable sauce, e.g. tomato, lyonnaise, diable etc.
  Cold service Garnish with salad vegetables and accompany with salad dressing.
Note: The eggs are often cut into halves for service.

Fish and shellfish

Dressed crab
(see Plate 2)

Yield: one portion

1	Cooked cold crab	1
1	Hard-boiled egg	1
75 ml	Mayonnaise	2½ oz
20 g	Fresh white breadcrumbs	¾ oz
	Chopped parsley	

Method
1 Remove the claws and legs from the crab.
2 Pull back and detach the bottom pincer of each claw, then crack the claws and remove the meat. The meat may also be removed from the legs, but this is time consuming.
3 Open the crab carefully pulling out the soft undershell (or purse).
4 Remove the gills and discard. Also remove the sack behind the eyes and discard.
5 Split the bony centre of the soft undershell with a knife and withdraw the white and brown flesh using a fork. Keep the white and dark meat separate.
6 Withdraw the soft dark meat and orange meat from the crab shell.
7 Wash the shell thoroughly then break along the natural line to extend the opening. This is done by pressing the outside of the shell along the natural line.
8 Mix the soft dark meat and orange meat with the white breadcrumbs and enough mayonnaise to form a paste.

Egg, pasta and fish dishes

9 Break up the white flesh and place aside.
10 Place the crab paste into both ends of the shell and smooth down the surface with a palette knife.
11 Dress the white meat in the centre.
12 Decorate with lines of sieved egg yolk, sieved egg white and chopped parsley.
13 Accompany with mayonnaise and any suitable salad if desired.

Potted shrimps These are usually prepared commercially, but may be made as required by mixing peeled shrimps with melted butter and seasoning with salt, pepper and nutmeg. Fill small pots with the seasoned shrimps, cover with the melted butter then allow to cool and set. Serve in the pots or turn out on to a bed of lettuce and garnish with tomato, cucumber, cress etc.

Grilled fish
Basic recipe for ten portions

10 × 400 g	*Flat fish*	10 × 14 oz
	sole, plaice, flounder etc.	
	Round fish	
10 × 225 g	Haddock, whiting, trout etc.	10 × 8 oz
	Fish steaks	
10 × 200 g	Salmon, cod, turbot etc.	10 × 7 oz
	Fish fillets	
10 × 175 g	sole, plaice, haddock, whiting etc.	10 × 6 oz
150 g	Seasoned flour	6 oz
125 g	Melted butter or margarine	5 oz
10	Pieces of lemon	10
	Branch parsley	
125 g	Parsley butter	5 oz

Method
1 Prepare the fish for grilling.
2 Pass the fish through the seasoned flour, shake off any surplus flour then coat with the melted butter.
3 Place the fish on to the grill tray.
4 Grill the fish on one side then carefully turn over and complete the cooking.
Note: Cook fish fillets at a higher temperature than whole fish or fish steaks.
5 When the fish is cooked and golden brown, remove from the tray and place on to the serving dish.
6 Arrange the garnish neatly around the fish.
7 Place a slice of parsley butter on top of each fish and serve immediately.

Compound butters These are flavoured butters which are used as an accompaniment to many grilled fish, meat, poultry and game dishes. Because they melt over the food they serve the same function as a sauce.

Anchovy butter 125 g (5 oz) butter, 25 g (1 oz) anchovy fillets, squeeze lemon juice and a pinch of cayenne pepper.
Garlic butter 125 g (5 oz) butter, 10 g (½ oz) pounded garlic (6 cloves) and a pinch of pepper.

Recipes for Pubs

Parsley butter   125 g (5 oz) butter, chopped parsley, pinch cayenne pepper, squeeze lemon juice and 15 g (¾ oz) finely chopped onion (optional).

Method
1. Cream the butter.
2. Add the flavouring ingredients and mix thoroughly together.
3. Place on to a sheet of dampened greaseproof paper, then roll into a neat cylinder approximately 25 mm (1 in) diameter.
4. Place into a cold cabinet or freezer and allow to harden.
5. When required for service cut into neat rondels.
6. Serve in a sauceboat in ice water or place on the grilled food when serving.

Sauced fish dishes   Fish dishes which contain flavoured and garnished sauces add variety and interest to a menu. A wide choice of flavourings and garnishes may be used to produce traditional dishes or house dishes.

Basic recipe for ten portions

	Fish fillets	
10 × 400 g	Sole, plaice, whiting etc.	10 × 6 oz
	Fish steaks	
10 × 225 g	Salmon, halibut, turbot etc.	10 × 8 oz
	Whole fish	
10 × 400 g	Sole, plaice, flounder etc.	10 × 14 oz
15 g	Butter or margarine	½ oz
125 ml	White wine	¼ pt
250 ml	Fish stock (or water)	½ pt
squeeze	Lemon juice	squeeze
	Salt and white pepper.	

Method
1. Prepare the fish for cooking.
2. Butter the base of a fish cooking utensil, then place the fish on top.
3. Season the fish then add the cooking liquor (wine, fish stock and lemon juice) up to about two-thirds of the height of the fish.
4. Cover with a piece of buttered greaseproof paper and lid, then place on top of the stove and bring almost to boiling point.
5. Place in an oven and cook at 175 °C (350 °F).
6. When cooked, remove the fish and drain then keep warm covered with the cooking paper.
7. Boil down the cooking liquor until thick and concentrated.
8. Add the reduced liquor to the fish sauce (see below).
9. Check the seasoning, consistency and temperature of the sauce.
10. Coat the serving dish or plate with a little of the sauce, then place the fish on top.
11. Coat the fish with the sauce.
12. Leave plain, gratinate or glaze under a hot grill as appropriate.
13. Add any garnish and serve.

Variations   *Fish bonne femme*   Decorate the serving dish with piped potatoes. Use bonne-femme sauce (Chapter 17) and brown under a hot grill.
Fish Dugléré   Use Dugléré sauce (Chapter 17) and garnish with crescents of puff pastry.

Egg, pasta and fish dishes

Fish Mornay Use cheese sauce (Chapter 17). Sprinkle the coated fish with grated cheese and gratinate under a hot grill. Garnish with crescents of puff pastry.
Fish Florentine Prepare the same as Mornay but place the poached fish on a bed of hot cooked spinach.
Fish with prawn sauce Use prawn sauce (Chapter 17) and garnish with crescents of puff pastry.
Fish with white wine sauce Use white wine sauce (Chapter 17) and garnish with crescents of puff pastry.
Fish Véronique Use white wine sauce (Chapter 17). Place skinned seeded grape halves on top of each piece of fish prior to coating with sauce. Brown the coated fish dish under a hot grill and garnish with crescents of puff pastry.

Fish pie
(see Plate 3)

An excellent method of preparing fish pies is to use one of the sauced fish recipes above. The fish and sauce is placed in a pie dish, covered with mashed potato and browned in a hot oven or under a hot grill. Cheese may be sprinkled on top of the potato as an alternative finish. This is a good way of preparing 'house' fish pies where one's own choice of flavourings and garnishes creates individuality.

Seafood skewers (brochettes aux fruits de mer)
(see Plate 4)

40	Scampi tails	40
10	Scallops (blanched)	10
40	Mussels (cooked)	40
10 slices	Lobster tail (cooked)	10 slices
30	Mushrooms	30
20	Bay leaves	20
75 g	Melted butter	3 oz
50 g	White breadcrumbs	2 oz
10 wedges	Lemons	10 wedges
	Braised rice	

Method
1 Cut each scallop into four neat slices.
2 Blanch the bay leaves and wash the mushrooms.
3 Neatly arrange the ingredients on the skewer, then lightly season.
4 Brush over with the melted butter, then roll in the breadcrumbs.
5 Grill on all sides until crisp and golden brown. Sprinkle with additional butter during cooking if required.
6 Serve on a bed of braised rice and garnish with the lemon wedges.
Note: A suitable sauce may be served as an accompaniment, e.g. white wine, prawn or tomato sauce.

19 Roasts, ethnic and featured dishes

Michael Davidson and Daniel Stevenson

Roasts

Oven roasting is quite a simple method of cooking, especially when the commodities to be roasted are *oven ready* and in addition easy to carve or portion. The basic procedures for roasting both butcher meats and poultry are listed below, followed by general cookery hints. The detailed preparation of the most common joints which are roasted has been included, although many pub caterers will purchase oven-ready commodities.

Basic procedure for roasting butcher meats and furred game

1. Prepare the joint ready for roasting.
2. Place the joint on the roasting tray and lightly coat with fat or oil.
3. Place the joint in a hot oven (225°C (440°F) approximately) and allow to brown slightly.
4. Add the seasoning and reduce the oven temperature to 175°C (350°F) approximately.
5. Cook slowly, basting as required until the correct degree of cooking is obtained.
6. Remove the joint from the oven and place into a hot-plate or store in a warm place for 15–20 minutes.
7. Carve the joint into neat slices across the grain of the meat and place on to the plate or serving dish.
8. Coat with a little hot gravy and decorate with watercress and any other suitable garnish. Accompany with the roast gravy and any other suitable sauces.

Basic procedure for roasting poultry and feathered game

1. Season the bird(s) inside and out with salt and place on the roasting tray. The bird(s) should be placed *on their sides*.
2. Lightly coat with fat or oil.
3. Place in the oven at a temperature suitable for the size of the bird:

Small birds	½–1 kg (1–2 lb)	220°C (425°F) approx.
Medium birds	1½–2 kg (3–4 lb)	190°C (375°F) approx.
Large birds	2½–5 kg (5–10 lb)	150°C (300°F) approx.
Very large birds	5½ kg + (11 lb +)	125°C (260°F) approx.

4. Allow to cook until a light colour is developed, then turn over on to the other side.

Roasts, ethnic and featured dishes

5 Continue cooking until both sides of the bird(s) have developed a light colour then turn breast up.
6 Complete the cooking, allowing a good colour to develop across the surface of the bird(s). Remove from the tray then sit the bird(s) vent up to allow the steam to escape.

Hints on oven roasting   Joints of butcher meat and furred game should be raised off the base of the roasting tray to prevent a dry hard surface being formed on the area of the joint touching the tray. Use a trivet, pieces of vegetables or the natural bone content of the joint. When roasting poultry or feathered game this is not essential as the *skinned* flesh develops a crisp golden-brown texture.

Salt attracts meat juices to the surface of a joint and therefore tends to delay browning. Season joints after colour has been developed, especially joints with a large area of surface flesh, e.g. topside. This is not essential for poultry and feathered game which can be seasoned prior to roasting.

Joints should be placed into the roasting tray with the fat side uppermost. This allows the joint to be basted with its own fat during cooking.

Joints are placed in a hot oven to develop colour. After this the temperature should be reduced and the joint cooked slowly to keep shrinkage and weight loss to a minimum. Initial colouring is less important when the joint has a good fat covering, e.g. rib of beef; here the joint can be cooked at the same temperature throughout coinciding cooking and colour development. The same procedure applies to poultry, where cooking and colour development are simultaneous.

Remember: the higher the roasting temperature, the greater the shrinkage and weight loss.

Poultry and feathered game should be turned during cooking to ensure that all parts of the bird are roasted evenly. The breasts of the birds are kept downwards for most of the cooking period for protection against excessive heat exposure, overcooking and loss of juiciness. Also the layer of fat on the back of the birds melts during cooking and runs down the bird, aiding basting.

The cooking times of roasts may vary considerably depending on many different factors; therefore the cook should treat suggested cooking times as a rough guide only. This requires the test for cooking to be made regularly at the latter part of the cooking period.

The most accurate means of testing a joint or bird for degree of cooking is to use a thermometer. Mechanical thermometers are inserted into the thickest part of the joint or bird prior to roasting and the temperature inspected during cooking. Digital display thermometers are the best and most versatile, but are the most expensive.

Temperature range   *Underdone:* beef, mutton, venison and hare 55–60 °C (130–140 °F)
Just done: beef, mutton, venison and lamb 66–71 °C (150–160 °F)
Well done: beef, veal and rabbit 75–77 °C (168–170 °F)
             pork 77–80 °C (170–176 °F).

Recipes for Pubs

The other means of testing the degree of cooking is the *pressure test* and *puncture* test. The pressure test requires considerable experience but the puncture test is more easily carried out.

Puncture test   Insert a small needle or cocktail stick into the joint or bird, then withdraw and press the surface, forcing the juices to escape. The amount of blood present in the meat juices indicates the degree of cooking; a considerable amount of blood present indicates the joint is very underdone, traces of blood indicate underdone up to just done, and no trace of blood indicates cooked through.

A joint or bird should be allowed to rest or settle in a warm place for a short period to facilitate carving or portioning and reduce the likelihood of the cook being burned.

Roast beef   Prepare the joint for roasting, then cook as stated in the basic procedure keeping underdone.
Cooking time: 15 minutes per ½ kg (1 lb).
Garnish: Garnish with watercress and Yorkshire pudding. Serve separately a sauceboat of gravy and a sauceboat of horseradish sauce.

Yorkshire pudding

200 g	Flour	8 oz
2	Eggs	2
250 ml	Milk	½ pt
	Salt and pepper	

Method
1. Sieve together the flour, salt and pepper.
2. Add the eggs and half the milk approximately.
3. Whisk until smooth.
4. Add the remaining milk to produce a smooth *thin* batter.
5. Place the Yorkshire pudding tins on a tray (or use a Yorkshire pudding tray), then add enough oil or dripping to cover the bottom of the tins to a depth of 5 mm (¼ in) approximately.
6. Place into a moderate oven 200 °C (400 °F) and allow to become very hot; 8–10 minutes in the oven.
7. Pour the batter into the hot oil and fill the moulds, then replace into the oven.
8. Allow to cook for 30 minutes approximately (until risen and set).
9. Turn the puddings upside down to remove the fat from the centres, and continue cooking until crisp – a further 10 minutes approximately.

Wing rib and fore rib of beef
1. Cut down between the eye of the meat and the flat piece of bone to the base of the backbone (A in Figure 59).
2. Remove the backbone along the base of the ribs with a saw or cleaver (B in Figure 59).
3. Remove the thick part of the sinew under the top layer of fat (C in Figure 59). Season under the fat.
4. Tie the joint securely. The bones which have been removed should be tied back on to protect the joint when roasting.

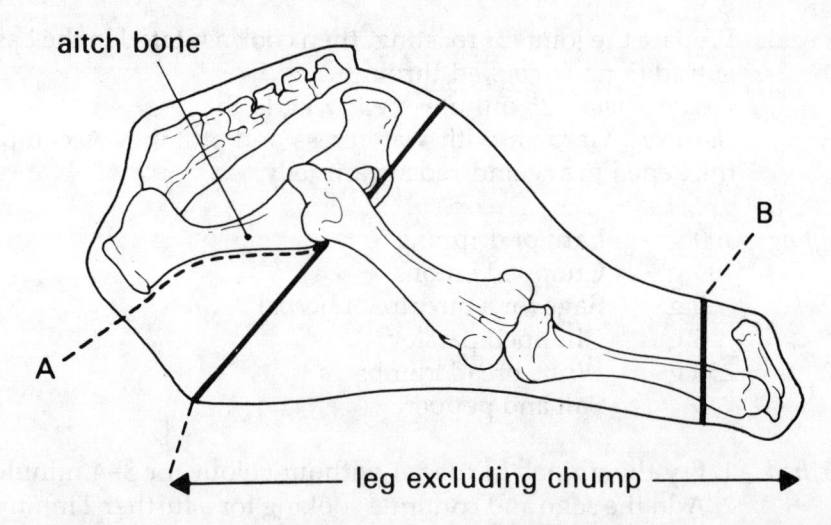

Roasts, ethnic and featured dishes

Figure 59 *Wing rib and fore rib of beef*

aitch bone

← leg excluding chump →

Boned and rolled joints   When time for preparation has to be kept to a minimum, boned and rolled joints may be purchased from the butcher. These include joints such as rib, sirloin, rump and good quality topside.

Roast lamb and mutton   Prepare the joint for roasting, then cook as stated in the basic procedure. Traditionally mutton is cooked a little underdone and lamb cooked through. However, nowadays lamb is sometimes also kept a little underdone.
Cooking time   20 minutes per ½ kg (1 lb).
Garnish   Garnish with watercress. Accompany lamb with gravy and mint sauce and mutton with gravy, onion sauce and redcurrant jelly.

Leg of lamb and mutton
1 Cut down along the aitch bone and through the ball and socket joint (A in Figure 60).
2 Bone out the aitch bone.
3 Trim the bottom knuckle and bone, then saw off the knuckle leaving a piece of clean bone (B in Figure 60).
4 Remove any excess fat, then season the inside.
5 Tie with string.
Important: In many instances it is advisable to ask your butcher to carry out the preparation of boning the joints for roasting. The above information can be used to indicate to the butcher the preparation required.

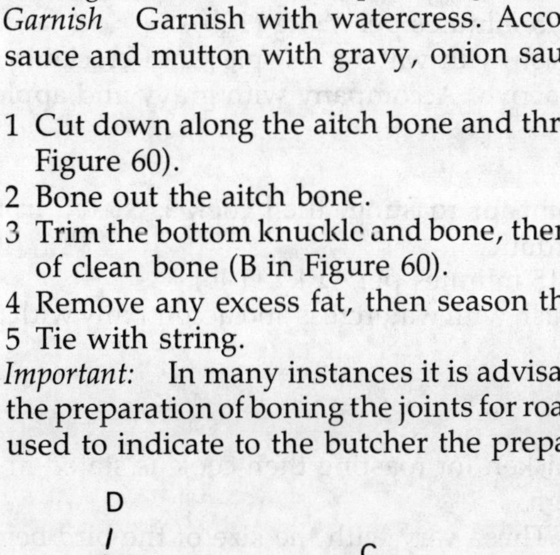

Figure 60 *Leg of lamb and mutton*

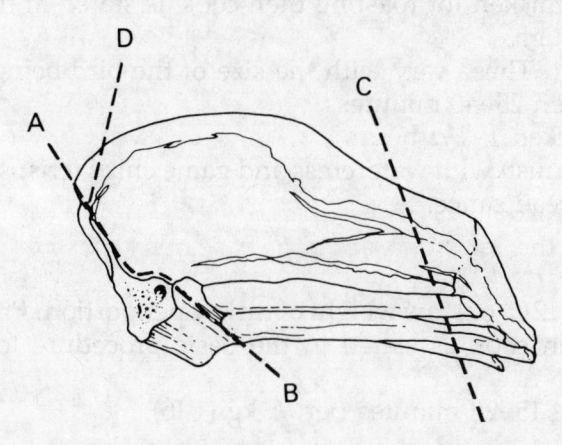

Recipes for Pubs

Roast veal Prepare the joint for roasting, then cook as stated in the basic procedure. Veal is traditionally cooked through.
Cooking time   25 minutes per ½ kg (1 lb).
Garnish   Garnish with watercress and stuffing. Accompany with gravy or thickened gravy and redcurrant jelly.

Stuffing

100 g	Lard or dripping	4 oz
100 g	Chopped onions	4 oz
5 g	Sage (or a mixture of herbs)	¼ oz
5 g	Chopped parsley	¼ oz
250 g	White breadcrumbs	10 oz
	Salt and pepper	

Method
1 Fry the onions in the fat without colour for 3–4 minutes.
2 Add the sage and continue cooking for a further 2 minutes approximately.
3 Add the breadcrumbs, seasoning and chopped parsley.
4 Combine all the ingredients and check the seasoning.
Note: Many different stuffings may be made by adding various flavouring ingredients, e.g. distinctive herbs, lemon zest, grated root ginger and spices etc.

Roast pork Prepare the joint for roasting, then cook as stated in the basic procedure. Pork should be cooked through. Also remove the scored crackling prior to carving.
Cooking time   25 minutes per ½ kg (1 lb).
Garnish   Garnish with watercress, pieces of crackling and sage and onion stuffing – see above. Accompany with gravy and apple sauce.

Roast venison Prepare the joint for roasting, then cook as stated in the basic procedure, keeping underdone.
Cooking time   15 minutes per ½ kg (1 lb).
Garnish   Garnish with watercress and accompany with gravy and redcurrant jelly.

Roast chicken Prepare the chicken for roasting then cook as stated in the basic procedure, cooking through.
Cooking times   These vary with the size of the bird being cooked, e.g.
Spring chicken 25–40 minutes.
Medium chicken 1–1½ hours
Garnish   Garnish with watercress and game chips (crisps). Accompany with gravy and bread sauce.

Roast turkey Allow 350 g (12½ oz) raw weight of turkey per portion. Prepare the turkey for roasting, then cook as stated in the basic procedure for poultry, cooking through.
Cooking time   15–20 minutes per ½ kg (1 lb).

Roasts, ethnic and featured dishes

Garnish   Garnish with watercress, slices of stuffing, cooked chipolata sausages and braised chestnuts (optional). Accompany with gravy, bread sauce and cranberry sauce.

Chestnut stuffing   Yield: 1 kg (2¼ lb) approx.

50 g	Butter	2 oz
125 g	Chopped onions	5 oz
75 g	Chopped suet	3 oz
200 g	White breadcrumbs	8 oz
2	Eggs	2
	Chopped parsley, good pinch	
300 g	Peeled chopped chestnuts	12 oz
200 g	Pork sausage meat	8 oz
	Mixed herbs, good pinch	
	Salt and pepper	

Method
1. Fry off the onions in the butter without colouring for 3–4 minutes.
2. Add the mixed herbs and cook for a further 2 minutes, then allow to cool.
3. Place the cooled onions and herbs in a bowl and add the rest of the ingredients except the egg.
4. Mix all the ingredients together then bind with the eggs.

Note: The stuffing may be cooked in the bird, or rolled in oiled paper then cooked in a tray with a little stock in an oven (or steamer).

Roast duckling   Prepare the duckling for roasting, then cook as stated in the basic procedure, cooking through. Garnish with watercress and game chips (crisps) and accompany with gravy, stuffing (see roast pork) and apple sauce.

Coq au vin

(see Plate 5)

10	Chicken portions	10
50 g	Butter	2 oz
50 ml	Oil	2 fl oz
2	Crushed garlic, good cloves	2
250 g	Finely chopped onions	10 oz
250 ml	Red wine	½ pt
750 ml	Brown sauce (Chapter 17)	1½ pt
	Garnish	
125 g	Button onions (peeled)	5 oz
125 g	Button mushrooms	5 oz
125 g	Bacon cubes (10 mm/½ in)	5 oz

Method
1. Place the bacon cubes in a saucepan, cover with cold water and bring to the boil.
2. Simmer until almost cooked then refresh under cold water and drain.
3. Heat the butter and oil in a suitable pan, add the button onions, mushrooms and blanched bacon pieces and fry until lightly browned.

4 Remove from the pan.
5 Add the chicken pieces to the same pan and shallow fry.
6 Add the chopped onions and crushed garlic and continue frying until the chicken pieces and onions are browned.
7 Decant off excess fat.
8 Add the wine and brown sauce and slowly simmer for 10 minutes.
9 Add the garnish and complete the cooking.
10 Check consistency and seasoning.

Note: Heart or diamond-shaped pieces of shallow-fried bread (croûtons) are often used to garnish the dish when serving.

Hot-pots

Yield: 10 portions

Lancashire hot-pot
(see Plate 6)

50 g	Lard or dripping	2 oz
1½ kg	Neck cutlets or lamb or mutton	3¾ lb
250 g	Sliced kidneys	10 oz
500 g	Onions	1¼ lb
1 kg	Potatoes	2½ lb
1¾ l	White stock/bouillon	3½ pt
	Chopped parsley	
	Salt and pepper	

See basic method to follow.
Cooking time 2–2½ hours.
Service Serve with pickled red cabbage.

Bolton hot-pot The same as Lancashire hot-pot, adding 200 g (½ lb) button mushrooms and 10–20 oysters. See basic method to follow.

Highland hot-pot

50 g	Lard or dripping	2 oz
3	Grouse	3
2	Rabbits	2
20	Streaky bacon rashers	20
250 g	Celery	10 oz
250 g	White cabbage	10 oz
250 g	Button onions	10 oz
800 g	Potatoes	2 lb
250 ml	Red wine	½ pt
1¾ l	Brown stock/bouillon	3½ pt
	Allspice, good pinch	
	Salt and pepper	

Roasts, ethnic and featured dishes

Basic method for hot-pots
1. Prepare the butcher meat or poultry:
   Lamb and mutton: Trim off excess fat
   Grouse and rabbits: Cut into joints
2. Wash, peel and slice the onions and any celery or cabbage.
3. Wash, peel and thinly slice the potatoes
4. Heat the fat in a frying pan, then brown the recipe flesh – meat and game etc. Reserve the frying fat for coating the potatoes.
5. Line the base of a large casserole or suitable dish with a layer of potatoes and add a layer of sliced onions (for Highland hot-pots – button onions) then lightly season.
6. Place the meat or game and any bacon rashers on top, then add any vegetable garnish – mushrooms, celery, cabbage etc. Season liberally then add the liquid to just below the top of the main item(s).
7. Place the remaining onions on top then cover with the rest of the potatoes neatly overlapping in rows. Brush over the top with melted fat.
8. Place in an oven at 200 °C (400 °F) and cook until lightly coloured. Reduce the temperature to 160 °C (320 °F) and cook slowly, occasionally pressing down with a fish slice. Use a lid for prolonged cooking times (over 1½ hours).
9. When cooked, clean round the sides of the casserole, brush over the top of the potatoes with a little more fat or margarine, and sprinkle with parsley.

Irish stew

1.6 kg	Boneless stewing mutton or lamb	4 lb
1¼ kg	Potatoes	3¼ lb
250 g	Onions	10 oz
250 g	White leeks	10 oz
250 g	White cabbage	10 oz
250 g	Button onions	10 oz
250 g	Shaped potatoes (from the potatoes above)	10 oz
to cover	White stock/bouillon	to cover
	Salt and pepper	
	Chopped parsley	

Method
1. Trim off excess fat from the mutton or lamb, then cut into a neat dice.
2. Wash and peel the vegetables.
3. Cut the potatoes into a neat dice 30 mm (1 in), reserving the trimmings.
4. Cut into small pieces the potato trimmings, ordinary onions, celery, white leek and cabbage.
5. Place the meat into a saucepan, cover with cold water and bring to the boil. Refresh under cold water, then drain.
6. Place the flesh back into the saucepan, then cover with the white stock.
7. Bring to the boil and skin if required.
8. Add the small pieces of potato, onion, celery, leek and cabbage and simmer for 1 hour (until the meat is almost cooked and the vegetable trimmings become a purée).
9. Add the button onions and shaped potatoes and complete the cooking.
10. Check seasoning, consistency and temperature.
11. When serving, sprinkle with chopped parsley and accompany with pickled red cabbage.

Recipes for Pubs

Figure 61 *Toad-in-the-hole – a cheap and simple hot dish*
Courtesy Flour Advisory Bureau

Toad-in-the-hole	750 ml	Yorkshire pudding batter (see earlier)	1½ pt
	60 g	Dripping or lard	2½ oz
	20 × 50 g	Sausages	20 × 2 oz

Method
1. Prepare the batter as given earlier in this chapter and allow to rest for 1 hour.
2. Heat the dripping in a shallow roasting tray or suitable cooking utensil, then add the sausages and lightly fry and colour.
3. Neatly arrange the sausages into portions then pour in the batter.
4. Cook in the oven at 200°C (400°F) for 30–40 minutes.
5. Serve accompanied with thin brown sauce (Chapter 17) or thickened gravy.

Sausages Sausages should never be pricked prior to cooking. Cook fairly slowly, allowing colour and cooking to take place simultaneously.

Avoid frying sausages in a deep fat fryer because the fat from the sausages causes deterioration of the frying medium; it considerably reduces the life of this expensive commodity.

Sausages may be served with onions and mash; with most of the brown sauce derivatives, e.g. lyonnaise, devil, piquant etc.; as toad-in-the-hole; as a sausage kebab; as a sausage risotto; and in buttered French bread, with or without onion.

Roasts, ethnic and featured dishes

Tripe and onions
(see Plate 7)

1¼ kg	Dressed tripe		3¼ lb
625 g	Sliced onions		1½ lb
65 g	Butter or margarine		2 oz
65 g	Flour		2 oz
¾ l	White stock/bouillon		1½ pt
½ l	Milk		¾ pt
125 ml	Cream (optional)		¼ pt
	Salt and white pepper		

Method
1. Cut the tripe into 30 mm (1 in) pieces, place in a saucepan and cover with the milk and stock.
2. Bring to the boil and simmer for 30 minutes.
3. Add the sliced onions and lightly season.
4. When almost cooked, drain off the cooking liquor.
5. In a suitable saucepan prepare a roux with the butter and flour.
6. Blend in the hot cooking liquor to the roux to prepare a veloute sauce.
7. Strain the sauce over the tripe and onions and complete the cooking.
8. Liaise with the cream (optional) and check consistency, seasoning and temperature.
9. When serving, sprinkle with a little chopped parsley.

Grills

A choice of one or more grilled dishes is a common feature on a pub menu. Examples are:

Beef steaks, e.g. rump, sirloin and fillet steaks
Lamb and mutton chops, e.g. single loin, double loin and chump chops
Gammon steaks
Hamburgers and other made-up products, e.g. king rib and ham steaks
Sausages – different types and local specialities
Liver and kidneys
See also barbecued chicken, spare ribs and kebabs.

Most items which are grilled or shallow fried can be bought precut or prepared into various portion sizes; steaks, chops, hamburgers, sausages and many other made-up items can also be purchased as ready-prepared graded frozen items.

Like deep frying, grilling is a simple method of cooking food. However, several important points should be considered:

Seasoning foods   Season foods after colour has developed, because salt draws moisture to the surface of the food and therefore retards colour development. This is important when using an over heat grill.

Do not season made-up items or salted products, e.g. sausages, hamburgers, gammon or bacon.

Coating foods with oil   Foods which are to be grilled should be coated with oil prior to cooking. Coating foods with oil reduces the likelihood of the food sticking to the grill bars, keeps the food moist, aids cooking and browning and gives a nice sheen to the food.

Recipes for Pubs

Speed of cooking   Grilled foods are usually cooked so that the appropriate degree of cooking and development of colour are achieved simultaneously; the smaller and thinner the food, the faster the speed of cooking. Also when foods are cooked underdone, the cooking must be fast to develop colour without cooking too far in to the flesh.

Degree of cooking   Chicken, pork and made-up items must be cooked through and never served underdone.

Testing steaks for the exact degree of cooking requires skill and experience. To avoid complaints regarding steaks being incorrectly cooked it is advisable to purchase a digital thermometer with a probe. These are relatively inexpensive and will given an immediate reading of the internal temperature.

Internal temperatures
Rare/blue
Beef   Raw inside, internal temperature up to 50 °C (122 °F).

Underdone
Beef, mutton and venison Pink inside leading to a raw centre: 55–60°C (131–140 °F) under the surface, with a centre temperature of 50 °C (122 °F) approximately.

Just done/medium
Beef, mutton, venison and lamb   Cooked inside but pink at the very centre: 66–71 °C (151–160 °F) under the surface, with a centre temperature of 59 °C (137 °F) approximately.

Well done
Beef, veal, rabbit and chicken   Cooked through, i.e. internal temperature of 75–77 °C (167–171 °F).
Pork   77–80 °C (171–176 °F).

Barbecue dishes

Barbecued chicken

	5 × 1 kg	Chickens (eviscerated)	5 × 2¼ lb
		Salt and mill pepper	
	250 ml	Oil/aromatic oil *or*	½ pt
		barbecue marinade (see below)	
	1 bunch	Watercress	1 bunch
	500 ml	Accompanying sauce, e.g. barbecue, devil or piquante	1 pt

Aromatic oil

200 ml	oil		8 oz
200 g	Onion		8 fl oz
2 cloves	garlic		2 cloves
1 lemon	zest and juice		1 lemon
2 tsp	Mustard paste		2 tsp
1 tsp	Worcester sauce		1 tsp
50 g	Honey		2 oz

Liquidize the ingredients to produce a smooth thick oil.

Roasts, ethnic and featured dishes

Method
1. Split the birds through the back with a large knife – insert the knife through the neck opening and cut towards the parson's nose.
2. Open out the birds and lightly flatten.
3. Remove the ribs with a small knife (optional).
4. Season the birds with the salt and mill pepper.
5. Brush over with the oil, aromatic oil or barbecue marinade.
   Note: The chickens may be allowed to soak in the aromatic oil or barbecue marinade for several hours prior to cooking.
6. Place the chicken on preheated grill bars and cook steadily for 15–20 minutes. Baste with the oil or marinade during cooking.
7. Turn over the chicken and continue cooking. This will take a further 10–20 minutes.
   Note: During cooking the chicken may have to be moved to a cooler part of the grill to avoid burning.
8. Serve with watercress and accompany with the sauce.

Devilled chicken
(see Plate 8)

Prepare as for barbecued chicken but coat the chicken during the latter stages of cooking with a mustard paste. Also sprinkle over white breadcrumbs, then complete the cooking.

Mustard paste

10 g	English mustard		½ oz
1 tsp	Worcester sauce		1 tsp
50 ml	Vinegar		2 fl oz
50 ml	Water		2 fl oz
	pinch cayenne pepper		

Mix the ingredients together to form a smooth paste.
Accompany with devil sauce.

Barbecued spare ribs

5 kg	Spare ribs		12½ lb
	Salt and pepper		
½ l	Barbecue marinade		1 pt

Barbecue marinade

125 ml	Oil		5 fl oz
75 g	Onion		3 oz
1 clove	Garlic		1 clove
125 ml	Vinegar		5 fl oz
50 ml	Soy sauce		2 fl oz
100 g	Tomato purée		4 oz
100 g	Honey		4 oz
10 g	Sugar		½ oz
1 tsp	Worcester sauce		1 tsp
1 tsp	French mustard		1 tsp
2 tsp	Chopped basil		2 tsp
	Dash red colouring (optional)		
	Salt and pepper		

Liquidize the ingredients to produce a smooth thick oil.

Method 1 Trim off any excess fat from the ribs, then place in the marinade for 4–6 hours.
2 Place the ribs on the preheated grill bars and allow to cook.
3 Coat with the marinade during cooking.
4 Turn over and complete the cooking.

Kebabs and skewers

Almost any combination of meat, poultry, game or fish may be arranged on a skewer with vegetables such as onions, mushrooms, peppers and tomatoes. Herbs such as bay leaves, thyme and mint are also usually added. Prior to cooking, the ingredients for the skewer may be marinaded in an aromatic oil.

Skewers may be served on boiled or braised rice or a bed of crisp salad vegetables.

Kebab orientale	500 g	Lean mutton	1 lb 4 oz
	500 g	Lean pork	1 lb 4 oz
	2½	Lamb's kidneys	2½
	40	Mushrooms	40
	20	Bay leaves	20
	50 g	Breadcrumbs	2 oz
	1 dspn	Parsley (chopped), (10 g approx)	1 dspn
Aromatic oil	200 ml	Oil	8 fl oz
	1	Lemon zest and juice	1
	100 g	Onion	4 oz
	50 g	Honey	2 oz
		Salt and pepper	

Method 1 Prepare the marinade: liquidize the ingredients to a smooth thick oil.
2 Cut the pork and mutton into squares or rondels 3 × 10 mm (⅜ in), then place in the marinade.
3 Remove any skin from the kidneys, then cut into quarters and place into the marinade.
4 Blanch the bay leaves in a little boiling water so that they can be pierced with the skewer without breaking.
5 Wash the mushrooms.
 Note: The vegetable garnish may also be placed in the marinade.
6 Leave the ingredients in the marinade for approximately 2 hours (if time permits).
7 Neatly arrange the ingredients on the skewers, then lightly season.
8 Grill on all sides until almost cooked, occasionally brushing with the marinade.
9 Mix together the parsley and breadcrumbs and sprinkle over the skewers and complete the cooking.
10 Serve the skewers on a bed of braised rise.
Note: When preparing meats such as pork it may be advisable to part cook

Roasts, ethnic and featured dishes

(grill) the pieces of flesh before assembling on a skewer. This is to avoid serving the meat underdone. Alternatively it shortens the cooking time, in turn reducing the risk of overcooking the vegetables.

Burgers

Hamburgers or Vienna steaks Also available as a frozen or tinned product.
Yield: 10 × 100 g (4 oz) hamburgers approximately.

1 kg	Lean minced beef	2½ lb
50 g	Finely chopped onion	2 oz
40 g	White breadcrumbs (optional)	1½ oz
25 g	Margarine or butter	1 oz
1	Egg	1
10 g	Salt (1 tsp)	½ oz
pinch	Pepper	pinch

Method
1. Lightly fry the onions in the margarine, then allow to cool.
2. Mix all the ingredients together thoroughly to a fine paste.
3. Divide the mixture into ten pieces, then shape into hamburgers.
4. Store on an oiled tray until required for use.
5. Shallow fry and use as appropriate, e.g. serve with French fries or in a bap with fried onions, tomato, selected relishes or piquant sauce etc.

Chip steaks Chopped meat instead of minced, sizes 3–5 oz.
Frozen.
Pure beef, shaped.
Seasoned and flavoured beef, shaped.

Chicken or turkey burgers (freeze stable) Also available as a frozen product.
Yield: 10 × 100 g (4 oz) burgers approximately.

650 g	Chicken/turkey flesh and skin	1 lb 10 oz
150 g	Ham	6 oz
100 g	Onion	4 oz
75 g	Mushrooms (white)	3 oz
20 g	Chicken bouillon	¾ oz
5 g	Salt	¼ oz
pinch	Pepper	pinch

Method
1. Ensure that the chicken or turkey flesh is free from gristle and sinew.
2. Peel onions and wash mushrooms.
3. Pass the flesh, skin, ham, onions and mushrooms through a mincer.
4. Place the mixture into a mixing bowl, add the chicken bouillon, salt and pepper, then thoroughly mix together.

Recipes for Pubs

5 Allow to rest for five minutes, then divide the mixture into 100 g (4 oz) pieces.
6 Shape into burgers and place on to an oiled tray.
7 Cook and serve the same as beefburgers.

Fish burger Available as a frozen product.
These consist of pieces of filleted fish which are breaded then shallow or deep fried. They are served in a bap in the same manner as a hamburger, with tomato, onion and lettuce and accompanied with a suitable sauce or relish, e.g. tartare, herb or tomato sauce, tomato, mustard, piccalilli or cucumber relish.

Vegeburger (freeze stable) Yield 10 × 75 g (3 oz) burgers approximately.

250 g	Carrots (peeled)	10 oz
100 g	Onions (peeled)	4 oz
1 clove	Garlic (peeled)	1 clove
5 g	Parsley (picked)	¼ oz
50 g	Peanuts (shelled)	2 oz
30 g	Sunflower seeds	1¼ oz
100 g	Porridge oats	4 oz
pinch	Nutmeg (grated)	pinch
5 g	Salt	¼ oz
25 ml	Lemon juice	1 fl oz
25 ml	Water	1 fl oz
20 g	Flour	¾ oz
20 g	Margarine (vegetable)	¾ oz
	Coating	
200 g	Sesame seeds	8 oz
40 g	Flour	1¾ oz
100 ml	Water	4 fl oz

Method
1 Place the water, lemon juice and margarine in a saucepan and bring to the boil.
2 Add the flour and mix to a smooth paste.
3 Cook for 1 minute, stirring continuously, then allow to cool.
4 Crush the garlic.
5 Grate the carrots.
6 Chop the onions, parsley and peanuts into 2 mm (⅛ in) pieces.
7 Place into a mixing bowl the carrots, onions, garlic, parsley, peanuts, whole sunflower seeds, porridge oats, nutmeg and salt and mix together.
8 Add the thick cold paste, then thoroughly combine all the ingredients.
9 Shape the mixture into burgers, i.e. roll out on a floured table until 10 mm (⅜ in), then cut with a round pastry cutter.
10 Prepare a coating batter with the flour and water.
11 Thinly coat the shapes with the batter, then pass through the sesame seeds.

Roasts, ethnic and featured dishes

12 Shallow fry in hot oil on each side until cooked and light brown in colour – approximately 3 minutes on each side.
13 Serve in a bap garnished with tomato and lettuce, and accompany with a suitable relish, e.g. cucumber, tomato, sweetcorn, mustard or piccalilli.

Ethnic dishes

Hara beef (freeze stable)
(see Plate 10)

700 g	Beef topside	1¾ lb
10 g	Meat tenderizer	½ oz
10 g	Garam marsala	½ oz
½ tsp	Chilli powder	½ tsp
5 g	Turmeric	¼ oz
15 g	Salt	¾ oz
1 tsp	Dry methi leaves	1 tsp
	Marinade	
30 g	Garlic (crushed)	1¼ oz
25 g	Root ginger (grated)	1 oz
15 g	Green chillies (chopped)	¾ oz
150 g	Coriander leaves (fresh)	6 oz
700 g	Spinach (frozen)	1¾ lb
500 ml	Yogurt (plain/natural)	1 pt
	Onion garnish	
500 g	Onions, roughly chopped	1 lb 4 oz
250 ml	Salad oil	½ pt

Method
1 Cut the topside into thin slices, place on to a tray, then sprinkle with the meat tenderizer. Leave for 30 minutes.
2 Prepare the marinade: allow the spinach to defrost, then place all the ingredients into a liquidizer or food processor and finely chop.
3 Mix together the beef, marinade, garam marsala, chilli powder, turmeric, salt and methi leaves. Allow to marinate for 1 hour.
4 Prepare the onion garnish: shallow fry the onions in the oil until golden brown. Allow to cool.
5 Add the onions to the beef, then place into a cooking dish with a tight-fitting lid.
6 Cook in a cool oven 170 °C (340 °F) for 1–1½ hours.

Moussaka Available as a ready-prepared frozen product.

(see Plate 11)

1¼ kg	Cooked lean mutton	3 lb 2 oz
50 g	Margarine or butter	2 oz
150 g	Onions	6 oz
3 cloves	Garlic	3 cloves
75 g	Tomato purée	3 oz
500 g	Tomatoes or tinned tomatoes	1 lb 4 oz
500 g	Aubergines	1 lb 4 oz
375 ml	Brown sauce (Chapter 17)	¾ pt

Recipes for Pubs

100 g	White breadcrumbs	4 oz
100 g	Grated cheese	4 oz
¼ l	Oil	½ pt
50 g	Melted butter	2 oz
	Salt and mill pepper	

Method
1. Wash, peel and chop the onions.
2. Crush the garlic.
3. Finely dice or mince the mutton.
4. Melt the margarine in a saucepan, add the onion and garlic and cook for 2–3 minutes.
5. Add the cooked mutton, tomato purée and brown sauce, and bring to the boil.
6. Simmer for 4–5 minutes, stirring occasionally to prevent burning.
7. Place the mixture in a serving dish.
8. Peel the aubergines then cut into 5 mm (¼ in) slices.
9. Place the oil in a pan and heat.
10. Pass the aubergines through flour, then fry in the hot oil.
11. Drain the aubergines well after frying.
12. Peel the tomatoes (if using fresh tomatoes) and cut into slices.
13. Neatly cover the moussaka mixture with the sliced tomatoes and fried aubergines.
14. Lightly season with salt and mill pepper, then sprinkle over the breadcrumbs and grated cheese.
15. Sprinkle over the melted margarine, then thoroughly reheat and gratinate in a hot oven. Sprinkle with a little chopped parsley when serving.
    Note: The moussaka may be dressed in porcelain or china containers and reheated in a microwave oven. The gratinated finish may be achieved by placing under a hot grill just prior to service.

Note: Raw lean mutton may be used. When this is the case, simmer the mutton in the sauce until cooked – approximately 1 hour. The mixture may have to be thinned with a little stock during cooking to prevent burning.

Samosas (freeze stable) Available as a ready-prepared product.

	Dough	
500 g	Bread flour	1 lb 4 oz
85 ml	Oil	3½ fl oz
5 g	Salt	¼ oz
300 ml	Water	12 fl oz
	Filling	
150 g	Potatoes	6 oz
150 g	Carrots	6 oz
100 g	Onions	4 oz
50 g	Lentils	2 oz
20 g	Garlic	¾ oz
100 g	Beansprouts	4 oz
2	Limes	2

Roasts, ethnic and featured dishes

50 g	Mango chutney	2 oz
20 g	Curry powder (standard)	¾ oz
15 g	Coriander seeds	½ oz
15 g	Cumin seeds	½ oz
15 g	Turmeric	½ oz
5 g	Salt	¼ oz
½ tsp	Black pepper	½ tsp
50 ml	Oil	2 fl oz

Method
1. Soak the lentils for several hours prior to cooking.
2. Prepare the dough:
   (a) Mix together salt and flour in mixing bowl.
   (b) Add the oil and two-thirds of the water and lightly mix.
   (c) Gradually add the remaining water to form a dough.
   (d) Knead thoroughly to form a smooth elastic dough.
   (e) Cover the dough and allow to rest for 30 minutes.
3. Wash and peel the carrots and potatoes, then cut into pieces.
4. Cook the carrots and potatoes until tender, then mash to a purée.
5. Peel and chop the onions and crush the garlic.
6. Finely crush (in a liquidizer or food processor) the coriander and cumin seeds.
7. Remove the zest from the limes with a grater, then squeeze out the juice.
8. Melt the oil in a saucepan.
9. Add the onions and garlic and cook for 4–5 minutes without colouring.
10. Add the crushed coriander, cumin seeds and curry powder and slowly cook for 3–4 minutes without burning.
11. Add the turmeric and lentils and barely cover with water.
12. Bring to the boil and cook until the lentils form a thick dry paste. Stir occasionally to prevent burning.
13. Add the remaining ingredients to obtain a thick well-flavoured mixture, then allow to cool.
14. Roll out the dough until paper thin, then cut into large 260 mm (10 in) circles.
15. Divide each circle into semicircles, then allow to rest for 5 minutes.
16. Lightly dampen the edges of each semicircle and fold into a coronet, sealing the sides and leaving the top end open.
17. Dampen the edges of the open end, then stuff with the mixture.
18. Seal samosa carefully to enclose the filling.
19. Deep fry in hot fat 180 °C (360 °F) until crisp and golden brown.
20. Drain and serve.

Tandoori chicken
(see Plate 12)

This chicken dish is usually prepared in a tandoor oven. However, a hot grill may be used as a good substitute in the pub kitchen.

5 × 1 kg	Small chickens	5 × 2¼ lb
10 g	Paprika	½ oz
	Salt and pepper, good pinch	
1½	Lemons	1½

Figure 62 *Spicy Indian foods prepared on a barbecue* Courtesy J A Sharwood & Co. Ltd

	Marinade	
250 ml	Yogurt (plain/natural)	½ pt
50 ml	Oil	2 fl oz
15 g	Garam marsala	¾ oz
5–10 g	Chilli peppers	¼–½ oz
25 g	Root ginger	1 oz
100 g	Onion	4 oz
2 cloves	Garlic	2 cloves
1	Lemon zest (see above)	1
	Salt and pepper, good pinch	

Roasts, ethnic and featured dishes

Method
1. Cut the chickens into halves, then remove the skin.
2. Cut slits in the flesh of the chicken to allow the marinade to penetrate.
3. Season the chicken with salt and pepper and sprinkle with the paprika.
4. Remove the zest of the lemon, then squeeze out the juice.
5. Brush over the surfaces of the chickens with the lemon juice.

Note: A little red and orange colouring may be added to the lemon juice.

6. Prepare the marinade:
   (a) Peel the onion, garlic and root ginger.
   (b) Remove the seeds and stalks from the peppers.
   (c) Place all the ingredients into a liquidizer and liquidize to a smooth thick liquid.
7. Place the chicken in the marinade for 4–8 hours (or overnight).
8. Remove the chicken from the marinade and cook under a hot grill. Turn when half cooked, then complete the cooking.
9. Serve the chicken with lemon wedges and a salad garnish consisting of strips of onion, lettuce, cucumber and tomato.

   Accompany with hot nan bread (to follow) and a yogurt chutney made with plain yogurt, chopped coriander leaves and chopped chilli peppers (to taste).

Stuffed pitta bread and stuffed nan bread

Available as packet mixtures. See also the recipe in Chapter 22.

These two breads may be used to produce popular pub snacks because they make good envelopes for a wide range of fillings: chilli con carne, goulash, ale stew, vegetable lasagne, hara beef, samosa filling, curried vegetable filling.

Service   *Stuffed pittas*   Split the hot pittas and stuff with the appropriate hot filling. Attractively garnish with salad vegetables.

Stuffed nans   Prepare as above but place the filling on one half of the hot nan, then fold the other half over to enclose the filling.

Stews

Chilli con carne
(see Plate 13)

Available as a ready-made chilled, frozen or tinned product.

1 kg	Minced beef	2½ lb
250 g	Onions (chopped)	10 oz
10 g	Garlic (crushed)	¼ oz
25 g	Tomato purée	1 oz
400 g	Tinned tomatoes	1 lb
25 g	Chilli powder	1 oz
35 g	Fat	1½ oz
35 g	Flour	1½ oz
500 g	Red beans (cooked) or	1 lb 4 oz
250 g	Red beans (raw)	10 oz
625 ml	Bean cooking liquor and brown stock/bouillon	1 pt 4 oz
	Salt and pepper	

The quantity of chilli powder may be adjusted depending on its strength.

Method
1. Using raw beans:
   (a) Soak the beans for several hours in cold water.
   (b) Drain, cover with cold water or brown stock then bring to the boil.
      Note: Carrot, onion, celery and bay leaf may be added for flavour.
   (c) Simmer until cooked.
2. Melt the fat in a saucepan, add the mince, fry to a light brown colour.
3. Add the onions, garlic and chilli pepper and fry for a further 3–4 minutes.
4. Add the flour and cook on a low heat for 2–3 minutes.
5. Mix in the tomato purée and tinned tomatoes.
6. Slowly blend in the hot stock, stirring smooth with each addition of liquid.
7. Bring to the boil and simmer for 45 minutes.
8. Add the beans and continue cooking.
9. When cooked, check the seasoning and consistency.
10. Serve accompanied with a garnish (or the garnish as a topping) of raw onion rings and heated chopped tomatoes.

Chilli con carne with crisp vegetables

Diced raw vegetables may be added to the chilli on completion of cooking to produce a dish of various tastes and textures. Vegetables which may be added are onions, celery and peppers. Nuts may also be added.

Hungarian goulash
(see Plate 14)

Available as a ready-made chilled, frozen or tinned product.

1¼ kg	Stewing beef or veal	3 lb 2 oz
250 g	Onions (chopped)	10 oz
10 g	Garlic (crushed)	½ oz
25 g	Tomato purée	1 oz
60 g	Paprika	2½ oz
60 g	Fat	2½ oz
60 g	Flour	2½ oz
1¼ l	Brown stock/bouillon	2½ pt
500 g	Raw shaped potatoes, e.g. cubes, squares or balls	1 lb 4 oz
125 g	Choux paste gnocchi	5 oz

Method
1. Trim off any excess fat or sinew from the meat, then cut into 20 mm (¾ in) cubes.
2. Heat the fat in a saucepan.
3. Add the cubed meat and fry till lightly browned.
4. Add the onions and garlic and continue cooking for 6–8 minutes.
5. Add the paprika and lightly cook for 2–3 minutes.
6. Mix in the flour and allow to cook for a further 4–5 minutes.
7. Mix in the tomato purée.
8. Slowly blend in the hot stock, stirring smooth with each addition of liquid.
9. Bring to the boil, then slowly simmer.
10. Skim as required during cooking.
11. Top up with additional stock/bouillon if required.
12. When almost cooked, add the potatoes and complete the cooking.
13. Check the seasoning and consistency.
14. When serving, sprinkle over the surface of the stew with the hot choux

Roasts, ethnic and featured dishes

paste gnocchi. A little chopped parsley may also be added to provide colour.

Choux paste gnocchi
1. Prepare the choux paste as in Chapter 22.
2. Place the paste into a piping bag containing a 5 mm (¼ in) diameter plain tube.
3. Pipe the paste into a shallow saucepan of very hot salted water. The mixture should be piped into strips which are 25 mm (1 in) in length approximately.
4. Poach the gnocchi very gently for 3–4 minutes. Do not allow the water to boil or the gnocchi will break up.
Note: The gnocchi may be prepared in advance of service and stored in cold water.

Rich brown beef stew

Available as a ready-made chilled, frozen or tinned product.

This recipe may be used for various meat stews, e.g. lamb, mutton, veal or venison. Replace the beef with the appropriate meat.

1¼ kg	Stewing beef	3 lb 2 oz
125 g	Onion	5 oz
125 g	Carrots	5 oz
60 g	Celery	2½ oz
60 g	Leeks	2½ oz
	Sprig of thyme, bay leaf and parsley stalks	
5 g	Garlic (optional)	¼ oz
1 clove		1 clove
60 g	Tomato purée	2½ oz
60 g	Fat	2½ oz
1¼ l	Brown stock/bouillon	2½ pt
	Salt and pepper	

Method
1. Trim off any excess fat or sinew from the meat, then cut into 20 mm (¾ in) cubes.
2. Wash, peel and chop the vegetables.
Note: Cut the vegetables into neat shapes if they are to be left in the stew as garnish.
3. Heat the fat in a saucepan.
4. Add the cubed meat and fry till lightly browned.
5. Add the vegetables and continue cooking for 6–8 minutes.
6. Mix in the flour and continue cooking for a further 4–5 minutes.
7. Mix in the tomato purée.
8. Slowly blend in the hot stock, stirring smooth with each addition of liquid.
9. Bring to the boil then slowly simmer.
10. Skim as required during cooking.
11. Top up with additional stock if required.
12. When cooked, remove the meat and place into a clean pan.
13. Strain the sauce over the meat.
14. Reboil and check consistency and seasoning.
Note: The colour of the sauce may be deepened with blackjack (gravy browning).

Recipes for Pubs

Rich brown beef stew in red wine sauce — Prepare as above but replace 200 ml (8 fl oz) of the brown stock with red wine.

Exeter stew — Prepare the basic stew as above, but strain out the vegetables when the stew is almost cooked. Add small suet paste dumplings well flavoured with parsley and a little mixed herbs (the recipe for suet paste is given in Chapter 22). Cover with a lid and complete the cooking.

Beef in ale (see Plate 15) — Use the basic recipe and method for brown beef stew but cut the vegetables into thin strips (use the bay leaf, parsley stalks and thyme as a bouquet garni). Add 125 g (5 oz) lean bacon cut into strips when frying the beef and replace half the stock with beer. Also add a good measure of port when cooking. Do not strain.

20 Vegetables

Michael Davidson and Daniel Stevenson

Vegetarian dishes

Country garden ratatouille (freeze stable)
(see Plate 16)

Yield: 15 × 200 g (8 oz) portions approximately.

500 g	Aubergines	1 lb 4 oz
650 g	Courgettes	1 lb 10 oz
400 g	Pimento (green)	1 lb
600 g	Turnip	1 lb 8 oz
600 g	Swede	1 lb 8 oz
650 g	Carrots	1 lb 10 oz
400 g	Celery	1 lb
600 g	Mushrooms	1 lb 8 oz
1 kg	Onions	2 lb 8 oz
750 g	Tinned tomatoes	1 lb 14 oz
200 g	Tomato purée	8 oz
200 ml	Vegetable oil	8 fl oz
15 g	Salt	¾ oz
	Pepper, good pinch	
10 g	Oregano	½ oz
10 g	Thyme	½ oz
50 g	Cornflour (see note below)	2 oz
200 ml	Water	8 fl oz

Method

1. Wash and peel the vegetables (see note below).
2. Cut the carrots, swedes and turnips into 15 mm (½ in) cubes, then lightly blanch in boiling water.
3. Cut the aubergines into 20 mm (¾ in) cubes.
4. Cut the courgettes into 15 mm (½ in) slices.
5. Cut the pimentoes into 20 mm (¾ in) squares.
6. Roughly cut the celery and onions.
7. Slice the mushrooms.
8. Heat the oil in a saucepan with a large surface area.
9. Add the onions and lightly fry for 2–3 minutes.
10. Add the remaining vegetables (except the tomatoes) and lightly fry for a further 3–4 minutes.
11. Mix in the tomato purée, then add the tinned tomatoes and herbs.
12. Add the seasoning and half the quantity of water, i.e. 100 ml (4 fl oz).
13. Bring to the boil.

Recipes for Pubs

14 Blend together the cornflour with the remaining water and stir through the vegetables.
15 Lightly cook, keeping the vegetables crisp in texture. When freezing the mixture, the vegetables should be left underdone.

Note: If the mixture is to be frozen it is desirable to use a starch which has been specifically developed for frozen products, e.g. Col Flo.

Note: Aubergines and courgettes may be left unpeeled to provide colour and dietary fibre.

Savoury baked potatoes
(see Plate 17)

Poultry, meat, game and vegetable

10 × 200 g	Potatoes	10 × ½ lb
500 ml	Sauce (tomato, béchamel, parsley or onion)	1 pt
250 g	Cooked chicken *or* alternative meat and/or	10 oz
250 g	Grated cheese	10 oz
250 g	Selected vegetables, e.g. diced onions, red and green peppers, mushrooms, sweetcorn, mushrooms and peas	10 oz
40 g	Margarine or butter	1½ oz

Method
1 Bake the potatoes.
2 Melt the margarine in a saucepan.
3 Add the onions, peppers and mushrooms and cook under cover for 2 minutes.
4 Add the diced chicken or meat, sweetcorn, peas and sauce, and bring to the boil.
5 Simmer for 3–4 minutes, then remove from the heat.
6 Add the cheese if present in the recipe and blend through the ingredients (alternatively add the cheese to the stuffed baked potatoes and gratinate under a hot grill).
7 Split the potatoes and place on the serving dish.
8 Fill with the garnish and serve.

Fish and shellfish These are prepared as above using fish or shellfish in place of meat or chicken. White wine fish sauce may also be used.

Note: Care should be taken to avoid overcooking the fish or shellfish when reheating in the sauce.

Pastry items

Quiches These are excellent for using ingredients which have been surplus to previous service requirements, e.g. peas, sweetcorn, beans, tomato pieces, peppers, cheese, cooked fish, meat, game or poultry.

Vegetables and savoury pastries

Quiche Lorraine	Available as a ready-made frozen of chilled product. Yield: 8–10 portions.		
	400 g	Savoury short pastry	1 lb
	2	Eggs	2
	250 ml	Milk	½ pt
	125 g	Diced streaky bacon	5 oz
	75 g	Cheese (usually Gruyère)	3 oz
	15 g	Margarine or butter	½ oz
	1 clove	Crushed garlic (optional)	1 clove
		Salt and pepper	

Method
1. Line a 250 mm (10 in) flan ring with the savoury pastry. Keep the pastry quite thin and ensure that there are no tears or splits or the egg mixture will run out.
2. Lightly fry the diced bacon in the margarine (and garlic) then place into the flan case.
3. Beat together the eggs and milk and season with the salt and pepper.
4. Pour the mixture into the flan case.
5. Grate the cheese, then sprinkle over the top of the egg mixture.
6. Bake in a moderate oven 190 °C (375 °F) approximately, until the mixture is set.

Note: It is deisrable to bake the quiche on a well-cleaned thin (black) baking tray. It is also advisable to regulate the oven to have a substantial amount of bottom heat to cook the pastry through and at the same time set the custard without overcooking.

Savoury vegetable quiche (see Plate 18)	Yield: 8–10 portions		
	400 g	Savoury wholemeal pastry	1 lb
	2	Eggs	2
	250 ml	Milk	½ pt
	25 g	Red pepper (diced)	1 oz
	25 g	Green pepper (diced)	1 oz
	25 g	Sweetcorn	1 oz
	50 g	Onion (chopped)	2 oz
	1 clove	Garlic (crushed)	1 clove
	100 g	Tomatoes (tinned or fresh)	4 oz
	50 g	Cheese (grated)	2 oz
	15 g	Margarine	½ oz
		Salt and pepper	

Method
1. Prepare the same as quiche Lorraine, lightly cooking the peppers, onion and garlic in the margarine.
2. Cut the tomatoes into dice then place all the vegetables into the flan.
3. Pour over the egg mixture, sprinkle the cheese on top then bake in a moderate oven.

Pasties

Cornish pasties (see Plate 19)

Available as a ready-prepared chilled or frozen product.
Yield: 10 pasties

800 g	Savoury short pastry	2 lb
375 g	Coarse minced beef	15 oz
125 g	Chopped onion	5 oz
250 g	Potatoes (peeled)	10 oz
	Salt and pepper	
	Eggwash	

Method

1. Prepare the filling:
   (a) Cut the potato into approximately 5 mm (¼ in) cubes.
   (b) Thoroughly mix together the potato cubes, chopped onion and minced beef. Season with the salt and pepper.
2. Roll out the pastry to a thickness of 3–4 mm (⅛ in), then cut into rounds with a 160 mm (6½ in) diameter plain round cutter.
   Note: To obtain the stated number of pastry shapes requires the trimmings to be used.
3. Place the filling on to the pastry shapes (75 g (3 oz) mixture per pastie), then lightly dampen around the edges with water.
4. Fold the pastry in half, bringing the edges upwards and over the filling, then seal together.
5. Notch the tops neatly with the fingers, then place on to a lightly greased and floured baking tray.
6. Brush over the pasties with eggwash, then bake at 200 °C (400 °F) for 40 minutes approximately.

Boffin: wholemeal curried vegetable pastie (freeze stable)

Yield: 10 pasties

800 g	Wholemeal savoury pastry	2 lb
15 ml	Oil	½ fl oz
200 g (each)	Small cubes of potato, onion, carrots and celery	8 oz (each)
200 g	Sweetcorn	8 oz
200 g	Tomatoes (tinned)	8 oz
5 g	Garlic	¼ oz
100 g	Tomato purée	4 oz
25 g	Curry powder	1 oz
100 ml	Stock/bouillon	4 fl oz

Method

1. Prepare the filling:
   (a) Blanch the carrots and potatoes in boiling water for 1 minute, then refresh in cold water and drain.
   (b) Heat the oil in a saucepan then lightly fry the garlic, onions and celery.
   (c) Add the curry powder and cook for 2–3 minutes.
   (d) Add the carrots, potatoes, sweetcorn, tomatoes and tomato purée.
   (e) Add only enough stock to moisten the ingredients, then bring to the boil and cook for 2 minutes.
   (f) Check the seasoning and allow to cool.
2. Roll out the pastry as for Cornish pasties.

Figure 63 (opposite)
Choice of hot savouries
Courtesy Alveston Kitchens. Photograph by Tony Robbins

Vegetables and savoury pastries

Recipes for Pubs

3 Lightly dampen around the edges of the pastry shapes.
4 Place the filling on to the pastry shapes, then fold over (half-moon shape) and seal edges.
5 Notch the edges neatly with the fingers, then place on to a lightly greased baking tray.
6 Brush over the boffins with eggwash, then bake at 200 °C (400 °F) for 30–40 minutes.

Pies

Chicken pie
(see Plate 20)

These may be attractively prepared in individual porcelain dishes or multiple portion pie dishes.
Yield: 10 portion pie

500 g	Puff pastry	1 lb 4 oz
	Eggwash	
10	Chicken quarters	10
10	Streaky bacon rashers	10
250 g	Button onions (peeled)	10 oz
125 g	Button mushrooms	5 oz
	Chopped parsley	
500 ml	Chicken stock/bouillon	1 pt
	Salt and pepper	

The pastry allowance is 50 g (2 oz) per portion.

Method

1 Season each chicken quarter, then wrap with a bacon rasher.
2 Place in the pie dish, then add the onions, mushrooms and parsley.
3 Add the stock until two-thirds the height of the chicken pieces.
4 Roll out the pastry to a thickness of 4 mm (3/16 in) approximately, then cut to a shape suitable to cover the pie dish.
5 Lightly dampen the rim of the pie dish with water, then cover with the pastry.
6 Cut a small hole in the top of the pastry to allow the steam to escape.
7 Notch the sides of the pie for decoration. The back of a knife may be used to mark the edge of the pastry to increase the flaky appearance.
8 Decorate the pastry if desired and brush over with eggwash.
9 Bake at 200 °C (400 °F) for 20–30 minutes until the pastry has fully risen, then reduce the oven temperature to 175 °C (350 °F) and complete the cooking (until the chicken is cooked through): approximately 1½ hours.
Note: The pastry may be covered with dampened greaseproof paper to avoid excessive colour development. This is done near the end of the cooking period when the pastry is fully cooked. The oven temperature may also be reduced at this stage.

Country pie Prepare as chicken pie but with a variety of ingredients used for the filling, e.g. pieces of rabbit, guinea fowl, turkey, leeks, celery, sweetcorn etc.

Steak and kidney pie Available as a ready-prepared chilled or frozen product.

Vegetables and savoury pastries

Like chicken pies, these may also be prepared in individual porcelain dishes or multiple portion pie dishes.
Yield: 10 portion pie

500 g	Puff pastry	1 lb 4 oz
	Eggwash	
1 kg	Stewing steack (diced)	2½ lb
250 g	Ox kidney (diced)	10 oz
50 g	Lard or dripping	2 oz
250 g	Onion (chopped)	10 oz
	Parsley (chopped), good pinch	
1 l	Brown stock/bouillon	2 pt
25 g	Arrowroot or cornflour	1 oz
	Worcester sauce, good dash	
	Salt and pepper	

Method
1. Cook the filling:
   (a) Melt the fat in a saucepan.
   (b) Add the steak and kidney and shallow fry until lightly browned.
   (c) Add the onion and cook for 6–8 minutes.
   (d) Add the stock, bring to the boil and simmer until almost cooked.
   (e) Add the Worcester sauce to produce a decided flavour.
   (f) Dilute the arrowroot or cornflour in a little cold water and pour into the mixture, stirring continuously until the mixture reboils.
   (g) When cooked, add the chopped parsley then check the seasoning.
   (h) Cool quickly and remove any solidified fat.
2. Place the filling into the pie dish.
3. Roll out the pastry to a thickness 4 mm (³⁄₁₆ in) approximately, then cut to a shape suitable to cover the pie dish.
4. Lightly dampen the rim of the pie dish with water, then cover with the pastry.
5. Cut a small hole in the top of the pastry to allow the steam to escape.
6. Notch the sides of the pie for decoration.
7. Decorate the pastry if desired and brush over with eggwash.
8. Bake at 200 °C (400 °F) for approximately 40 minutes.

Steak, kidney and mushroom pie

This is prepared the same as steak and kidney pie, adding 125 g (5 oz) washed and quartered mushrooms to the steak mixture just prior to adding the Worcester sauce.

Puddings
Steak and kidney pudding (see Plate 21)

Available as a ready-made tinned, chilled or frozen product. To prepare fresh on a large scale, this dish requires the use of a steamer. Therefore it may be unsuitable for many small operations.
Yield: 10 portions

800 g	Suet pastry	2 lb
1 kg	Stewing steak	2½ lb
250 g	Ox kidney	10 oz
250 g	Onion (chopped)	10 oz
	Parsley (chopped), good pinch	

25 g	Flour	1 oz
15 ml (1 tbsp)	Worcester sauce	½ fl oz (1 tbsp)
375 ml	Brown stock/bouillon (cold)	¾ pt
	Salt and pepper	

Method
1. Prepare the filling:
   (a) Trim any fat or gristle from the beef, then cut into small slices or cubes.
   (b) Mix together the beef, onions, parsley, seasoning and flour.
   (c) Add the Worcester sauce, then mix in the cold stock.
   (d) Allow to stand for 1–6 hours before use.
2. Prepare the suet pastry (Chapter 22).
3. Lightly grease a large pudding basin, then line with three-quarters of the pastry.
4. Place the filling into the lined basin leaving a 15 mm (¾ in) gap from the filling to the top of the basin.
5. Dampen around the edges of the paste with a little water.
6. Roll out the remaining paste and cover the top.
7. Seal down around the edges, then neatly trim if required.
8. Cover with a circle of greased greaseproof paper and a pudding cloth which is secured with string – and with the ends tied together.
9. Steam for 4½–5 hours (depending on the quality of the meat used).

Vegetables

Fresh vegetables
1. Ensure that the vegetables you purchase are as fresh as possible.
2. Remove the outer leaves or peel the skin only when it is essential to do so, i.e. with older winter vegetables. Young spring vegetables should only be cleaned in fresh cold water, and this applies to potatoes as well.
3. If vegetables have to be cut, ensure that the knife is sharp; a blunt knife will bruise them and spoil the quality.
4. With the exception of roots, which can be prepared up to 12 hours in advance, do not prepare vegetables too early since cut vegetables deteriorate rapidly.
5. Green leaf and fresh leguminous vegetables, i.e. cabbages, sprouts, peas, green beans etc. should be cooked by placing them in a small amount of boiling salted water to which a little sugar is added.
6. Use as little water as possible with green vegetables to avoid all the flavour ending up in the water; do not overcook them.
7. If vegetables are not to be used immediately, cool them rapidly in fresh cold running water.
8. Fresh green vegetables should still be slightly crisp when cooked, to retain the maximum flavour and texture.
9. If preparing mixed fresh vegetables, cook them separately and then cool them down in cold running water. Drain and mix them together, and then reheat them by (a) plunging in boiling salted water in a basket or strainer and brushing with melted butter, (b) heating with a little butter, salt and pepper in a shallow saucepan on the stove, or (c) heating in a microwave oven in an earthenware dish with added seasoning and butter.

Vegetables and savoury pastries

10 Do not cook vegetables in large quantities, and remember that keeping them hot for any length of time leads to colourless, tasteless, soggy or tough vegetables.

Frozen vegetables

1 Always cook frozen vegetables from the frozen state, putting them straight into boiling salted water.
2 Use a minimum of water.
3 Remember that they have already been blanched or partly cooked, so check for cooking regularly.
4 Frozen vegetables can be cooked with seasoning and butter from the frozen state in a covered earthenware dish in a microwave oven. Cooking and reheating times vary with different ovens, therefore consult your handbook. There is no need to add water.
5 Serve frozen vegetables in the same way as fresh ones.

Made-up vegetables Apart from fresh cooked single vegetables or those to which seasoning and a little butter is added, there are vegetarian dishes and those that can be enhanced with a sauce.

Cauliflower Sauces: cheese, parsley, polonaise. Cover the cooked hot cauliflower with fresh white breadcrumbs tossed in a little butter to which the sieved white and yolk of a hard-boiled egg and some chopped parsley is added.

When cooking cauliflower there is usually some left over, or bits which have broken off from the whole cauliflower. In order to use this up, place it in a bowl when it is cold and mix lightly with salt and pepper. Make it into 40 mm (1½ in) round-shaped mounds by scooping it out with an ice cream scoop. Place these on a greased tray and coat them with cheese sauce sprinkled with grated cheese and place them in the top of a very hot oven, 230 °C (450 °F) until they are heated through and browned on top.

Broad beans and carrots Sauce: parsley. Allow 300 ml (½ pt) sauce per four portions.
Add the heated cooked broad beans to the preheated sauce and serve sprinkled with chopped parsley.
Treat carrots in the same way.

Haricot beans Soak the beans overnight, strain away all the water, and cook them until they are tender in boiling salted water together with an onion 'spiked' with two cloves and a large carrot. Drain and add a rich tomato sauce to them, 300 ml (½ pt) to four portions.

Boston baked beans Add 100 g (4 oz) of bacon pieces per four portions (cut this as for coq au vin, blanched in hot water and browned in a little oil) to the beans and then pour on a barbecued tomato sauce.

French style peas Using tinned or frozen baby peas, heat up 300 ml (½ pt) of water per 225 g (8 oz) of peas with a teaspoon of sugar. Add one medium sized onion cut into 20 mm (¾ in) dice or 5–6 button onions and poach this until the onions are tender. Add one or two outside leaves of lettuce shredded with a sharp knife into thin strips. Season with salt and add the peas. Thicken the liquor with

Recipes for Pubs

30 g (1 oz) butter and 25 g (1 oz) flour creamed together and dropped in as small lumps. Shake the pan backwards and forwards to blend the thickening and then test for seasoning and serve with a little chopped parsley.

Celery (braised) Cut some stick celery down to 150–200 mm lengths. Divide these vertically into 2 or 3 portions and place them in boiling salted water for 2–3 minutes. Lay this on a bed of sliced onion, carrot and bay leaf and cover with a beef or veal stock; braise in a covered dish in a medium oven 185–200 °C (375–390 °F) until tender. Serve the celery whole with a little brown sauce thinned with the cooking liquor and garnish with chopped parsley.

Courgettes (Portugaise) Prepare, per 900 g (2 lb) of courgettes: peel then slice the courgettes into 15 mm (½ in) slices.

1 large onion, medium chopped
1 400 g (14 oz) tin tomatoes
1 clove garlic (optional)
2 dstsp oil
salt and pepper to taste
1 tsp sugar

1. Heat the oil, place the onion and garlic in this and cook it without colour for 2–3 minutes.
2. Add the courgettes and continue cooking without colour for 2 minutes.
3. Roughly chop the tomatoes, add to the courgettes and complete the cooking. Sprinkle with chopped parsley.

Courgettes (fried)
1. Prepare the courgettes as for Portugaise.
2. Dip them in seasoned flour and then into batter as if frying fish. Fry at 185 °C (370 °F) until they are golden brown.

Stuffed marrow
1. Cut the marrow (with skin) into 100 mm (4 in) portions.
2. Scoop out the centre.
3. Blanch for 2–3 minutes in boiling salted water and drain.
4. Fill the centre with cooked savoury mince.
5. Bake in a moderate oven, 180 °C (350 °F). Leave the marrow plain or sprinkle it with a mixture of brown breadcrumbs and grated cheese topped with a little melted butter.

Rice
1. Place a large pan of salted water on the heat and bring to the boil.
2. When it is boiling pour in the weighed and washed rice and allow this to boil fairly rapidly for 17–20 minutes, adding a little lemon juice.
3. Rinse the rice thoroughly under the cold tap and drain it; spread it out on a flat sieve.
4. Cover the rice with a clean tea towel and heat it slowly in a low oven, 140 °C (290 °F).

Potatoes
Creamed potatoes
1. Using old, well-peeled, potatoes, cut them into golfball-sized pieces.
2. Rinse them thoroughly, place in a saucepan and cover them with water. Bring them to the boil, adding a good helping of salt.

Vegetables and savoury pastries

3 Simmer gently for 15–20 minutes until they are tender.
4 Drain the potatoes thoroughly and put them back into the saucepan.
5 Add (per ½ kg (1 lb) of peeled potatoes):

30 g (1 oz) butter
2 tbsp milk
½ tsp salt
¼ tsp pepper
¼ tsp grated nutmeg.

6 Mash the potatoes with a potato masher or an electric mixer using a beater attachment.
7 For immediate service place the mash in a vegetable dish and smooth it into a pyramid with a pallet knife, finishing it off by 'scalloping' it all round with the knife.

For the hot-plate, place a generous splash of milk in the bottom of a casserole (preferably the enamelled cast iron type), add the hot potatoes, a further splash of milk on top and a couple of knobs of butter. This will keep them moist during service.

Roast potatoes
1 Peel and cut the potatoes into golfball-sized pieces.
2 Bring a large pot of salted water to the boil and then add the potatoes and simmer for 5–6 minutes. Thoroughly drain them in a colander.
3 Meanwhile add some good meat dripping to a roasting tray and heat this up in the oven until it is smoking.
4 Carefully place the drained potatoes into the hot fat and turn them so that they are coated with the fat.
5 Sprinkle them with salt and roast them in the top of a hot oven, turning them occasionally until they are golden brown. (Do not overcook them or they will fall to pieces.)

Baked potatoes
The potatoes can simply be washed and then baked in a moderate oven. If desired they can be cooked in tin foil, but this is expensive and unnecessary. Baked potatoes can also be cooked (and reheated) in a microwave oven.

To serve baked potatoes, cut a deep cross in the top of the potato and pinch the sides to open this up. Insert a generous knob of butter, a sprinkle of salt and a pinch of parsley. You can also use cream cheese or sour cream (1 dessertspoon per potato) with chives.

Baked potato au gratin
Either sprinkle the cut pinched potato with a mixture of breadcrumbs and cheese (50/50) and place them under the grill to brown; or scoop out the soft inside, mix it with grated cheese and seasoning and place this back in the potato skin. Coat the potato with cheese and breadcrumbs as above and grill until golden brown.

Pan Haggerty
This is an old North Country potato dish. It would have been served as a complete dish on its own in the days when meat was not always available. Yield: 8 portions.

1 kg	Prepared potatoes (old ones)	2 lb
2	Large onions	2

Recipes for Pubs

200 g	Cheddar cheese	½ lb
50 g	Dripping	2 oz
	Seasoning	

Method
1. Thinly slice the potatoes, no more than 3 mm (⅛ in) thick, and thoroughly wash them under running water to remove excess starch.
2. Drain them well and pat dry with absorbent paper; add the sliced onion and seasoning and half of the grated cheddar cheese. Mix together well.
3. Place this into a greased casserole, arranging the top potatoes in a neat flat layer.
4. Pour in the melted dripping and sprinkle with the remaining cheese.
5. Bake in the bottom of a moderate oven for 20–30 minutes.
6. Transfer it to the top and increase the heat to 185 °C (370 °F) for a further 15–20 minutes until the potatoes and cheese are golden brown.

Boulangère potatoes

The ingredients are the same as for pan Haggerty but without the cheese and with 600 ml (1 pt) of good beef stock. Prepare the ingredients as for pan Haggerty up to and including stage 3. Add the stock to a height just short of the top of the potatoes, then brush over with the fat. Bake in a moderate oven until cooked and golden brown.

Hash browns

Yield: 8 portions.

1 kg	Prepared potatoes	2 lb
100 g	Butter or good dripping	4 oz
	Salt and pepper to taste	

Method
1. Scrub the potatoes and set them to boil in a covered saucepan and cook them for about 6 minutes. Remove them and allow to cool.
2. Remove the skin and grate the potatoes using a cheese grater. Form the gratings into small round cakes.
3. Melt the butter in a large frying pan and gently lay the cakes in the butter, allowing them to brown nicely on one side; turn them over and repeat the operation.
4. Press the cakes firmly in order to keep them in one piece. When thoroughly brown on both sides remove them from the butter, drain on absorbent paper and serve with chopped parsley. They are delightful with fried chicken.

Variations
1. A small finely chopped onion with this mixture gives added flavour.
2. A tin of sweetcorn, bound together with a sprinkling of flour to prevent it breaking up the potato cake during frying.
3. Diced cooked streaky bacon, well drained of fat on absorbent paper.

Boiled potatoes
1. Thoroughly clean and wash the potatoes.
2. Place them in a pot of boiling water containing a generous sprig of fresh mint and salt.
3. Cook them gently until they are tender.
4. Serve them with butter and sprinkle with chopped parsley or cooked mint leaves.

21 Buffet items, sandwiches and cheese

Michael Davidson and Daniel Stevenson

Dishes offered on a buffet vary depending on the type of operation. Some offer a small selection of cold dishes, e.g. meat, pâtés, sandwiches, salads, gâteaux and fruit salad etc. as buffet service, but serve hot dishes plated in an out-of-sight kitchen. Here the hot dishes rely on written menus for sales.

Alternatively the buffet may include plated hot and cold items for the customer who has seen what he wants. With this type of buffet service almost any type of hot dish can be served, and the use of attractive silver, copper, porcelain or china dishes may be used to create a style in keeping with the image that an establishment wishes to project, e.g. the use of copper or porcelain casseroles to serve meat or game stews in an old-fashioned country pub.

Buffet items

Starters

Fruits

Avocado pear with salad dressing Avocado pear halves served on a bed of lettuce garnished with salad vegetables (optional) and accompanied with vinaigrette.

Avocado pear with gherkins and walnuts (epicurean style) Avocado pear stuffed with a mixture of the pear flesh, gherkins, small pieces of walnuts, paprika and mayonnaise. Decorated with a pickled walnut and served on a bed of lettuce.

Avocado pear with crab meat (see Plate 22) Avocado pear stuffed with a mixture of the pear flesh, flaked cooked crab meat, lemon juice, pinch cayenne pepper, whipped cream and mayonnaise. Garnished with lettuce and lemon wedges.

Hot grapefruit with red pimento (Mexican style) Half grapefruit sprinkled with sherry and brown sugar and allowed to macerate. Covered with strips of pimento, sprinkled with caster sugar and browned under a grill.

Chilled melon Melon half or wedge decorated with a cherry and served well chilled. Ground ginger may be served separately.

Melon with port Half melon filled with port and allowed to macerate for 20–30 minutes

Recipes for Pubs

Eggs

Egg mayonnaise
(starter/main course or snack)
Halves or quarters of hard-boiled eggs dressed on lettuce and coated with mayonnaise. A garnish of salad vegetables, e.g. tomato, cucumber, cress and spring onion, is also usually included.

Fish

Fish mayonnaise
Cooked flaked fish mixed with a dice of hard-boiled eggs and cucumber and bound with mayonnaise. The mixture is dressed on a bed of lettuce and decorated with olives, anchovies, capers and chopped parsley.

Shellfish mayonnaise
salmon mayonnaise
trout mayonnaise
Prepared as above using appropriate fish or shellfish.

Potted shrimps
Available as a ready-prepared chilled product.

Shellfish cocktail
(shrimp, prawn, scampi etc.)
(see Plate 23)
Cooked shellfish bound with Marie-Rose sauce and dressed in a cocktail glass or dish. The mixture is coated with Marie-Rose sauce and decorated with olive, anchovy, lemon or appropriate shellfish etc.
Note: A dice of cucumber, gherkin, pimento, onion etc. may be added to the shellfish to produce individuality.

Pâtés
(see Plate 24)
Chicken liver, duck, game, country, mushroom pâtés etc. All available as ready-prepared products.

Main course dishes, snacks and salads

Fish and shellfish

Soused herring
Filleted herring (usually rolled with the skin side outwards) cooked in a pickling liquor consisting of carrots, onions, bay leaf, peppercorns, thyme, salt, sugar, vinegar and water. The fish is served cold with the liquor and vegetables.
Available as a ready-prepared product.

Rollmops and Bismark herring
(see Plate 25)
Filleted herring which is pickled in a marinade consisting of onion, bay leaf, peppercorns, cloves, lemon juice, salt, vinegar and white wine. The raw herring is pickled in the marinade (which has been boiled, cooled and strained) together with sliced onions, bay leaves, mustard seeds, peppercorns, sliced salt cucumber and a little shredded chilli pepper.
Available as a ready-prepared product.

Smoked mackerel
Thin slices of smoked mackerel fillets garnished with lemon wedges and salad vegetables. Served with buttered brown bread.

Buffet items, sandwiches and cheese

	Alternatively, lightly cooked whole mackerel fillets garnished with salad vegetables.
Smoked trout (see Plate 26)	Whole smoked trout with the skin removed. Served with lemon wedges, cress, salad vegetables and horseradish sauce.
Cold salmon with mayonnaise (or other suitable fish)	Portion of cooked cold salmon dressed on lettuce and garnished with salad vegetables, e.g. tomato, cucumber, peppers, spring onions, radishes, cress and quarters of hard-boiled eggs (optional). Served with mayonnaise.
Cold lobster with mayonnaise (see Plate 27)	Half or halves of boiled lobster with the intestines removed. The intestinal cavity is lined with lettuce or shredded lettuce, then filled with the flesh from the claws. The lobster is dressed on a bed of lettuce, decorated with anchovy fillets and capers and garnished with salad vegetables. Serve with mayonnaise.

Meat, poultry and game (cold)

Roast beef, lamb, pork and venison	Slices of cold roast meat arranged on a platter and garnished with salad vegetables. Served with appropriate sauces, e.g. horseradish, Oxford, Cumberland, mayonnaise or redcurrant jelly.
Roast chicken, turkey, guineafowl, duckling, pheasant, partridge etc.	Slices or pieces of cold roast poultry or game birds dressed on a platter and garnished with salad vegetables. Served with appropriate sauces (see above).
Boiled meats and offal	Slices of cold boiled brisket, ham and tongue dressed on a platter and garnished with salad vegetables.

Pies (cold)	Available as ready-prepared chilled products.
Game, pork, veal, ham and veal, ham and egg etc.	Small pies served whole and large pies cut into slices or portions. The pies or portions of pie are dressed on a platter and garnished with salad vegetables.
Scotch eggs	Scotch egg cut into halves, dressed on lettuce and garnished with salad vegetables.

See also pâtés, egg mayonnaise and fish mayonnaise in the starters section.

Quiches	Available as ready-prepared products.

Salads

Simple salads Beetroot, French bean, cucumber, potato, red bean, rice salad etc.

French salad Lettuce, cucumber, tomato, quarters of hard-boiled eggs and salad dressing.

Green salad Green salad vegetables in season, e.g. lettuce, watercress, curly chicory, chives, spring onions etc.

Mixed salad All types of salad vegetables in season.

Niçoise salad Diced cooked potatoes, cooked green beans and diced tomato flesh bound with salad dressing. Dress the mixture in the service bowl and decorate with olives, capers and anchovies. Tuna fish is sometimes added to the potato mixture for this salad.

Coleslaw Shredded white cabbage mixed with shredded carrots and onions and bound with mayonnaise. Additional ingredients may include slices of pimento, apple, raisins and nuts.

Potato and watercress salad Slices of boiled potato and watercress leaves mixed together and dressed in a serving dish. The potatoes and cress are sprinkled with hard-boiled eggs and chopped parsley. Serve with salad dressing. Alternatively, bind the potatoes and watercress leaves with the salad dressing.

Waldorf salad Diced dessert apples, celery or celeriac and half walnuts bound together with mayonnaise and dressed on lettuce.

Caesar salad Pieces of cos lettuce, diced celery, pimento, peas, grated parmesan, crumbled blue cheese, crisp cubes of bread cooked in the oven with a little garlic oil, chopped pickle and chopped anchovy fillets.
The ingredients are mixed with a dressing consisting of garlic oil, raw egg (or lightly cooked boiled egg), lemon juice, salt and ground black pepper.

Types of buffet

Listed below are the main types of buffet normally associated with the licensed trade. They include items ranging from the highly priced dishes for select pub location to much simpler ones.

Hot and cold fork buffet Cold whole decorated fish.
Whole shellfish, cold or hot fried.
Cold carving joints.
Cold savoury pies.
Hot carving joints.
A selection of mixed green salads.

Buffet items, sandwiches and cheese

Boiled new potatoes or baked potatoes.
Gâteaux, cold sweets and cheeses.

Hot and cold finger buffet
Small items of fried seafood and seafood canapés.
A range of fancy decorated open and closed sandwiches.
Puff pastry savoury bouchées.
A variety of sharp-tasting savouries on sticks, both hot and cold.
Small decorated pastries.

Hot and cold high-quality luncheon or supper buffet bar
Carving joints on the bone and pâtés.
Various shellfish and smoked fish.
Hand-raised pies.

Cold Salads.

Hot Rich home-made traditional pies, pasties, casseroles and hot-pots, sausages and a hot carving joint.
A choice of fresh vegetables and potatoes.
Various freshly made sandwiches and a ploughman's lunch.
Hot or cold sweets and a cheese board.

Standard hot and cold luncheon and supper buffet

Cold 'Easicarve' cold joints.
Pâtés.
Peeled and prepared seafood.
Various salads.

Hot Cold pies, Scotch eggs, sandwiches, ploughman's lunch.
Home-made and convenience pies, pasties, hot-pots, casseroles.
Sausages.
A hot and a cold sweet.

Small hot and cold luncheon and supper buffet

Cold Sliced meats and cheeses.
Salads.
Possibly one type of seafood.
Sandwiches, rolls and a ploughman's lunch.

Hot One or two made-up dishes and sausages.

Vegetables and potatoes.
A cold sweet.

Hot and cold carving or fork buffet

Cold whole decorated fish Salmon, trout, salmon trout.
   The fish should be poached in a court-bouillon (a mixture of water, vinegar, vegetables, herbs and seasoning). When cold it should be taken out and, with the head and tail on, the skin and fins should be removed. The brownish flesh on either side of the backbone and in the indentation down the side of the fish should be removed with the tip of a knife. The fish is dressed upright or divided into two down the backbone. All the bones are removed, and the fish is then dressed flat on two dishes.

Suggested decorations *Vegetables* Sliced cucumber, cooked carrot, radishes, tinned red peppers, strips of cucumber skin (for leaves or stalks of flowers), hard-boiled eggs, lemon.
Fish Prawns (shell on or off).
Piping A mixture of butter and mayonnaise (50/50).
Glaze Aspic, chilled down until it becomes oily, but not set.

Using a combination of these items, decorate the fish on a flat silver or attractive china meat plate.

Salmon This requires a simple decor. Using cucumber strips as stalks and long daffodil type leaves, make a floral decoration down the length of the salmon. This is ideal for the filleted flat dressing. Dip the items in aspic before applying them to the fish. The whole upright fish lends itself to decoration with overlapping slices of round vegetables and eggs.
   Allow the fish to cool thoroughly in the fridge before attempting to glaze it with the aspic. This can be brushed on to the plain fish and poured gently from a ladle or spoon over the decoration. This method of decoration and finish applies to all fish and the design can be varied according to taste and imagination.

Lobster For an attractive centrepiece, use two cooked lobsters. All the meat is removed from one and cut up into small portions, including the tail and claw meat. The other is left whole and is dressed in the centre of an oval dish on top of a large wedge-shaped croûton of fried bread or other edible socle (e.g. stiff semolina). This lifts the head of the lobster up. The portions of lobster are placed around the centrepiece and the whole dish is decorated with lemon and cucumber.

Prawns Prawns are best left whole and hung around the edge of a large Paris goblet. The goblet is filled with shredded outer leaves of lettuce and the prawns are then placed with their tails in the glass and their heads hanging down over the edge. They are held in place with half a lemon and a piece of parsley in the top.

Dublin Bay prawns These should be placed in a glass or silver bowl full of crushed ice; a dish of

Buffet items, sandwiches and cheese

(see Plate 28) mayonnaise or cocktail sauce is placed in the centre and the prawns lie in a circle round the bowl. Decorate the dish with lemon and parsley.

Cold carving joints and poultry The preparation and cooking of joints is fully described in Chapter 19. The following are suggestions for presentation and carving for the colf buffet.

Beef Fore rib (3–5 bone), carvery trimmed.
Pork A whole leg 5½–6½ kg (12–15 lb), with the crackling removed.
Turkey A 9–13½ kg (20–30 lb) cock bird.
Ham Smoked or green gammon, plain or glazed and decorated.
Chicken Capon; 2½ –3 kg (5–6 lb) bird.

Finishing

Beef Trim any unsightly bits and pieces from the cold roasted joint. Glaze it with aspic and slice 6–10 pieces. Lay them overlapping around the base of the joint on a flat oval dish and decorate it with radishes and watercress. Accompany the joint with stoned black olives, maraschino cherries and stoned green olives placed alternately on the stem of a decorative skewer.

Pork Remove the crackling from the joint and trim off the excess fat. Cut 8–10 slices for decorating the dish. Decorate the leg with sliced blanched eating apples cut into rings (no core) and with a cherry placed in the centre hole; lay these on the joint in an overlapping pattern.

Turkey Make up a ruff for the legs by folding a white or coloured serviette in half to form a rectangle and then cutting it at 6 mm (¼ in) intervals with a pair of scissors. Fold the serviette back the other way and wrap the ruff round the top of the turkey's leg with the cut sections pointing upwards. The ruff can be secured with a pin.

Decorate the turkey on the flat section between the front of the breast with sliced tomato and parsley and the dish with watercress and fried heart-shaped croûtons dipped in cranberry sauce.

Ham or gammon If you have cooked your own ham, remove the rind and trim off the excess fat. Trim round the knuckle end of the skin to expose 60 mm (2 in) of the shin bone. Thoroughly dry and chill the gammon and stand it on a wire tray.

Add decorations to the joint using vegetables and fruit such as slices of orange, pineapple and maraschino cherries. Dip the items in aspic before applying them to the surface of the ham. A floral decoration or a design that has a connection with the organization of person for whom the buffet is being provided is attractive and suitable.

Allow the decoration to set and coat it carefully with aspic. Put the ham aside to set once more and then place an angled carving stand on a flat dish and decorate the dish with slices of ham, orange or pineapple segments and watercress.

Capon Remove the two whole cooked breasts from the bone, skin them and cut the meat into medallions about the circumference of a standard cup. Remove the breast bone and fill the space left with pâté shaped like the original meat. Set

Recipes for Pubs

the bird on a wire tray. The remade chicken and the medallions should be decorated using the same vegetable items as for a ham, glazed with aspic.

Hot carving joints If hot joints are to be carved in front of the customer, pay attention to their appearance. Ensure correct carving of the joint in order to serve attractive portions; give value for money and keep wastage to a minimum. A good well-cooked joint should be carved across the grain or it will produce tough slices of meat – even a fillet of beef cut with the grain can be tough. The garnishes and sauces can be found in Chapter 17. If there is more than one joint a certain amount of precarving to save time would be sensible.

Saddle of lamb, venison or baron of beef can also be used, but the butcher will need plenty of notice for the latter.

Finger buffet

Ensure:

1 That each item can be eaten with grace in one mouthful.
2 That items can be picked up with one hand and held without getting one's fingers messy or losing half the garnish.
3 That you design your buffet so that items are well spaced about. This enables people to eat without using a plate, taking only one item at a time.
4 That if you have hot items, plenty of cocktail sticks are provided to pick them up by; this avoids burnt and greasy fingers.

Seafood canapés

Bases These must be dry and crisp, and should be sealed with butter or a butter and mayonnaise mixture to prevent the dampness of the seafood making the base soggy.

Savoury biscuits Round or square, no more than 40 mm (1½ in) across.
Toast Slow toasted thin dry white or brown bread, toasted whole and then cut into squares while still hot or into fingers no more than 20 mm (¾ in) wide and 70 mm (2½ in) long.
Fried bread Cut to the same dimensions as the toast.

Toppings	*Finish and garnish*
Prawn	Celery, tomato, hard-boiled egg, anchovy and cucumber
Smoked salmon	Lemon, butter/mayonnaise decoration and cayenne
Smoked mackerel	Lemon, horseradish, candied cherry and cucumber
Smoked eel	As for salmon, plus horseradish.
Smoked salmon pâté	Lemon, olive and gherkin
Kipper pâté	Lemon, olive and gherkin
Crab pâté	Hard-boiled egg, parsley and lemon

Buffet items, sandwiches and cheese

Salmon pâté	Mayonnaise decoration, cucumber and grapes
Anchovies	Gherkin, sour cream, lemon and cucumber
Lumpfish roe (or caviar)	Lemon, hard-boiled egg and finely chopped onion
Soused herrings	Apple, sour cream and onion
Smoked oysters	Lemon, mayonnaise and cucumber
Lobster	Anchovy butter and cucumber
Sardines	Anchovy butter, tomato and gherkin

Finishing
1 Achieve a contrast in colour and texture with the toppings. Decide first on the main ingredient and then add the contrasts.
2 Start by preparing all the ingredients ready for use. Canapés require a certain amount of time to prepare, but because they are on a base which will go soft they cannot be made up too far in advance. Therefore, if all the items are prepared in advance, ready for immediate use, time can be saved and it will be possible to make some more up after the buffet has started.
3 Dress the canapés on to a wire tray and seal them by coating them with a light aspic (this will prevent the garnish falling off as well as preserving the finish of the canapés by keeping the air away from items that can discolour in a warm room).

Other canapés

Toppings	*Finish and garnish*
Ham	Pineapple, apricot and coleslaw
Turkey	Cranberries, chestnuts and orange slices
Salami	Gherkin and cherry
Liver sausage	Radish, watercress, cucumber and celery
Pâté	Gherkin, olives and onion
Chicken	Stuffing, bacon, tomato and orange.

Sandwiches for finger buffet The difference between sandwiches for a finger buffet and standard sandwiches over the bar (see later) is in their preparation and finish.

Sandwiches for a finger buffet are reduced to one mouthful, and so must be cut into small squares, fingers or triangles. This is not easy with the standard square sandwich, and it is time consuming.

1 Take a long uncut sandwich loaf (not too fresh) and cut off all the crusts; but do not throw them away!
2 Cut the loaf into slices 5–15 mm (¼–½ in), thick, lengthwise.
3 Butter the inside surfaces of each pair of slices.
4 Fill them with the required filling, either one whole loaf of one filling or alternate sandwiches of different fillings:

If the loaf is for immediate use then it can be cut into sandwiches. If it is not required straight away, place the crusts back on the loaf and wrap it in tin foil and keep it in a refrigerator until it is required.

For a special occasion, spread the outside surfaces of the made-up sandwich loaf with a mixture of butter and mayonnaise, but leave the underneath dry. Place some of the mixture in a piping bag with a small shell design tube and

Recipes for Pubs

decorate the loaf. To finish, you can add colour by decorating the top, sides and either end with a flower or cucumber leaf design, or simply with thin slices of cucumber and tomato. To serve, just cut the loaf into 13 or 19 mm (½ or ¾ in) slices.

See also the section on sandwiches later in this chapter.

Sundries A selection of whole cheeses, mainly English with a few continental types: e.g. Stilton, Gloucester, Sage Derby, Brie.
Salami.

Ploughman's lunch and variations

At the bottom end of the scale the ploughman's lunch comes in a plastic and tin foil wrapping: it is colourless and tasteless. At the top end is the wholemeal crusty loaf with good cheese cut from a large, mature Cheddar and served with generous helpings of fresh butter, salad and a little pickle.

Standard formula
(see Plate 29)

Bread
1. Best white cottage loaf. The top piece is cut in two and the bottom cut into four or six pieces.
2. Brown wholemeal cob loaf, cut into four.
3. Good quality French bread.

Cheese Any cheese may be served with a ploughman's lunch, but most people expect to be served with Cheddar. It might be worth trying others, such as Stilton, Gloucester, Cheshire, Derby or Wensleydale.

Cheddar sizes

Farmhouse cloth or black waxed	25 kg (56 lb)
Farmhouse quarters	6.25 kg (14 lb)
Oblong block, 3–4 quality	4.5 kg (10 lb)
Truckle, small cloth wrapped	4 kg (9 lb)
Baby truckle, small cloth wrapped	2 kg (4 lb)
Miniatures, round white wax coated	400 g (14 oz)

The 4 kg (9 lb) truckle is recommended for pub use. Remove the outer cloth and cut it into 25 mm (1 in) rings and then into wedges. A wire cheese cutter, once you get used to it, is the easiest and safest way to cut cheese.

If you use the 4.5 kg (10 lb) block, do not cut it into squares, which are reminiscent of bars of soap, cut into triangles.

Salad There is no need to serve a large salad with a ploughman's lunch. The main

Buffet items, sandwiches and cheese

reason for it is to add colour to the dish, and therefore all you require is:

1 small lettuce leaf
1 quarter of tomato
2–3 slices of cucumber or pieces of celery
2–3 rings of onion

Butter For a ploughman's lunch you need at least 25 g (1 oz) butter. Cut a 250 g (10 oz) pack into ten pieces and place them in a large bowl with ice cubes and a little water. You will find that these portions are larger and cheaper than the standard butter pats.

Pickle Sweet, onion or mixed pickle are the usual varieties which are offered. Do not serve them automatically but offer them as an extra. As an alternative you can serve any of the made-up wet salads, or gentleman's relishes.

Variations with additions required

Frenchman's lunch	Pâté and onion soup
Beefeater lunch	Corned beef and oxtail soup
Italian shepherd's lunch	Italian cheese and minestrone soup
Italian shepherd's lunch	Salami and minestrone
Pigman's lunch	Pork sausage and kidney soup
Pigman's lunch	Pork brawn and kidney soup
Fisherman's lunch	Smoked salmon pâté and crab soup
Crofter's lunch	Kipper pâté and cock-a-leekie soup
Gamekeeper's lunch	Game pie or pâté and duck orange soup

Sandwiches

Plain sandwiches

Triangular, square and finger sandwiches (white and brown bread)   *Examples of fillings*   Tomato, tomato and lettuce, cucumber, cheese, cheese and chutney, boiled eggs, roast beef, chicken or turkey, salmon and smoked salmon (brown bread).

Rolled sandwiches   *Examples*   Asparagus rolls, salsify rolls and palm heart rolls.
Production   Spread the bread with cream cheese and trim off the crusts. Place the selected vegetable at the bottom of each slice then roll up.

Pinwheel sandwiches   *Examples of fillings*   various fillings or spreads, e.g. pâté, cheese, chicken, tongue, sardine etc.
Production   Long thin slices of buttered bread spread with filling (different fillings giving colour variation). The slices are rolled up tightly similar to a Swiss roll, then cut into slices.

Recipes for Pubs

Figure 64 *Selection of sandwiches*
Courtesy Flour Advisory Bureau

Buffet items, sandwiches and cheese

Toasted sandwiches *Bookmaker sandwich* Grilled or sautéd minute steak spread with mustard.
(see Plate 30) *Broadway sandwich* Mayonnaise, smoked salmon, shredded lettuce and slices of hard-boiled eggs.
Club sandwich Mayonnaise, shredded lettuce, sliced tomatoes, grilled rashers of streaky bacon, slices of cooked breast of chicken and a final layer of shredded lettuce.

Open sandwiches Using a good tasty wholemeal or rye bread as a base (for slimmers use crispbread type biscuits), cut it into slices about 15–20 mm (½–¾ in) thick and spread them with mayonnaise and butter or mustard butter. The toppings are the same as for the canapés.

Sandwich platters For example, a cheese platter with a variety of bread/rolls and salad accompaniments.

This list of sandwiches and snacks, developed by adding possible combinations of meat, salad, fish and dairy produce, indicates their potential.

In putting together a comprehensive sandwich menu there could be waste. Establish those basic ingredients which are used up quickly as the basis for all combinations.

Preparation First prepare all the fillings, garnishes, bread and butter and lay them out on a table so that everything is near at hand. Place the butter in a mixing bowl and cream it with a whisk. This should make it easier to spread and also help it to go further.

Sandwich ideas There are many combinations, but the general rules are:

1 Try to mix two different textures, i.e. soft and crisp, like pâté and cucumber.
2 The stronger the flavour of the items, the less you need to use. Again, try to combine complementary soft and sharp flavours such as beef and horseradish.
3 Do not be afraid to use sweet items in savoury sandwiches; for example, orange or pineapple with ham, raw apple with pâté, redcurrant jelly with sausage.

Fish *Sardine and cucumber* In white or brown bread. Mash the sardines with a little anchovy essence and seasoning, spread them on buttered brown bread, top with cucumber slices, cover with buttered white bread, garnish with cucumber slices and prawns.
Prawn, coleslaw and lettuce double Butter some brown bread with a butter–mayonnaise mixture, cover it with peeled prawns, add buttered sliced white bread, cover it with coleslaw and lettuce, add buttered sliced brown bread and garnish it with whole prawns and lemon wedges.
Egg and crab sandwich or bap Butter some brown bread (or baps); cover it with crab meat and sliced hard-boiled egg. Top this with a slice (or bap top) spread with butter or mayonnaise, and garnish it with small cress and tomato slices.

Recipes for Pubs

Kipper pâté, horseradish and cucumber Butter some brown or white bread or baps with butter and horseradish sauce, mixed. Spread this with kipper pâté and top it with sliced cucumber. Cover all this with a butter or horseradish-covered slice of bread or bap top and garnish with radish and watercress.

Meats   *Country ham and cheese* Spread a mixture of cottage cheese and chives, or cottage cheese and chopped pineapple, on buttered brown bread and ham and garnish it with radish and watercress.
Chicken or turkey, stuffing and coleslaw Spread some bread with butter mixed with sage and onion stuffing; lay slices of dark and white chicken or turkey meat on top of this. Cover it with a slice of brown bread and add a layer of coleslaw and then a slice of buttered white bread. Garnish it with watercress and tomato quarters.

Hot sandwiches

Toasted open   This consists of hot meat, dairy products or fish on top of toasted bread.

Grilled open   This consists of cold produce on top of a bap or bread, French stick or roll and placed under the grill to heat and brown.

Toasted closed   This consists of a variety of items placed between two slices of bread and then toasted.

This small selection of sandwiches can be extended considerably.

Hot dogs   The smoked frankfurter sausage in a soft roll is normally poached in salt water, but it can be grilled or fried. However, cooked in this way it can easily split. Serve with onion, mustard or tomato ketchup.

The frankfurter has other uses: cut up into a risotto; served with sauerkraut as a main meal; served with bread, salad and pickle as a variation on the ploughman's lunch.

22 Pastry, puddings and sweets

Michael Davidson and Daniel Stevenson

Doughs, pastries, frying batter and sweet sauces

Choux paste Yield: 500 g (1¼ lb) approximately.

200 ml	Water	8 fl oz
80 g	Fat, e.g. margarine, butter or lard	3¼ oz
120 g	Flour (bread)	5 oz
3–4	Eggs	3–4

Method
1. Place the water and fat into a saucepan and bring to the boil.
2. Add all the flour at one time and mix over a low heat for 1 minute approximately. The mixture should leave the sides of the pot cleanly.
3. Allow the mixture to cool slightly, i.e. to a temperature which will not cause any of the egg to coagulate.
4. Add the eggs a little at a time while beating the paste. Scrape down the bowl occasionally when adding the eggs.
5. Test the paste for consistency – it should be soft with the ability to *hold its shape* (just and no more) when piped.

Short pastry Available as a packet mixture or a ready-prepared frozen product.

Savoury short pastry (non-lard recipe) Yield: 600 g (1½ lb) approximately.

400 g	Plain flour (sieved)	1 lb
200 g	Margarine or butter	8 oz
	Salt, good pinch	
80 ml	Water (cold)	3½ fl oz

Method
1. Place half the flour 200 g (8 oz) into a mixing bowl with the margarine or butter and thoroughly cream together.
2. Dissolve the salt in the water.
3. Add the water to the creamed fat and flour and mix until completely combined. Scrape down the bowl as required.
4. Add the remaining flour and mix together to a smooth dough.

Wholemeal pastry Yield: 600 g (1½ lb) approximately.

| 400 g | Wholemeal flour | 1 lb |

Recipes for Pubs

200 g	Margarine or butter	8 oz
	Salt, good pinch	
120 ml	Water (cold)	4½ fl oz

Method
1 Place the flour into a mixing bowl, then rub in the fat to a sandy texture.
2 Dissolve the salt in the water.
3 Add the water to the fat and flour and mix together to a smooth dough.
4 Allow to rest for a short period before use.

Sweet short pastry (high quality)   Yield: 400 g (1 lb) approximately.

200 g	Plain flour (sieved)	8 oz
125 g	Butter or margarine	5 oz
70 g	Caster sugar	2¾ oz
½	Egg	½
	Grated lemon zest, good pinch	

Method
1 Place 50 g (2 oz) of the flour into the mixing bowl with the butter or margarine and thoroughly cream together.
2 Add the remaining flour and lightly mix together (do not form a dough).
3 Mix together the egg, sugar and lemon zest.
4 Add and mix together until a smooth dough has been obtained.

Plain sponge   Yield: 2 × 200 mm (8 in) diameter baking tins.

5	Eggs	5
200 g	Caster sugar	8 oz
200 g	Plain flour (sieved) (see note below)	8 oz

Method
1 Place the eggs and sugar into a mixing bowl, then place over hot water and stir until warm – 32 °C (90 °F) approximately.
2 Whisk the eggs and sugar until very light and stiff, i.e. the mixture when held on the whisk shows fairly stiff peaks which slowly drop when held upright.
3 Fold the flour gently through the whisked eggs and sugar until combined.
4 Place the mixture into greased and floured baking tins.
5 Bake at 200 °C (395 °F) for 25–30 minutes.
6 Allow to cool on a cooling wire.
Note: 25 g (1 oz) of the plain flour may be replaced with self-raising flour to help counteract the loss of aeration which occurs when handling, dividing or shaping the mixture.

Génoise sponge   This is prepared the same as plain sponge with the addition of 75 g (3 oz) of melted butter, which is folded very gently through the sponge mixture *after* adding the flour.

Chocolate or almond génoise   Replace 25 g (1 oz) of the flour in the recipe with cocoa powder for chocolate génoise or 40 g (1½ oz) of the flour with ground almonds for almond génoise.

Pastry, puddings and sweets

Suet paste   Yield: 800 g (2 lb) approximately.

400 g	Plain flour	1 lb
200 g	Beef suet (chopped)	8 oz
10 g	Baking powder (see note below)	½ oz
	Salt, good pinch	
250 ml	Water (cold)	½ pt

Method
1 Sieve together the flour, baking powder and salt.
2 Add the suet and mix through the flour.
3 Add the water and lightly mix together to a stiff paste.

Note: The quantity of baking powder may be doubled, i.e. 20 g (1 oz) when a light paste is desired.

Yeast doughs

Nan bread   Yield: 6 large nans

500 g	Plain flour	1 lb 4 oz
5 g	Salt	¼ oz
10 g	Baking powder	½ oz
40 g	Caster sugar	1½ oz
150 g	Yogurt	6 oz
70 ml	Oil	2¾ fl oz
½	Egg	½
30 g	Yeast	1¼ oz
140 ml	Milk	5½ fl oz
25 g	Sesame seeds	1 oz

Method
1 Sieve together the flour, salt and baking powder.
2 Mix together the sugar, oil, egg and yogurt (room temperature).
3 Break down the yeast in the milk (room temperature).
4 Mix all the ingredients together to form a smooth dough.
5 Allow to rest under cover for 15 minutes at room temperature (18 °C (65 °F) approximately).
6 Divide the dough into six pieces, then roll out thinly using flour and sesame seeds. Traditionally the dough is shaped like large teardrops.
7 Place on to oiled plates and allow to dry prove at room temperature for 30–40 minutes.
8 Carefully turn each nan out of the plate and into a hot, very lightly greased frying pan and cook until the base is brown (45 seconds–1 minute).
9 Place under a hot grill and brown.

Note: This is a suitable procedure when no tandoor oven is available.

Pizza dough   Available as a packet mixture or as a ready-prepared frozen product.
Yield: 1¾ kg (4½ lb) approximately.

| 1 kg | Plain flour | 2½ lb |
| 10 g | Salt | ½ oz |

Recipes for Pubs

30 g	Milk powder	1¼ oz
150 g	Margarine	6 oz
1	Egg	1
50 g	Yeast	2 oz
560 ml	Water (cold 18 °C (65 °F))	22 fl oz

Method
1. Sieve together the flour, salt and milk powder.
2. Rub in the margarine to a sandy texture.
3. Break down the yeast in a little of the recipe water.
4. Add the egg, yeast water and almost all of the remaining water and mix together.
5. Add the remaining water if the dough is too stiff.
6. Mix to a smooth dough, then allow to rest and ferment under cover for 15 minutes.
7. Use the dough to prepare the pizzas as in Chapter 18.

Frying batter Yield: 1 l (2 pt) approximately

800 g	Plain flour	2 lb
40 g	Baking powder	1½ oz
20 g	Salt	¾ oz
20 g	Milk powder (see note below)	¾ oz
1 l	Water (cold)	2 pt

Method
1. Sieve together the dry ingredients and place into a mixing bowl.
2. Add approximately half the water and mix to a smooth thick paste.
3. Add the remaining water in stages, whisking between each addition of liquid until a smooth coating batter is obtained.

Note: Milk may be used in place of the milk powder and water.

Sweet sauces Yield: 1 l (2 pt).

Almond sauce

1 l	Milk	2 pt
40 g	Cornflour	1¾ oz
100 g	Sugar	4 oz
3–4 drops	Almond essence	3–4 drops

Chocolate sauce

1 l	Milk	2 pt
40 g	Cornflour	1¾ oz
200 g	Sugar	8 oz
60 g	Cocoa powder	2¼ oz
20 g	Butter	¾ oz

Custard

1 l	Milk	2 pt
40 g	Custard powder	1¾ oz
100 g	Sugar	4 oz

Pastry, puddings and sweets

Spirit sauces, e.g.	1 l	Milk	2 pt
brandy, sherry	40 g	Cornflour	1¾ oz
whisky	100 g	Sugar	4 oz
	100 ml	Spirit or fortified wine	4 fl oz

Basic method
1. Place a little of the cold milk into a bowl, add the cornflour or custard powder and blend together.
   Chocolate sauce: Add the cocoa powder at this stage and blend together with the milk and starch.
2. Place the remaining milk into a saucepan and bring to the boil.
3. Stir in the diluted starch mixture to the hot milk. Stir constantly until a smooth mixture is obtained.
4. Reboil and simmer for 2–3 minutes, stirring occasionally to prevent burning.
5. Remove from the boil, add the recipe sugar and any essence, spirit, wine or butter.

Jam sauce, e.g.	700 g	Jam	1 lb 10 oz
Apricot, raspberry,	350 ml	Water	14 fl oz
strawberry	35 g	Arrowroot	1½ oz

Syrup sauce	450 g	Golden syrup	1 lb
	600 ml	Water	24 fl oz
	2	Lemons	2
	35 g	Arrowroot	1½ oz

Basic method
1. Place the water and any jam, golden syrup or lemon juice in a saucepan.
2. Bring to the boil.
3. Dilute the arrowroot in a little cold water.
4. Stir the diluted arrowroot mixture into the hot liquid. Stir constantly until smooth.
5. Reboil and simmer for 2–3 minutes, stirring occasionally to prevent burning.

Sweet dishes

The popularity of sweet dishes varies from one pub establishment to another; from few if any sweets on offer, to a comprehensive selection of sweets served from a trolley or buffet service area.

It may be worth while for some publicans to further their wine sales by offering a selection of sweet dishes with matching wines.

The points made regarding buffet service apply to the presentation of sweet dishes.

Cheesecake (high quality) Available as ready-prepared frozen products.
Yield: 2 × 250 mm (8½ in) cheesecakes.

		Biscuit base	
	400 g	Wholemeal biscuits	1 lb

Recipes for Pubs

100 g	Butter (unsalted)	4 oz
	Filling	
300 g	Cream cheese (firm)	12 oz
500 ml	Cream (double)	1 pt
100 g	Icing sugar	4 oz
5 ml	Lemon juice	¼ fl oz

Method
1. Prepare the base:
   (a) Crush the biscuits.
   (b) Melt the butter and mix through the biscuit crumbs.
   (c) Line 2 × 250 mm (8½ in) flan rings with the biscuit mixture (including the sides) and allow to set firm.
   (d) Carefully remove the flan rings.
2. Cream the cheese with the icing sugar, then mix in the lemon juice.
3. Whip the cream until quite stiff.
4. Fold together the cream mixture and the cream.
5. Place the mixture on to the biscuit bases, then place into the refrigerator for approximately 1 hour.
6. Decorate to taste.

Fruit cheesecakes (see Plate 31) Neatly garnish the top of the cheesecake with the appropriate fruit, e.g. strawberries, raspberries, sliced peaches, lightly cooked blackcurrants etc. Lightly cover with a little fruit glaze (fruit syrup thickened with arrowroot) or quick-gel glaze.

Éclairs and profiteroles

Chocolate éclairs (see Plate 32) Available as a ready-prepared frozen product.
Yield: 12 éclairs approximately.

500 g	Choux paste	1¼ lb
300 ml	Cream (whipping or double)	12 fl oz
125 g	Chocolate (cooking)	5 oz

Method
1. Prepare the choux paste as given earlier in the chapter.
2. Place the choux paste into a piping bag with a 15 mm (½ in) diameter plain tube.
3. Pipe the paste in lengths about 100 mm (4 in) on to a lightly greased baking tray.
4. Bake at 220 °C (425 °F) until very crisp and golden brown, i.e. approximately 25 minutes.
5. Allow to cool, then slit along one side of each éclair.
6. Whip the cream until stiff.
   Note: The cream may be lightly sweetened and flavoured with vanilla essence (Chantilly cream).
7. Fill each éclair with the whipped cream using a piping bag and star tube.
8. Melt the chocolate over warm water. Do not overheat.
9. Dip the top of each éclair in the melted chocolate, then remove the surplus by lightly running a palette knife across top.

Pastry, puddings and sweets

Profiteroles with chocolate   These are small choux paste buns which are prepared in the same manner as éclairs. The buns (3–4 per portion) are dressed on the serving dish or plate, then coated with the chocolate. Alternatively, they may be dusted with icing sugar and coated with cold chocolate sauce when serving.

Egg custard dishes

Cambridge cream (also called crème brûlée)

Yield: 10 portions.

10	Egg yolks	10
75 g	Caster sugar	2¾ lb
750 ml	Cream	1¼ pt
3–4 drops	Vanilla essence	3–4 drops
100 g	Soft brown sugar	3½ oz

Method
1. Mix together the yolks, caster sugar and vanilla essence.
2. Heat the cream.
3. Whisk the hot cream through the egg yolks.
4. Pour the mixture into individual portion dishes (e.g. soufflé cases).
5. Place the dishes into a tray half full of water and cook in a cool oven, 130–140 °C (265–285 °F). Cook until lightly set.
6. Sprinkle the brown sugar over the surface of each cream, then glaze (brown) under a grill.
7. Serve hot or cold.

Caramel creams (see Plate 33)

Available as a packet mixture.
Yield: 10 portions

	Egg custard	
5	Eggs	7
750 ml	Milk	1¾ pt
75 g	Caster sugar	3½ oz
3–4 drops	Vanilla essence	3–4 drops
	Caramel	
250 g	Granulated sugar	10 oz
100 ml	Water	4 fl oz

Method
1. Prepare the caramel:
   (a) Place the sugar and water into a saucepan and bring to the boil.
   (b) Boil quickly. Do not stir, and keep the sides of the pan clean by occasionally brushing down with a brush dipped into a little clean water.
   (c) Boil to a good golden colour.
   (d) Place the pan into water to stop the boiling action.
   (e) Carefully add 75 ml (2¾ fl oz) hot water to the caramel.
   (f) When the water has thoroughly combined with the caramel, pour into the cooking containers and allow to cool.
2. Prepare the custard:
   (a) Whisk together the egg, sugar and vanilla essence.
   (b) Heat the milk.
   (c) Whisk the hot milk through the eggs and sugar.

Recipes for Pubs

3 Strain the custard into the prepared moulds.
4 Place the dishes into a tray half full of water and cook in a cool oven, 130–140 °C (265–285 °F). Cook until set.
5 Allow to cool, then store in a refrigerator until required for service.
6 Lightly press down the sides of the custard to free from the cooking container, then turn out on to the serving dish. Decorate if desired.

Bread and butter pudding (see Plate 34)

Yield: 10 portions
Prepare the basic egg custard mixture given under caramel creams. Line a suitable pie dish with five slices of buttered bread (crusts removed) and 100 g (4 oz) sultanas. Strain the custard over the bread and sultanas and allow to stand until the bread absorbs the custard. Bake in a cool oven 150 °C (300 °F). When serving, dust over the top of the pudding with icing sugar.

Pancakes

Yield: 10 portions

	Batter	
500 ml	Milk	1 pt
200 g	Flour	8 oz
30 g	Butter or margarine	1¼ oz
2	Eggs	2
pinch	Salt	pinch
50 ml	Oil	2 fl oz
100 g	Caster sugar	4 oz

Method
1 Prepare the batter:
   (a) Sieve together the flour and salt.
   (b) Add the egg and half the quantity of milk, and mix to a smooth paste.
   (c) Add most of the remaining milk, and mix to a smooth thin batter.
   (d) Correct the consistency to produce a thin batter (similar to a single cream).
   (e) Melt the butter and whisk into the batter until completely combined.
   (f) Allow to rest for approximately 1 hour.
2 Heat the pan, adding a little oil. When hot pour off the surplus oil.
3 Add only enough batter to form a thin coating on the base of the pan.
4 Tilt the pan to spread the batter evenly across the base of the pan.
5 Cook until golden brown, then turn over and cook the other side.
6 Turn the pancake out of the pan on to a large plate. Cover with a second plate and keep hot.
7 Repeat the operation until the required number of pancakes is obtained.
8 Sprinkle with caster sugar, then fold in half, then half again.
9 For stuffed pancakes, spread the centre of each pancake with the hot filling then roll up. Trim the ends if required.

Flans, pies and tarts

Available as ready-prepared products.

Pastry, puddings and sweets

Fruit flan Yield: 1 × 250 mm (8½ in) flan (8–10 portions)
(see Plate 35)

| 500 g | Sweet short pastry | 1 lb 4 oz |
| 500 g | Fruit, e.g. tinned apricots, cherries, peaches, pears, pineapple etc. | 1 lb 4 oz |

Pastry cream 400 ml (1 pt)

2	Egg yolks	2
80 g	Caster sugar	3¼ oz
40 g	Flour	1½ oz
400 ml	Milk	1 pt
3–4 drops	Vanilla essence	3–4 drops
75 ml	Glaze	3 fl oz

Method
1. Prepare the sweet short pastry as given earlier in this chapter.
2. Line the flan ring with pastry and bake blind:
   (a) Pierce over the bottom of the pastry with a docker or fork.
   (b) Line with a circle of greaseproof paper, then fill with dried beans or peas.
   (c) Bake at 200 °C (395 °F) until almost cooked, approximately 25 minutes.
   (d) Carefully remove the paper and beans, then place the flan back into the oven and complete the cooking – a further 5 minutes approximately.
   (e) Remove the flan ring and wipe clean, then allow the flan to cool.
3. Prepare the pastry cream:
   (a) Place the sugar, yolks and essence into a mixing bowl, then cream together.
   (b) Mix in the flour.
   (c) Boil the milk in a saucepan, then whisk on to the yolks, sugar and flour. Ensure the ingredients are well mixed.
   (d) Return the mixture to a clean saucepan then bring to the boil, stirring continuously. Boil for 1 minute approximately.
   (e) Pour the mixture into a basin, cover with a piece of greaseproof paper and allow to cool.
4. Prepare the fruit: drain cooked or tinned fruit, and if required cut into slices or suitable pieces.
5. Spread the pastry cream over the base of the flan, then neatly arrange the fruit on top.
6. Prepare the glaze: thicken the drained fruit juice with arrowroot blended together with a little cold water (a little sugar and lemon juice may be added to improve flavour).
7. Lightly coat the fruit with the hot glaze then allow to cool.

Lemon meringue pie Available as a ready-prepared product.
(high quality) Yield: 1 × 250 mm (8½ in) flan (8–10 portions)
(see Plate 36)

| 500 g | Sweet short pastry | 1 lb 4 oz |

Lemon curd

250 ml	Water	½ pt
125 g	Caster sugar	5 oz
50 g	Cornflour	2 oz
2	Lemons	2

327

Recipes for Pubs

30 g	Butter or margarine	1¼ oz
1	Egg yolk	1
	Meringue	
125 ml	Egg whites	¼ pt
250 g	Caster sugar	10 oz

Method
1. Line the flan ring with the pastry and bake blind – see fruit flan above.
2. Prepare the lemon curd:
   (a) Remove the zest from the lemons with a grater.
   (b) Place the water, lemon juice, zest and sugar into a saucepan and bring to the boil.
   (c) Blend the cornflour in a little cold, water, then whisk into the boiling lemon and water solution.
   (d) Simmer for 1 minute, stirring continuously.
   (e) Remove from the heat then blend through the egg yolk and butter.
3. Place the curd into the flan case.
4. Prepare a meringue with the egg whites and sugar, then pipe neatly across the top of the flan.
5. Place the flan back in the oven and bake until the meringue is a good colour.

Apple meringue pie This is prepared the same as lemon meringue pie, replacing the lemon curd with apple purée.

Fruit pies Available as ready-prepared products.
Yield: 8–10 portions

500 g	Sweet short pastry	1 lb 4 oz
1 kg	Fruit, e.g. apples, blackcurrants, blackberries, cherries, gooseberries, rhubarb	2 lb 8 oz
250 g	Caster sugar (see 1 below)	10 oz
50 ml	Water (see 1 below)	2 fl oz
	Eggwash	

Method
1. Wash and prepare the fruit, then mix together with the sugar and water. The exact quantity of sugar and water will depend on the type of fruit used.
2. Place the fruit mixture into a suitable pie dish. The fruit mixture should fill the pie dish.
3. Roll out the pastry to a thickness of 5 mm (¼ in).
4. Cut the pastry to a size suitable to cover the pie.
5. Lightly dampen the rim of the pie dish, then cover with the pastry.
6. Notch or mark the edges of the pastry, then cut a small hole in the centre to allow the steam to escape.
7. Brush with eggwash, then place on a baking tray.
8. Bake at 200 °C (395 °F) for 30–40 minutes.

Fruit tarts Available as ready-prepared products.

450 g	Sweet short pastry	1 lb 2 oz
750 g	Fruit – examples as above.	1 lb 14 oz
175 g	Caster sugar (see 2 below)	7 oz

Pastry, puddings and sweets

25 ml	Water (see 2 below)	1 fl oz
	Eggwash	

Method
1. Wash and prepare the fruit.
2. Place the fruit in a saucepan, then add the sugar and water. The exact quantity of sugar and water will depend on the type of fruit used.
3. Lightly stew the fruit, keeping it underdone, then allow to cool.
4. Line a flan ring or lightly greased tart plate with two-thirds of the pastry, ensuring that the edge of the ring or plate is overlapped with pastry.
5. Place the fruit mixture into the pastry case, then lightly dampen around the edge of the pastry with water.
6. Roll out the remaining pastry and cover the top of the tart.
7. Press down to seal the edges, then trim off the surplus pastry.
8. Decorate around the edge of the pastry by marking or notching with the fingers, then cut a small hole on top to allow the steam to escape.
9. Eggwash the top of the pastry, then bake at 200°C (395°F) for approximately 30 minutes.
10. Allow to cool slightly, then carefully detach from the ring or plate.
11. Sprinkle with caster sugar if desired.

Fruit crumbles (see Plate 37)
Prepare the fruit filling as for fruit pies, then sprinkle over the following mixture:

300 g	Flour	12 oz
150 g	Butter or margarine	6 oz
100 g	Caster sugar	4 oz

Method
1. Rub the butter into the flour to produce a crumbly texture.
2. Mix through the sugar.
3. Sprinkle the crumble mixture over the fruit, then lightly press smooth.
4. Bake at 200°C (400°F) for approximately 40 minutes.

Fruit fritters Yield: 10 portions

1 l	Frying batter	2 pt
	Fruit, e.g. apples, pineapple, bananas	
	Flour	
	Caster or icing sugar	

Method
1. Prepare the frying batter (see earlier in this chapter).
2. Prepare the fruit:
   Apples Peel, core then cut into slices or rounds, 5 mm (¼ in) approximately. Allow half a medium-sized cooking apple per portion approximately.
   Pineapple Circles of pineapple either tinned or fresh. Allow 1–2 slices per portion.
   Banana Peel the banana, then remove the strings. Leave whole or cut in half (usually on a slant). Allow one banana per portion.
3. Pass the fruit through flour, then coat with the frying batter.

Recipes for Pubs

  4 Deep fry at 180 °C (355 °F) until golden brown, about 4 minutes.
  5 Remove from the fryer and drain, then place on a cooking tray.
  6 Sprinkle over the surface with caster or icing sugar.
  7 Glaze under a grill.
  8 Serve with a suitable sauce, e.g. apricot or fresh cream.

Fruit salad   Available as a tinned or frozen product.

  Allow 1¼ kg (3 lb) of fresh fruit per 10 portions approximately, e.g. 3 apples, 3 pears, 3 oranges, 50 g (2 oz) each, black and green grapes, 50 g (2 oz) cherries and 1 banana, etc.

Method
1. Prepare a syrup by boiling together 250 ml (½ pt) water and 100 g (4 oz) sugar.
2. Add a good squeeze of lemon juice and allow to cool.
3. Cut large fruits into slices and small fruits such as grapes and cherries into halves, and remove the seeds.
4. Place the fruits into the cold syrup as soon as prepared.

Note: Bananas are added to the fruit salad just prior to service.

Gâteaux   Available as a chilled or frozen ready-prepared product.

Chocolate gâteau
(see Plate 38)

Yield: 8–10 portions

2 shapes	Chocolate génoise	2 shapes
250 ml	Cream	½ pt
25 g	Caster sugar (optional)	1 oz
200 g	Chocolate (melted)	½ lb
100 g	Chocolate vermicelli	4 oz

Method
1. Whip the cream until stiff. If desired, sweeten the cream with the caster sugar.
2. Sandwich together the two pieces of sponge with the cream.
3. Apply a thin coat of cream around the sides of the sponge.
4. Cover the sides with the vermicelli.
5. Neatly coat the top with the melted chocolate.
6. When the chocolate is almost set, scroll over the surface with a serrated plastic scraper to produce an attractive finish.

Note: The sponge shapes may be dampened with a little fruit juice; this will produce a gâteau with a moist eating texture.

Black Forest gâteau   Recipe as above, adding black cherries, kirsch and grated chocolate.

Method
1. Dampen the sponge shapes with the juice from the cherries and the kirsch.
2. When sandwiching the sponge shapes together with the cream, add a layer of cherries.
3. Coat the sides with cream and grated chocolate.
4. Decorate the top of the gâteau with whipped cream, black cherries and grated chocolate.

Pastry, puddings and sweets

Coffee gâteau (see Plate 39)	2 shapes	Génoise	2 shapes
		Coffee butter cream	
	400 g	Unsalted butter	1 lb
	400 g	Icing sugar	1 lb
	to taste	Coffee extract	to taste
	400 g	Nib almonds (roasted)	1 lb

Method
1. Prepare the butter cream:
   (a) Cream together the butter and icing sugar until very light and fluffy.
   (b) Mix in the coffee essence.
2. Dampen the sponge with a little fruit juice (optional).
3. Sandwich together the two pieces of sponge with the coffee butter cream.
4. Apply a thin coat of butter cream around the sides of the gâteau.
5. Cover the sides with the roasted nib almonds.
6. Coat the top with a smooth layer of butter cream.
7. Pipe around the top edge of the gâteau with butter cream.
8. Pipe the word 'coffee' on top of the gâteau. Alternatively, decorate to taste with butter cream and roasted nib almonds.

Sweets incorporating ice-cream: coupes

Alexandra — Place fruit salad flavoured with a little kirsch into the coupe, add a ball of strawberry ice cream and decorate with whipped cream.

Jacques — Place fruit salad in the coupe and flavour with a little maraschino. Add a ball of ice cream consisting of half lemon and half strawberry. Decorate with a rosette of whipped cream and a black grape.

Jamaique — Place pineapple slices which have been macerated in rum in the coupe, add a ball of coffee ice-cream and decorate with whipped cream and crystallized violets.

Venus — Place a half peach flat side up in the coupe, and sit a ball of vanilla ice cream on top. Decorate with a large fresh strawberry and surround with whipped cream.

Sweets incorporating meringue

Shaped, cooked, meringues are available as ready-made products.

Meringue with ice cream and Chantilly cream — Sandwich together two meringue shells with a ball of ice cream, then decorate with Chantilly cream (lightly sweetened whipped cream flavoured with vanilla essence).

Vacherins — Cooked vacherin cases are available as ready-made products.

The meringue cases may be filled with whipped cream, ice cream, fruit salad, fresh summer fruits or poached/tinned fruits. Decorate to taste.

Recipes for Pubs

Sweet mousses Available as ready-prepared chilled or frozen products. Also available as packet mixtures.
(see Plate 40)

Vanilla mousse Yield: 10 portions approximately

750 ml	Milk	1½ pt
125 g	Sugar	5 oz
20 g	Cornflour	¾ oz
30 g	Gelatine (leaf)	1¼ oz
250 ml	Cream (lightly whipped)	½ pt
4–5 drops	Vanilla essence	4–5 drops
2–4	Egg whites (optional)	2–4

Method
1 Place the milk in a saucepan and bring to the boil.
2 Blend the cornflour with a little cold milk, then stir into the boiling milk.
3 Bring to the boil and simmer for 2–3 minutes.
4 Add the sugar and vanilla essence.
5 Soak the leaf gelatine in cold water until soft and pliable.
6 Squeeze out the water from the gelatine and add to the hot sauce.
7 Stir until the gelatine is completely dissolved, then strain into a clean bowl.
8 Allow to cool, then place in ice water.
9 Stir until setting point is almost reached, then fold through the whipped cream.
10 If egg whites are to be used, whisk to a stiff snow and fold through the mixture.
11 Place the mixture into moulds, then allow to set in a refrigerator.
12 When set, turn out on to a serving dish and decorate to taste.
Note: Alternatively, the mixture may be set in individual serving dishes, e.g. coupes or Paris goblets, then decorated. When this is the case the gelatine should be used reduced to 20 g (½ oz).

Chocolate mousse Prepare as stated but omit the vanilla essence. Blend together 50 g (2 oz) of cocoa powder and a little of the cold recipe milk. Stir into the hot milk before adding the diluted cornflour.

Fruit mousses Prepare as vanilla mousse but replace the vanilla essence with the desired fruit essence, e.g. lemon, orange, pineapple etc. A little food colour may be necessary depending on the mousse being made, e.g. orange. Decorate to taste (using the appropriate fruit if desired).

Further reading

Stevenson, D., *Professional Cookery: The Process Approach*, Hutchinson, 1985.
Fuller, J. and Renold, E., *The Chef's Compendium of Professional Recipes*, Heinemann, 1984.
Fuller, J. (ed.), *H. P. Pellaprat's Modern French Culinary Art*, Virtue, 1984.
Fuller, J. (ed.), *Meat Dishes in the International Cuisine*, Virtue, 1984.
Simms, A. E. (ed.), *Fish and Shellfish*, Virtue, 1985.

Index

à la carte menu, 98, 99
accidents procedure, 66
acoustics, 83
advertising, 28, 34
    materials, 33–4
alterations:
    implementing, 59–61
    planning, 49–51
audits, internal, 148, 190

bakery goods selection, 125
bar snacks, 105
Bayley Arms, case history, 40–8
bill presentation, 161
bookings, 45, 102
    function diary, 157
booths, 87
breakfasts, 105
brochures, 149
budgeting, 179–81
buffets, 165–6, 201–2
    menus, 308–14
business lunches, 167

carpets, 84–5
carving procedure, 221
cash and carry suppliers, 118
catering policies, 39
chairs, 156
champagne, 233
charcuterie displays, 206
charges, 14–16, 113
checklist, premises, 29–30
checks, control, 190
cheese, serving, 222
chilled foods, 77
cloakroom staff, 172
closing stock, 184
coach parties, 44–6
coffees, liqueur, 223
cold buffet, 201–2
cold display counter, 204–7
colour selection, 83
competition, 39
complaints, handling, 214
consumer-based pricing, 189
containers, charging for, 135
control, systematic, 190–1, 224–5
convenience foods, 128–30, 168–9
cost-based pricing, 188–9

cost control:
    finished dishes, 178
    purchasing, 131
    stores, 146–7
costing, 44, 176–81
    convenience foods, 129
    food, 162–3
    functions, 162–4
    outside catering, 173
    revenue check, 181–2
    to monitor consumption, 182–5
covers, lay-up of, 218–19
crockery, 91–2
curtains, 86
cutlery, 90

dairy produce selection, 125–6
deep frying, 264–5
delivery note, 135
demand, assessing, 31, 32
design, functional, 82
deterioration of food, 138
dinner dances, 164
dispensing points, 216
disposables, 78, 90, 156, 200
drinks, at receptions, 169–71
    see also under wines
dry goods, 126–7

energy:
    costs, 71
    efficient use, 53
entertainment, 46
Environmental Health Department, 51
equipment:
    catering, 69–79
    hiring, 156–7
    maintenance, 66–7
    storage, 92
ethnic dishes, 33

family appeal, 23, 25
fare, types of, 33
fast food operations, 93, 203
fire precautions, 49–50, 65
first aid precautions, 66
fish:
    buying, 123–4
    serving, 219–20
flat ware, 90

food:
    costing, 177
    issuing, 145–7
    ordering, 119–20
    receiving, 133–7
    serving, 197
    specifications, 116–17
    standards, 131
    stock levels, 119, 141–2
    storing, 137–9
    supply sources, 117–18
Food and Drugs Act 1955, 227
'food percentage', 183
    report, 185
food service staff, 172
formal functions, 164–5
franchised operations, 27
fraudulent practices, 136–7, 143
free houses, 17
freezers, 76–7, 139
fruit:
    selection, 125
    serving, 223
    storage, 141
fry plates, 72
frying oils, 127
fuels, alternative, 62–3
fume extraction, 89
functions:
    costing, 162–3
    forms, 157
    menus, 167–9
    organizing, 150–1, 157–61
    publicizing, 149–50
    space requirements, 153–4
    staffing, 154–5
furnishings, 83–4

glasses, 219, 233, 234
goods received book, 136
griddles, 72
grill and griddle bar, 201
grilling procedures, 279–80
grills, 72–3
groceries, buying, 126–7
gross profit, 177
guéridon service, 217

hazard prevention, 64–6
heating and ventilation, 53, 87, 89
heat transfer methods, 71

333

Index

high teas, 105
hollow-ware, 90
hors d'oeuvres, 219, 223–4
hot buffet, 202
hot snacks, 207–8
house wines, 230
hygiene standards, 51

ice cream supplies, 130
illumination levels, 83
image co-ordination, 29
informal service, 197–8
internal audits, 148, 190
internal check control, 147
inventory, *see* stock-taking

kitchens, 112–13
    equipment, 42, 61–3, 72–8
    materials, 62
    planning, 51–9
    staffing, 171

labour costs, 163
laying up, 218–19
licence, occasional, 173
licensing justices, 50
lighting arrangements, 83
liner menu, 98, 99, 105
liqueur coffees, 223

main courses, serving, 220–1
maintenance of equipment, 66–7
market identification, 32, 38, 97–8
marketing, 27, 47
mark-up, 177, 178
meat:
    buying, 121–3
    displays, 205
menus, 218
    grill and griddle bar, 201
    functions, 167–9
    planning, 98–102
    pub food, 109
    steak bar, 199
merchandising, 38
metrication, 130
microwave ovens, 71, 75–6
milk, buying, 125
mixing machines, 77–8
multiple costing, 181

opportunity times, 31
outside catering, 173–4
ovens, 73–4
    microwave, 71, 75–6
overheads, 163

party groups, 34, 35
payment checklist, 225

pies, displays, 205
pilferage, 145
pizzas, 207
place mats, 33–4
planning consent, 49
plate service, 216–17
poultry buying, 123
premises checklist, 29–30
preparation equipment, mechanical, 77–8
pressure fryer, 74–5
price calculations, 115, 177, 178, 188–9
price displays, 208
Price Marking (Food and Drink on Premises) Order 1979, 98
prime cost, 180–1
private house service, 217
processed goods, 129–30
profit, 115, 179–80, 204
    mark-up, 39
    nett, 192
    on functions, 152, 163–4
profits tax, 192
publicity events, 35–6
purchases, paying for, 120
purchasing food, 116, 118–19

recipes, *see separate* recipe index
refrigerators, 76–7, 138
retailers, use of, 117
returns notes, 135
roasting procedures, 270–6
room preparation, 214–16
rubbish disposal, 140

safety precautions, 70
salad displays, 207
salads, serving, 221–2
sandwiches, 208–9
sauces, 248
seafood displays, 206
seating plans, 154–5, 164
security, stock, 142–3
self-service, 202–3
service:
    organizing, 213–14
    types, 169, 219–24
service tables, *see* sideboards
serviettes, 219
sideboards, 215
signs, displays, 33
silver service, 89, 90, 217
snacks, 202, 206
soups, buying, 126
staffing, 40
    appearance, 213
    food, 184
    instructions, 171–2
    uniforms, 213

statement of account, 191–2
statutory regulations, 49–50
steak bars, 21–2, 198–201
    menus, 199
steaks, buying, 121
steamers, 74
stock card, 143
stock security, 142–3
stock-taking, 144, 185
stores, layouts, 63, 139–41
stores requisitions, 146
sweet dishes, serving, 22
systems catering, 19–20

table cloths, 215
table d'hôte menu, 98, 99
table mats, 33–4
table planning, 153–4, 164
table service, 216–18
tables, 87, 155–6
tableware, 89–90, 156
taxation, 192–3
themed pubs, 22–3, 25, 81, 93
tips, 41
toastmaster, 171
tourists, 34
Trade Descriptions Act 1968, 99

uniforms, 213
unique selling proposition (USP), 27–9
unit costs, 179

Value Added Tax (VAT), 113, 193
variance analysis, 185–7
vegetables:
    preparation, 77, 300–1
    selection, 124–5
    storage, 141
vending machines, 37
vermin protection, 137

washing-up facilities, 63, 92
wedding receptions, 166–7
wholesalers, use of, 118
wine bars, 209–10, 235–7
wine measures, 230, 231–2
wines, 170–1, 234–5
    bottle types, 227
    categories, 226
    choice, 226–7
    decanting, 228–9
    labelling, 233
    promoting sales, 227–8
    sales by the glass, 229–32
    serving, 232–4
    storage, 232
'work triangle' (in kitchen), 53

Recipe index

barbecue dishes, 282–3
barbecue sauce, 255
batter, frying, 324
bechamel sauce, 249
beef stew, 291–2
boffin, 296
bolognese sauce, 253
bonne femme sauce, 250
bread and butter pudding, 326
broths, 244
brown sauce and derivatives, 252–5
buffet items, 305–6, 308–9
burgers, 283–4

canapés, 312–13
carving buffet, 311–12
chasseur sauce, 254
cheesecakes, 323–4
chicken pie, 298
chilli con carne, 289–90
choux paste, 319
cold meat, 307
cold pies, 307
consommés, 242–4
country pie, 296
curry sauce, 251–2

deep fried items, 264–5
devil sauce, 254
devilled chicken, 281

eclairs, 324
egg custard dishes, 325

finger buffet, 312–14
fish and shellfish, 266–9, 306–7
fish pie, 269
flans, 325
flavoured butters, 267–8
fork buffet, 310
fried fish, 265–6
fruit fritters, 328–9
fruit pies and tarts, 327–8
fruit salad, 329

gateaux, 329–30

grilled fish, 267
grilled foods, 279–80

hara beef, 285
hot dogs, 318
hot-pots, 276–9
Hungarian goulash, 290–1

irish stew, 277

jam sauces, 323
joints, carving, 311

kebabs, 282

lyonnaise sauce, 254

mayonnaise sauce and derivatives, 255–6
meringue pie, 227
minestrone, 244
moussaka, 285
mousses, 331

nan bread, 321

omelettes, 257–60

pan Haggarty, 303
pancakes, 326
pasta dishes, 360–2
pasties, 296
pastry items, 294–9
piquante sauce, 255
pizza dough, 321
pizzas, 263–4
plain sponge, 320
ploughman's lunch, 314–15
potato soup, 246
potatoes, 302–4
  baked, 294
profiteroles, 325
puddings, 299
purée soups, 245

quiches, 294–5

ratatouille, 293
rice pilaffs, 262–3
risottos, 262–3
roasting procedures, 270–6
roux-thickened sauces, 248–9

salad dressings, 256
salads, 308
samosas, 286–7
sandwiches, 313, 315, 317, 318
sauced fish dishes, 268–9
sausages, 278
Scotch eggs, 266
seafood canapés, 312
seafood skewers, 269
short pastry, 319–20
skewers, 282
soups, 241–8
  personalizing, 242
spirit sauces, 323
spring vegetable soup, 245
starters, 305–6
steak and kidney pie, 298–9
steak and kidney pudding, 299–300
stuffed breads, 289
suet paste, 321
sweet sauces, 322
sweets, 330–1

tandoori chicken, 287–9
toad-in-the-hole, 278
tomato sauce, 251
tomato soups, 247–8
tripe and onions, 279

vegetable cream soups, 246–7
vegetables, 300–2
vegetarian dishes, 293–6
veloute sauces, 250–1

white sauces and derivatives, 249–50

yeast dough, 321